THE
ENTREPRENEUR'S
GUIDE TO
BUSINESS LAW

CONSTANCE E. BAGLEY
Graduate School of Business
Stanford University

CRAIG E. DAUCHY
Cooley Godward LLP
Palo Alto, California

WEST

WEST EDUCATIONAL PUBLISHING COMPANY

An International Thomson Publishing Company

Publisher/Team Director: Jack W. Calhoun
Acquisitions Editor: Rob Dewey
Senior Developmental Editor: Jan Lamar
Production Editor: Sharon L. Smith
Production House: DPS Associates, Inc.
Internal Design: Ellen Pettengell
Cover Design: Joe Devine
Marketing Manager: Scott Person

1 2 3 4 5 WST 1 0 9 8

Printed in the United States of America

ISBN: 0-314-22316-9

Bagley, Constance E.
     The entrepreneur's guide to business law / by Constance E. Bagley,
Craig E. Dauchy.
          p.   cm.
     Includes index.
     ISBN 0-314-22316-9
     1. Business law—United States. 2. Business enterprises—United
States—Popular works. I. Dauchy, Craig E.,   . II. Title.
KF390.B84B34   1997   97-10421
346.7307—dc21   CIP

I(T)P®

International Thomson Publishing

Contents

Preface iii

1 Taking the Plunge 1
Putting It into Practice 4

2 Leaving Your Employer 8
Restrictions While Still Employed 9
Postemployment Restrictions and the Covenant Not to Compete 14
Trade Secrets 19
Invention Assignment Agreement 22
Strategies for Leaving on Good Terms 24
Putting It into Practice 27

3 Selecting and Working with an Attorney 29
The Need for an Attorney 30
Choosing an Attorney 31
Working Cost Efficiently with an Attorney 36
Attorney-Client Privilege 44
Putting It into Practice 47

4 Deciding Whether to Incorporate 49
The Forms of Business Entity 50
Corporations 51
Partnerships 55
Limited Liability Companies 59
Making the Selection from Among the C Corporation,
  S Corporation, Partnership, and Limited Liability Company 61
Conducting Business in Other States, Local Licenses,
  and Insurance 64
Choosing and Protecting a Name for a Business 65
Putting It into Practice 69

5   Structuring the Ownership 71

Incorporation 71
Splitting the Pie 80
Issuing Equity, Consideration, and Vesting 83
Agreements Relating to the Transfer of Shares 92
Voting Agreements 95
Employment, Proprietary Rights, and Noncompete Agreements 95
Putting It into Practice 97

6   Raising Money 101

Sources of Funds 101
Pitching to Investors 110
Issues Related to Investment Securities 115
Federal Securities Registration Requirements and Exemptions 123
Blue Sky Laws 129
Putting It into Practice 141

7   Creditors' Rights and Bankruptcy 144

Types of Loans 145
Loan Agreements 147
Secured Transactions Under the UCC 147
Security Agreements 149
Perfecting a Security Interest 152
Filing Procedure 154
Types of Creditors and Their Rights 155
Personal Guaranties 158
Strategies for Responding to a Financial Crisis 158
Bankruptcy 164
The Chapter 11 Bankruptcy Process 167
Running a Business in Bankruptcy 174
Effect of Bankruptcy on Director and Officer Litigation and
   Indemnification 176
Chapter 11 Plan of Reorganization 177
Prepackaged Bankruptcy and Plans of Reorganization 182
Business Combination Through Chapter 11 Bankruptcy 184
Loss of Control and Other Risks in Bankruptcy 185
Bankruptcy Pros and Cons 186
Putting It into Practice 187

8   Venture Capital 189

Deciding Whether to Seek Venture Capital 190
Finding Venture Capital 191
Selecting a Venture Capitalist 194
Determining the Valuation 197
Rights of Preferred Stock 202
Other Protective Arrangements 225

Putting It into Practice 228
Getting It in Writing: Sample Venture Capital Term Sheet 230

9   Forming the Board 237
The Benefits of Having an Independent Board 238
The Size of the Board 240
Frequency of Board Meetings 240
Type of Representation Desired 241
The Responsibilities of the Board 243
Business Judgment Rule 246
Compensation of Board Members 247
Types of Information Directors Need 249
How to Make the Most Effective Use of the Board 252
Putting It into Practice 256
Getting It in Writing: Sample Indemnity Agreement 259

10   Contracts 267
The Main Principles of Contract Law 268
Written Contracts Versus Oral Contracts 275
Advantages of Putting a Contract in Writing 277
Written Contracts: The Form and Terms to Include 279
Checklist for Contract Analysis 292
Effect of Bankruptcy 295
Remedies 296
Promissory Estoppel 301
Quantum Meruit 303
Special Types of Contracts and Their Characteristics 303
Sales of Goods 315
Putting It into Practice 317

11   Product Liability, Warranties, and Advertising 320
Warranties 320
Magnuson-Moss Warranty Act 325
Liability for Defective Products 325
Advertising 332
Putting It into Practice 337

12   Business Torts 339
Elements of Negligence 339
Defenses to Negligence 341
Intentional Torts 343
Strict Liability 352
Toxic Torts 352
Vicarious Liability and Respondeat Superior 353
Remedies 354
Liability of Multiple Defendants 356
Reducing Tort Risks 357
Putting It into Practice 359

13   Human Resources 361

Employees Versus Independent Contractors 362
Major Employment Legislation 366
Equal Employment Opportunity Commission (EEOC) 381
Preemployment Practices 382
Employment At-Will and Wrongful Discharge 389
Reducing Litigation Risk 391
The Employment Agreement 393
Agreements Not to Compete 398
Works Made for Hire 398
Nondisclosure and Invention Assignment Agreements 400
Foreign Employees 402
Employer Liability for Employees' Act 404
Equity Compensation 404
Other Employee Benefits 409
Putting It into Practice 414
Getting It in Writing: Sample Independent Contractor Services
   Agreement 417

14   Intellectual Property 432

Trade-Secret Protection 433
Copyrights 443
Patents 450
Trademarks 462
Comparison of Types of Protection 470
Unfair Competition 472
Licensing Agreements and Other Transfers of
   Intellectual Property 474
Safeguarding Computer Software 481
Putting It into Practice 492

15   Going Public 494

Why Go Public? 494
IPO Versus Sale of the Company 496
Is the Company an IPO Candidate? 498
The IPO Process 499
Restrictions on Sales of Shares 515
Contents of the Prospectus 517
Liability for Misstatements in the Prospectus 521
Preparing for an IPO 522
Responsibilities of a Public Company and Its Board of Directors 526
Putting It into Practice 537

Index 541

Preface

*I*ndividuals starting a new business or expanding an existing one face a sometimes daunting set of legal hurdles. The purpose of this book is first to identify the legal challenges inherent in entrepreneurial activities, then to suggest strategies for meeting those challenges while achieving the core business objectives.

Apart from sharing a name based on the French word *entreprendre* (to undertake), entrepreneurs may at first appear to have nothing in common. Entrepreneurial ventures range from the small start-up firm operating on a shoestring budget to a fully developed enterprise ready to take advantage of the public equity markets. Yet, however one defines entrepreneurship, the heightened interest in entrepreneurship and the economic strength and continued growth of entrepreneurial ventures cannot be questioned. As more companies downsize and restructure, the idea of starting and running one's own company has become more attractive than ever.

In recent years, entrepreneurship has been an engine for growth in the United States, creating thousands of new jobs at a time when millions of workers were laid off by the largest companies. Peter Lynch, vice chairman of Fidelity Management & Research Co., has identified ten companies that have led this growth. They include Amgen (biotech), Circuit City (retail), Compaq Computers (computers), Federal Express (air courier), and MCI (communications). Amazingly, half of them did not exist in 1975, and the balance employed only 6,300 people altogether. In 1995, they employed 279,000 people.[1]

Venture capital is just one of many sources of capital for entrepreneurs, but its size and growth illustrate the magnitude of entrepreneurial activity. According to VentureOne, the leading venture capital investment research firm, more than 1,250 private equity financings were completed in 1996, and more than $10 billion was raised by venture-backed companies. These companies spanned many industries, including health care, biotech and pharmaceuticals, software, environmental, electronics and computer hardware, retailing, and consumer products. The year 1996 marked the sixth consecutive year in which more than 100 venture-backed firms made initial public offerings; $11.8 billion was raised by 206 firms.[2] In 1996, a total of $52 billion was raised by all companies that went public, a new record.[3]

INTENDED AUDIENCE

Persons involved in start-ups and others interested in making the law work for them will benefit from reading this book. It is intended not only for entrepreneurs but also for their investors, attorneys, consultants, advisors, and board members. This book will enable CEOs, managers, and other businesspersons to spot legal issues before they become legal problems, and to achieve savings and efficiencies when operating in the legal environment of business.

WHAT DISTINGUISHES THIS BOOK FROM OTHERS

Numerous other self-help and reference books for entrepreneurs cover a host of legal issues, and many are quite good. However, the available literature is often too general or too technical, impractical, or incomplete. Often the authors are not acknowledged experts in their fields and may have unproven track records. There is a need for a single definitive source that covers the main legal aspects of starting and growing a business, written in a manner that allows the reader to efficiently learn about the relevant law and at the same time benefit from the practical tips based on experience. We have designed this book to meet this market need. We offer the reader a comprehensive book that presents the substantive and practical legal guidance necessary to excel in business.

In particular, our book distinguishes itself from the current literature in the following ways:

- **Integration of Law**   Much of the relevant literature sees the legal aspects of business as distinct from such aspects as sources of capital or intellectual property. Because we see the law as integral to these other important aspects, we have interwoven the law and its business applications by relating real-life business examples that illustrate the pitfalls to watch out for.

- **From the Trenches**   Throughout this book, a number of examples appear in a boxed feature called "From the Trenches." When the example is based on a reported court case, we have provided the citation to the legal reporter in which the case can be found. However, many examples are drawn from our own practice representing entrepreneurs and venture capitalists. Sensitivity to confidentiality often required us to use fictitious names, but rest assured that the entrepreneurs and companies involved are real and that everything described in the "From the Trenches" examples actually occurred.

- **Examples That Challenge the Nuances of the Law**   We use examples from the high-tech arena that push the edge of the envelope as the law is applied to new products and services.

- **Running Hypothetical**   A hypothetical that runs throughout the book follows the progress of Alexandra Scott as she leaves her former place of employment, starts an Internet-related software company, raises money from venture capitalists, and ultimately takes the company public in an initial public offering (IPO). Much of working effectively with the law entails knowing the appropriate questions, and when to ask them. This hypothetical, which is presented at the end of each chapter under the heading "Putting It into Practice," highlights the key concerns the entrepreneur needs to contemplate as the business progresses. By following the thought processes and progress of this hypothetical entrepreneur, the reader learns how to spot the issues and put them in a factual context.

- **Getting It in Writing**   Samples of certain key legal documents appear in a feature called "Getting It in Writing." They include a venture capital term sheet and an independent contractor services agreement.

- **Crucial Information in One Source**   Current literature with more detailed information exists, but often the entrepreneur has to search many books to find it. We believe that it is important to have the key information contained in one book. We have worked hard to achieve this balance—providing a practical source of information without overloading the reader.

PURPOSE

The purpose of this book is twofold. The first is to provide guidance regarding the legal considerations of which entrepreneurs should be aware when launching a new enterprise. The second is to serve as a source and reference book to those who are already active in the entrepreneurial world.

The format of the book is designed to heighten the understanding of the substantive law while offering practical guidance. Interwoven throughout the book are tips from entrepreneurs and attorneys whose experiences highlight valuable lessons.

This book is intended to encompass all phases of the entrepreneurial journey. It is not intended to take the place of an attorney but to help the entrepreneur select one with whom he or she can work in an intelligent, informed, efficient, and economic manner.

CONTENTS

The book contains 15 chapters that follow the progression of a start-up and anticipate its legal concerns through the stages of growth up to an initial public offering. Each chapter is self-contained and may be read on its own.

The book begins with a brief description of the rewards and risks of entrepreneurship, and introduces the hypothetical that will be discussed throughout the book under the heading "Putting It into Practice." Chapter 2 explores the steps that an entrepreneur who is contemplating leaving an employer can take to make the departure amicable, and it offers guidance regarding the significance of documents (such as a non-compete clause or an assignment of inventions) that the entrepreneur may have signed. The chapter also offers insights into intellectual property issues involved in leaving a company to form a new venture and how the entrepreneur might safely (i.e., legally) go about recruiting colleagues.

Chapter 3 focuses on when and whether the entrepreneur should retain an attorney. It also explores how to find an appropriate attorney and how to work effectively with him or her. The next two chapters detail the considerations entailed in choosing an appropriate legal form for the business and offer suggestions on how to structure the ownership of the business among the founders and the investors. Chapter 6 discusses sources of funds, and the pros and cons of different ways of raising money, including the effects of federal and state securities laws. Chapter 7 deals with creditors' rights and gives an overview of bankruptcy. Chapter 8 explores venture capital in depth and highlights the aspects of the term sheet and other venture capital documents of greatest importance to the entrepreneur. Chapter 9 deals with ensuring that the entrepreneurial venture has the proper governance structure and examines the role of the board of directors.

Chapter 10, on contracts, explains what is necessary for a legally binding agreement and highlights contractual issues often faced by entrepreneurs. Chapter 11 highlights special issues associated with the sale of goods, including warranties under article 2 of the Uniform Commercial Code and product liability. Chapter 12 discusses a variety of business torts that an entrepreneur may face and explains the environmental law risks associated with purchasing or leasing real property. Chapter 13 considers the legal issues faced by a growing company when dealing with employees and independent contractors.

Chapter 14 takes an in-depth look at intellectual property; it includes sections on how to protect and license different kinds of intellectual property, as well as an integrated discussion that applies the law of intellectual property to the software industry. Chapter 15 concludes the book with insights on one common exit strategy, the initial public offering.

ACKNOWLEDGMENTS

The authors gratefully acknowledge the helpful comments on the manuscript for this book provided by the following professors:

Robert J. Borghese, University of Pennsylvania
Frank Cross, University of Texas at Austin
Kiren Dosanjh, National University

Richard P. Mandel, Babson College
Sandra J. Perry, Bradley University

The authors owe a particular debt of gratitude to Marilyn Gildea, faculty assistant at the Stanford Business School. Marilyn typed, proofed, and edited the entire manuscript. We could not have done this book without her.

Connie Bagley gratefully acknowledges the contributions to this book of her Stanford Law School and Stanford Business School research assistants P. Y. Nicole Chang, Josh Feldman, Diane Hutnyan, and Ellen Leznik.

Craig Dauchy gratefully acknowledges the contributions of the following Cooley Godward LLP attorneys who helped in the writing of this book: Bill Morrow (chapter 4), Dan Frank (chapter 5), Bob Eisenbach (chapter 7), Jeff Zimman (chapter 8), Laura Owen, Erica Rottenberg, and Dan Westman (chapter 13), Diane Savage (chapter 14), Deborah Marshall (chapter 15), and, in addition, Cooley Godward attorneys John Cummerford, Bill Freeman, and Mark Pitchford.

The authors would like to thank Clyde Perlee, publisher of West Educational Publishing; Rob Dewey, acquisitions editor; Jan Lamar, senior development editor; and Sharon Smith, production editor. As always, working with the pros at West Publishing was a pleasure.

CONCLUSION

This area of the law is exciting and challenging. We have done our best to bring to life the power of the law and the strategies necessary to make the law work for the entrepreneur. We had a lot of fun writing this book, and we hope the reader will have just as much fun using the book as a guide when embarking on the exciting but sometimes perilous journey of entrepreneurship.

NOTES

1. *See* Peter Lynch, "The Upsizing of America," *The Wall Street Journal,* Sept. 20, 1996, at A14.
2. VentureOne, *1996 Report on Venture-Backed Companies* (1997). *See also* Stephanie N. Mehta, "Venture Capitalists Step Up Role in IPOs," *The Wall Street Journal,* Jan. 7, 1997, at B2.
3. *See* Tom Lowry, "Bonus Bonanza," *USA Today,* Jan. 23, 1997, at B1.

About the Authors

Constance E. Bagley has been a member of the faculty at Stanford University's Graduate School of Business since 1988, and was selected as first runner-up for the Distinguished Teaching Award in 1993. Her M.B.A. courses include "Legal and Regulatory Challenges in Entrepreneurship," "Managers and the Legal Environment," and "Corporate Governance, Power, and Responsibility." Connie also teaches in the Stanford Executive Program, the Stanford Executive Program for Growing Companies, and the Stanford Marketing Management Program. She is a member of the Faculty Advisory Board of the *Stanford Journal of Law, Business & Finance* and a member of the Advisory Boards for the Bureau of National Affairs Corporate Practice Series and *The Internet Lawyer*. Prior to joining the Stanford faculty, Connie was a corporate securities partner in the San Francisco office of McCutchen, Doyle, Brown & Enersen LLP, a 250-lawyer law firm. She was a member of the faculty of the Young Presidents' Organization (YPO) International University for Presidents in Hong Kong and is the author or coauthor of more than 75 books and publications, including one of the leading business-law textbooks, *Managers and the Legal Environment: Strategies for the 21st Century*, 2nd ed. (St. Paul, Minn.: West, 1995). Connie has a J.D., *magna cum laude*, from Harvard Law School and an A.B., with Honors in political science and Distinction, from Stanford University, where she was elected to Phi Beta Kappa in her junior year. She is a member of the State Bar of California and the State Bar of New York.

Craig E. Dauchy is the managing partner of Cooley Godward LLP's Menlo Park office located in the heart of Silicon Valley, and is in charge of Cooley Godward's venture capital practice firmwide. With more than 325 lawyers and additional offices in Palo Alto, San Francisco, San Diego, Boulder, and Denver, Cooley Godward is one of the nation's leading law firms providing counsel to entrepreneurs and venture capitalists. The firm has represented both issuers and underwriters in more than 250 public offerings in recent years and, in each of the last five years, ranked among the top ten firms in the United States for serving as company counsel in the greatest number of venture-backed initial public offerings. In 1996 alone, Cooley Godward represented either the company or the underwriters in 76 public offerings, ranking it second in the United States. Craig has represented entrepreneurs, emerging companies, and venture capitalists in diverse industries, including medical devices, software, health care, electronics, and consumer products, for more than 20 years. He was featured in the 1987 *Venture* article "Don't Call Just Any Lawyer" and on the CD-ROM *Venture Capital* (INFON, 1994). Craig is a frequent lecturer on matters relating to securities law and public offerings, mergers and acquisitions, and venture capital. He also serves on a number of advisory boards and boards of directors. Craig has a J.D. and an M.B.A. from Stanford University and graduated *magna cum laude* with a B.A. in history from Yale University. He is a member of the State Bar of California.

To My Mother, with Love.
C.E.B.

To My Wife, Sue Crawford, and to My Mother
and Father, Philippa and Walter Dauchy.
C.E.D.

Taking the Plunge

I

*I*ndividuals start businesses for any number and combination of reasons: to be their own boss, to achieve financial reward, to establish a new livelihood after corporate downsizing, to fill an unmet need with an innovative product or service, or simply to create something. For example, Greg Steltenpohl and his childhood friend, Gerry Percy, started Odwalla, a fresh-juice maker, in 1980 as a way to raise money to produce musical programs in schools. Starting with a crate of oranges from the local farmers' market and a $250 juicer, the two squeezed the oranges in their backyard and delivered the fresh-squeezed juice to local restaurants. The concept caught on, and Odwalla went public in 1995. Today Odwalla is a $100-million company distributing more than 24 types of fresh-packed juices and blends throughout the western United States.

Despite the vast variety of entrepreneurs and their companies, once individuals decide to become entrepreneurs, they will be forced to confront the same issues. These issues will include whether to work alone or with one or more partners, what products or services to provide, and where to obtain the necessary capital.

One recent example of a company that resolved these issues successfully is Netscape Communications, the maker of Netscape Navigator®, a popular Internet browser. Netscape's founding team included James Clark, founder of Silicon Graphics, Inc., who provided the start-up capital, and Marc Andreessen, who helped create Mosaic, a graphical Internet browser, while an undergraduate at the University of Illinois. In April 1994, Andreessen reassembled his Mosaic research team by hiring five other former students and staff to work on the Netscape browser. In 1995, Netscape went public after attaining a dominant position with 80% market share in the Internet browser market. After the first day of trading, Netscape's market capitalization was $2.2 billion, and Clark and Andreessen owned stock worth more than $1 billion and $50 million, respectively.

Before taking the plunge, the would-be entrepreneur must also consider the sacrifices, both professional and personal, that will be required. These sacrifices may include accepting several years of low pay and long hours in exchange for a large potential payoff later. Successful entrepreneurship also requires a willingness to take risks. As Sandra Kurtzig, founder of Ask Computer Systems (a company she grew to $400 million in sales), points out, the act of quitting one's job and starting a new business is only the beginning.[1] An entrepreneur must continually take risks

---

FROM THE TRENCHES

Debbie Fields, the founder of Mrs. Fields Cookies, started her company at the age of 20. Fields had been baking cookies since she was a child, testing recipes on neighbors and her five sisters. She knew nothing about business, so she talked to local retired business owners, attended management seminars, and read every book she could find on starting a business. With $50,000 of start-up capital from her husband, Fields rented and renovated a small store in downtown Palo Alto, California. She canvassed auctions for bargains on ovens and cooking equipment, and carefully chose all the ingredients for her cookie recipes. Fields opened the store in 1977 and, together with her next-door neighbor, baked and sold cookies and managed the business. During the evenings she created new cookie recipes.

At first business was slow. Fields started handing out samples to passersby. Within a few weeks business picked up dramatically, and Fields decided to delay her return to college to concentrate on the store.

In 1979, Pier 39, a San Francisco shopping complex on Fisherman's Wharf, asked her to open a store. Fields had not thought of expanding, but after several months of consideration, she accepted Pier 39's offer. Rather than franchising, which would not allow her to easily control quality, she established Mrs. Fields Cookies, Inc., and hired and trained store managers. The Pier 39 store quickly generated the highest sales per square foot of all stores in the shopping complex.

Today, Mrs. Fields is a multimillion-dollar company with more than 500 stores in seven countries.

and be prepared to make the bet-the-company decisions that will determine the venture's ultimate success or failure.[2]

Regardless of how carefully one deliberates before making decisions, an entrepreneur will make mistakes. As Kurtzig puts it, "Screwing up is part of the process."[3] One key to being successful is to make fewer mistakes than the competition. Because legal risks are among the most important of the many risks faced by a young company, an entrepreneur can increase the likelihood of success by understanding and minimizing legal risk; that is, by spotting legal issues before they become legal problems.

The law, when harnessed correctly, can be a positive force that creates opportunities by making it possible for entrepreneurs to enforce agreements, protect creations, and shield themselves from liability.

FROM THE TRENCHES

Pete's Brewing Co. began in 1979 when Pete Slosberg decided to make homemade red wine. After pressing 200 pounds of cabernet grapes, squeezing the juice through a cheesecloth, then fermenting and bottling it, he realized he would have to wait five to ten years for it to mature before he could taste his creation. Agitated, he called the equipment company and learned that, with some modifications, the equipment would be suitable for beer-making. He joined a home-brewing club, and by 1986 his ale recipe had become so popular that he and a partner decided to start their own microbrewery.

Slosberg borrowed $50,000 from family and friends to rent a local commercial brewery, and he and 15 friends worked around the clock for four days to produce 500 cases of beer. The cases quickly sold out. Slosberg quit his job, and by 1991 Pete's Wicked Ale was selling 200,000 cases a year. Sales have doubled every year since.

Originally, Slosberg used a picture of his pet bull terrier, Millie, on his bottle label. About six months later, Anheuser-Busch, the world's largest beer manufacturer, launched an advertising campaign around the dog Spuds McKenzie. After lawyers on both sides exchanged numerous letters, Slosberg decided it was not worth taking on Anheuser-Busch, and he replaced Millie with a picture of himself.

The company went public in 1995, a year in which it sold approximately 115 million 12-ounce bottles for total revenues of $59 million.

Putting It into Practice

Alexandra Scott (our fictitious entrepreneur) has been an employee of Creative Software Solutions, Inc. (CSS), a corporation headquartered in Massachusetts, for the past seven years. CSS is a successful software company that develops programming kits for sale to software developers. It had revenues of $600 million in 1995. Alexandra began as a software development programmer and now heads CSS's Internet Applications Group. She is in charge of all CSS software development for the Internet. Most of her time is spent developing programming kits to write applets—small cross-platform programs written in Sun Microsystem's Java language. During her time at CSS, Alexandra has made full use of the company's tuition reimbursement program, and recently earned a Master of Science degree in computer science.

Eighteen months ago, while on a company-sponsored outing, Alexandra spoke with a friend from the Customer Service Group, Bill Ramseyer, about a problem identified by customers who were interested in writing applets that would rapidly retrieve proprietary content over the Internet. Shortly after that discussion, Alexandra decided the problem would make a challenging thesis project, and she began working on it at home during her spare time. She devised a revolutionary software application that allows applets to rapidly retrieve graphic and audio content from the Internet. Currently, limitations on bandwidth restrict the speed with which graphics and other large files are retrieved. This new method would facilitate the creation of applets and significantly decrease the user's Internet access costs. For example, one applet that Alexandra plans would automatically retrieve sports scores and photographic highlights of the sports and teams chosen by its user.

To develop her application, Alexandra worked alone and outside of regular work hours until six months ago, when Paul Eagle (a CSS Internet Applications Group programmer) and his spouse, Sheryl (a Stanford MBA), began working with her. The three signed a brief, handwritten agreement to form a partnership to develop what Alexandra dubbed the Internet Rapid Retrieval System (IRRS). The agreement stated that they would "divide any profits fairly." Alexandra was careful not to discuss her outside project with coworkers but occasionally borrowed technical manuals from work and attended CSS in-house presentations on related topics.

continued

continued

Alexandra has just returned from a six-week leave of absence, during which she prepared a presentation for potential investors and completed plans for commercializing the technology. Alexandra envisions her company using the technology to develop and sell specialized applets utilizing her breakthrough technology. She estimates that she will need $1.25 million to purchase the necessary equipment and hire programmers to create beta-test versions of a dozen applets that will form the nucleus of her virtual applet storefront. Alexandra believes that it is important to get her new venture under way as soon as possible, and realizes that, to do so, she and Paul must leave CSS. For geographic and family reasons, Alexandra, Paul, and Sheryl have decided to set up their new business in California.

In preparation for her departure, Alexandra asked to review her personnel file to determine what agreements with CSS she had signed. Alexandra vaguely remembers that on her first day she was given a stack of papers to sign and return. In her file she found forms for health insurance and tax withholdings, along with a long nondisclosure agreement that she had signed without reading. Now she sees that the agreement contains provisions for the assignment of inventions, a nondisclosure provision, a one-year covenant not to compete, and a no-raid provision, which prohibits the signee from actively hiring the company's employees. (For a further discussion of these provisions, see chapter 2.)

Before taking any action, Alexandra knows she must investigate some crucial issues. Below are some of the questions Alexandra ponders in the initial stages of forming her business and the corresponding chapters of this book in which her questions are addressed.

1. Who owns the Internet Rapid Retrieval System? What rights, if any, can CSS claim to it? (Chapter 2: Leaving Your Employer)
2. What can Alexandra do to make her departure from CSS amicable? Should she have left sooner? What ongoing obligations does she have to CSS? (Chapter 2: Leaving Your Employer)
3. Can Alexandra ask some of her colleagues at CSS to join her new enterprise? (Chapter 2: Leaving Your Employer)
4. Should Alexandra hire an attorney? How does she select one? (Chapter 3: Selecting and Working with an Attorney)

continued

continued

5. Given her limited budget, can Alexandra afford an attorney? Can she afford not to have one? (Chapter 3: Selecting and Working with an Attorney)

6. What would be an appropriate legal form for the business from a liability and tax standpoint? (Chapter 4: Deciding Whether to Incorporate)

7. How should Alexandra approach the issue of splitting the equity in her new venture among the three founders? (Chapter 5: Structuring the Ownership)

8. How will the three manage the venture? What happens if one of the founders leaves? (Chapter 5: Structuring the Ownership)

9. What are Alexandra's options to finance the new venture? (Chapter 6: Raising Money)

10. What happens if the company runs out of cash and cannot pay its debts? (Chapter 7: Creditors' Rights and Bankruptcy)

11. If Alexandra seeks venture capital financing, how should she approach the venture community? What business and legal provisions in the term sheet and other financing documents should concern her? What is negotiable? Are any of the terms a deal breaker? (Chapter 8: Venture Capital)

12. What are the advantages and disadvantages of having an active board of directors? Who should sit on the board, and what should Alexandra expect the directors to do? (Chapter 9: Forming the Board)

13. How can Alexandra ensure that her customers pay her on time and that her suppliers ship goods in the quantity and of the quality she needs for her business? What should she consider before signing a standard-form lease for office space? (Chapter 10: Contracts)

14. What warranties are implied when the company sells a product? Can the company disclaim all warranties and limit its liability to replacement of the product or refund of the purchase price? Can the company in its advertising speed up a videotape of the product in operation so that the product appears to retrieve images at a faster speed than it actually does? (Chapter 11: Product Liability, Warranties, and Advertising)

15. Does the company need to be concerned that the property it is considering leasing was previously used by an automotive store that sold

continued

continued

oil and other lubricants? How should the company resolve a claim for assault, battery, and false imprisonment arising out of an altercation with one of the company's employees, and how can the company protect itself against such claims in the future? (Chapter 12: Business Torts)

16. Does the company have to pay software engineers minimum wage and overtime? When is the company required to withhold taxes from a worker's check and pay Social Security taxes? What accommodations must the company make for workers with physical or mental disabilities? How should the company resolve a claim by a 41-year-old Hispanic woman that she was laid off because of her age, race, national origin and gender, and how can the company protect itself against such claims in the future? How should the company resolve a sexual-harassment claim brought by a male employee with a female supervisor? (Chapter 13: Human Resources)

17. How can the company protect its proprietary technology? Does the company need to worry about violating other companies' patents or copyrights? (Chapter 14: Intellectual Property)

18. How does the company provide its investors with a fair and liquid return? When is an initial public offering an appropriate exit strategy? When is it preferable to sell the business to a larger competitor? What is involved in going public? What does it mean to be a public company? (Chapter 15: Going Public)

Notes

1. Sandra L. Kurtzig, *CEO: Building a $400 Million Company from the Ground Up* (Boston, Mass: Harvard Business School Press, 1994), at 2.
2. Id. at 2-3.
3. Id. at 3.

Leaving Your Employer

2

Sometimes an entrepreneur will start a new business right out of school or while between jobs. More often, a person decides to start his or her own company while still employed by a more established company. The idea for a new business may come from something the person was working on for the current employer. Depending on the agreements the entrepreneur has with his or her current employer, the entrepreneur's position, and the nature of the proposed new business, the entrepreneur may not be free to work on the venture while still employed or for some time thereafter.

For example, the employee may have signed an agreement containing a *no-moonlighting clause*, which prohibits the employee from engaging in any business activities (even after-hours activities) unrelated to the employee's job with the employer. A signed nondisclosure agreement (discussed later) prohibits the entrepreneur from using or disclosing any of the employer's trade secrets (such as a customer list) unless the employer authorizes it. The prohibition continues even after the entrepreneur quits. In some cases, the entrepreneur may have signed an agreement in which he or she agreed not to compete with the former employer for some period of time after leaving the employer (a *covenant not to compete*). The entrepreneur's ability to recruit former coworkers to join the new enterprise may also be restricted.

Awareness of these restrictions is crucial. A lawsuit arising out of the entrepreneur's duties to his or her former employer can result in a level of expense and drain on management time sufficient to sink the venture. At a minimum, the new company would be greatly impeded by the threat of a lawsuit by the former employer.

This chapter discusses the restrictions that are applicable while a person is still employed by another, and postemployment restrictions, including a covenant not to compete. It then presents strategies for leaving on good terms.

RESTRICTIONS WHILE STILL EMPLOYED

The employer-employee relationship is based on confidence and trust, which gives rise to certain legal duties. For example, the employer has a duty to maintain a good working environment and to compensate the employee for his or her efforts. In return, the employee has a duty to use his or her best efforts on behalf of the employer, and not to act in any way that is adverse to the employer's interests. The extent of the duties that an employee has to a former employer depends on the position held at the company and whether the new venture will compete with the employer. In addition, the employee needs to consider the issue of solicitation of coworkers.

Position with the Company

Absent a covenant not to compete and a no-moonlighting clause, the employee's position will largely determine what he or she can legally do while contemplating starting a new business. This determination is made in large part on the basis of which of three main categories of positions the employee falls into: key employees, skilled employees, and unskilled employees.

Key employees (such as officers, directors, or managers) and *skilled employees* (such as software engineers, marketing specialists, or sales representatives) owe a duty of loyalty to the company. This duty, which exists regardless of whether there is an employment contract, prohibits an employee from doing anything that would harm the employer while he or she is still employed. This includes operating a business that competes with the employer or that usurps any business opportunities that the employer might be interested in exploring. A key or skilled employee may make plans to compete with an employer but may neither actually compete nor solicit employees to work for the new business during the period of employment.

The duties of *unskilled employees* (and other employees not in positions of trust) are generally confined to the period of time during which they are actually working. Their off-hour activities are not restricted unless these activities are detrimental to the employer's interests. However, even unskilled employees can be restricted from competing with the company during their nonworking hours by a covenant not to compete or a no-moonlighting clause in an employment agreement.

Type of New Venture

The activities in which an employee can engage to further a new venture while still employed also depend on whether the venture will compete

---

FROM THE TRENCHES

When cofounder Steve Jobs left Apple Computer Inc. in 1985, he outraged Apple's board by persuading five top Apple managers to join in starting NeXT, Inc. Jobs had been chairman and CEO, but was stripped of the CEO position and control over day-to-day operations in May 1985. Thereafter, he began planning his new company. Five days before resigning as chairman, Jobs gave then Apple CEO John Scully a list of the five employees who would be joining him at NeXT. Jobs also inquired about the possibility of licensing Apple technology for his new venture. Apple responded by suing Jobs for breach of his fiduciary responsibilities as chairman and for misappropriation of confidential and proprietary information. Four months later, Apple agreed to settle the suit in return for Job's promise that NeXT would not hire any additional Apple employees for a six-month period and would not solicit Apple employees for a year. NeXT also granted Apple the right to inspect NeXT's products before they were marketed.

with the current employer. If the new enterprise is a noncompeting business, the employee (whether a key employee, skilled employee, or unskilled employee) is essentially free to establish and operate the new venture so long as it does not interfere with current job performance or violate any provisions (such as a no-moonlighting clause) in any employment agreement. An employee may make telephone calls, rent an office, hire employees (but not coworkers, except as explained below), and retain attorneys and accountants provided that two conditions are met. First, the employee may not use any of the employer's resources (e.g., telephone, fax machine, printer, copying machine, laptop or home computer supplied by the employer, or conference room). Second, all activities must be conducted after hours.

What constitutes *after hours* is not always clear. For an employee with specified work hours, defining what is after hours may be easy. It becomes more difficult when the entrepreneur is a key employee whose working hours are not strictly defined and who has a duty to use best efforts to further the interests of the employer. For example, software engineers are famous for doing their best work between midnight and dawn. For them, there may be no clear after hours during the workweek. Instead, vacations may provide the only truly free time to develop an outside venture.

On the other hand, if the new venture will compete directly with the current employer, the entrepreneur's actions are significantly more restricted. Key employees and skilled employees may not prepare for and plan the new venture if doing so would interfere with their job responsibilities. Under no

---

FROM THE TRENCHES

A consultant wanting to open a new restaurant explicitly worked out with his employer arrangements for his new venture. He told the consulting firm that he was involved in starting a new, noncompeting business, and that, if it did well, there was a possibility that he would work on it full time. The parties agreed that he would be responsible for fulfilling his duties as a consultant while working on his culinary interest after hours.

circumstances may they be involved in the actual operation of a competing venture while still employed by the employer.

Once plans for the competing business are in place, it is almost always advisable to terminate the employment relationship. Although it may be tempting to continue working, the potential liability and the time required to straighten out any legal or business conflicts that may arise will probably outweigh the benefit of the extra income.

The rules are summarized in Exhibit 2.1.

Solicitation of Coworkers

Solicitation of coworkers to leave their employment and come to work for the new company can be a sensitive issue. If the coworker has an employment contract for a definite term (e.g., two years), the entrepreneur

---

EXHIBIT 2.1

Summary of Permissible Activities While Still Employed by Another

	TYPE OF VENTURE	
TYPE OF EMPLOYEE	**NONCOMPETING VENTURE**	**COMPETING VENTURE**
Key Employee Skilled Employee	Can prepare for and operate the venture so long as it does not interfere with responsibilities and fiduciary duty. If subject to a no-moonlighting clause, the employee cannot operate it.	Can prepare for the venture so long as it does not interfere with responsibilities and fiduciary duty. Cannot operate it.
Unskilled Employee	Can prepare for and operate the venture so long as it does not interfere with responsibilities. If subject to a no-moonlighting clause, the employee cannot operate it.	Can prepare for the venture so long as it does not interfere with responsibilities. If under covenant not to compete or a no-moonlighting clause, the employee cannot operate it.

seeking to lure the coworker away may be liable for damages for intentionally and improperly encouraging the coworker to break that contract and to leave the employer before the specified term is over. The employer could sue for intentional interference with contract, a tort discussed further in chapter 12.

Even if the coworkers do not have a written employment contract and their employment is terminable *at-will* (i.e., at any time, by either party, for any reason), an entrepreneur can still be held liable if the entrepreneur's conduct leads coworkers to violate any applicable restrictive covenants. For example, an entrepreneur may want to hire away a coworker who has access to the company's confidential information and who has developed special expertise that could be of great value to the new business. However, this may result in the violation of the coworker's nondisclosure agreement or of a covenant not to compete. (As discussed below, even in the absence of a nondisclosure agreement, the entrepreneur and the coworker may be opening themselves up to liability for misappropriation of trade secrets.)

Key employees are even more restricted in how they may approach coworkers. Generally, if a key employee induces another employee to move to a competitor, and the inducement is willfully kept from the employer, the conduct is a breach of fiduciary duty. Everyone who has participated in or benefited from that breach may be held liable. In one case, several key management employees induced several coworkers to leave their employer and enter into employment with their newly formed competing air-freight forwarding company. The management employees were held liable to the former employer for breach of fiduciary duty, fraud, and interference with contractual relations. The fact that none of the employees had employment contracts was irrelevant.

There is a distinction generally drawn between soliciting coworkers and telling them about future plans. Although pretermination solicitation may be problematic, some courts would not prevent an entrepreneur from discussing his or her plans with coworkers. If coworkers are interested, they can contact the entrepreneur later and discuss any potential job opportunities.

Often employees are asked to sign an agreement expressly prohibiting them from soliciting coworkers, inducing coworkers to leave, or hiring them for some stated period of time after leaving the former employer. Such a provision is referred to as an *antipiracy* or *no-raid clause*. If the entrepreneur has signed such an agreement and solicits or hires in violation of it, the former employer could successfully sue for breach of contract, and perhaps even obtain an injunction or court order preventing the personnel from working for the entrepreneur.

POSTEMPLOYMENT RESTRICTIONS AND THE COVENANT NOT TO COMPETE

Once an entrepreneur leaves the former place of employment, he or she still may be restricted by an antipiracy clause (discussed above) or by a covenant not to compete (also known as a *noncompete covenant*). A covenant not to compete is an agreement between an employer and an employee designed to protect the employer from potentially harmful competition from a former employee. Prohibited competition usually includes dealing with or soliciting business from the former employer's customers, or using the former employer's confidential business information for the benefit of the new employer.

To be binding and legally enforceable, the covenant not to compete must meet certain requirements. It must be ancillary to some other agreement; designed to protect a legitimate interest of the employer; reasonably limited in scope, geography, and duration; and not contrary to the interests of the public. In addition, it must be supported by adequate consideration, that is, the person agreeing to the covenant must receive something of value from the other party. If the court finds that a legally valid covenant has been breached, the court may issue an injunction ordering the entrepreneur to stop the offending activities and/or award damages.

Ancillary to Another Agreement

For a noncompete covenant to be valid, it must be subordinate to some lawful contract that describes the relationship between the parties, such as a formal employment agreement, a sale-of-business contract, or an agreement dissolving a partnership. A stand-alone covenant not to compete is a naked restraint on trade, which is, in many states, *per se*, or by itself, invalid. For example, a court refused to enforce a noncompete covenant executed during an employment-at-will relationship (which is characterized by the absence of an employment contract) because the covenant was not ancillary to an otherwise enforceable agreement.[1]

Legitimate Interests

A noncompete covenant may legally protect only legitimate interests of the employer. A general interest in restricting competition is insufficient. For the employer to enforce a restrictive covenant, the employee must present a substantial risk either to the employer's customer base or to confidential business information. Employer interests that have been found to be legitimate include protection of trade secrets and other confidential information, long-term customer relationships, and customer lists and other confidential customer information, as well as protection of the goodwill, business reputation, and unique skills associated with the company.

Limited in Scope

The restrictions imposed by the noncompete covenant must be reasonably related to the interests protected. To be valid, these restrictions must be limited in time, geographical area, and scope of activities affected. In case of a dispute, the court will scrutinize closely the imposed restrictions to determine how they relate to the employer's business. If the court finds the restrictions overly broad, it will typically either modify some terms of the covenant to make them reasonable (e.g., shorten the duration) or declare the whole covenant invalid. A well-drafted covenant will contain a provision that invites the court to enforce the covenant to the greatest extent possible under applicable law and to modify the covenant as needed to make it enforceable. This is called a *blue-lining clause*.

The determination of the validity of restrictions varies greatly from case to case and is very fact specific. For example, one court upheld a two-year covenant not to compete whereby a dermatologist was prohibited from practicing dermatology within a thirty-mile radius of the offices of the doctor for whom he had worked. Two years was considered reasonable to erase from the public's mind any identification of the dermatologist with his former employer's practice and to allow the former employer to reestablish his relationship with patients who had been referred to the dermatologist. The thirty-mile radius covered the territory from which the dermatologist's former employer drew most of his patients.[2]

With respect to the time restriction, courts have generally found one year or less to be a reasonable limitation, while a court probably would never enforce a covenant for a period of more than five years, except perhaps in connection with the sale of a business.

Some courts will not enforce a covenant extending beyond the geographical area where the employer currently does business. One court refused to enforce a covenant prohibiting an employee who was fired for poor performance from competing with his former employer for two years in a 300-mile area. The court held that it was unreasonable "to permit the employer to retain unfettered control over that which it has effectively discarded as worthless to its legitimate business interests."[3]

FROM THE TRENCHES

Maria started a successful computer export company that built an enormous client base in Latin America. When she decided to cash out a number of years later by selling her company to a multinational computer exporting company, she was required to sign a noncompete agreement that, among other things, prohibited her from competing against her company's acquirer in the export of computers to Latin America. Rather than try to learn a completely different industry, she applied her experience to a new company she founded in Africa, thereby replicating her Latin American success in another part of the world.

Interests of the Public

In determining the validity of a noncompete covenant, the court will also look at the interests of the public affected by the covenant. Noncompete covenants can prevent the uninhibited flow of labor necessary for a competitive market. The public policy of preserving free labor markets disfavors any such restraints on trade and puts limits on the use of restrictive covenants. In addition, there is a basic belief that a person must be able to ply his or her trade to earn a living. But covenants not to compete also help deter unethical business practices, such as stealing trade secrets, and lack of adequate protection may make it less likely that persons will start new businesses and spend time and money to develop and market better and cheaper products that increase consumer wealth. The balance struck between these competing public policies varies from state to state and is reflected in each state's legislation and judicially created law (called *common law*).

State-Enacted Legislation A number of states have enacted legislation restricting the enforceability of noncompete covenants. Such legislation generally falls into three categories. Some states, such as California, have statutes that broadly prohibit covenants restraining anyone from engaging in a lawful profession, trade, or business. Some credit this California law as being the impetus for the growth of Silicon Valley, as many companies were founded by the former employees of older companies. Other states, such as Oregon, have statutes that do not contain such a broad prohibition but rather regulate only some aspects of employee covenants not to compete. Texas and a number of other states have taken yet another approach, adopting statutory reasonableness standards that must be satisfied for the covenants to be enforced. Some states prohibit enforcement of noncompete covenants in their state constitutions. States that do not have special legislation or a constitutional provision governing the use of the covenants not to compete have judicially created, or common law, rules of reason for determining the validity and enforceability of such covenants.

Some states will not enforce a covenant not to compete against an employee living in that state if the covenant from another jurisdiction is not consistent with the law of the state where the employee lives, even if there is an employment agreement specifying that the law of the employer's principal place of business should govern. For example, a California court would probably not enforce a covenant not to compete against a California resident even though the employer's principal place of business is in Massachusetts (which does honor postemployment covenants) and the employment agreement provides that Massachusetts law will apply.[4]

Exceptions to Legislation Many states that have broad prohibitions against covenants not to compete have exceptions to permit such covenants in certain limited circumstances. For example, California has statutory exceptions permitting reasonable restrictions not to exceed five years in duration in connection with the sale of the goodwill of the business; the sale of all of the covenantor's shares in a corporation (the covenantor is typically the owner selling the business and, upon the sale, may be restricted from starting a similar business in a certain location); and the dissolution of a partnership or the sale of a limited liability company. California's statutory exceptions have been further narrowed by judicial rulings that limit restraints against the pursuit of an entire or substantial part of a profession, trade, or business, and allow restrictions only if the effect is not significant.

Breach of a Noncompete Clause

If the court finds that the employee breached a valid noncompete covenant, it will impose liability on the offender. The most common form of relief for an employee's breach of a noncompete covenant is an injunction that would require an employee to stop competing against the former employer. In some cases, actual damages may be assessed against an employee in an amount calculated to put the employer in the same position that it would have been in had there been no breach.

TRADE SECRETS

Most states expressly prohibit the misappropriation of trade secrets as a matter of law, regardless of whether the employee signed an agreement prohibiting use or disclosure. Unauthorized use or disclosure of the employer's trade secrets is generally prohibited both during and after employment. Even if a particular state will not enforce a covenant not to compete, all courts will generally enforce an agreement by an employee not to disclose or use trade secrets belonging to the former employer.

A *trade secret* is information used in one's business that provides the business owner an economic advantage over competitors who do not have access to this information. (Trade secrets and programs for their protection are discussed further in chapter 14.) Information is considered secret when it is neither generally known nor readily ascertainable in the industry. What constitutes a trade secret is not always evident. A trade secret can be a formula, pattern, program, device, method, technique, process, or customer list. The two critical factors in determining whether a trade secret exists are (1) the value of the information to the business owner and competitors and (2) the amount of effort made to maintain the secrecy of the information. These two factors are closely related, because the more valuable a certain piece of

FROM THE TRENCHES

Collagen Corp., a biomedical product company, sued Matrix Pharmaceutical Inc., a drug delivery company, in 1994 for theft of trade secrets after Matrix hired 10 former Collagen employees. In its amended complaint, which named two of the employees as additional defendants, Collagen alleged that Matrix was in possession of several boxes of files and other material taken from Collagen by Collagen's former director of manufacturing. Collagen claimed that these documents contained details about Collagen's proprietary manufacturing process as well as proposed budgets, production and sales forecasts, and a capital allocation plan.

information is to a business owner, the more likely he or she will make efforts to keep it secret.

Security procedures that the owner implements are generally the most important evidence of the existence of a trade secret. Both external and internal security procedures can be used by a company to ensure the integrity of its trade secrets. External security procedures protect trade secrets from being disclosed to parties outside of the company, such as customers and competitors. The goal of these procedures is to ensure that dissemination of information to third parties does not result in the loss of trade secret status. Procedures controlling the publication of news releases, manuals and sales brochures, and third-party confidentiality agreements are examples of external security procedures.

Internal security procedures provide clear notice to employees that they are dealing with confidential information, and they control dissemination of such information within the company. Some examples of internal security procedures include storing confidential information in locked files; requiring employees to keep a clean desk; programming special access codes into computer systems and changing them regularly; limiting access to certain information on a need-to-know basis; requiring employees to wear identification badges; and having guards on the premises.

A prohibition on the use or disclosure of trade secrets and confidential information is usually included in a specialized agreement called a *nondisclosure agreement* (or *NDA*). The purpose of this agreement is to put employees on notice that they are exposed to trade secret information in their work, to inform employees about their duties with regards to such information, and to create a covenant restricting their disclosure or use of trade secrets or other confidential information after the termination of their employment. The validity of a nondisclosure agreement is conditioned on the existence of the trade secrets it is designed to protect. If trade secrets do exist, then a reasonable nondisclosure agreement will be upheld.

A court may enjoin a former employee from working for a competitor firm if the former employer is able to prove that the employer's new employment will inevitably lead him or her to rely on the former employer's trade secrets. For example, one case involved a former PepsiCo employee who was privy to sensitive, confidential strategic, marketing, distribution, and pricing plans relating to PepsiCo's sports drink All Sport and its ready-to-drink tea products and fruit drinks. He left PepsiCo to work for Quaker Oats, seller of market leaders Gatorade and Snapple. The court concluded that the former employee would necessarily rely on his knowledge of PepsiCo's trade secrets when making decisions at Quaker Oats about Gatorade and Snapple. This put PepsiCo "in the position of a coach, one of whose players has left, playbook in hand, to join the opposing team before the big game."[5] The court prohibited him from working at Quaker Oats for a period of six months.

People who steal trade secrets risk not only civil liability but also may face criminal penalties. For example, Guillermo "Bill" Gaede, a former

---

FROM THE TRENCHES

Peak Computer maintained computer systems, including MAI Systems Corporation computers, for its clients. Peak's maintenance of MAI computers accounted for between 50% and 70% of Peak's business. MAI also maintained MAI computers for its customers. MAI's customer service manager and three other employees left to join Peak. Thereafter, MAI began to lose maintenance business to Peak. MAI sued Peak and its former employees for, among other things, copyright infringement, misappropriation of trade secrets, trademark infringement, and unfair competition.

MAI sought and received a temporary restraining order and preliminary injunction. The preliminary injunction was ultimately converted to a permanent injunction. The permanent injunction enjoined Peak from infringing on MAI copyrights, misappropriating MAI trade secrets, maintaining MAI computers, soliciting MAI customers, and maintaining certain MAI customer contacts.

The court determined that MAI's customer database was a protectable trade secret which had potential economic value because it allowed a competitor such as Peak to direct its sales efforts to those potential customers that were already using MAI's computer system. The fact that Peak contended that the former customer service manager never took MAI's customer database or put such information into the Peak database was not sufficient to affect the court's ruling.

Source: MAI Systems Corporation v. Peak Computer, Inc., 991 F.2d 511 (9th Cir. 1993).

©1996 Washington Post Writers Group. Reprinted with permission.

Intel Corp. software engineer, pleaded guilty in March 1996 to mail fraud and interstate transportation of stolen property for stealing copies of Intel's designs for its 486 and Pentium microprocessors and sending them to Advanced Micro Devices, Inc. (AMD), a rival microprocessor company. AMD returned the plans to Intel and contacted the FBI. The engineer faced a maximum penalty of 15 years in prison and $500,000 in fines and restitution.

Even if there is no nondisclosure agreement, most states have passed statutes, such as the Uniform Trade Secrets Act (UTSA; adopted by 37 states), that prohibit an employee from disclosing or using trade secrets belonging to the former employer. In those states that have not adopted the UTSA or comparable legislation, there are common-law rules judges have developed that prohibit misappropriation of trade secrets.

INVENTION ASSIGNMENT AGREEMENT

The *invention assignment agreement* is another type of agreement an employee often is asked to sign. This document requires the employee to assign to the employer all inventions conceived, developed, or reduced to practice by the employee while employed by the company. Some states restrict the scope of such agreements. California, for example, prohibits the application of such agreements to inventions that the employee developed entirely on his or her own time without using the employer's equipment, supplies, facilities, or trade secret information, except when such

---

FROM THE TRENCHES

General Motors Corp., a U.S. automobile manufacturer, was involved in a heated dispute with Volkswagen AG, a German carmaker, over the defection of GM's former purchasing chief to Volkswagen. GM filed suit in March 1996 against VW, Jose Ignacio Lopez de Arriortua, and ten former GM managers, alleging that Lopez and the other former employees took numerous boxes of secret GM documents when they quit GM to join VW. The documents in question allegedly contained confidential GM information about prices for parts, new models, and marketing strategies. The parties settled in early 1997, with VW agreeing to pay GM $100 million and to buy at least $1 billion worth of GM parts over seven years. Lopez resigned from VW and was criminally indicted by German authorities.

Source: Gabriella Stern and Brandon Mitchener, "GM Agreed to VW Pact to Avoid Further Costs, Risks," The Wall Street Journal, Jan. 13, 1997, at B4.

---

inventions relate to the employer's business or to current or demonstrably anticipated research and development, or result from any work performed by the employee for the employer. Thus, if, for example, an employee of a software development company involved in developing database management software creates, on her own time and using her own home computer, a new and improved way to input files, that new program will belong to her employer because it is related to her employer's business.

Invention assignment agreements may provide for the assignment of inventions not only during the period of employment but also within a certain time, typically one year, after the termination of employment. Such agreements are not *per se* invalid. One court found, for example, that an agreement was valid and enforceable as it related to ideas and concepts based on secrets or confidential information of the employer even if conceived within one year after the termination of employment. It is important, however, that any restriction on an employee's further inventive activities be limited in time. Thus, although some agreements providing for assignment of inventions made within one year of employment termination have been found valid, other agreements requiring

---

FROM THE TRENCHES

Exxon Corp. and Fina Inc., two rival oil companies, engaged in litigation over the ownership of patents covering polymer molecules, which are used to make plastic. Exxon claimed that a former employee breached a nondisclosure agreement. John A. Ewen, who was involved in polymer research for Exxon, left in 1983 and was hired by Fina as its director of research. Within five years, Fina had filed thirty patents for polymers based on Ewen's work. One significant patent being contested covered a new substance for making super-hard, impact-resistant, clear plastic. When Exxon learned of Ewen's discoveries in 1989, it hired intellectual property lawyers to determine if Ewen had breached his agreements with Exxon. Exxon's investigation led to a lawsuit against Fina and Ewen. In 1993, Fina and Ewen settled with Exxon, agreeing to allow Exxon to use the disputed technology when it was commercially viable.

Source: Bridget O'Brien, "Material Obsession: Battle Over Patents Pits Two Oil Concerns Against One Scientist," The Wall Street Journal, March 1, 1996, at A1.

---

assignments for longer periods have not been enforced. One court, for example, found a contract provision requiring an employee to assign ideas and improvements conceived by him for five years after termination of employment to be unreasonable and void as against public policy.

Even if there is no assignment-of-inventions agreement, by law the patent to any invention by a person expressly "hired to invent" belongs to the employer. The courts construe this narrowly, holding, for example, that a person "hired to improve" was not subject to this rule. Similarly, as a matter of copyright law, the copyright to any work created by an employee acting within the scope of employment belongs to the employer, even if the employee has not signed an assignment-of-inventions agreement.

STRATEGIES FOR LEAVING ON GOOD TERMS

To the extent possible, an employee should try to leave the current employer on good terms. To do this, the employee must be honest with the employer about the real reasons for leaving. If the employee lies and says she is going to set up a noncompeting business, then in fact starts a competing company, the employer is likely to think the worst of the former employee. This will spark fears of stolen trade secrets and other misdeeds.

When the employee tells the employer of his future plans, it may be appropriate to offer the employer an opportunity to invest in the employee's new venture. The employer will be most likely to invest if the entrepreneur's prospective business will make products that are complementary to the employer's products. Complementary products can increase a product's market and help establish it as an industry standard. For example, Autodesk's AutoCAD (Computer Aided Design) program has been so successful in part because it contains "hooks" that allow other software companies to design applications for AutoCAD. The availability of these additional applications has helped make AutoCAD an industry standard.

Having the employer invest in the new business offers several benefits. First, it may provide an easy source of funding for the entrepreneur. In addition to money, the employer may contribute technology, commercial expertise, and industry contacts. Second, it generates goodwill between the parties by aligning the interests of the employer with those of the entrepreneur. This alignment is important because the employer may be a valuable customer or supplier of the entrepreneur's business. Additionally, with an equity interest in the new enterprise, the employer may be more willing to allow the entrepreneur to hire other current employees. The entrepreneur should be careful,

---

FROM THE TRENCHES

Two employees of a software company told their employer that they were leaving to start a restaurant. In fact, they founded a competing software company. Their former employer was furious—in part because he had been lied to and in part because he suspected misappropriation of trade secrets—and was successful in getting a court to issue an injunction that prevented the closing of the start-up's financing.

FROM THE TRENCHES

When Chiron Corp., a leading biotechnology company, bought Cetus Corp., a neighboring biotechnology firm, for $300 million in 1992, it did so based largely on the strength of Cetus's cancer research. Shortly after the acquisition, Frank McCormick, the head of cancer research, and his staff decided to leave Chiron to start a new venture-capital financed cancer research company. When Chiron learned of the pending defection, it persuaded McCormick and the venture backers to restructure the deal to give Chiron a noncontrolling 42.8 percent stake in the new company, named Onyx Pharmaceutical. In return for the equity stake and first rights to diagnostics and vaccines developed by Onyx, Chiron contributed $4 million and technology to the new venture.

---

however, about how much of an ownership stake and control he or she gives his or her former employer. Allowing the former employer to be more than a passive investor may create the same situation that the employee left in the first place, namely that the entrepreneur will again be working for someone else.

The entrepreneur should avoid soliciting coworkers while still employed. Active solicitation of employees by skilled or key employees during employment constitutes a breach of the entrepreneur's duty of loyalty and could lead to an injunction preventing the entrepreneur from hiring anyone from his prior employer. A good strategy is for the entrepreneur to tell people that he is leaving. If people ask him what his future plans are, it is OK for him to tell them he plans to start a new business and to give them a phone number at which he can be reached. Through this method, employees of the entrepreneur's former employer will contact the entrepreneur directly, thereby shielding the entrepreneur from allegations of solicitation.

Putting It into Practice

Alexandra decided that the time had come to inform her boss at CSS of her future plans. Before discussing her departure, she contacted Adele Washington, a college roommate who had graduated from law school, for advice on the enforceability of the agreement that she had signed. Adele told her that the agreement specified that Massachusetts law governed its interpretation and enforcement. However, Adele believed that a California court would not enforce a posttermination noncompete covenant against a California resident, even though the contract stated that Massachusetts law governs the employment relationship. The California courts strongly favor employees when faced with ruling on noncompete covenants.

Adele told Alexandra that she was bound, however, by the provisions covering the assignment of ownership of inventions, and by the no-moonlighting, nondisclosure, and no-raid clauses. Of the four provisions, the one covering assignment of inventions was potentially the most problematic. Even though Alexandra developed the IRRS technology on her own time, because the invention related to CSS's business and she used some of CSS's resources (the technical manuals), CSS probably owned the technology.

Adele explained that the no-moonlighting clause prohibited Alexandra from starting her business while employed at CSS. Alexandra breached this agreement when she and the Eagles signed a partnership agreement to develop the IRRS technology. Although it would have been all right for Alexandra to make plans for her new venture before quitting, she should not have begun operating until she left. The nondisclosure provision prohibited Alexandra from using or disclosing any confidential information that she learned while working for CSS. The no-raid clause prohibited Alexandra from soliciting employees from CSS. She was permitted, however, to hire employees if they contacted her about a potential job. Alexandra and the Eagles did not plan to hire any other employees in the initial phases, so this was not an issue.

Armed with this advice, Alexandra went to see her supervisor. After she informed her supervisor of her plans, the supervisor told her that she would need to speak to the director of research regarding the rights to the IRRS technology. A few days later Alexandra and Adele met with the director of research and CSS's corporate counsel. After some negotiating,

continued

continued

both parties agreed to the following arrangement. CSS would transfer all of its rights to the IRRS technology to Alexandra's new company in exchange for 15% of the equity.

Satisfied with the agreement she had reached, Alexandra gave official notice of her resignation. She informed people who asked that she was leaving to start a new business and gave them a phone number at which she could be reached.

Alexandra realized that if she took any CSS documents or disks she could be accused of stealing trade secrets. She returned all non-IRRS-related documents and disks to her supervisor, deleted all non-IRRS-related information on the hard drives of her office and home computers, and walked out of CSS carrying only her personal effects.

Although Adele had been helpful in advising Alexandra about issues related to leaving CSS, she was not experienced in representing start-ups. Alexandra next turned her attention to selecting a lawyer for her new venture.

NOTES

1. *Travel Masters, Inc. v. Star Tours, Inc.*, 827 S.W.2d 830 (Tex. 1991).
2. *Weber v. Tillman*, 913 P.2d 84 (Kan. 1996).
3. *Insulation Corp. of America v. Brobston*, 667 A.2d 729 (Pa. Super. Ct. 1995).
4. *See, e.g., Hollingsworth Solderness Terminal Co. v. Turley*, 622 F.2d 1324 (9th Cir. 1980).
5. *PepsiCo, Inc. v. Redmond*, 54 F.3d 1262 (7th Cir. 1995).

Selecting and Working with an Attorney

3

*E*arly in the development of the business, the entrepreneur should consider the need for an attorney. Depending on what the entrepreneur is looking for and the ability of the attorney, the role of a corporate attorney can be varied. The corporate attorney can be someone who is called on periodically to address a potential legal issue or, at the other extreme, can be someone who provides invaluable assistance by acting as a sounding board for both business and legal issues. In the long run, a good attorney can enhance the bottom line of the enterprise by providing sound advice and preventing unforeseen liabilities. Yet, no matter what the capacity of the attorney, the costs associated with retaining legal counsel can be substantial. Many attorneys charge hundreds of dollars per hour for legal guidance.

This chapter explains the need for an attorney and suggests how to choose the right one. It addresses the challenge of deciding when and to what extent to work with an attorney, given the financial constraints of the new enterprise. It summarizes typical billing options and provides suggestions for keeping fees under control. The chapter concludes with a brief description of the attorney-client privilege, which is key to keeping communications with an attorney confidential.

The authors gratefully acknowledge the contributions of P. Y. Nicole Chang to this chapter. Ms. Chang received her J.D. and M.B.A. degrees from Stanford University, and is an associate with McKinsey and Company, an international consulting firm.

THE NEED FOR AN ATTORNEY

Although there is no scarcity of published legal guides and prefabricated forms on the market, it is highly advisable that the entrepreneur not rely on these materials to the exclusion of expert legal guidance. The law can be quite complicated, and mistakes are costly. Although an entrepreneur may feel that he or she can turn to published sources for specific answers, often the value of a corporate attorney is having someone point out potential problems that the entrepreneur never thought about.

Furthermore, at a certain stage, most start-ups need attorneys. Certain matters require the legal experience and skills that only an attorney can provide. In addition, as the business grows, issues related to real estate, employment, intellectual property, securities, tax, and other areas of specialty may arise. They can be quite complicated and are best delegated to an outside expert so that the entrepreneur can focus on the day-to-day running of the business.

In assessing when to start looking for an attorney, an entrepreneur must weigh the financial costs and administrative hassle of finding an attorney against the potential benefits in terms of business and legal advice and document production. Although certain firms may offer reduced rates and deferred-payment plans until the entrepreneur gets started, typically the costs are significant.

FROM THE TRENCHES

One entrepreneur knew the time was ripe for getting an attorney on board when he was attempting to put together a financing package and structure a founders' agreement. The entrepreneur wanted an agreement that would appreciate the complexity of the founders' situations. When the business was initially starting, each of the four founders was putting in differing amounts of time because of their diverse strengths. The cofounders wanted to capture the value-added that each was adding to the business during its different stages of risk.

CHOOSING AN ATTORNEY

As is the case with finding an appropriate doctor, finding an appropriate attorney is not as easy as looking in the yellow pages of the local telephone book. Although any attorney licensed to practice in the state can theoretically fulfill many of the legal requirements of the entrepreneur, only a small percentage of them have the experience and expertise necessary to provide adequate legal guidance.

An efficient search requires diligence on the part of the entrepreneur. First, the entrepreneur should consider whether he or she wants to work with a large or small firm and then identify through referrals some attorneys to investigate. Next, the entrepreneur should interview as many of them as possible.

Large Firm or Small Firm

The two main differences between a large and small firm are the difference between working with a specialist and a generalist, and the costs and billing procedures.

Large firms typically have many groups of attorneys who specialize in discrete areas of law. Smaller firms, on the other hand, typically have practitioners who have a greater breadth of knowledge. Small boutique firms usually specialize in a specific area, such as patents. Thus, the trade-off may be seen as depth versus breadth. However, in a large firm each attorney has access to many specialists, which in turn gives the entrepreneur access to a vast amount of internal knowledge. Also, some large firms have attorneys who specialize in representing entrepreneurs, and thus have the breadth of knowledge found in smaller firms. For the young start-up with general and common business issues, the difference may be inconsequential. Initially, an entrepreneur may want to focus on finding an attorney who has experience in meeting the entrepreneur's immediate concerns in an efficient and timely manner.

The cost and billing structure of large and small firms may differ greatly. Larger firms tend to charge more per hour but may be better able to accommodate a deferred payment structure and may be more efficient

---

FROM THE TRENCHES

A small entertainment company that wanted to incorporate and have ownership agreements drafted went to a major San Francisco Bay Area firm. The founders were directed to a second-year associate who was assigned the work. After a few weeks it was apparent that the associate was listening to one founder and not the other. When the entrepreneurs complained to a partner, they were told that the firm does not usually handle clients as small as their company. The partner, however, said that the firm was not used to people being dissatisfied with its work and so would not charge the entrepreneurs. The entrepreneurs went to a solo practitioner who was able to meet their needs. They continue to use the solo practitioner.

(thereby spending fewer billable hours) because of their expertise. In addition, attorneys from larger firms have lower-paid assistants helping them, which, again, brings down the cost of services. On the flip side, although an entrepreneur may benefit from this cheaper-by-the-hour help, the inefficiencies of involving more persons who are also less experienced may outweigh the benefits.

Referrals

Although it may seem that the numerous lawyer referral services or law directories could help the entrepreneur make a good decision, these sources are usually insufficient. Choosing an attorney is a very personal decision, and these sources are impersonal and often untested. The choice of the best attorney depends on the entrepreneur's type of business and his or her own business expertise, personality, and skills. One of the best sources for finding a good lead is to ask friends, colleagues, and other entrepreneurs in the geographic area who have used a particular law firm and attorney for similar purposes. For example, an entrepreneur starting a high-tech company should find an attorney with prior experience in this realm. Find out what others like or do not like about their attorneys and what they consider the most important factors in an effective working relationship. Also ask whether they have had any bad experiences.

Local community groups or universities may be able to provide good leads. Attorneys who specialize in working with start-ups often frequent local entrepreneur conventions or meetings. Consider attending these and meeting with these attorneys. Classes on entrepreneurship at local colleges often feature attorneys as guest speakers.

The director of the state bar's continuing legal education (CLE) program, the local chamber of commerce, accountants, or the local bar committee for business lawyers also may provide some good leads. In addition, entrepreneurs should keep an eye on the trade journals or newspapers for articles written about or by attorneys who have the experience they seek.

Shopping Around

It is important to sit down with potential attorneys to determine which one best meets the entrepreneur's needs for a provider of legal work and legal (and perhaps business) advice, and a potential information broker. Personality and a compatible working relationship are among the most important factors entrepreneurs should look for when choosing an attorney. If a person has not worked with an attorney before, it makes sense to bring along someone who has. When first exploring a relationship with an attorney, the entrepreneur should take advantage of an opportunity to have lunch with members of the law firm to become better acquainted with the attorney(s) and to obtain some free legal advice.

Factors many entrepreneurs consider important in deciding which attorney to retain include:

- *Personality.* Most entrepreneurs look for an attorney who is a good listener, can communicate, understands what the entrepreneur wants from the relationship, and is trustworthy.
- *A Compatible Working Relationship.* It is important to determine whether, and if so, how, the attorney uses assistants. If assistants are used extensively, the entrepreneur may want to meet with them also. An effective working relationship between the entrepreneur and the

law firm may involve a legal team consisting of an experienced partner and a more junior associate who would do most of the actual drafting. In this case, the entrepreneur should focus on whether there is a good personality fit with the associate. Some tasks, such as registration of a trademark, state securities filings, and drafting of minutes, are best done by a legal assistant or paralegal.

- *Use of Technology.* The level of technology at a law firm can make a significant difference in deciding which attorney to choose. Having up-to-date computer systems and software allows attorneys to rapidly retrieve and modify documents, and easily customize standard agreements and forms, thereby creating significant cost savings for the entrepreneur. For companies with divisions in different time zones, or that are international or contemplating international expansion, it scarcely matters where the attorney is located.

  The entrepreneur may also want to find a firm that has e-mail. Entrepreneurs who use e-mail find it very efficient, as it is often difficult to reach attorneys over the telephone, and leaving a long voice message can be awkward. Correspondence via e-mail is less interruptive, response time is typically within the day, and the entrepreneur (and the attorney) have written documentation for reference. Using e-mail may reduce legal fees, as many attorneys do not bill the time they spend reading e-mail but start the meter running as soon as they pick up the phone.

- *Timeliness in Returning Telephone Calls.* Often an entrepreneur needs to resolve a legal question or issue quickly. A timely response from an attorney, ideally within a day, is critical. To some clients, a prompt reply reflects the importance of the entrepreneur to the attorney. If the attorney is not timely in returning phone calls, the entrepreneur may conclude that his or her business is not a high priority for the attorney.

- *General Business Acumen and Understanding of Industry.* Some entrepreneurs view their attorneys as solely legal consultants, while others view them as an important source of business acumen and, in some cases, a partner. For some entrepreneurs, especially those who do not have a business partner, it is important to have an attorney with whom they can discuss ideas and go over the business plan. For example, one entrepreneur in the restaurant business finally chose an attorney because of the attorney's prior experience with clients in a retail business similar to that of the entrepreneur. For entrepreneurs involved in very technical ventures, it is important to have an attorney who understands the technology and the industry involved. Such an understanding typically implies the attorney has contacts in the industry. In addition, it shows that the attorney knows how to view the business and which contingencies to consider. On a more practical level, familiarity with the industry jargon helps minimize the legal costs.

- *Information Brokerage and Network with Potential Investors and Venture Capitalists.* Attorneys can serve an important information brokerage function and provide a path to potential investors and venture capital funds. They have the personal and business connections in the industry that an entrepreneur may need to tap into later to finance the business. For the entrepreneur who may consider venture capital, it is advantageous to work with a firm that has good relations with the venture capital community and can provide introductions. Attorneys who have done prior work with entrepreneurs may also be able to provide other good networking leads such as commercial bankers, accountants, business partners, and investment bankers.

- *Cost Sensitivity.* It is important to have an attorney who understands the business in terms of budgetary constraints. Having an attorney who watches costs carefully and has a good sense of the appropriate amount of time to spend on a matter is important.

- *Cost.* Attorneys charge different rates per hour and per task. These rates can appear to differ vastly. However, even though an attorney may charge significantly less by the hour, he or she may take significantly longer to accomplish the task if he or she has to move up the learning curve on the start-up's dime. In that event, the "cheaper" lawyer ends up costing more than the "expensive" but experienced lawyer. An appropriate way to assess this component is to comparison shop and ask each candidate how much the firm typically charges to do certain basic legal work such as drafting incorporation documents and shareholder agreements. The entrepreneur should also ask the candidate about his or her recent experience in drafting such documents.

WORKING COST EFFICIENTLY WITH AN ATTORNEY

Most start-ups monitor their spending carefully, so it can be daunting for the entrepreneur to be faced with thousands of dollars in legal fees. Although many firms will negotiate a fee arrangement with an entrepreneur, the legal fees can nonetheless be a significant component of the operating expenses of a start-up. However, there are many things an entrepreneur can do to prevent unpleasant surprises and to keep the fees at a manageable level.

The cost of an attorney can be broken into time- and nontime-related costs. Although nontime-related costs can be substantial, the bulk of the costs come from being billed for someone's time.

The Structure of Billing Time Costs

A client is typically charged for the time spent by attorneys and legal assistants on that client's affairs. Firms differ in how they structure fees. Generally, fees fall into one of four categories: hourly fees, flat fees, contingent and deferred fees, and retainers.

Law firms generally charge by the hour, and depending on the firm and the seniority of the attorneys working with the entrepreneur, prices can

---

FROM THE TRENCHES

In April 1980, three venture capitalists and a UCLA scientist met at the law firm Cooley Godward for the purpose of starting a biotechnology company to be called Amgen. Cooley Godward's partners aided Amgen in recruiting a Scientific Advisory Board for the company and Dr. George B. Rathmann as CEO. In January 1981, Cooley helped Amgen obtain $18.9 million in its only round of venture capital financing. The firm designed Amgen's equity program, dealt with several critical personnel matters, and assisted in preparing Amgen to go public in 1983, which resulted in $39 million in capital being raised. In ten years, Amgen became the nation's leading independent biopharmaceutical company.

range from $100 to $500 per hour. Any time that an attorney or other staff member spends on the entrepreneur's affairs may be considered billable time. Thus, for example, the clock may be considered to be running for the time spent in meetings or on the telephone, researching a topic or writing a memo or e-mail message, traveling, and discussing matters with other attorneys or legal assistants in the firm. As discussed in greater detail below, hourly fees of $150 to $350 are not uncommon, so it is important for the entrepreneur to inquire about what services are considered billable.

Flat fees often can be arranged for discrete tasks such as drafting a specific contract or registering a trademark. In this case, the attorney will charge a fixed rate, barring unforeseen circumstances, no matter how much time he or she spends on the matter.

A contingent fee structure may be arranged, whereby the attorney receives a fixed payment or a certain percentage of some potential cash flow when a certain event occurs. A contingent payment structure is not uncommon in a trial setting (such as a personal injury case), where, for example, an attorney may receive 40% of the settlement. An entrepreneur may wish to structure the fee so that the attorney can continue to bill at the normal high hourly rates but will not expect payment for the bulk of the fee until (and perhaps unless) venture capital or other investor funding is provided. This type of fee structure may be ideal for the entrepreneur who is still testing the feasibility of his or her venture.

An attorney may agree to defer billing but not make payment contingent on financing. For example, one large Silicon Valley firm gave a start-up client a break on the up-front time charged and agreed that the entrepreneur could defer all payments without interest for up to nine months. Sometimes a firm will ask for stock in the enterprise in exchange for deferring its billing. This can create a conflict of interest as the law firm itself becomes an investor, so the entrepreneur should proceed cautiously.

Some attorneys will request an up-front payment called a *retainer* to ensure that they get paid. Because cash is tight in start-ups, the entrepreneur should resist this arrangement and agree only to advance out-of-pocket costs (such as filing fees) as incurred.

The entrepreneur can use the attorney more economically if he or she minimizes the time the attorney spends on the work by being organized, preparing an outline for a term sheet, doing a rough draft of some documents, and otherwise remaining proactive in all legal affairs. Sometimes an attorney will agree to attend one board meeting a month at no charge. This keeps the attorney abreast of business developments and available for a certain amount of free legal advice without bankrupting the start-up.

Nontime-Related Costs Besides charging for the time spent directly on the legal matter, law firms typically will bill for other costs that the entrepreneur may not expect to pay for separately. Nontime-related costs may include charges for photocopying, word processing, on-line research, faxing, long-distance telephone calls, messenger service, and travel, as well as filing fees. Firms usually bill these costs directly to each client rather than absorb them and raise rates for all clients to cover the added expense. The entrepreneur should determine the protocol of the firm and negotiate how he or she will be billed for these other incidental costs. The entrepreneur can try to negotiate better rates, to pay only for faxing and not photocopying, for example, or to propose paying a fixed monthly fee or a fee based on a percentage of the professional fees incurred that month.

Hidden Head Counts Even though the entrepreneur may have spoken initially only to a particular attorney, it is likely that some of the work will be farmed out to others in the firm. This delegation has positive and negative aspects. More senior attorneys are typically more adept at looking at the big picture and setting up business structures, whereas mid-level associates are typically more efficient in preparing documentation. The junior associates gain experience by working on assignments under the supervision of more experienced attorneys. Although this process is beneficial to junior associates, the cash-poor entrepreneur needs to be careful that he or she is not financing this training. At meetings and on conference calls, the entrepreneur may find junior associates sitting in. The entrepreneur should find out whether anyone is unnecessarily involved, and if so, whether the entrepreneur is being charged for that person's presence. The entrepreneur may wish to establish a policy that no new person may be brought in without the entrepreneur's approval. The entrepreneur should not hesitate to say that he or she does not think a certain person should be on the clock.

In most law firms, each attorney is responsible for billing a certain number of hours per month and per year. Attorneys record how they spend their time, often in six-minute increments, and then the firm bills the individual clients for the attorneys' time. Junior attorneys bill out at lower rates than the more senior attorneys. Many entrepreneurs prefer working with partners because of the prestige and because they believe they are in more knowledgeable hands. However, seniority does not necessarily ensure that the best or ideal person is handling a certain transaction. Use of junior associates, who are cheaper per hour and often have more free time to focus on the entrepreneur's concerns and to return phone calls, is often appropriate.

However, sometimes the cheaper per-hour rate is not worth the extra time that a less experienced person may take. Usually a first-year associate is not cost efficient unless the billing partner is willing to write off substantial blocks of time as training. Once an associate has two or three years' training, he or she usually will have a level of competency that, coupled with the lower rate, makes him or her a good choice for drafting and negotiating documents.

Drafting

Accurately drafting a document that includes all the necessary nuances and covers all possible contingencies can be difficult and time-consuming. Typically, the entrepreneur knows the company's business issues, and the lawyer knows the legal issues. A thorough understanding of both is critical to drafting certain documents, such as shareholder agreements. No document is completely standardized to the extent that a form can just be churned out. There is always some customization to be done, depending on potential risks. Even if no extensive customization is needed, the entrepreneur should understand the significance of the terms and their application to his or her business because ultimately the contract will become legally binding. Thus, by the time the document is finalized and the signatures

"Better not dawdle. Mr. Dewlap has already started billing."

From *The Wall Street Journal* Permission, Cartoon Features Syndicate

obtained, the entrepreneur could end up spending a significant amount of money for what may seem at first to be a simple document.

Although lawyers can be instrumental in drafting documents, the impecunious entrepreneur may want to handle the bulk of the drafting. Depending on the type of document being produced, the entrepreneur could write the first draft, using the most appropriate and detailed sample forms from the attorney, preferably on a disk, as a sample from which to work. By working with the most detailed forms, the entrepreneur will gain a better understanding of all the issues to consider. Although the sample forms may have many terms that are not relevant to the entrepreneur, it is much more efficient to cross out unnecessary terms than to risk forgetting to include a salient feature. The entrepreneur might want the attorney to quickly summarize the main features of the document before attempting to customize terms for the entrepreneur's business. The attorney should then review the draft to ensure legal compliance and to consider whether there are legal or business issues not adequately covered. It should be noted that if a firm has standardized documents, such as a certificate of incorporation and bylaws, it may be far more expensive to have the attorney review the entrepreneur's draft than to just plug the company information into the lawyer's standard form.

Furthermore, the entrepreneur, when negotiating a term sheet with another business party, should draft the most detailed term sheet possible before passing it off to the attorney. It is much more expedient if the entrepreneur puts in the terms, as opposed to saying nothing about a certain issue and then having the lawyer negotiate something without knowing what the entrepreneur would have wanted.

Finalizing standard employment forms is one area in which the entrepreneur can save money. The entrepreneur should ask the attorney whether employees will need to sign a standard agreement. If so, the entrepreneur should obtain the standard forms on disk and then insert the employee's name. This method may be appropriate for certain assignment of invention agreements, nondisclosure agreements, and letters offering employment.

Another area in which drafting can often be left to the entrepreneur is letters that are legally significant but that also contain substantial business content. Certain letters of intent, strongly worded demand letters, or contract proposals can be substantially prepared by the entrepreneur before any legal review.

Organization

Because lawyers often keep track of their time in six-minute increments, it is prudent to be as organized as possible to avoid wasting time. The entrepreneur will be billed for the time spent describing an issue. Thus, he or she should prepare before calling the attorney. This preparation includes having the necessary documents on hand and being able to explain the situation in a clear and concise manner. By keeping chronological notes on what has been covered with the attorney, the entrepreneur can help ensure that no important details are omitted. The entrepreneur should also consider minimizing the frequency of interactions by maintaining a running list of questions and being prepared to discuss various issues during one meeting or conversation.

Being Proactive

The entrepreneur's working relationship with his or her attorney is often enhanced if the interaction is not always on a specific legal issue. As important as it is to try to educate one's self before seeing an attorney and avoid asking unnecessary questions, the client should not err on the side of being too independent. It is a good idea to keep the attorney informed of important business issues that may have seemingly insignificant legal implications. On the one hand, there may be legal implications that are unrecognized by the entrepreneur. More important, keeping the attorney informed keeps him or her excited about the client and keeps the entrepreneur's business in the forefront of the attorney's mind should any pertinent legal issues arise or new legal developments occur.

An entrepreneur can be proactive in keeping the attorney current on the relevant law. In scouting industry-specific trade journals, an entrepreneur may run across legal issues or precedents. Legal research time can be reduced if the entrepreneur makes it a habit to send relevant clippings to the attorney and asks the attorney to do the same.

The Billing Process

Attorneys and the legal realm can be overwhelming and intimidating. However, it is important to remember that the client is paying an attorney for a service, and, as when visiting a doctor, it is good to speak up about any concerns.

Especially when first starting to work with a law firm, the client should ask for a price estimate or upper price limit on a certain assignment. Although the attorney can never be sure how much time a certain task will take, barring unexpected contingencies, he or she should be able to provide a reasonable cost estimate. Asking for an estimate is important for several reasons. First, as when purchasing anything, it is always a good idea to get

*"Look, I'm not saying it's going to be today. But someday—someday—
you guys will be happy that you've taken along a lawyer."*

Drawing by Ziegler; ©1986 the New Yorker Magazine, Inc.

a sense of how much something costs. Second, it forces the attorney to anchor around a reasonable price. For competitive reasons, a law firm will not quote a ridiculous price for a certain transaction. Third, if the task takes longer than anticipated, the law firm may just absorb the extra costs rather than charge a higher price than originally quoted.

When first negotiating the fee structure for the business, the entrepreneur should ask to see a sample bill. Ideally, the bill should be detailed enough so that the client knows exactly for what he or she is being charged. The comments should not be vague, such as "produced documents," but should contain specifics about the agreements being drafted. Some firms have a policy of establishing minimum billable hours, whereby they charge a minimum for a certain task, and more if the assignment takes more time. If this method seems inappropriate, the entrepreneur should voice concern. The entrepreneur may desire to pay only for the time actually spent and may ask that work be billed in tenth-of-an-hour increments, as is done in many firms. Some entrepreneurs go to the extent of writing out how they are to be billed. They might specify that all clerical activities performed by an attorney are to be billed out at a paralegal's hourly rate, telephone calls fewer than a certain number of minutes are not billable, express-mail or air-courier costs will be paid only if such a service was requested by the client, and any charge over a certain number of minutes will be broken out separately and described.

The entrepreneur should examine each invoice closely. If the amount of time billed for a particular task seems out of line, challenge it. Firms will often write down (or adjust) bills to keep the client happy. Of course, if the partner on the account is asked to spend an inordinate amount of time delving into billing minutiae, it may be harmful to the relationship.

Given that many start-ups live month to month, the entrepreneur should demand monthly billing. Although the entrepreneur should keep a written log of incurred legal expenses, if the bill comes too long after the service, he or she may not be able to recall the work the bill covers.

ATTORNEY-CLIENT PRIVILEGE

When retaining an attorney, it is important to be clear about who the client is. Communications with a lawyer are not protected by the *attorney-client privilege* unless they are between a lawyer and a client seeking confidential legal advice. If the client is a corporation, the privilege protects the communications or discussions of any company employee with counsel so long as the subject matter of the communication relates to that employee's duties and the communication is made at the direction of a corporate superior. For example, if a corporation hired a lawyer to do an internal investigation of possible misconduct, and an officer instructed an employee to cooperate in the investigation, a third party (such as the government or a competitor) could not compel the disclosure of the communication between the employee and the lawyer. However, because the privilege belongs to the corporation as client, the corporation may require the disclosure of the communication between the employee and the lawyer in a case brought by the corporation against the employee.

An attorney retained to incorporate a company will normally view the company as the client, at least once it is organized. This relationship should be clearly spelled out in an engagement letter with the attorney.

Although the founders may initially be the sole representatives of the company, they are usually not considered to be the client. This means that if there were a dispute down the road and the board of directors voted to fire a founder, the attorney could not ethically represent both the founder and the company. In addition, any conversations between the attorney and the founders would not be privileged.

Attorneys often recommend that each founder retain separate counsel from the outset, especially when structuring the ownership and negotiating buy-sell agreements. In practice, this rarely happens because it is too expensive. A founder should, and usually will, retain separate counsel if there is a dispute or threatened dispute with the company or its board of directors.

The attorney-client privilege applies only to legal advice, not business advice. It does not protect client communications that are made to further a crime or illegal act. For example, if an entrepreneur were to ask his or her attorney the best way to steal trade secrets of a competitor, that conversation would not be privileged. A client loses the attorney-client privilege if the client shares the attorney's advice with outsiders or permits outsiders to listen in on a discussion between the client and the attorney.

FROM THE TRENCHES

Company X and Company Y were the majority and minority shareholders, respectively, of Company Z. Under the terms of a contract between companies X and Y, Company X had the right to appoint a majority of Company Z's board of directors. Company X determined that an initial public offering (IPO) of stock would be in the best interest of Company Z. Company X retained counsel to advise it on its rights under certain contracts between companies X and Y, and under Company Z's articles of incorporation, to cause Company Z to initiate the IPO process. In the course of the discussion, Company X realized that it would be prudent to invite Company Z's management into certain of the discussions so that Company Z's management could be part of the IPO planning process.

A dispute arose between Company X and Company Y. Company Y made a motion to require Company X's directors to answer questions about the discussions with counsel and produce their notes of those discussions. Company X asserted attorney-client privilege.

The court held that the attorney-client privilege, which would otherwise have protected Company X's communications with its counsel, was waived as to those conversations in which Company Z's personnel participated. Although Company X was entitled to receive confidential advice from its own counsel concerning its rights and obligations, Company Z's personnel were not strictly necessary to the accomplishment of this end, and their presence destroyed the privilege. As a result, Company X's directors were required to give deposition testimony concerning the conversations with their attorneys in which Company Z's representatives participated and to turn over their notes of those conversations.

Putting It into Practice

Because Alexandra thought that an attorney would be useful in the initial structuring of the company and issuance of equity, she decided to find an attorney before officially launching her business. She believed that it would be helpful to develop a relationship with an attorney sooner rather than later. In addition, she had been told by another entrepreneur that even though you think you do not need an attorney until you are raising money, an attorney can handle many matters in the beginning, from making sure that stock is issued properly to reviewing a lease for office space.

To find a suitable attorney, Alexandra asked friends and business associates for recommendations, then pruned her options down to two: a solo practitioner and a partner in a large regional firm. Alexandra made an appointment to talk with both attorneys, who each agreed to meet with her free of charge.

At her meeting with Janet Winslow, the solo practitioner, Alexandra learned that she had a generalized legal practice. Janet said that she would do all the legal work herself at a rate of $225 per hour. She warned Alexandra that her practice was quite busy, so her turnaround time on documents would vary depending on other client demands. Janet explained that she had done a number of jobs for start-up companies and that, in most cases, she would be able to modify existing documents to meet Alexandra's needs. However, Janet would have to draft certain documents from scratch. Janet had contracted with a local patent firm that would handle any patent applications that Alexandra needed filed. Janet promised that regardless of how busy she was, she would always return Alexandra's phone calls the same day.

Although Janet did not yet have e-mail, she was considering getting it as part of a general upgrade of her computer system. In terms of a payment plan, Janet said she could be flexible for a couple of months but ultimately would have to be paid.

Alexandra's second meeting was with Michael Woo, a highly regarded corporate partner in a large regional firm. Michael explained that although he would ultimately be responsible for Alexandra's company's legal work, a third-year associate, Josh Austin, would actually draft the documents, which Michael would then review. Michael said his billing rate was $330 per hour, and Josh billed at $150. Michael told Alexandra

continued

continued

that the firm's resources allowed it to turn around documents as quickly as Alexandra needed them. His firm had recently added patent counsel to its roster of partners, and the firm was capable of handling all patent work that Alexandra would need.

Michael also explained that the firm had invested heavily in technology and had a computer program that allowed an associate to enter certain information about a company and its needs, after which the program automatically generated customized documents. The firm also had e-mail and a Web site. Michael said that because of his schedule, which entailed significant travel, it might take a day or two to return phone calls. Josh, however, would be able to respond to calls immediately and would have access to Michael for advice. In addition, Michael offered his and Josh's home phone numbers to Alexandra, and said that if time-sensitive issues arose, she should not hesitate to call them at home.

Michael said that his firm would agree to postpone billing Alexandra until her company received venture capital or other financing. If the company did not receive financing, the company would still be responsible technically for the legal fees, but Michael assured Alexandra that his firm would not expect the company or the entrepreneur to pay the full amount of the fees.

Michael then introduced Alexandra to Josh. Alexandra was impressed by his enthusiasm and intelligence.

After the two meetings, Alexandra decided to hire Michael. She was particularly impressed by the firm's commitment to technology and felt that the improved efficiency would offset the higher billing rates. She also felt that because most work would be done by the associate, she would save money. Although Michael might not be accessible at all times, she felt comfortable knowing she would be able to reach the associate whenever she had a legal question or concern. Finally, she thought the firm would have the flexibility and sophistication to accommodate the company's growing legal needs. Alexandra discussed her thoughts with the Eagles, and they agreed with her decision.

Content with her choice, Alexandra called Michael, told him of her decision, and set up an appointment to discuss what form of legal entity would be best for the new business.

Deciding Whether to Incorporate

4

By carefully considering the forms of business entity that are available and then intelligently choosing the most appropriate one, the entrepreneur can reduce exposure to liabilities, minimize taxes, and ensure that the business is capable of being financed and conducted efficiently. In addition, formalizing the business helps prevent misunderstandings among the participants by defining their ownership stakes, roles, and duties in the business.

The primary considerations in the choice of business entity will be the degree to which the entrepreneur's personal assets are protected from liabilities of the business; how best to pursue tax strategies such as maximizing the tax benefits of start-up losses, avoiding double (or even triple) layers of taxation, and converting ordinary income into long-term capital gain, which is taxed at lower rates; attractiveness to potential investors and lenders; availability of attractive equity incentives for employees and other service providers; and costs (start-up and ongoing).

This chapter first describes each of the principal business forms and then explores the considerations and strategies involved in making an appropriate selection. A brief discussion of name selection and protection follows.

THE FORMS OF BUSINESS ENTITY

A business may be conducted as a corporation (including the S corporation, which has special flow-through tax attributes), a general or limited partnership, a limited liability company (LLC), or a sole proprietorship. Each state has its own laws under which businesses may organize and operate. A corporation is a distinct legal entity owned by its shareholders and managed by a board of directors. A partnership is a separate entity for some purposes and a group of individual partners for other purposes. It does not pay taxes on its activities; instead, its partners pay taxes on its activities based on their respective interests in its profits. The LLC, one of the newest forms of business organization, attempts to combine the best attributes of the corporation and the partnership. If properly structured, an LLC is taxed the same as a partnership.

A *sole proprietorship* is a business owned by one person. It has little legal significance separate from its owner and usually requires no governmental filing except a fictitious-business-name statement, which discloses the name under which the business will be conducted and the owner's name and address. The sole proprietorship is probably the most prevalent form of small business in the United States.

Most large business organizations operate as corporations despite the tax incentives to use the partnership or LLC form of doing business. The corporation is the most familiar business entity and is governed by the most highly developed laws. A principal attraction to the corporate form is the limited liability it provides to its shareholders: Creditors are limited to the assets of the corporation for payment and may not collect directly from shareholders if corporate assets are insufficient to pay all debts and liabilities. Other advantages of the corporate form include its familiarity and well-understood governance laws, its permanence, and the ability to transfer corporate stock more easily than partnership or LLC interests (particularly in the public securities markets). In addition, many venture capital and other investment funds are unable to invest in partnerships and LLCs because their major investors are pension and profit-sharing trusts and other tax-exempt entities that are subject to certain tax restrictions.

However, partnerships, proprietorships and, increasingly, LLCs are also widely used for smaller businesses and when tax and other considerations warrant. Exhibit 4.1 sets forth the relative advantages and disadvantages of the various forms of business organization.

CORPORATIONS

A *corporation* is a distinct legal entity owned by its shareholders. Unlike a partnership, a corporation may be owned by a single person who can be the corporation's sole director and serve as any required officer (e.g., president, treasurer, and secretary). The shareholders elect the corporation's board of directors but are not otherwise active in the management of the corporation. The board of directors is responsible for major corporate decisions. Day-to-day management is carried on by the corporation's officers, who are appointed by, and serve at the pleasure of, the board of directors. A corporation has an unlimited life so that it is not terminated or changed on the death of a shareholder or other changes in its ownership. Instead, shares are transferred upon a shareholder's death to the shareholder's heirs.

Unless a corporation elects to be taxed as an S corporation, it is taxed as a separate legal entity. (A corporation that does not elect S corporation treatment is sometimes referred to as a *C corporation* because it is taxed under Subchapter C of the Internal Revenue Code.) Under current federal income tax law, a corporation is taxed on its net income (gross income less allowable deductions) at rates ranging from 15% to 35% (the rate is 34% on income over $75,000 up to $10,000,000). Property, other than money, contributed to a corporation will be subject to tax unless the person, or group of persons, contributing the property owns at least 80% of the corporation. Money or other property distributed by a corporation to its shareholders is subject to tax again when distributed in the form of dividends; shareholders pay that tax.

Preserving Limited Liability: Piercing the Corporate Veil

The proper operation of a corporation limits the liability of the shareholders because the creditors of the corporation cannot usually reach the shareholders to satisfy the corporation's obligations. However, under the *alter ego doctrine,* a court may disregard the corporate entity and hold the shareholders personally liable for the corporation's obligations if the shareholders used the corporation to perpetuate a fraud or promote injustice. In determining whether to *pierce the corporate veil,* that is, whether to disregard the corporate form and make the shareholders directly liable for the corporation's obligations, a court will examine many factors, such as:

1. Was the corporation undercapitalized, given the risks inherent in its business?
2. Were corporate assets used for personal reasons?
3. Were corporate assets commingled with personal assets?
4. Were the corporate and personal books kept separately?
5. Were corporate actions properly authorized by the board of directors or the shareholders?

To preserve limited liability for its shareholders, the corporation should observe at least the following procedures:

1. Obtain and record shareholder and board authorization for corporate actions. An annual shareholders' meeting and regular board meetings should be conducted, and accurate minutes should be prepared and kept as part of the corporate records.
2. Keep corporate funds separate from personal funds.
3. Maintain complete and proper records for the corporation separate from personal records.
4. Make it clear in all contracts with others that they are dealing with the corporation, and sign all contracts as shown:

[CORPORATE NAME]

By: _____

[Name and Title]

5. Maintain an arm's-length relationship between the corporation and any principal shareholder. Transactions with any of the directors or principal shareholders (or entities in which they have an interest) should be subject to approval by the disinterested members of the board, if any, without the vote of the interested directors, after all the facts material to the transaction are fully disclosed.
6. Start the business with an amount of equity and liability insurance sufficient in light of the future capital needs of the business and its inherent risks.

S Corporations

The Internal Revenue Code permits certain shareholders to operate as a corporation while taxing them as individuals. Such corporations, known as *S corporations*, generally do not pay federal income tax but pass the tax liability for their profits to their shareholders. Consequently, profits earned by an S corporation will be taxed only once. Similarly, an S corporation's losses flow through to the shareholders and may be deducted by the shareholders on their individual tax returns (subject to certain significant limitations). Profits and losses are required to be allocated based on share ownership for taxation purposes. The shareholders must include as individual income the profits earned by the S corporation regardless of whether any cash amounts were distributed to shareholders. A distribution of earnings by an S corporation to its shareholders is generally not taxed a second time. In contrast, a similar distribution by a corporation other than an S corporation will be taxed twice: The C corporation must pay federal corporate income tax on profits when earned, and shareholders must treat distributions as dividends subject to tax. An S corporation is the same as any other corporation except for the manner in which it is taxed.

Shareholders generally elect S corporation status when the corporation is profitable and distributes substantially all of its profits to the shareholders, or when the corporation incurs losses and the shareholders wish to use the loss deductions on their personal income tax returns. The case for S-corporation status is weaker when the corporation is owned solely by insiders who work for the company and receive their share of the profits in the form of deductible salary and bonuses. The presence of outsiders, who do not receive their share of profits in the form of deductible salary and bonuses, makes the technique of extracting profits by paying salaries and bonuses unavailable and the argument for an S corporation more compelling. However, because the overall maximum individual income tax rate (39.6%) is higher than the corporate income tax rate (35%), using an S corporation may not be the best choice if the corporation is profitable and expects to accumulate its earnings, rather than distribute them currently.

There are substantial limitations on the availability of the S corporation election and the allocation and deduction of S corporation losses by its shareholders. To qualify for S corporation status, a corporation must satisfy the following requirements:

1. The corporation must have no more than 75 shareholders, all of whom are individuals, certain tax-exempt organizations, qualifying trusts, or estates, and none of whom are nonresident aliens.
2. The corporation must have only one class of stock (although options and differences in voting rights are generally permitted).
3. The corporation may generally not own 80% or more of any other corporation unless special requirements are satisfied.

The requirement that an S corporation have no shareholders other than individuals will prevent any business that intends to raise equity capital from venture capital funds, corporations, or other institutional investors from qualifying as an S corporation. In addition, because an S corporation can have only one class of stock, it cannot issue inexpensively priced founders' stock to key employees. Founders' stock is discussed in chapter 5.

As discussed further in chapters 6 and 8, most corporations that raise money from outside investors issue two classes of stock: convertible preferred stock to the investors and common stock to employees. The common stock is typically issued at a small fraction of the price of the preferred stock because it lacks the liquidation, dividend, voting, and other preferences that the preferred stock possesses. Because an S corporation can issue only common stock, it must issue the stock to employees at the same price paid by the investors (unless sold to the founders well in advance of the sale to the investors) if the employees are to avoid being taxed on their receipt of their shares. Accordingly, the S corporation is most commonly used for family or other closely owned businesses that obtain capital from their individual shareholders and/or debt from outside sources and do not provide equity incentives to their employees on any significant scale.

A qualified corporation may elect to be taxed as an S corporation by filing form 2553 with the Internal Revenue Service, together with the written consent of all the shareholders. This election must be filed on or any time before the fifteenth day of the third month of the taxable year of the corporation for which S corporation status is to be effective. If a corporation does not meet all of the S corporation requirements during the entire year, the election will not be effective until the following year.

PARTNERSHIPS

A partnership is a business carried on by at least two persons. For some purposes, a partnership is treated as a distinct legal entity separate from its partners. For example, a partnership can sue and be sued, and can own property in its own name; a creditor of a partner must proceed against a partner's interest in the partnership, rather than directly against the assets of the partnership. For other purposes, a partnership is treated as an aggregate of its individual partners. For example, a partnership dissolves on the death of any partner (but as discussed below, the partnership business need not terminate as the result of such an event).

A partnership may be a general partnership or limited partnership. In a *general partnership*, each partner is a general partner, each has unlimited liability for the debts of the partnership, and each has the power to incur obligations on behalf of the partnership within the scope of the partnership's business. Some liability concerns, such as potential claims for personal injuries or those resulting from errors or omissions, can be alleviated through insurance. Each general partner acts as an agent for the other partners and the partnership. As a result of this mutual agency principle, great care must be exercised in the selection of general partners.

A *limited partnership* has one or more general partners (each of whom has the same liability and power as a general partner in a general partnership) and one or more limited partners. Limited partners' liability is limited to the amount of their capital commitment. Generally, limited partners may not participate in the control of the partnership, or they will be treated as general partners for liability purposes.

Although each state has a general partnership and limited partnership act (many of which are patterned on uniform acts), the partners may generally establish their own business arrangements among themselves by entering into a written partnership agreement. The partners may thereby override most provisions in the partnership acts both in terms of how a partnership is managed and how profits and losses are allocated and distributed. In the absence of an agreement to the contrary, profits and losses are split evenly among the partners.

Unlike a corporation, a partnership will dissolve (cease to be) on the death or withdrawal of a partner. However, a partnership agreement can, and should, provide for alternatives to liquidation after dissolution. For example, the partnership agreement can provide for the buyout of a deceased or withdrawn partner, the election of a new general partner, and the continuation of the business of the partnership by the remaining partners. In a limited partnership, the death of a limited partner typically does not result in the liquidation of the partnership; the limited partnership interest can be passed on to the deceased limited partner's heirs.

Partnerships require few legal formalities. A general partnership does not even require a written agreement; it can be formed with nothing more than a handshake and a general understanding between the partners. For example, students agree to work together on a business plan; a baker and a chef agree to open a restaurant together; two software programmers agree to collaborate on writing a program. In each case, a partnership of sorts is formed. However, the intention of one party alone cannot create a partnership. There must be a meeting of the minds: Each party must intend to establish a business relationship with the other. A limited partnership requires the filing of a certificate with the applicable secretary of state and a written partnership agreement.

For the protection of the parties, a detailed written partnership agreement is strongly suggested for both general and limited partnerships. In the absence of a written agreement, state partnership laws will govern the partnership. Some provisions of the laws may lead to unfavorable results. For example, state laws may require partners to share the profits and losses equally regardless of their original capital contributions. A written partnership agreement can prevent future misunderstandings by including the term of the partnership's existence, the division of profits and losses between partners, the allocation of responsibility for any needed capital contributions, the payment of partnership salaries or withdrawals of capital, the duties of the partners, and the consequences to the partnership if a partner decides to sell his or her interest or becomes incapacitated or dies. It can also provide for a dispute resolution mechanism. As a practical matter, because a partnership is largely governed by the partnership agreement, which will vary significantly with each partnership, there is more expense involved in forming a partnership than a corporation, because a corporation's governance is largely controlled by statute. Standard or *boilerplate* forms should be avoided.

A key attraction of the partnership is that it pays no income tax. Income or losses flow through to each partner and are reported on each partner's individual tax return. Unlike an S corporation, which allocates income or loss based on stock ownership, a partnership can allocate income and loss flexibly. For example, income can be allocated differently from losses. In a partnership in which one partner contributes services and another contributes money, the tax losses generated from the expenditure of funds contributed by the cash partner can all be allocated to the cash partner. In addition, allocations can provide for preferred returns to a certain partner or class of partners, and can change over time or as higher profit levels are achieved.

Even though partnership losses flow through to the partners based on the loss sharing arrangements in the partnership agreement, a number of limitations restrict the ability of a partner to deduct these losses on his or her personal tax return. For example, the tax code restricts the ability of partners (or shareholders in an S corporation) to deduct passive losses against most income. A partner's losses from a partnership are passive losses unless the partner materially participates in the partnership's business. A limited partner will rarely be able to treat partnership losses as other than passive. Other tax limitations prevent a partner from deducting losses that exceed his or her tax basis (the amount paid for his or her partnership interest plus his or her share of partnership liabilities, as adjusted over time). In certain circumstances, a limited partner may not deduct losses attributable to nonrecourse debt (debt for which the debtor is not personally liable).

Property can generally be contributed to and distributed from a partnership without being subject to tax. Section 351 of the Internal Revenue Code permits a partnership to convert into a corporation without tax if the incorporation is properly structured. However, once a partnership is converted into a corporation, upon a distribution from the corporation there will generally be two levels of tax: a corporate tax and a shareholder tax.

A partnership has limited sources of operating capital available to it. It is generally restricted to capital contributed by partners and funds loaned by partners and outsiders. It is uncommon for a partnership to raise capital in a public offering, in part because publicly traded partnerships are taxed as corporations. Most venture capital funds have tax-exempt investors who would receive disadvantaged tax treatment if the fund invested in a partnership. Therefore, a business that expects to attract capital from a venture capital fund generally should not organize as a partnership. Foreigners are generally disinclined to invest in a partnership that is carrying on an active business because their participation as a partner causes them to be treated as being engaged in a U.S. trade or business. The result is that foreigners are taxed by the United States on any U.S. income they receive that is connected with the trade or business. Foreigners generally do not pay tax on the income of U.S. corporations in which they invest.

Until recently, limited partnerships have been the entity of choice for activities such as investing in real estate or securities where flow-through tax treatment is desired. In addition to permitting profits and losses to flow through directly to the owners of the business, partnerships can distribute property in kind without incurring tax on the partnership or the partner. Many investment funds distribute highly appreciated securities to their partners after a liquidity event (e.g., an initial public offering or acquisition by a public company in a tax-free reorganization), thereby allowing each partner to make an individual decision as to when to sell the securities he or she receives. The advent of the LLC, discussed below, is resulting in many businesses organizing as an LLC instead of as a limited partnership to achieve limited liability for all members, even those who actively participate in the business.

LIMITED LIABILITY COMPANIES

The limited liability company (LLC) is a form of business organization that is rapidly gaining popularity in the United States. All but a handful of states now have laws that permit the organization and operation of a business as an LLC. A properly structured LLC combines the pass-through federal tax treatment of a partnership with the liability protections of a corporation. Thus, an organization that would otherwise organize as a general or limited partnership, or as an S corporation if it met the requirements, will generally derive the most benefit from organizing as an LLC, because it will have limited liability protection while retaining favorable partnership tax treatment.

The owners (referred to as *members*) of the LLC have no personal liability for the obligations of the LLC (but, as is also true for corporate directors and officers, members will still have personal liability for their individual acts and omissions in connection with the LLC's business). For all practical purposes, an LLC operates as a limited partnership without the legal requirement of having a general partner who bears ultimate liability for the obligations of the partnership. As discussed above, an S corporation also has both the limited liability and most of the federal tax pass-through features found in the LLC, but ownership is limited to 75 shareholders, all of whom

---

FROM THE TRENCHES

Adobe Systems Incorporated, the leading desktop publishing software company, was founded as a partnership in 1982. It was initially organized as a partnership so that its investors, Hambrecht & Quist Investors, and its founders, John Warnock and Charles Geschke, could deduct the losses against their individual taxes. It operated as a partnership until December 1983, when its partners traded their interests for stock in the newly formed corporation. Adobe went public in 1986.

must be individuals, certain tax-exempt organizations, qualifying trusts, or estates, and none of whom may be foreigners; in addition, the S corporation can have only one class of stock. An LLC has none of these restrictions.

An LLC has two principal charter documents. The first is a short (one to two pages) document filed with the secretary of state, which sets forth the name of the LLC, its address, its agent for service of process, the term, and whether it will be governed by the members or managers appointed by the members. This document is generally called the *certificate of formation* (Delaware) or *articles of organization* (California).

The second charter document for an LLC is its *operating agreement*, which is analogous to, and closely resembles, a partnership agreement. The operating agreement specifies how the LLC will be governed, the financial obligations of the members (e.g., additional capital calls could be forbidden, voluntary, or mandatory), and how profits, losses, and distributions are shared. As with a partnership agreement, the operating agreement for an LLC will be tailored to suit the needs of each individual LLC, with the attendant expense of a specialized legal agreement. Again, boilerplate documents should be avoided.

The IRS recently issued regulations that generally allow limited liability companies and partnerships that are not publicly traded to be taxed as flow-through entities unless they elect to be taxed as corporations.

The LLC is not suitable for businesses financed by venture capital funds because of tax restrictions on the funds's tax-exempt partners. But an LLC can be very attractive for businesses financed by corporate investors and to a lesser extent (because of the passive-loss limitations) wealthy individuals. The LLC is the entity of choice for the start-up entity seeking to flow-through losses to its investors because (1) it offers the same complete liability protection to all its members as does a corporation; (2) it can have corporations and partnerships as members (unlike an S corporation) and is not subject to any of the other limitations that apply to S corporations; and (3) losses can be specially allocated entirely to the cash investors (in the S corporation losses are allocated to all the owners based on share ownership). In addition, the LLC can be incorporated tax-free at any time. For example, after the initial start-up losses have been allocated to the early round investors, the LLC could be incorporated to accommodate investment from a venture capital fund in a conventional preferred stock financing. Alternatively, incorporation could be deferred until a public offering.

MAKING THE SELECTION FROM AMONG THE C CORPORATION, S CORPORATION, PARTNERSHIP, AND LIMITED LIABILITY COMPANY

The three most critical factors in selecting the form of business entity are (1) who the owners of the business will be; (2) how the earnings of the business will be returned to its owners; and (3) whether the business is expected initially to generate profits or losses.

Who Will Be the Owners?

If a business is owned by a few individuals, any of the above entities may be the appropriate business form, and factors other than the type of owner will be determinative. If the business will be widely held, the C corporation is usually the entity of choice for a variety of reasons. A corporation has unlimited life and free transferability of ownership. The corporation's existence is not affected by changes in its ownership resulting from transfers of

---

FROM THE TRENCHES

Two entrepreneurs had been reading about a new form of legal entity, the limited liability company. The flood of articles in the business press made LLCs sound like the only way to go, so the entrepreneurs formed an LLC that was classified as a partnership for tax purposes, with enough cash to fund product development for about a year. Nine months later, while negotiating the first round of venture financing, they learned that venture capital funds that have tax-exempt investors as partners could not invest in their LLC. As a result, the business had to be restructured at the last minute, resulting in unnecessary costs and delays in the financing.

stock (by a living shareholder or upon a shareholder's death) or the issuance of new shares (i.e., additional shares issued directly by the corporation). On the other hand, free transferability of interests and unlimited life are more difficult to achieve in a partnership or LLC and, if provided for in a partnership or LLC, can adversely affect flow-through tax treatment. An S corporation is not suitable for a widely held corporation because it cannot have more than 75 shareholders (all of whom must generally be U.S. citizens or resident aliens or eligible trusts).

If the business is so widely held that its ownership interests become publicly traded, the corporation is the entity of choice. Investors are more receptive to offerings of corporate stock than partnership or LLC interests because they are easier to understand. In addition, publicly traded partnerships and LLCs lose their tax advantages and thus are taxed as a corporation (i.e., no flow-through tax treatment).

If ownership interests in the business will be provided to employees, the C corporation will generally be the preferred entity for several reasons. First, stock ownership is easier to explain to employees than equity interests in partnerships and LLCs. Second, creating favorably priced equity incentives is easiest to accomplish in a C corporation, because ownership can be held through various classes of stock. It is quite common for a corporation to issue preferred stock to investors and common stock to management and other employees. If properly structured, the common stock can be sold at a substantial discount from the preferred stock because of the special rights and preferences of the preferred stock. For example, preferred stock will usually have a liquidation preference equal to the price paid for the preferred stock. This liquidation preference must be paid to preferred-stock shareholders if the corporation is sold or liquidated, before any funds can be paid to common-stock holders. Preferred stock is usually convertible into common stock at the option of the holder, and conversion would ordinarily occur in an upside situation in which the company is successful and goes public or is sold.

Finally, the tax law gives favorable tax treatment to incentive stock options (ISOs) granted by a corporation. The holder of an ISO generally incurs no tax until the shares purchased through an option exercise are sold. The recognized gain is taxed at the more favorable long-term capital gain rate, rather than as ordinary income. Incentive stock options are available only for corporations, not partnerships or LLCs. When options do not qualify as incentive stock options, the option holder recognizes ordinary income when the option is exercised and must pay tax on the difference between the exercise price of the option and the fair market value of the underlying stock at the time the option is exercised.

If the business raises capital from a venture capital fund, the business will usually be formed as a corporation, because most venture capital funds raise money from tax-exempt entities such as pension and profit-sharing trusts, universities, and other charitable organizations. These nonprofit entities would incur taxable unrelated business taxable income if the venture fund invested in a flow-through entity such as a partnership or LLC.

How Does the Business Expect to Return Its Profits to Its Owners?

A business can either distribute earnings currently to its owners or accumulate and reinvest the earnings with the goal of growing the business so that it can either be taken public or sold to another business for cash or marketable stock of the acquiring business. Current earnings are taxed as ordinary income, whereas the gain on the sale of stock is taxed at the more favorable long-term capital gain rate.

A tax flow-through entity such as a partnership, LLC, or S corporation is the entity of choice for a business that intends to distribute earnings currently so that the earnings can be distributed without incurring a second level of tax. If a C corporation is used, earnings can be paid out without being taxed at the corporate level only if they are paid as salary or other reasonable compensation to shareholders who work for the business. (Such compensation is deductible by the corporation against its taxable income.) On the other hand, distributions of earnings by a corporation to its shareholders, other than as compensation for services, will not be deductible by the corporation and will be taxed as ordinary dividend income to its shareholders. Most small businesses that distribute the business's earnings currently and do not have owners who work for the business have a strong incentive to use a tax flow-through entity such as an S corporation, partnership, or LLC.

The income tax law provides an additional incentive for businesses that seek to build long-term value, rather than the current distribution of earnings, to organize as a C corporation. With a C corporation (but not any other business entity) that qualifies as a small business corporation (SBC), stock issued after August 1993 that is held for at least five years is generally eligible for a 50% capital-gains tax deduction, reducing the effective tax rate to approximately 14%. High-income-tax payers subject to the alternative minimum tax may incur a higher rate.

Is the Business Expected Initially to Generate Profits or Losses?

If the business is expected initially to generate losses, then a tax flow-through entity such as a partnership, LLC, or S corporation is the entity of choice, because it allows the owners to deduct the losses from their taxable income. For example, biotechnology companies frequently operate at a loss because of the extraordinary costs of product development, clinical trials, and FDA approval. A biotechnology company will typically experience several years of multimillion-dollar losses before reaching profitability even in the best-case scenario. Depending on the sources of start-up funding, use of a flow-through entity may be attractive, as it allows the investors to deduct the start-up losses against taxable income. Otherwise it may be years before the business earns a profit and can use tax loss carryforwards.

CONDUCTING BUSINESS IN OTHER STATES, LOCAL LICENSES, AND INSURANCE

Before commencing operations in other states, the business should determine whether such operations will require it to register as a foreign corporation, partnership, or LLC in those states. Some states have significant penalties for failure to register properly. Even if it need not register as a foreign business entity, the company may be required to pay income and other taxes (including sales and use taxes) in such states for operating therein. If the business has employees in other states, it may be subject to requirements with respect to withholding from employees' wages, workers' compensation insurance, and other regulatory requirements. If the business owns real or personal property in other states, it may be required to pay property taxes in those states.

State licensing is required for a wide variety of businesses and professions. Cities, counties, and other municipal agencies require local licenses. Because licensing requirements vary greatly among cities and counties, a business may wish to consider local licensing requirements and taxes before choosing a location for doing business.

New businesses should obtain insurance coverage for all anticipated contingencies, not only to protect the individual participants from personal liability but also to protect the assets and future retained earnings of the business. The coverage may include general liability insurance (including product liability), errors and omissions insurance for directors and officers, fire and casualty insurance, business interruption insurance, key-personnel life and disability insurance, insurance to fund share purchases in the event of the death or disability of a shareholder, and workers' compensation insurance.

CHOOSING AND PROTECTING A NAME FOR A BUSINESS

Proposed names for new corporations, LLCs, and limited partnerships should be precleared through the secretary of state office's name-availability section before filing documents. The preclearance and/or reservation of a name is necessary to avoid the rejection of the filing documents by the secretary of state because of a name conflict.

Most secretaries of state maintain a consolidated list of the following: (1) the names of all corporations, LLCs, and limited partnerships organized under the laws of that state in good standing; (2) the names of all foreign corporations, LLCs, and limited partnerships qualified to transact intrastate business in the state and in good standing; and (3) the names reserved for future issuance. Charter documents will not be accepted for filing if the stated name resembles closely, is confusingly similar to, or is the same as any name on the consolidated list.

A further consideration in selecting a name is whether that name is available for use in other states in which the organization will be conducting business. State laws generally provide for the use of an assumed name in a foreign state when an organization's true name is not available in that state. If a corporate, limited partnership, or LLC name is not available because that name or a similar one is in use, it may be possible to still use that name by obtaining the consent of the entity using the name.

It is important to understand the difference between the actions of a secretary of state in allowing the use of a name and the issues involved in the use of a name or trademark for purposes of identifying a good or service. The determination of a secretary of state in approving the use of a name merely means that an entity has complied with the state law prohibiting a business from using a name that closely resembles the name of another business organized or qualified to do business in the state. Therefore, the fact that a secretary of state does not object to the use of a particular name as the name of a business does not necessarily mean that other people or entities are not already using the proposed name in connection with goods or services. If they are, the law of trademarks (discussed in chapter 14) will prohibit the new company from using the name. A promising start-up business may find its business plan abruptly derailed when it receives a demand to change its name or faces an injunction and penalties for trademark infringement. To prevent this, the entrepreneur should conduct a search of the existing names in his or her proposed area of activity to determine, prior to its adoption, how protectable a particular name or trademark will be, and whether it will infringe the rights of others.

Exhibit 4.1

Choice of Business Entity: Pros and Cons

The following chart lists the principal considerations in selecting the form of business entity and applies them to the C corporation, S corporation, general partnership, limited partnership, and limited liability company. The considerations are listed in no particular order, in part because their importance will vary with each business formation depending on the nature of the business, sources of financing, and the plan for providing financial returns to the owners (e.g., distributions of operating income, a public offering or a sale of the business). Other factors that are not listed will also influence choice of entity. In addition, the "yes or no" format oversimplifies the applicability of certain attributes.

	C Corp	S Corp	General Partnership	Limited Partnership	Limited Liability Company
Limited Liability	Yes	Yes	No	Yes[a]	Yes
Flow-through Taxation	No	Yes	Yes	Yes	Yes
Simplicity/Low Cost	Yes	Yes	No	No	No
Limitations on Eligibility	No	Yes	No	No	No
Limitations on Capital Structure	No	Yes	No	No	No
Ability to Take Public	Yes	Yes[b]	No[c]	No[c]	No[c]
Flexible Charter Documents	No	No	Yes	Yes	Yes
Ability to Change Structure Without Tax	No	No	Yes	Yes	Yes
Favorable Employee Incentives (including incentive stock options)	Yes	Yes/No[d]	No[e]	No[e]	No[e]
Qualified Small Business Stock Exclusion for Gains	Yes[f]	No	No	No	No
Special Allocations	No	No	Yes	Yes	Yes
Tax Free In Kind Distributions	No	No	Yes	Yes	Yes

continued . . .

EXHIBIT 4.1 (CONTINUED)

a. Limited liability for limited partners only; a limited partnership must have at least one general partner with unlimited liability.
b. S corporation would convert to C corporation upon a public offering because of the restrictions on the permissible number of S corporation shareholders.
c. Although the public markets are generally not available for partnership offerings, a partnership or LLC can be incorporated without tax and then taken public.
d. Although an S corporation can issue incentive stock options (ISOs), the inability to have two classes of stock limits favorable pricing of the common stock offered to employees.
e. Although partnership and LLC interests can be provided to employees, they are poorly understood by most employees. Moreover, ISOs are not available.
f. Special low capital gains rate for stock of U.S. C corporations with not more than $50 million in gross assets at the time stock is issued if the corporation is engaged in an active business and the taxpayer holds his or her stock for at least five years.

Source: Bill Morrow of Cooley Godward LLP. Reprinted from Constance E. Bagley, Managers and the Legal Environment: Strategies for the 21st Century, 2nd ed. (St. Paul, Minn.: West, 1995), at 165. Used by permission.

Putting It into Practice

Michael Woo outlined the forms of business organization available and their pros and cons. He told Alexandra and Paul and Sheryl Eagle that they had probably already formed a general partnership by signing the brief handwritten agreement and carrying on joint business activities. No special form of agreement or governmental filing is required to establish a general partnership. They did, however, need to quickly reorganize their business as an LLC or a corporation to protect themselves from the liabilities of the business, because in a general partnership each partner has unlimited liability for the obligations of the business and obligations incurred by the other partners in conducting the partnership business. In addition, reorganizing as an LLC or a corporation would formalize their ownership interests by specifying how they will share profits, losses, and distributions and what their respective roles, powers, and obligations will be in the business. (These topics are discussed in more detail in chapter 5.)

The choice between an LLC and a corporation depended primarily on from where the anticipated $1,250,000 start-up funding would come. If the financing is to come from venture capital funds, the business should be organized as a C corporation, because most venture capital funds cannot invest in businesses that are taxed as flow-through entities such as partnerships and LLCs. If the financing is to come from other sources, such as corporate investors, wealthy individuals, debt, or some combination of these, an LLC would be attractive from a number of perspectives.

The LLC offers the same liability protection as the corporation. An LLC would likely be organized with Alexandra and the Eagles as the managers and with the investors as passive members (the voting and other participation rights of the investors would, of course, be the subject of negotiation). As a flow-through entity for tax purposes, start-up losses would be allocated in the LLC operating agreement to the LLC members who provided the financing. A corporate investor would generally be able to deduct start-up losses allocated to it against its other income, whereas an individual investor would generally have to carry his or her share of start-up losses forward to use against future income from the LLC, because of the limitations on losses from passive activities. However, an individual could use such losses sooner if he or she had qualifying passive income from other investments.

continued

continued

The LLC would be the appropriate entity if Alexandra and the Eagles expected to license the application kit to another business solely for royalties and did not create specialized applets for sale. In a royalty-only situation, earnings would be distributed to the owners, rather than retained to grow the business with the view toward selling it or taking it public.

Because the LLC is not a separate taxpayer, the royalty income would be taxed only once (although at ordinary income rates). In a C corporation, the royalties would be taxed first at the corporate level and shareholders would be taxed again (at ordinary income rates) on all dividends they received.

Because Alexandra and the Eagles planned to grow the business with a view toward taking it public, they planned to reinvest their earnings in the company and thereby shelter substantial amounts of the business's income. When the business is sold or they sell their stock to the public, the gains of Alexandra and the Eagles would be taxed at the long-term capital gain rate, which is lower than the ordinary-income rate.

An LLC might have an additional attraction to Alexandra. Because she is the one contributing the IRRS technology to the business for all or part of her equity, she may want to keep a string on it so that the IRRS technology reverts to her if the participants elect to dissolve the business. However, institutional investors such as venture capital funds are highly unlikely to permit Alexandra to retain any reversionary interest in the IRRS technology. If the business were financed internally, such an arrangement would not be unusual. Using an LLC would permit the business to be dissolved and its assets divided among the owners without any tax (either to the entity or the members). On the other hand, if the business were a corporation, Alexandra and the Eagles would be taxed twice if they parted ways and dissolved the business.

Notwithstanding the advantages of pass-through taxation of an LLC, Alexandra and the Eagles decided to organize their business as a C corporation named WebRunner Inc. They planned to seek venture capital financing within twelve months. That financing would not be available if they organized as a partnership or LLC. Organizing as an S corporation was not an option because WebRunner would have a corporate shareholder, CSS. In addition, Alexandra and the Eagles wanted to issue founders' shares at a fraction of the price to be paid by investors and to be able to issue easily understood and tax-favored employee stock options.

Having decided to use a C corporation, the founders now turned to understanding the issues involved in incorporating and in dividing the equity.

Structuring the Ownership 5

*A*fter selecting the form of organization best for the new business, the entrepreneur's next important step is structuring the initial ownership and the relationship among the founders. If done correctly, the resulting structure will protect the rights of each founder, provide incentives for hard work, and divide the rewards fairly. In addition to formalizing the relationship among the existing founders, the process should be forward-looking and include considerations such as whether additional founders or new employees will be added in the near future and whether the company will seek venture capital financing. The structure that is ultimately put in place should anticipate these events and provide the flexibility to deal with them.

The process of structuring the initial, formal relationship is often the first point at which the founders are forced to sit down and discuss the details of their deal. In the early stages, when there is often little more than an idea, founders tend to be vague and informal in their relationship. If the topic is not discussed formally, each participant probably expects to be treated equally and to receive a pro rata share of the equity and control. Even when discussed, the result may be nothing more than an oral agreement to "divide any profits fairly." The problem, of course, is that fairness is in the eye of the beholder. When the time comes to formalize the relationship, hard questions must be addressed to minimize future disputes. These questions include:

- Who will own what percentage of the business?
- Who will be in the position of control?
- What property and how much cash will be contributed to the business?
- How much time will the participants be required to devote to the business?
- What incentives will there be to remain with the company?
- What happens if a founder quits?
- What protections will a founder have against being forced to leave the company?
- Is there a *wayward* or *forgotten founder,* someone who was involved with starting the venture and may have put work into the project, but is no longer actively involved?

In some ways, the mechanics of implementing these decisions may appear trivial to entrepreneurs who simply want to get on with the important tasks of developing and marketing a product or service. However, thoughtful consideration at this stage will minimize serious problems in the future, problems that can threaten the very survival of the business. An added benefit of careful planning of the initial structure can also come when venture financing is sought. A well-planned structure can anticipate the concerns of the venture capitalist, make for smoother venture financings, and provide evidence that the founders can work through difficult issues as a team and "have their act together."

This chapter describes the basic documents that need to be prepared and the decisions that must be made to get the new business launched, including where to incorporate, how to allocate the equity among the founders, what vesting arrangements to impose, and what restrictions to impose on stock transfer.

INCORPORATION

Most entrepreneurs view the formal paperwork of starting a new business as a necessary evil best left to lawyers. After all, there are more important things for the entrepreneur to be doing than reviewing documents. Although much of the incorporation paperwork may be boilerplate, entrepreneurs should recognize that careful attention to initial structuring details can help avoid future misunderstandings. On a very basic level, founders should understand the critical terms of the business's *charter documents* (the certificate of incorporation and bylaws, discussed below). A thorough understanding of all of the details probably is not necessary; however, a general understanding of the controlling documents is important.

The formal documents required to form a new company will, of course, depend on the type of entity that will be used. Chapter 4 describes the various forms of entities available and the pros and cons of each. This section provides a brief description of the documents necessary to legally establish a corporation and sets the ground rules by which the owners will deal with each other. It assumes that the decision has been made to form a corporation, rather than a partnership, a limited liability company, or some other entity. However, even if a non-corporate entity is used, most of the issues discussed must still be addressed.

Where to Incorporate

As a preliminary matter, the state of formation must be chosen. Generally, it is best to form the entity either in the state where its principal business will be located or in another state with a well-developed body of corporate law, such as Delaware.

Delaware is chosen by many larger companies that are not based in that state because of its favorable corporate law which can, in certain instances, increase the power of management and give the majority shareholders more flexibility in dealing with the minority. Delaware allows a corporation to have only one director while California, for example, requires at least three directors unless there are fewer than three shareholders. Other areas where state laws differ include the type of consideration that can be used to purchase stock, the enforceability of voting agreements among shareholders, the ability of less than all of the shareholders to act by written consent, the ability to elect directors for multiple-year terms (and thereby *stagger* the election of directors), the availability of arrangements regarding indemnification of directors and officers, the ability to have certain kinds of *poison pills* (anti-takeover defenses), and the ability of shareholders to demand appraisal rights upon certain events.

The choice of a state of incorporation other than the state of the principal place of business usually results in somewhat greater taxes and other costs because of the need to comply with certain tax and regulatory requirements in both states. Finally, if a corporation operates in a state other than the one in which it is incorporated, it will still need to qualify as a foreign corporation and pay a filing fee. The founders should review their choice of state of incorporation with counsel.

The California corporations law has several restrictions worth noting. A California corporation may buy back shares or pay dividends only to the extent that it has accumulated earnings. Companies that have negative retained earnings are prohibited from paying dividends, repurchasing shares, or making other distributions. The penalties for violating this provision are stiff, and directors are personally liable for any violations of this law. Privately held California corporations must give shareholders the right to vote cumulatively, which may give minority shareholders the opportunity to elect one or more directors. Under *cumulative voting*, each shareholder can cast a total number of votes equal to the number of shares owned multiplied by the number of directors to be elected; the shareholder can allocate those votes to such nominees as he or she sees fit. (Cumulative voting is discussed more fully below). All directors must be elected yearly so there can be no staggered *(classified)* board.

A privately held corporation is subject to California corporate governance laws regardless of where it incorporates if more than 50% of its shares are owned by California residents and more than 50% of its business is conducted in California. For this reason, a corporation that will be owned primarily by California residents and will have most of its property, employees, and sales in California is often best advised to incorporate initially in California and then reincorporate in Delaware in the event of a public offering.

Certificate of Incorporation

The legal steps needed to form a corporation are surprisingly simple. Once the state of incorporation is chosen, most state statutes simply require that a very short *certificate of incorporation* (sometimes called *articles of incorporation*) be filed with the secretary of state in the state of incorporation, together with payment of a filing fee. Although laws differ from state to state, the certificate of incorporation normally sets forth the following.

First, the certificate must state the name of the corporation, which typically must include the word "Corporation," "Company," or "Incorporated" (or an abbreviation thereof) and usually cannot contain certain words such as "insurance" or "bank" unless the corporation satisfies certain other criteria. In some states a person's name may not be used as the corporate name without adding a corporate ending, such as "Inc.," or some other word or words that show that the name is not that of the individual alone. The corporate name also must not be so similar to an existing name as to cause confusion and must not infringe anyone's trademarks. (The desirability of doing a name search is discussed in chapter 4.)

Second, the business purpose of the corporation must be described. In most states, including California and Delaware, the purpose can be as broad as "engaging in any lawful activity for which corporations can be organized in the state."

Third, the certificate must state the authorized capital of the corporation, including the aggregate number of shares that can be issued, the par value of the shares, and the classes of shares if shares are divided into classes. If the company expects to seek venture financing, the founders can avoid the need for an amendment to the certificate by providing for preferred stock in the certificate at the outset even though only common stock will be issued to the founders. Because the terms of any preferred stock issued in a venture financing will be negotiated, it is best, if the law of the state of incorporation allows, to authorize so-called *blank-check preferred stock*. One authorizes blank-check preferred stock by providing in the certificate that classes of preferred stock are authorized and will have such rights, preferences, and privileges as the board of directors sets in board resolutions; no further action by the shareholders is required.

Fourth, the certificate must list the name and address of an agent resident in the state for purposes of service of legal process (such as delivery of a summons). Although it is tempting to use an individual who is otherwise involved with the company, this would require amending the company's certificate of incorporation promptly if the individual moves or is no longer in a position to accept service of process on behalf of the company. Otherwise, default judgments could be entered by a court against the corporation on behalf of plaintiffs who were unable to serve process on the company. As a result, it is advisable to use one of the many professional service corporations that perform this service for a small fee rather than naming an individual.

Fifth, the certificate should set forth provisions providing indemnification for directors, officers, employees and other agents, and limiting the monetary liability of directors with respect to certain breaches of the duty of care. *Indemnification* means that the company will reimburse the parties indemnified for certain damages and expenses (including attorneys' fees) resulting from their activities on behalf of the corporation.

Certain statutory provisions can be varied only if express language is included in the certificate of incorporation. For example, to impose *supermajority voting requirements* (which require more than a simple majority vote) for shareholder or director actions in California, a provision requiring a supermajority vote must be included in the corporation's certificate of incorporation. In Delaware, cumulative voting of shares is permitted only if expressly provided for in the certificate of incorporation.

Some states give all shareholders preemptive rights unless the certificate of incorporation provides otherwise. *Preemptive rights* give each shareholder the right to participate in future rounds of financing and to buy that number of shares as would be needed to maintain the shareholder's percentage ownership interest. This can wreak havoc when the entrepreneur goes out to raise more money in future financings.

The certificate of incorporation may be signed by anyone. The person signing is called the *incorporator*.

Bylaws

Although the certificate of incorporation establishes the legal existence of the corporation, it provides little guidance for determining how the shareholders, officers, and directors deal with each other and with third parties. The operating rules of the company generally are set forth in a document called the bylaws. However, the applicable corporation statute will establish certain operating rules that cannot be violated or that will apply by default if the bylaws do not provide otherwise. In most cases, the standard bylaws prepared by legal counsel working with the company will both comply with the applicable statute and sufficiently address most issues of concern to the start-up company. As corporation statutes impose very few restrictions on what can be contained in the bylaws, the founders should not hesitate to propose specific provisions needed to effectuate their business deal. The founders should carefully review the bylaws before they are adopted to confirm that their intent is reflected accurately.

The founders should focus on a variety of subjects governed by the bylaws, including matters relating to the number of directors, calling board meetings, directors' voting rights, the process for filling board vacancies and removing directors, the term for which directors are elected, and whether there will be different classes of directors. Most states permit the bylaws to specify a fixed number of directors or a range (e.g., not less than three and not more than five). The board of directors normally controls all but the most crucial decisions for the company; these decisions, such as a sale of substantially all of the corporation's assets, are left to a vote of the shareholders. Thus, even if a founder owns a significant amount of stock, that ownership alone may not guarantee a real influence on many decisions. Instead, each founder should carefully consider whether he or she should sit on the board and, if so, how to guard against removal or replacement if there are disagreements. The minimum number of directors that must be present at a board meeting to legally transact business (known as a *quorum*) and provisions for supermajority votes should also be considered.

The founders should review shareholder voting provisions for an understanding of how directors are elected, what matters require a vote of the shareholders, whether there will be separate class voting on certain matters, how a quorum is determined, and the degree of shareholder approval needed for each action. If a founder believes that, by reason of his or her stock ownership, he or she is ensured a seat on the board or will be able to elect more than one director, special attention should be given to how the shareholder votes are counted in the election of directors.

If cumulative voting is either allowed or required, the ability of a relatively small shareholder to elect a director might be surprising. For example, under cumulative voting, if there are five board seats being voted on, a shareholder owning as little as 17% of the stock will be able to elect a director. The percentage of stock ownership required to elect one director under cumulative voting can be calculated by taking the number 1 and dividing it by the sum of the number of directors being elected plus one. The formula to determine the percentage interest necessary to elect one director (x) is:

$$x = \frac{1}{\text{the number of directors being elected} + 1}$$

Accordingly, if six directors are being elected, a shareholder holding 14.3% of the stock (1 ÷ (6 + 1)) could elect one director; a shareholder would need to hold at least 28.6% of the stock (14.3% x 2) to elect two directors. Given the importance of this issue, it is often best to have a separate voting agreement among shareholders to ensure that the board's composition will be as expected.

While forming the company, the founders typically will have expectations as to who will fill various officer positions (although these appointments are technically made by the board of directors). The bylaws will specify the principal duties and responsibilities of the officers, and the founders should confirm that particular provisions accurately describe the functions that each officer will perform.

Bylaws will often contain restrictions on the transferability of shares and may grant a right of first refusal to the company or its assignees to purchase shares at the time of a proposed transfer to a third party. Such provisions can be especially important in a new company when it is vital that stock be owned by those individuals and entities that are directly involved in the success of the business. This right should be assignable by the company in case the company is not able to exercise the right when it arises due to capital constraints or corporate law restrictions on the repurchase of shares.

Bylaws are generally prepared to provide for the broadest indemnification of directors, officers, and agents allowed by the controlling state statute. The founders should consider whether such indemnification should be mandatory or permissive and whether it should extend to employees and agents of the company. They should also consider whether the company should be required to advance attorneys' fees if a director, officer, or agent is sued.

Each founder should fully understand the mechanics of amending the bylaws. The fact that an important provision is included in the initial bylaws provides little comfort if the provision can easily be deleted or amended later.

Mechanics of Incorporation

In a document generally called the *action by incorporator,* which can be executed as soon as the certificate of incorporation has been filed with the secretary of state of the state of incorporation, the incorporator named in the certificate of incorporation adopts the bylaws and appoints the first directors and then resigns. The board of directors then usually elects officers, authorizes the issuance of stock to founders, establishes a bank account, and authorizes the payment of incorporation expenses. In addition, at the first

---

FROM THE TRENCHES

A disaffected founder of a California computer peripheral start-up company proposed to transfer a large block of stock to a third party. The company was unable to exercise its right of first refusal because it had negative retained earnings, meaning that a repurchase would have been an illegal distribution under California law, subjecting the company's directors to possible personal liability to creditors. However, because the bylaw right of first refusal was assignable, the company was able to transfer its repurchase right to a major shareholder, who exercised the right and purchased the founder's shares. The major shareholder later sold the stock back to the company at cost when the company could legally make the purchase. The stock was then used by the company as an incentive for new employees.

meeting the board may adopt a standard form of proprietary information agreement for use by employees and consultants; a form of restricted stock purchase agreement, which typically imposes vesting and rights of first refusal on employee stock; and an employee stock purchase and/or stock option plan. The board may also select the fiscal year of the corporation and determine whether to elect to be taxed as an S corporation. These actions are generally taken by the board of directors at a meeting called and noticed in accordance with the new bylaws; written minutes of the meeting should be approved by the board at its next meeting. However, many states permit actions to be taken by the board without a meeting if all directors sign a document approving the action, called an *action by unanimous written consent*.

A closely held corporation's organizational documents (i.e., the certificate of incorporation, bylaws, and organizational minutes) are largely boilerplate, and canned organizational documents are readily available for entrepreneurs who desire to incorporate without hiring a lawyer. However, because this documentation is usually straightforward, experienced counsel can prepare it inexpensively. Experienced counsel's real value is less in preparing the basic documentation and more in the advice he or she can provide on choosing an appropriate capital structure, allocating ownership among the founders, transferring assets to the corporation in the most tax-efficient manner, recommending appropriate equity incentive programs, and generally avoiding pitfalls.

SPLITTING THE PIE

Perhaps the most difficult decision in structuring the new business is how to divide the equity ownership, which will determine who participates in the financial success of the business and at what level. The participants often avoid this topic initially due to its sensitivity. However, delaying working out these details can be disastrous. When the time comes to formally structure the ownership of the business, the founders must be forthright in their discussions.

The founders should take into account almost any contribution to the business that they believe should be recognized. Factors commonly considered include the following:

FROM THE TRENCHES

In the early 1980s, four individuals—A, B, C, and D—decided to build a cogeneration power plant to take advantage of available tax subsidies. A and B hired a lawyer to prepare incorporation documents. The lawyer prepared the documents, which listed his secretary as the incorporator. She signed the articles of incorporation and filed them with the California Secretary of State.

A and B then ended their involvement with the project. The two remaining individuals, C and D, then signed a document they called "Action by Incorporator," in which they purported to adopt bylaws and elect themselves as directors. In their capacity as directors, they issued themselves stock and elected officers. The corporation subsequently entered into a joint venture with a large Canadian electric company to build the plant.

The construction was financed with a permanent loan from a bank. When interest rates fell and retail power prices also declined, the company needed to renegotiate the loan to make the plant economically viable. The lender requested an opinion from counsel for the joint venture that the cogeneration plant was owned by the joint venture. After reviewing the corporation's organizational documents, counsel for the joint venture discovered that the person who signed the articles of incorporation was different from the persons who had signed the action by incorporator appointing the directors. This error created doubt about the legal status of the corporation's directors and the officers they had appointed, and thus their ability to enter into the joint venture.

A and B, the original two partners who had dropped out of the partnership, learned of the mistake and claimed that they owned 50% of the corporation. The joint venture could not get the refinancing closed without resolving the two former partners' claim, and the joint venture ended up settling with them for a substantial sum.

Comment: Although having the wrong person sign the action by incorporator designating the directors is a seemingly simple mistake, it created a massive problem, generating very high legal bills. This costly mistake could have been avoided by following the correct legal formalities.

- What cash and property will be contributed at the outset?
- If property is contributed, what is its value and how was it acquired or developed?

- What contributions to the business are the founders expected to make in the future, whether in terms of cash, property, *sweat equity* (time and effort), technical or business expertise, or any other valuable addition?
- What opportunity costs will the founder incur by joining the business?

In the end, the objective should be to treat each founder as fairly as possible. It is not necessarily in the best interest of an individual to negotiate the best deal possible for himself or herself. Success of the company will depend on the hard work of each member of the team over a long period of time. If the business is to grow and be successful, each founder will need to be satisfied that the equity allocation was fair. If members feel slighted, they may be tempted to look for opportunities elsewhere or may not be as dedicated to the business as the other founders.

In addition to considering ownership among the initial founders, the founders need to determine how they will "split the pie" with future employees. If the management team is incomplete and one or more high-level participants will be recruited, the dilutive effect of issuing additional stock and the impact of that issuance on voting control should not be overlooked. For example, if the initial team consists solely of technical people, a chief executive officer (CEO) will be needed. Depending on the caliber of the person recruited, the company may have to issue 5% to 10% of the equity to that person. Similarly, venture capitalists who invest in the first round of financing could negotiate for up to 40% to 60% of the company and may require that 10% to 20% of the equity be reserved for employee stock options. The dilutive effect of these potential events should be considered when allocating equity among the founders.

Finally, the expectations of persons who may have contributed to the enterprise at its preincorporation phase but who are no longer part of the founder group must be considered. It can be very harmful to the company if such a so-called wayward or forgotten founder suddenly appears at the time of a venture financing or, worse, at the time of the company's initial public offering and asserts an ownership right. The claim could be based on oral promises by the other founders or, more

---

FROM THE TRENCHES

Two young entrepreneurs received $50,000 from a wealthy individual (an angel investor) to finance the test marketing of a new handheld device containing updatable financial information. It was the understanding of the parties that the cash would purchase equity in a new entity if the device proved promising but that the money would not have to be repaid if the venture did not proceed. The equity split was not discussed. The test marketing was successful, and the two entrepreneurs incorporated the company. They issued 45% of the company's stock to each of them and proposed issuing the angel investor the remaining 10% of the stock in exchange for his $50,000. They reasoned that because they conceived of the product concept and would be the driving force behind the company, 10% for the angel investor was fair.

However, the angel investor believed that advancing the initial risk capital for the enterprise entitled him to be an equal partner. He sued the founders and the company. The entrepreneurs offered to pay back the $50,000. The angel would not settle and insisted that he was entitled to one third of the equity of this now-promising enterprise. The litigation remains pending.

Comment: This situation could have been avoided if the parties had either incorporated and issued shares earlier or set forth their deal in writing at the time the $50,000 was advanced.

---

commonly, on early contributions to, and therefore partial ownership of, the company's underlying technology. If such persons exist, it is best to settle their claims at the incorporation stage rather than having to deal with them at a time when the company has increased in value or when their claims could destroy a pending transaction.

ISSUING EQUITY, CONSIDERATION, AND VESTING

Once a decision has been made as to how the ownership of the new business will be divided, it is time to formally issue the stock.

Types of Stock

Stock initially issued to founders upon formation of a new company is almost always common stock, while stock issued to venture capital investors is usually preferred stock. There are two primary reasons for this structure.

First, the risk to the venture investors is reduced by purchasing preferred stock that includes a liquidation preference over the common stock. A *liquidation preference* gives the preferred shareholders first claim on the company's assets in the event that the company is dissolved. Thus, if the business does not succeed but retains some valuable assets (e.g., patents or other intellectual property), the preferred shareholders may be able to recoup some or all of their investment.

Second, by issuing venture investors stock that has preferential rights over the common stock, the common stock can be valued at a discount to the price paid by these venture investors. As a result, even if the preferred stock is issued at a premium over what the founders paid for their common stock, the founders can still maintain that they paid fair market value and should not be taxed on the acquisition of the common stock.

The benefit of valuing common stock at a discount to the preferred stock continues as the company expands and begins to grant stock options. As additional employees are hired, it is often desirable to switch from issuing common stock to granting stock options. The exercise price of these stock options usually must be at or near fair market value either for tax or securities laws reasons. Once again, by issuing preferred stock in venture financing rounds, the company can keep the common stock's value relatively low, resulting in a lower option exercise price for employees.

Consideration for Stock

The applicable state statute under which the corporation was formed will contain certain restrictions on the type of consideration that can be used to pay for stock. Cash is always acceptable, as are most types of property. Past services may be acceptable. Under both Delaware and California law, future services are not valid consideration, and promissory notes are acceptable only in certain cases. Given these restrictions, care must be taken to ensure that each founder provides adequate consideration to purchase his or her allocable portion of the company's stock.

Contributions of Property If property is to be contributed to the company, the founders should understand the tax considerations. An exchange of property for stock will be tax-free if it qualifies under section 351 of the Internal Revenue Code, which imposes two requirements. First, the property must be transferred solely in exchange for stock (or securities) of the company. Second, immediately after the transfer the transferor(s), including those contributing cash but not those contributing only services, must own stock possessing at least 80% of the combined voting power of all classes of stock entitled to vote and at least 80% of the total number of shares of each non-voting class.

When there is more than one transferor, the contributions of property do not have to be simultaneous. However, when there are nonsimultaneous contributions, the rights of the parties must have been previously defined, and the execution of the documents necessary to effect the transfer must proceed at a speed consistent with orderly procedure. As a result of these rules, if property is contributed by a founder who alone will not meet the 80% tests, sufficient other contributions should be made at or around the same time by others so that the group satisfies the 80% tests.

An additional concern when property is to be contributed is confirming that the person contributing the property has the right to do so and that the transfer is complete and binding. If technology or intellectual property is being contributed and will be improved upon, the founders should be absolutely certain that the company has obtained adequate ownership of the property so that the company can both use the property in development efforts and retain and exploit any advances or improvements made by the company.

Stock Versus Stock Options

At the formation stage of the business and for some time thereafter, it is usually best to issue stock outright rather than to use stock options. Stock can be issued for little cost and thereby provide the founders certain benefits of direct stock ownership and avoid some of the drawbacks of stock options. As the company matures and the value of the stock goes up, stock options are used extensively to allow employees and others the opportunity to participate in the growth of the business without putting up cash or otherwise having their capital at risk.

If stock is issued to an individual providing services to the company, the recipient must either pay the fair value of the stock or recognize ordinary taxable income to the extent that the value of the stock exceeds the amount paid. If the stock has more than a nominal value, the purchase price or the amount recognized as income can be quite high. Consequently, companies whose stock has more than a nominal value will normally elect to use options as a way to allow employees to participate in the growth of the business.

For a newly formed company, the value of the underlying stock is normally not an issue. Upon formation, the company's assets usually consist of a limited amount of cash and property. The prospects of the new business are still in doubt. As a result, the value of the company's stock often is low enough that early participants can either afford to pay for the stock

> **FROM THE TRENCHES**
>
> A young entrepreneur made an informal deal with a retired engineer to exploit proprietary technology owned by the engineer. The entrepreneur formed a company and spent more than $100,000 to develop and market a product. When the entrepreneur went back to the engineer to negotiate a formal transfer of the technology to the company, the engineer not only refused to complete the transfer but threatened to sue the company and the entrepreneur for misappropriation of the intellectual property. As a result, the company was never launched and the entrepreneur lost the $100,000.

or recognize taxable income on receipt of the stock. There will continue to be a low valuation until there is an event that indicates a higher value for the stock. Although the valuation event may be as undefined as advances in product development, increased sales, and the like, more concrete valuation events can occur, such as a round of venture capital financing in which third parties put a higher value on the business. As explained in chapter 4, to take full advantage of this ability to issue *cheap stock* or *founders' stock,* entrepreneurs should attempt to incorporate the business and issue the initial equity as early as possible. The greater the time that separates the founders' stock acquisition from a subsequent event that establishes a higher value, the less the risk that the founders will be treated as purchasing their stock at a discount with resulting taxable income.

Until the value of the stock is high enough to cause the purchase price or tax consequences to be prohibitive, direct stock ownership has a number of advantages over stock options. Upon receipt of stock, whether for cash or in exchange for property or services, the stock becomes a capital asset in the hands of the recipient (assuming that the stock is vested or a section 83(b) election is made, as described below). As a result, any increase in the value of the stock will be treated as a capital gain when the stock is sold. If the stock is held for more than one year, the gain will be a long-term capital gain, which is taxed at a lower rate than ordinary income.

Additionally, stock in a start-up company can often be classified as *qualified small business stock.* Upon the sale of qualified small business

stock that has been held for at least five years, and subject to certain limitations, one half of the gain is excluded from taxation. By owning stock
rather than receiving a stock option, the founder can start the holding
period for both this exclusion and for purposes of various securities laws,
thereby making it easier to sell the stock later.

The receipt of an option by a service provider is normally not a taxable
event, and the option itself is not a capital asset. Generally, to realize the
value of the option, the holder must first exercise the option and then sell
the underlying stock. The tax consequences of exercising an option and
selling the underlying stock depend on whether the option is an incentive
stock option or a nonstatutory stock option. To qualify as an *incentive
stock option (ISO)*, the option must be granted to an employee (not a nonemployee director or consultant, who can get nonstatutory options) and the
exercise price must be at 100% of fair market value at the date of grant
(110% if the grantee is a greater-than-10% owner of the company). Any
options that do not meet these requirements are called *nonstatutory* or *nonqualified stock options (NSOs)*. An incentive stock option generally
receives more favorable tax treatment than a nonstatutory stock option.

Upon exercise of a nonstatutory stock option, the optionee normally
recognizes ordinary taxable income, which, if the optionee is an employee,
is subject to income and employment tax withholding. The optionee must
pay tax on the difference between the fair market value of the stock purchased on the date the option is exercised and the amount paid to exercise
the option (the *spread*). Any additional gain on the sale of the stock, or
any loss, is a capital gain or loss that is long term or short term depending
on whether the stock was held for more than one year from the date of
exercise. As a result, appreciation in the value of the stock from the
option's grant date through the exercise date is taxed as ordinary income.
This results in a lower after-tax return than would be achieved if stock had
been issued directly at the outset.

Incentive stock options allow the optionee to avoid ordinary income
recognition at the time the option is exercised (although alternative minimum tax might be due). Income is not recognized, and thus generally no
tax is due, until the underlying shares are sold. The optionee then pays tax
on the difference between the fair market value of the underlying shares on

the date they are sold and the exercise price (the *gain*). For the optionee to achieve capital gain treatment on the ISO gain, the stock must be held for more than one year from the date of exercise and more than two years from the date the option was granted; otherwise, the gain at the time of sale will be taxed as ordinary income.

Vesting

When individuals form a new business based on their own ideas, assets, and labor, many founders at first believe that the stock they acquire should be theirs no matter what happens in the future. After all, the business would not exist but for their initial efforts, so why should their ownership be subject to forfeiture? On the other hand, most founders would also agree that if a cofounder were to leave the business shortly after it began, he or she should not continue to own a large part, or perhaps any part, of a business that will require substantial future efforts to grow and be successful. Consequently, a mechanism is needed that recognizes that forming the business is only the beginning and that to earn the right to participate in the future rewards the recipients of stock, including the founders, should have to continue working for some period of time.

If the founders expect to seek venture capital financing in the future, they should also recognize that the venture investors will have similar concerns. Venture capitalists invest in people as much as in ideas and technologies. The typical venture capitalist will spend as much time evaluating the team as the product and, before investing, will want to make sure that incentives are in place to keep the team intact. If the founders do not impose restrictions on the stock owned by themselves or other important team members, they can be sure that the venture capitalist will raise this issue before investing. Except in the most unusual situations, a vesting requirement must be imposed before the venture capitalists will invest.

Consequently, although there are exceptions, stock issued in a start-up company is usually subject to some type of vesting. In its most common form, vesting occurs if the individual holding the stock continues to be employed by or otherwise performs services for the company over a specified period. In these cases, vesting usually occurs gradually. A very common vesting schedule is for the stock to be completely unvested at the time of issuance with one fourth of the stock vesting after one year (so called *cliff vesting*) and the remaining stock vesting monthly over the next thirty-six months. If the employee leaves before becoming fully vested, the company will have the right to repurchase the unvested stock at the lower of the stock's market value and the cost of the stock to the employee. The purchase price may be paid in cash or, in some cases, the company may be allowed to repurchase the stock with a promissory note. The use of the promissory note alternative is especially important if the purchase price is high and if the company is cash poor. Often, if the company is unable to purchase the stock due to a cash shortage or legal restrictions, the company will be allowed or required to assign its repurchase right to the shareholders.

As stated earlier, an individual who receives stock in connection with the performance of services is normally taxed at ordinary income tax rates to the extent that the value of the stock when received exceeds the amount paid for the stock. However, if the stock is subject to a *substantial risk of forfeiture,* the taxable event (including the measurement of taxable income) is normally delayed until the risk of forfeiture lapses. This is true even if the recipient pays full value at the time the stock is received. In general, a substantial risk of forfeiture exists if the recipient's right to full enjoyment of the stock is conditioned upon the future performance of substantial

---

FROM THE TRENCHES

Three founders formed a new company to develop adapter cards for connecting high-performance workstations and personal computers over local area networks. Their initial contributions carried the business for eighteen months. When venture financing was sought, the potential investors insisted that stock owned by the founders be subject to vesting over a four-year period. One founder refused, arguing that he had already devoted two years to the business, counting time before the company was formed, and that that should be enough for full vesting. After long negotiations, it was agreed that four-year vesting would be imposed but that one year's credit would be given for past services.

services. Therefore, if stock issued to founders or others is subject to repurchase by the company at less than fair market value upon the termination of employment (i.e., the stock is subject to vesting), the stock will be treated as subject to a substantial risk of forfeiture.

Under these rules, if a founder is issued stock that will vest over a period of time, he or she could recognize taxable income on each vesting date. For example, assume that the founder pays $25,000 for 500,000 shares of common stock ($0.05 per share) and that one fourth of this stock will vest after one year with the balance vesting on a monthly basis for the next three years. Assume that $0.05 per share was the value of the stock on the date the stock was issued, and that at the end of the first year the value of the stock has increased to $1.00 per share. Unless the founder has filed a timely section 83(b) election (discussed below), he or she will recognize taxable ordinary income at the end of the year when one fourth of the stock vests in an amount equal to $118,750 (the value of one fourth of the stock [$125,000] minus one fourth of the exercise price [$6,250]). This income will be recognized even though the stock is still held by the founder. Similarly, on each monthly vesting date occurring thereafter, the founder will recognize additional ordinary taxable income measured by the then current value of the shares that become vested minus the amount paid for those shares. This income will be treated as if it were wages paid by the company in cash, and (assuming that the founder is an employee) it will be subject to income and employment tax withholding.

As an alternative to recognizing taxable income upon each vesting date, the founder always should consider filing an election under section 83(b) of the Internal Revenue Code within 30 days of the initial purchase of the shares. By filing a timely *section 83(b) election,* the founder is electing to pay tax at the time the stock is purchased in the amount that would be due if the stock were not subject to vesting. If the founder paid full market value at the time of the purchase, no tax would be due because the value of the stock on that date would not exceed the purchase price. Once this election is made, subsequent vesting of the stock will not be taxable. The founder will only be required to pay tax when the stock is ultimately sold, and any gain recognized on the sale will be a capital gain. Thus, the filing of a section 83(b) election both allows a deferral of tax beyond the vesting dates and allows all appreciation in the stock's value to qualify for capital-gains tax treatment.

AGREEMENTS RELATING TO THE TRANSFER OF SHARES

Unvested stock normally is not transferable due to restrictions contained in the purchase agreement for the stock. In addition, it is quite common for other restrictions on transfer to continue even after the stock has become vested. The primary reasons for these restrictions are to keep the ownership of the company with those individuals and entities that are directly involved in the success of the business, to provide liquidity to shareholders in certain situations, to allow other shareholders to participate in transfers of a controlling interest in the company, and to maintain the balance of power among shareholders. Although a separate document might be prepared for each of these restrictions and provisions, they also can be reflected in a single agreement among shareholders. Common agreements include a right of first refusal, buy-sell agreements, and co-sale agreements.

Right of First Refusal

The most common form of transfer restriction imposed on shareholders of a newly formed company is a right of first refusal. This type of restriction

---

FROM THE TRENCHES

A number of employees of a software company received stock subject to vesting. By making a section 83(b) election, they were able to value the shares at the time purchased at a fraction of the value established when the company went public eighteen months later. Those who did not make a section 83(b) election had their shares valued at the public trading price on the date the shares became vested. Because they had paid a fraction of that price of the shares, these employees realized very substantial amounts of ordinary income as the shares became vested. This tax expense could have been avoided with careful tax planning.

is so common that in many cases it is contained within the bylaws of the company. Sometimes a more elaborate right of first refusal is contained in a separate agreement among shareholders. Under a *right of first refusal,* if a shareholder wishes to transfer his or her stock in the company, either the company, its assignees, or the other shareholders (depending on the agreement) must first be given the opportunity to buy the stock pursuant to the terms being offered by the third-party purchaser. Typically, the party or parties with the right have thirty to sixty days to purchase the stock after receiving notice of the pending sale. If they fail to purchase the stock, the selling shareholder is free to sell to the identified third party on the terms presented to the company and the other shareholders within a designated period of time. If the sale to the third party is not consummated within the designated period of time, any subsequent sale may again be made only after application of the right of first refusal.

The primary benefit of a right of first refusal is that it allows the company and other shareholders to prevent transfers to outsiders who might be uninterested in, or disruptive to, the business. On its face, a right of first refusal appears to allow an existing shareholder to sell his or her stock at its fair value. As a practical matter, however, the effect of a right of first refusal is to severely limit the transferability of stock. A potential third party buyer is often disinclined to negotiate a potential purchase knowing that the negotiated terms will then have to be offered first to the company and/or the other shareholders. Even if the right of first refusal is not exercised, the delays caused by the procedures are often enough to dissuade a potential purchaser.

Buy-Sell Agreements

Buy-sell agreements are another device used to provide a liquidity option to shareholders while limiting stock ownership to a small group. Buy-sell agreements typically contain three operative provisions. First, the signing shareholder is prevented from transferring his or her shares except as permitted by the agreement. Second, transfers to certain parties (e.g., family members or controlled entities) or upon certain events (e.g., death) are permitted, subject in most cases to the transferee's agreeing to be bound by the buy-sell agreement. Third, the company or the other parties to the agreement are either granted an option or are obligated to purchase at fair value another party's stock; that other party is obligated to sell the stock upon certain events (e.g., termination of employment).

Often the most difficult aspect of a buy-sell agreement is determining the price to be paid for stock purchased under the agreement. Because the event giving rise to the purchase and sale does not involve a third-party offer, as with a right of first refusal, there usually is no arm's-length evidence as to the stock's value. Alternatives for determining value include valuation formulas based on a multiple of earnings, revenues, and the like; the use of outside appraisers; good-faith determination by the board of directors; and a price to be agreed on. In some agreements the method for determining or paying the purchase price will vary depending on the event giving rise to the sale. For example, selling stock as a result of voluntarily leaving employment might result in a lower price than selling stock as a result of extenuating circumstances (e.g., death).

Co-Sale Agreements

Co-sale agreements are commonly used by venture capital investors to allow them to participate in sales by other shareholders. These agreements are especially common when one or more of the founders owns a controlling interest in the company. Such a controlling interest could, absent transfer restrictions, be sold to a third party, thereby leaving the venture investors in a minority position in a business that has lost at least one of its founders. Conversely, a founder concerned that the venture capitalists might sell out to a third party and leave the founder as a minority shareholder could propose a co-sale agreement covering the venture capitalist's shares; however, many venture capitalists are unwilling to agree to such a provision.

Co-sale agreements in venture capital deals are discussed further in chapter 8.

VOTING AGREEMENTS

Although effective control of a business is often tied to the level of equity ownership, this is not always the case, particularly after a venture financing has occurred and one or more of the investors has been granted the right to designate directors through voting agreements. Even before the first venture financing it may be appropriate to implement a voting agreement to ensure that the composition of the board is defined. Such an agreement is normally entered into by all or a group of the shareholders. Under the agreement, the parties pledge to vote their shares for designated individuals as directors. The individuals can be named in the agreement, or the agreement can allow one or more of the shareholders to nominate the director at the time of each election.

When the company is being structured initially, the number of shareholders may be small enough that a voting agreement appears to be unnecessary. For instance, if there are three equal shareholders and three board seats, then if there is cumulative voting, each shareholder will be able to elect himself or herself to the board. Even in these simple cases, however, a voting agreement could be useful. If, for example, two of the three shareholders are related and are expected to vote together at the board and shareholder levels, the third shareholder might demand that a fourth board seat be established and that, pursuant to a voting agreement, the third shareholder be entitled to designate two of the board members.

EMPLOYMENT, PROPRIETARY RIGHTS, AND NONCOMPETE AGREEMENTS

In structuring and forming a new business, the founders should not only focus on equity ownership and control issues but should also consider the appropriateness of individual agreements between the company and founders and other employees. (Employment agreements are discussed further in chapter 13.)

At the very least, a proprietary information and inventions agreement should be required from all employees, including the founders.

The proprietary information provisions will require the employee to keep the company's proprietary information confidential and to use such information only as authorized by the company. Provisions dealing with inventions will effectively assign to the company any inventions that result from work performed for the company, are discovered during company time, or arise from the use of company materials, equipment, or trade secrets. Protection of trade secrets and other types of intellectual property is discussed further in chapter 14.

Employment agreements at the very early stages of the company are uncommon but, in the right circumstances, can be useful. Under the law of most states, employment is considered to be at-will unless there is an express or implied agreement to the contrary. *At-will employment* means that the company can terminate the relationship at any time, with or without cause. As a result, the company may have little incentive to implement an employment agreement if it has otherwise obtained a proprietary information and inventions agreement and, if allowed under state law, a noncompete agreement. However, a founder who feels vulnerable to the whims of his or her cofounders may find some comfort in such an agreement. On the other hand, care should be taken that any employment agreement is not so airtight that the employee, including a founder, cannot be terminated even for good reason. If the contract effectively guarantees employment, or imposes substantial costs on the company for terminating employment, venture investors could be concerned. These investors must believe that if personnel changes are necessary as the business grows, they can be made without the company paying too high a price.

In states in which an agreement not to compete with a previous employer is enforceable, the founders should consider whether such an agreement between themselves and the company is appropriate. The initial reaction will probably be against noncompete agreements because each founder should believe, at this stage of the company's development, that he or she will be with the company for a long time. In addition, if a founder is forced out, he or she may want to be able to establish a competing venture. Founders should not be surprised if venture investors in the first financing round seek to impose these agreements as yet another way of protecting their investment. (Covenants not to compete are discussed in chapter 2.)

Putting It into Practice

As a first step in structuring their new enterprise, Alexandra, Paul, and Sheryl met to discuss their expectations for the business. Their simple agreement to "divide any profits fairly" might have given them some comfort on an informal basis, but they recognized that it was now time for them to be clear and forthright about their expectations as to equity ownership and control. Given that Alexandra devised the initial software application for the Internet Rapid Retrieval System and had been working on the project longer than Paul and Sheryl, she indicated that she expected a disproportionate piece of the equity. The group concluded that Alexandra should be given 43% of the equity, Paul, 20%, and Sheryl, 20%. Alexandra had already agreed to give CSS a 15% stake in return for licensing the IRRS technology. They decided that Bill Ramseyer, the CSS engineer who gave Alexandra the idea for the IRRS, should be offered 2% of the equity in exchange for his release of any claims to the IRRS and WebRunner.

After working out the business deal among themselves, Alexandra, Paul, and Sheryl met with their legal counsel Michael Woo and his associate Josh Austin to discuss incorporating the enterprise. Michael asked them to describe clearly the agreements they had reached and their expectations as to foreseeable events (e.g., whether they would seek venture capital financing and, if so, when). Alexandra said that WebRunner intended to seek venture capital financing in about six months. Paul indicated that until the company received venture financing, it would be financed by family loans and a modest equity investment by a wealthy family friend. The founders asked Michael and Josh what legal documentation was needed to ensure the equity ownership and board structure they had agreed upon. Because stock was being issued upon the expectation of continued employment, they asked about mechanisms to keep the stock with the company if one of them were to leave. Finally, Alexandra said that she wanted to talk about an employment agreement for herself.

Michael began with a discussion of the pros and cons of incorporating in Delaware or in California, and suggested that California be chosen. He pointed out that for at least for the next few years, significant aspects of California corporate law likely would apply to the company no matter where it was incorporated because of the company's

continued

continued

location and the fact that most of its stock would be held by California residents.

To reflect the agreement regarding equity, Michael proposed that 10,000,000 shares of common stock be authorized in the company's articles of incorporation, and that 1,000,000 shares of common stock be issued, with 430,000 to Alexandra, 200,000 to Paul, 200,000 to Sheryl, 150,000 to CSS, and 20,000 to Bill (assuming he signs a release). He also suggested the authorization of 1,500,000 shares of blank-check preferred stock based on his assumption that the initial venture investors would seek 40% to 60% of the equity. (Michael explained that to sell 60% of the company's equity to the venture investors, the company would issue 1,500,000 shares of preferred stock convertible one-for-one into shares of common stock, so that after the closing, the 1,000,000 shares held by the founders would be 40% of the 2,500,000 shares outstanding.) This capital structure would enable the board of directors to issue convertible preferred stock to venture investors without the need for a shareholder vote and would leave a cushion of shares of common stock available to issue to venture investors upon conversion of their convertible preferred stock and to new employees directly or through options.

The situation with Bill was briefly discussed. Michael expressed the view that 2% of the initial common stock was quite generous, given Bill's contribution, but that obtaining his release was certainly a good idea, particularly if it could be accomplished quickly. At Michael's suggestion, Alexandra agreed to contact Bill immediately to discuss the founders' plans and to seek Bill's release of any claims to the IRRS technology in exchange for common stock.

Michael next discussed the board arrangements, pointing out that cumulative voting would apply as this was a California corporation. Alexandra, Paul, and Sheryl reported their conclusion that a four-person board would make the most sense, with Alexandra having the right to elect two directors, and Paul and Sheryl together having the right to elect two directors. Under this arrangement, neither group could control the board if disputes arose. Josh told the founders that with a four-person board, Alexandra automatically would be able to elect two directors because she held at least 40% of the stock, and that Paul and Sheryl each would be able to elect one of the four directors because they each owned

continued.

continued

at least 20% of the stock. Nevertheless, he advised the parties to sign a voting agreement to reflect their decision on board composition because the ownership percentages would change as additional shares were issued to employees, consultants, or investors. Paul asked Alexandra if he could have a veto over Alexandra's choice of a fourth director; Alexandra agreed, subject to her right to veto any director nominated by Paul or Sheryl if Paul and Sheryl did not nominate themselves.

Josh said that he could include all of these provisions in the proposed voting agreement. He suggested that the agreement expire at the time of the company's initial public offering, because the company's investment bankers would insist on this. He also advised that the even number of directors could result in a deadlocked board which would be unable to take any action. Alexandra said she would rather have a situation where the directors were forced to agree to an action than one where one of the two sides could dictate a decision, or where an outside director would have the swing vote on any important issue. Michael said he was not particularly troubled by the deadlock possibility because these voting arrangements would most certainly change once the company received venture capital financing.

Josh then discussed vesting on the common stock to be issued to the founding group. He started to say that the venture investors would insist on vesting, but Paul interrupted to state that the founders did not need to be persuaded to install vesting now. The founders decided that, for Paul and Sheryl, monthly vesting over four years would be fair and would set an example for future employees, but that vesting for Alexandra should be shorter because she had been the driving force behind the project and had been involved for a longer time. The parties agreed to vest one fourth of Alexandra's shares immediately, with the balance to vest monthly over the next three years. Josh asked whether any credit toward vesting should be given in the event of death, but the founders decided against it because of the need to use unvested shares to attract replacements for key personnel who left the business regardless of reason.

Next, Michael raised the need for controls on the shares to be issued to the founders and future shareholders. All agreed that it made sense to prevent transfers of shares outside of the existing shareholder group. Michael suggested an assignable right of first refusal in favor of the

continued

continued

company, with exceptions for estate planning transfers, gifts, and transfers to existing shareholders. Alexandra thought that there should be no exceptions to the right, even for gifts to family members. The others agreed, as long as the board could waive the right of first refusal in particular cases. Josh said he would include the right of first refusal, and the ability of the board to waive it, in the company's bylaws. Michael pointed out that venture investors might not agree to a right of first refusal on their convertible preferred stock but suggested that for now the right should apply to all stock of the company.

Finally, Alexandra asked about an employment agreement for herself. She was concerned that the venture investors might insist on board control and then use their power to terminate her without compensation. Michael stated that employment agreements for executives were uncommon in Silicon Valley start-ups and such an agreement would probably have to be eliminated before a venture capitalist would invest. Alexandra said she would rather face that issue at the time of financing than have nothing in place. Paul and Sheryl reluctantly agreed, and Josh was instructed to prepare a three-year agreement providing for basic compensation of $75,000 per year and a year's severance pay in the event of termination by the company without good cause. Sheryl asked Alexandra if the commencement of salary payments could be postponed until the company was able to raise capital. Alexandra agreed.

The final step was for Alexandra, Paul, and Sheryl to review carefully the legal documents prepared by Josh as a result of their meeting. The founders believed that they had communicated their deal clearly to counsel and asserted that they did not feel a need to review the resulting documents in any detail. Josh explained that it was much better to discover any differences between what was intended and what the documents said at this early stage rather than in the future, when it may be more difficult to reach an agreement.

Alexandra, Paul, and Sheryl then carefully reviewed the documents and asked questions about several of the more technical drafting points. With one minor modification, they agreed that the documents reflected their intentions. Having successfully divided the ownership, the three founders turned their attention to their biggest challenge yet, raising money to launch their venture.

6

Raising Money

R aising capital for a new or expanding early-stage company with unknown management and no track record may be one of the greatest challenges facing the entrepreneur. It is likely that loans from commercial banks will be either insufficient for the new company's needs or available only on unacceptable terms. For these reasons entrepreneurs often must seek alternative funding sources.

This chapter discusses the advantages and disadvantages of several major alternatives, including the sale of stock to private investors, venture capital financing, self-financing, and strategic alliances and joint ventures. The chapter sets forth the types of information usually contained in a business plan, which is used to attract investors. The chapter concludes with a summary of federal and state securities laws that must be complied with when issuing stock. (Chapter 7 discusses borrowing alternatives and issues raised by loan agreements, as well as bankruptcy.)

SOURCES OF FUNDS

Several major sources of funds are available to start-up companies: money from private investors, venture capital financing, self-financing and credit, and strategic alliances and joint ventures. Each of these sources of funding has advantages and disadvantages, and more than one source of funding may be suitable for a given company. Before making a final decision on which source to pursue, the entrepreneur should consider the degree of control over the company he or she wishes to retain, the amount of equity dilution (decrease in percentage ownership) he or she is willing to bear, whether assistance is desired with such tasks as recruiting talent or managing the company, and to what extent a more seasoned company may be interested in a joint venture or strategic alliance with the start-up.

Sometimes an entrepreneur will engage a broker-dealer as a placement agent to help raise money. A *placement agent* distributes a document describing the company and the offering to suitable persons, and assists in the private sale of securities. Commissions for placement agents are negotiable and commonly range from 8% to 15% of the amount raised. Placement agents are used most often in later-stage rounds.

Private Investors

Private sales of debt or equity securities directly to qualified individual investors (commonly called *angel investors* or *angels*) may be an appropriate way to raise funds, especially if only modest amounts of money are required and the entrepreneur is acquainted with the persons interested in investing in the start-up. The entrepreneur may also want to borrow money from or sell stock to family and friends.

Advantages Angel financing is often a relatively cheap and quick source of seed capital. It is usually preferable when the management team wants to maintain control and manage the day-to-day business of the enterprise without input from the investors. Private investors are typically primarily interested in a return on their investment, rather than an active role in the

---

FROM THE TRENCHES

A 38-year-old entrepreneur left his job managing a $400 million division of a multinational corporation to start a retail business. He funded the first two stores with money he had saved. After exhausting his own resources, and unwilling to seek venture-capital financing, the entrepreneur borrowed money from his father to continue the expansion. At this writing, the entrepreneur had opened three stores and plans to purchase three more.

business. They seldom insist on board representation or the right to approve or select key employees. They usually require no more than the right to veto major changes in the business, restrictions on increases in top management's salary, and limits on the amount of equity to be available for incentive programs (such as stock option plans). Also, they generally do not demand as much equity as a venture capitalist, so dilution is minimal.

Offerings to private investors usually take the form of preferred stock, with the company's founders holding shares of common stock. Sometimes the investment is structured as a limited partnership, with the founders as general partners and the investors as limited partners. Alternatively, a limited liability company may be used. (Factors to consider when choosing an appropriate form of business entity are discussed in chapter 4.)

Disadvantages Private individual investors usually do not bring as much to the company as venture capitalists do in terms of expertise, talent, and

---

FROM THE TRENCHES

After graduating from Stanford Law School at the age of 23, Christy Haubegger decided that she did not want to practice law. Instead, she dreamed of publishing a high-quality magazine for Hispanic women such as herself. She formed Alegre Enterprises, Inc. One of her first investors was angel Mel Lane. Mel and his brother Bill had just sold their tremendously successful Western lifestyle magazine *Sunset* to Time Warner for about $225 million. Mel not only provided capital but also critiqued drafts of Christy's business plan (including the projections and the assumptions underlying them) and served as an advisor on how to roll out a successful magazine. Mel was also a great source of encouragement during the tough times when money was in short supply and Christy's "to do" list seemed endless.

A few years later, Alegre Enterprises, Inc. entered into a joint venture with Essence Communications, publisher of the very successful African-American women's magazine *Essence*. The joint venture was structured as a limited liability company (called Latina Publications L.L.C.) and was funded by Essence Communications with Christy as president and publisher. The first issue of her magazine *Latina* hit the newsstands in May 1996.

recruitment. The amount of money they are willing to invest is usually smaller than what a venture capital firm will invest. Moreover, they may be more difficult to find without engaging in prohibited forms of solicitation.

Venture Capital Financing

Venture capital is money provided by professional investors for investment in new or developing businesses. In deciding whether to invest, venture capital firms differ widely in their preferred technologies, products, industries, size of investment, and the stage of development of the company in which the investment is made. Reference materials are available that list the names, addresses, and specialties of venture capital funds. Often the entrepreneur's professional contacts, such as attorneys and accountants, can direct him or her to an appropriate firm. (Chapter 8 discusses venture capital in greater detail.)

Advantages   Venture capital firms often have the resources to provide the funds needed to finance research and development and growth. Many venture capital firms work closely with young companies and can assist with formulating business strategy, recruiting additional management talent, assembling a board of directors, and providing introductions in the

---

FROM THE TRENCHES

Brad Jendersee left Pfizer in late 1991 to form Arterial Vascular Engineering (AVE), a company that manufactures and sells coronary arterial stents (metal prostheses designed to hold open arteries) and balloon angioplasty catheters. Because of control and dilution concerns, Brad chose not to pursue venture financing. Instead, he financed AVE with money from angel doctors, many of whom were heart surgeons who understood the need for the company's products. The average price paid by the angels was less than $1 per share. In April 1996, AVE went public at a price of $21 per share. The value of the company at $21 per share was $600 million. Jendersee and his two cofounders together owned approximately 25% of AVE's stock at the time of the public offering.

financial community. They are often able to recommend strategies and approaches that make the company more profitable than the founders alone could have made it.

Disadvantages   In addition to sharing in the equity, most venture capitalists insist on sharing in the control of the company. They may want the right to have one or more representatives on the board of directors. They often require veto power over any major changes to the company's business operations or financial arrangements. They may insist on approving or even selecting candidates to fill key management positions in the company. Venture capitalists generally desire registration rights, which will enable them to liquidate their investment when the company makes a public offering of its stock. (Registration rights are discussed more fully in chapter 8.)

One of the most troubling issues for the aspiring entrepreneur is the decision of whether to give up autonomy in exchange for the necessary funding for the start-up. Often the entrepreneur has no choice. Losing control of the company may be a prerequisite to financing the cash-starved emerging business. Entrepreneurs are reminded constantly that having a minority position in a well-financed start-up is preferable to being firmly in control of a venture that goes bankrupt because it was underfinanced.

Venture capitalists will generally not be interested in investing unless the expected return is in the range of 35% to 45% compounded annually. The venture capitalist must produce at least a 20% compounded return for his or her investors, and not all investments will turn out to be winners. In addition, there must be an exit vehicle available, usually within five years of the date of the investment, because most venture capitalists invest through funds with only a ten-year life. An *exit vehicle* is a way for investors to get their money back without liquidating the company, for example, through the sale of the company to a larger company or through an initial public offering of the company's securities.

Self-Financing and Credit

In a few types of businesses, such as distributorships, it may be possible to self-finance, that is, to generate capital by carefully managing the

FROM THE TRENCHES

Jerry Yang and David Filo, the founders of Yahoo! Inc., an Internet directory service for the World Wide Web, started the company while doctoral students at Stanford University. The pair founded Yahoo! after Filo started keeping track of the cool sites he found while surfing the Net. Initially they kept the directory on Yang's university workstation, but soon so many people were connecting with Yang's computer that he found it impossible to study. At that point they realized Yahoo!'s commercial potential and decided to seek venture capital financing.

They were about to accept a $500,000 valuation from a venture capitalist when they received a $1 million buyout offer from America Online, Inc. Yang and Filo went back to the venture capitalists and convinced them to also offer $1 million, but for just a part of the company. With the funding in hand, Yang and Filo dropped out of their doctoral programs to work full-time on Yahoo! Today the index has grown to more than 20,000 categories.

The company went public in April 1996 and the closing price at the end of the first day valued the company at about $850 million. Yang's and Filo's shares of the company were worth $138 million each.

Source: Todd Copilevitz, "On-Line Gold Mine; Surfing Instead of Studying, Yahoo!; Team Struck It Rich," Dallas Morning News, Feb. 18, 1996.

company's internal funds. For example, a business that sells goods or services may be able to obtain payment within fifteen days of shipment, rather than the more customary thirty or forty-five days. The business may even be able to structure contracts with its customers to require advance payments or deposits, although this feature may require price discounts.

In some cases, favorable trade credit arrangements can be made with the business's suppliers whereby suppliers do not require payment until sixty or ninety days after a shipment is received. In addition, it may be possible to eliminate unnecessary expenses, reduce inventories, or improve inventory turnover. To conserve working capital, an entrepreneur may lease equipment rather than purchase it.

Sometimes a finance company will lend money even to a young company if it has current accounts receivable or readily salable inventory. The lender takes a security interest in the accounts receivable and inventory, which serve as collateral; the lender has a right to keep the collateral if the loan is not repaid. (Secured borrowing is discussed more fully in chapter 7.)

Advantages The main advantage of self-financing is that it does not involve sharing the control or the equity of the business. For example, the contractual restrictions and affirmative covenants under an equipment lease may be less restrictive than the rights granted to holders of preferred stock. In addition, because no securities are offered or sold, an equipment lease requires no disclosure document describing the company.

Disadvantages Self-financing alone may not generate sufficient funds to cover salaries and other overhead expenses. Obtaining favorable trade credit terms is more difficult for a new enterprise than for an established business. Customers may object to making advance payments or deposits.

"*Beg.*"

Drawing by Ziegler; ©1986 the New Yorker Magazine, Inc.

Experience shows that it is difficult to make self-financing work. Self-financing should be attempted only if the company's business plan contains realistic projections demonstrating that it can be done successfully.

Strategic Alliances and Joint Ventures

A less common source of financing is a collaborative arrangement with an established company that has complementary needs or objectives. In such a strategic alliance or joint venture, the parties commit themselves to sharing resources, facilities, or information, as well as the risks and rewards that may accrue from the alliance.

Strategic alliances can take many forms. A strategic alliance may be structured as a minority investment by the established company in the young company through the creation of a separate joint-venture entity. Alternatively, an established company may agree to fund a young company's research costs in return for the right to market or exploit the product or technology developed. If both parties are required to conduct extensive research, the alliance will often provide that the parties may cross license each other's technology. Strategic alliances generally require the parties to accept a substantial loss in autonomy, at least with respect to the project under joint development.

A strategic alliance may be used in any situation in which one party has an essential technology or resource that the other party does not have and cannot readily obtain. For example, if an undercapitalized company is developing a technology that has promising applications in an established company's business, the two companies may agree to collaborate. The established company may provide financing as well as access to personnel, equipment, and certain preexisting and future technologies. The young company may correspondingly provide access to its personnel and its preexisting and future technologies.

Advantages A strategic alliance may provide a young company with less costly financing than a venture capital investor. This advantage is most pronounced when the established company anticipates some synergistic benefit to its existing business from exploiting the new technology. The young company often benefits from the more mature company's technical and marketing expertise, and the young company may earn more from the product through a strategic alliance than it would from a licensing agreement.

Disadvantages   One difficulty with almost any strategic alliance is that it requires two companies to cooperate and agree on the development and marketing of a product; this can give rise to management problems. The respective management teams may be unwilling to give up their autonomy to the extent necessary. Furthermore, because there will be two parallel management groups trying to control the same personnel, it may be difficult to manage the alliance effectively without the creation of a supermanagement group.

In a strategic alliance each party may be liable for the other party's wrongdoing. For example, if one company supplies a technology that takes advantage of a third party's trade secret, the other company will be liable for its use of the misappropriated information, regardless of its intent. This risk can be reduced if each party makes certain representations and warranties, and enters into indemnity agreements, regarding the

---

FROM THE TRENCHES

Noah's New York Bagels Inc., a San Francisco Bay Area bagel store chain, sold a 20% stake to Starbucks Coffee Co. in March 1995 for $11 million. The money was used to open another twenty-four stores.

The partial sale made sense for a number of reasons. First, Starbucks and Noah's were a good strategic fit. Their clientele is the same, and bagels and coffee are complementary rather than competitive products. At the time of the purchase, Starbucks and Noah's had two adjacent stores in two areas, with more side-by-side outlets under development. The control of Noah's did not change, and there were no venture capitalists to whom Noah's had to answer.

Source: Wendy Sheanin and Kenneth Howe, "Starbucks Takes Bite of Noah's Bagels: Coffee Giant Buys Stake in Local Chain," San Francisco Chronicle, March 7, 1995, at D1.

technology it will supply. The established company will usually want absolute representations and warranties concerning infringements of other parties' intellectual property rights. However, it may be possible instead to get the established company to accept a qualified representation and warranty that "to the best of Party A's knowledge" there is no violation of others' intellectual property rights.

Strategic alliances also raise antitrust concerns, and experienced counsel should be consulted before talking with competitors or entering into a strategic alliance.

PITCHING TO INVESTORS

The Business Plan

A start-up's success in attracting funds is determined in part by the care and thought the entrepreneur demonstrates in preparing a business plan and presenting it to potential investors. The entrepreneur and his or her colleagues must effectively communicate the nature of the company and its business, markets, and technology; the qualifications of the key members of the management team; the financial goals of the venture; the amount of capital required to achieve these goals; and, in detail, how the required capital will be spent. The business plan should also include such information as the potential market for the company's product, the competition, the barriers to entry, and any research-based projections. Preparation of a formal business plan will greatly assist the initial management team by focusing its planning efforts and offering its members the opportunity to discuss goals and set appropriate milestones. Once in place, the business plan will guide management and enable it to measure the company's progress.

Federal and state securities laws prohibit the sale of securities through the use of any misleading or inaccurate information, even if it is only in a business plan. As a result, when preparing the business plan, the entrepreneur should take care to include all material information about the company, its management, and the risks of the investment. The business plan should describe all of the assumptions on which its projections are based, and it should contain only those projections for which management has a reasonable basis. In addition, it is important to point out any material risks or weaknesses of the enterprise and its products, in addition to mentioning the strengths. For example, the product may still be in the development stage; there may be a shortage of a raw material or component required for its manufacture; or another company may produce or be able to produce a competing product. It is important to disclose such facts. Often the entrepreneur is the only one who really knows these details, and he or she should volunteer such information to the lawyers or other persons preparing or reviewing the offering document.

The Private-Placement Memorandum

The company seeking funding through the sale of securities may also be required to prepare an offering document (usually called a *private-placement memorandum*) that meets the requirements of federal and state securities laws. Although the private-placement memorandum is both a selling document and a disclosure document, its primary purpose is disclosure of both the benefits and the risks of the investment. Consequently, the memorandum may not be as upbeat as the entrepreneur might like.

The particular exemption from federal securities registration requirements being relied on will determine the content of the private-placement memorandum. State securities laws may also influence the content and format of a private-placement memorandum. Because laws requiring disclosure are technical in nature, the entrepreneur should always consult with an attorney before preparing the private-placement memorandum and request that the attorney review drafts of it.

In many circumstances, a private-placement memorandum is not technically required. Even if not required by the state or federal securities laws relating to the registration or qualification of securities, however, an issuer should disclose all material information and risks associated with the enterprise in a business plan or private-placement memorandum. Under the antifraud provisions of the federal and state securities laws (which apply even to offerings exempt from registration, qualification, or any other requirement for approval by a federal or state authority), an issuer is liable if, in connection with the offer or sale of securities, it either makes an untrue statement of a material fact or makes a misleading statement by omitting a material fact. By explaining the company's business and management and the risks of the investment in writing in an offering document, the entrepreneur can avoid a swearing contest in court later about what oral statements were made by the entrepreneur to the investor.

Requirements of the Business Plan

Set forth below are many of the required components of a business plan. A discussion of business plans prepared for venture capitalists is included in chapter 8.

Description of the Company The business plan should contain a detailed description of the company and its history and goals. It should clearly point out the enterprise's limited history and the lack of assurance that the stated goals will be met. A clause similar to the following is sometimes used.

> *The Company is in the development stage and its proposed operations are subject to all of the risks inherent in the establishment of a new business enterprise, including the absence of an operating history. The likelihood of the Company's success must be considered in light of the problems, expenses, difficulties, complications, and delays frequently encountered in connection with the formation of a new business, and the competitive and regulatory environment in which the Company will operate. Although forecast revenues and expenses are set forth in this Memorandum, the actual amounts may vary substantially from those projected and no assurance can be made that the results forecasted in this Memorandum will be achieved.*

This clause and other sample language in this chapter are for illustrative purposes only. Legal counsel should be consulted in connection with any offering of securities.

Description of the Product The business plan should describe the market for the company's product, the technology behind it, how it differs from other products, and how and by whom it will be manufactured and marketed. The business plan should discuss the product's stage of development, the status of any patent or trademark applications, whether and by what means the enterprise has protected its rights to the underlying technology, and any known obstacles to production. A detailed description of the company's market research (if any) should also be included in a business plan, with projected sales figures for an appropriate period and a discussion of the market for the product, its customer appeal, and competitive strategies. This description should be cautious and factual, and should include certain disclaimers and information about competitors and competing products.

Discussion of the Management Team The business plan should contain a detailed discussion of the strengths and the weaknesses of the management team and its members' responsibilities and track records. It should also describe the respective ownership interests of management in the enterprise, the prices each person paid for his or her ownership interest, management's salary and other remuneration, and any existing agreements between members of the management team and the enterprise. If the founders received equity in exchange for noncash consideration (such as rights to ideas or technology), it is important to disclose that fact together with a statement about how the consideration was valued.

Identification of Risks The specific elements that make an investment in the enterprise speculative must be clearly stated. These factors may include the lack of operating history and the inexperience of management, as well as the undeveloped status of the company's product. A review of prospectuses prepared for public companies in the same industry (which may be ordered from services such as Disclosure, Inc. of Washington, D.C., or accessed through the Internet) may help identify particular industry factors that make the investment risky. Full and prominent disclosure of risk factors can help reduce the likelihood of being sued later for fraud in connection with the sale of securities.

Description of the Competition The competition may consist of competing products, other producers of the same or a similar product, and even defensive measures that other producers might take in response to the company's proposed efforts. All of these should be described in detail.

Avoidance of Unsupported Statements It is essential to avoid including statements in the business plan for which there is no evidence. For example, an enterprise should not be referred to as "the only company" that produces an item unless there is tangible evidence to support such an assertion. Entrepreneurs should not refer to their company as "the largest" when it is impossible to be certain that it is the largest. Such statements may be reworded to refer to the enterprise as "one of the largest," or better yet, to state the actual facts. For example, rather than referring to itself as the "largest owner of privately owned pay telephones in Florida," an issuer could state the number of such phones it owns and the percentage it is of the total, citing an industry study as the source for the total.

Backup File It is important to establish a backup or due diligence file that documents the basis for the statements made. For example, if an issuer's business plan states that the company owns the technology behind its product, someone should locate the actual patent or other source of those rights for the file.

Further Requirements The business plan should describe the securities being offered and the intended use of the proceeds from the offering, including any commissions to be paid (for example, to a broker-dealer) for privately placing the securities. Any material litigation involving the issuer must also be disclosed. A supplement to the business plan

FROM THE TRENCHES

One company thought that its founder owned the technology behind its proposed product because the founder had personally conducted the research that led to its discovery and development. The founder even filed the patent application. In attempting to document the founder's ownership of the technology for potential investors, however, it was discovered that, under the terms of his prior employment contract, he had actually assigned those rights to his former employer. Discrepancies of this nature are best discovered before, rather than after, presenting a proposal to potential investors.

should be prepared if there is any material change in the information in the plan.

ISSUES RELATED TO INVESTMENT SECURITIES

Many businesses operate as corporations because of their flexibility and limited liability. Greater discussion of the attributes of corporations can be found in chapter 4. The investors in a corporation may own shares of one or more classes of stock, and they may have purchased certain debt securities.

Often the type of security to be issued will be determined by the investor. Most investors will desire to purchase preferred stock or some type of convertible debt instrument, such as a promissory note, that can be converted into stock. Some will want warrants (options to acquire stock) or at least a right of first refusal to purchase any new securities that may be issued by the company. Most investors will require the company to make extensive representations and warranties about itself, and many investments will be conditioned on certain corporate changes, such as expansion of the board of directors, or the hiring or resignation of certain key persons.

Generally, investors have greater bargaining power than entrepreneurs because there are more start-ups competing for funds than investors looking for deals. Investors are typically more familiar than entrepreneurs with the form and substance of a financing and the points that are open to negotiation. The percentage of voting power to be acquired by the investors and the price per share are based on the investors' valuation of the company. The extent of board representation granted to the investor, the type of security purchased, and the rights, preferences, privileges, and restrictions afforded to the securities to be purchased are all negotiable. It is therefore helpful for the entrepreneur to know as much as possible about the way a financing works before commencing negotiations. In addition, the entrepreneur should identify the acceptable levels of *dilution* (i.e., the amount by which the founders' percentage interest in the company will be reduced); learn the extent to which the principals desire to retain, or relinquish, management and control of the enterprise; identify those persons who will be directors and officers of the corporation; and designate the corporation's accountants, lawyers, bankers, and public-relations consultants.

After the founders and investors reach agreement on the terms of the securities and the investment, these terms are memorialized in a *term sheet*. The term sheet allows the parties to agree on the principal terms of the investment before the lawyers proceed to draft a stock purchase agreement and any necessary amendment to the corporate charter.

Equity Financing

Classes of Stock If all shares of stock have the same rights, then there is only one class of stock, known as *common stock*. If the issuer wishes to give all of the investors the same rights and restrictions, the company should issue only common stock. In this case, the number of votes per share, the shareholders' rights to vote on various decisions, the dividends to shareholders, and their rights to the corporate assets if the corporation is liquidated will be the same on a share-by-share basis for all shareholders.

Many start-up companies issue shares of common stock to their founders. Subsequent investors, however, often require additional rights, such as the right to elect a certain number of directors, the right to approve major corporate changes, and the right to priority of payment if the corporation is liquidated. Such additional rights can be provided by amending the corporation's certificate of incorporation to authorize a second class of stock, called *preferred stock*.

Venture capital firms and institutional investors commonly invest in start-up companies by purchasing *convertible preferred stock*, that is, preferred stock that may be converted into common stock at a specified exchange ratio. In the typical case, outside investors will purchase preferred shares for cash after the company's founders have received shares of common stock in exchange for services, for transferring their rights to technology to the new enterprise, and for modest amounts of cash. Issuing convertible preferred stock to outside investors can create a tax advantage to the founders. As explained in chapter 5, a person, such as a founder, who receives stock in exchange for services to the corporation is required to pay income tax on the difference between the fair market value of the stock and the price he or she paid for it. If preferred stock is used, the founders can argue that the price they paid per share for their stock was lower than the price investors paid per share, not because the founders paid less than the fair market value but because they bought common stock with no special advantages, while the investors bought preferred stock with valuable additional rights and protections.

Warrants A *warrant* is a right, for a given period of time, to purchase a stated amount of stock at a stated price. The price is often equal to the fair market value of the stock when the warrant is issued, permitting its holder to benefit from any increase in value of the securities. A warrant differs from a stock option only in that options are granted to the company's employees, whereas warrants are sold to investors. If used in an initial financing, warrants typically will be issued to purchase lower-priced common stock in conjunction with the investor's purchase of higher-priced preferred stock. The warrant in this situation is sometimes called an *equity sweetener* because, if exercised, it lowers the investor's average price paid per share.

Employee Compensation Plans Many start-up companies find it desirable to have an equity compensation plan, usually in the form of a stock option plan, to attract key technical and executive personnel. Such a plan can be a very significant component of employee compensation because the company's stock will appreciate if the company is successful. Employee stock plans are explained further in chapter 13. Because the equity compensation plan will have tax consequences, legal counsel should be consulted before implementing such a plan.

Rights of Holders of Preferred Stock

State laws impose few requirements on the creation of preferred stock. California law, for example, requires either a dividend preference or a liquidation preference over common shares, without any requirement as to the type of dividend (cumulative or noncumulative) or the amount of the dividend or liquidation preference. Convertible preferred stock gives investors various rights that, depending on the circumstances and bargaining position of the parties, may be structured differently in each transaction.

Liquidation Preference If the corporation is liquidated, any assets remaining after payment of all debts and obligations are distributed first to the holders of preferred stock and then to the holders of common stock. Investors buying preferred stock often will require a liquidation preference in an amount at least equal to their original investment plus all accrued and unpaid dividends.

Dividend Preference Holders of preferred stock are often entitled to a dividend preference, which means that a specified amount of dividends must be paid to holders of the preferred shares before any dividends may be paid on the common shares. These dividend rights are often *cumulative*, so that amounts not paid in one year are added to the amounts that must be paid in the following years before any dividends may be paid to common shareholders.

Redemption Rights Redemption occurs when the corporation buys back shares from a shareholder. *Voluntary redemption rights* permit the investor to require the corporation to redeem his or her shares for cash at a specified price, provided that the corporation is not prohibited by law from buying back stock or making distributions to its shareholders. To protect creditors and preferred shareholders against dissipation of corporate assets, the corporation codes of many states, including California, prohibit distributions to shareholders unless the corporation is able to meet certain specified financial tests, often based on retained earnings. Thus, unless a corporation is able to meet such tests, it may be unable to pay a dividend or redeem any of its outstanding shares.

Involuntary redemption rights permit the corporation, at its option, to redeem the shares for a specified price either after a given period of time or upon the occurrence of certain events. This right may have the effect of forcing the investor to convert the shares to common stock to avoid redemption. By forcing conversion, the corporation can eliminate the liquidation and dividend preferences of the preferred stock. Accrued but unpaid dividends, however, generally must be paid upon conversion. In addition, automatic conversion may be triggered by specified events, such as an initial public offering or the company's achievement of stated milestones. The specific events resulting in automatic conversion are a subject of negotiation between the issuer and the investor. (Redemption rights are discussed further in chapter 8.)

Conversion Rights Holders of preferred stock normally have the right to convert their preferred stock into common stock at any time. The preferred stock is usually automatically converted into common stock when the company does an initial public offering. Sometimes conversion can also be required upon the vote of a majority or supermajority of the preferred stock. (Conversion rights are discussed further in chapter 8.)

Antidilution Provisions Antidilution provisions adjust the conversion prices at which convertible preferred shares may be exchanged for shares of common stock in the event of certain actions taken by the corporation. *Structural antidilution provisions* come into play when the corporation undergoes structural changes such as stock splits and stock dividends. An antidilution provision's purpose can be to protect against either percentage dilution or the economic dilution of the investor's interest.

The investor in an early-stage start-up is typically looking for protection against percentage dilution. This protection assures the holders of convertible preferred stock that they can exchange their shares for the same percentage of the total common stock after the dilution event as they would have received before the dilution occurred.

In addition to protecting against structural dilution, many investors demand some kind *of price antidilution provision* that is triggered if the corporation issues additional common or preferred shares at a price less than the *conversion price* (typically the per share price paid by the investor). There are two main types of price antidilution provisions: the ratchet method and the weighted-average method. The *ratchet method* is onerous from the company's point of view because, in the event of a dilutive financing, the conversion price of the protected stock is adjusted downward to the issuance price of the dilutive financing. The *weighted-average method* reduces the conversion price in proportion to the amount that the new, lower-cost stock dilutes the total amount of stock outstanding.

Sometimes the company will insist on *pay-to-play provisions*, which require the investor to participate pro rata in certain subsequent financings to retain antidilution protection for his or her shares. (Antidilution provisions are discussed further in chapter 8.)

Voting Rights It is quite common for holders of preferred stock to be entitled to voting rights equal to those of common shareholders and, in addition, to be entitled to (l) vote as a separate class on major corporate events, such as amending the corporate charter or selling substantially all of the corporation's assets; and (2) elect certain members of the board without input from common shareholders. Under the law of most states, any special voting rights afforded to holders of a class of stock are effective only if they are specified in the corporation's charter. (Voting rights are discussed further in chapter 8.)

Charter Amendment The rights of the holders of preferred stock must be set forth in detail in the corporate charter. If the certificate of incorporation provides for a class of blank-check preferred stock, then the directors must set the rights, preferences, and privileges of the securities in a document—often called the *certificate of determination*—that is filed with the secretary of state in the state in which the corporation was incorporated. If preferred shares are not authorized, then the certificate of incorporation must be amended to authorize a class of preferred stock with specified rights, preferences, and privileges.

The Stock Purchase Agreement

Investments in shares are governed by a stock purchase agreement signed by the company and the investors. The first draft is usually prepared by the company's lawyers after the parties have negotiated the basic terms and reduced them to a term sheet.

Description of Security   The typical stock purchase agreement will begin with provisions concerning the type of security to be purchased, the purchase price per share, the number of shares to be purchased, and the expected date of purchase (the *closing date*).

Representations and Warranties   The company, and often the founders as well, will be required to make extensive representations and warranties about such things as the business, financial, and legal condition of the company. Any exceptions to the representations and warranties are listed on a schedule of exceptions attached to the stock purchase agreement. The founders should review the representations and warranties carefully and ensure that the schedule of exceptions accurately states all respects in which the true state of affairs differs from that stated in the standard representations and warranties. Otherwise the company, and perhaps the founders, could be liable for damages to the investors if a representation made in the stock purchase agreement turns out not to have been completely true.

Conditions to Closing   The investors' *conditions to closing* are events that must take place before the investors will go forward with the deal, such as an amendment of the corporate charter to authorize the additional class of securities to be purchased, or an amendment of the bylaws to provide for an expanded board of directors. The conditions will often include items related to the operation of the business, such as employment contracts (with assignments of inventions and confidentiality clauses) with key employees; sometimes the resignation of certain key people; usually a legal opinion from the company's counsel; and often, if the investment will be made by several persons or entities, the raising of a specified minimum amount of capital.

Covenants The typical preferred-stock-purchase agreement will contain both affirmative and negative covenants on the part of the company. An *affirmative covenant* is a promise to do something; a *negative covenant* is a promise to refrain from doing something. These covenants often remain in effect as long as a substantial portion, such as 25% or more, of the securities purchased by the investors remain outstanding. Affirmative covenants may include promises by the company to pay its debts, to meet its obligations under contracts with third parties, to keep its assets in good condition, to deliver specified financial information on a regular basis to the investors, to maintain a certain minimum net worth, and to meet other stated financial tests. Such provisions contractually bind the company to do these things; if it does not, the investors can sue for breach of contract.

Negative covenants may include promises not to increase top management's salaries, make loans to affiliated persons or entities, make substantial changes in the company's business, borrow amounts above a stated level, or enter into contracts outside the ordinary course of business without the consent of the investors.

Investors' Rights The stock purchase agreement may provide for one or more investor representatives to sit on the board of directors. It may grant the investors a right to participate in future rounds of financing. It may grant them the right to impose certain controls and restrictions on the company.

Investors make investments with a view to the company's appreciating in value and providing an exit vehicle that will enable them to realize that appreciation. Some investors will require a *right of co-sale,* which means that if one of the founders decides to sell any of his or her shares, the investor is entitled to participate pro rata as a seller. This right protects an investor from being left with an investment in a company whose founders have sold out. (Co-sale agreements are discussed generally in chapter 5 and in the context of venture capital financings in chapter 8.)

The stock purchase agreement may impose obligations on the founder or employees. For example, an officer who is a minority shareholder may be obliged to sell his or her shares to the majority shareholder upon termination of employment.

The stock purchase agreement will frequently grant the investors *registration rights,* that is, the right to require the company to register, under applicable federal and state securities laws, the shares of common stock into which the preferred stock is convertible. These rights permit the investors to sell their stock in a public offering. (Registration rights are discussed in chapter 8.)

Investors' Representations   The stock purchase agreement will contain representations by the investors that the securities are being purchased for investment and not with a view to further distribution. This requirement is necessary for the securities to be exempt from federal and state registration or qualification requirements, which are discussed further below.

FEDERAL SECURITIES REGISTRATION REQUIREMENTS AND EXEMPTIONS

The Securities Act of 1933 (the *1933 Act*) was adopted during the Great Depression. In adopting the 1933 Act, Congress sought to give the purchaser adequate information relating to the issuer and the offering. The act requires that promoters of securities offerings register them with the Securities and Exchange Commission (SEC), an agency of the U.S. government, and provide to prospective purchasers a prospectus containing material information about the issuer and the offering, unless the security or the type of transaction is exempt from registration.

Because registered public offerings are very expensive (often costing more than $900,000), sales of securities to private investors or venture capitalists are almost always structured to be exempt from the federal registration requirements. An offering of securities may be exempt if it is a private offering, a limited offering (not more than $5 million), an offering to qualified investors, or an offering confined to a single state. These exemptions (which are summarized in Exhibit 6.1) are quite technical in nature, and failure to comply can have disastrous consequences. Each purchaser in the offering would have a right to *rescind* (undo) the purchase and get his or her money back or to recover damages.

Even if an offering is exempt from registration under the federal securities laws, state securities laws *(Blue Sky laws)* may impose their own registration or qualification requirements. Limited-offering exemptions under the Blue Sky laws of California, Connecticut, Massachusetts, New York, and Texas are summarized in Exhibit 6.2.

As noted earlier, even exempt transactions are subject to federal and state antifraud rules. For example, rule 10b-5 under the Securities Exchange Act of 1934 (the *1934 Act*) imposes liability if, in connection with the sale of securities, the issuer makes an untrue statement of a material fact or makes a misleading statement by omitting a material fact. Because federal and state registration requirements and antifraud rules are complicated and subject to strict limitations, it is strongly suggested that the entrepreneur consult with an attorney before soliciting funds.

Private Offerings

Section 4(2) of the 1933 Act provides an exemption for private offerings. A *private offering* (also called a *private placement*) is a transaction not involving an offer to the public but rather an offer to only selected qualified investors who can understand and bear the risk of the investment. A private offering can be consummated more quickly and much less expensively than a public offering. However, to qualify as a private offering, the issuer must be able to prove that all offerees, even those that do not eventually purchase the securities, had the ability to comprehend and bear the risk of the investment. This proof requires a pre-offering qualification through an offeree questionnaire that includes questions about the potential offeree's education, investment experience, and financial situation.

Regulation D: Safe-Harbor Exemptions

Regulation D, promulgated by the SEC, provides greater certainty to companies seeking to do private placements by offering them very specific safe harbor exemptions from registration. An issuer that fails to comply with all the requirements of the applicable rule may still qualify for an exemption if the transaction meets the more burdensome conditions of section 4(2).

Regulation D contains three separate exemptions from registration. These exemptions are outlined by rules 504, 505, and 506.

Accredited Investors   A key element of regulation D is the concept of an accredited investor. Offerings to accredited investors are exempted from the registration requirements on the theory that certain investors are so financially sophisticated that they do not need all of the protections afforded by the securities laws.

Rule 501 defines an *accredited investor* as any one of the following:

1. any national bank;
2. any corporation, business trust, or charitable organization with total assets in excess of $5 million;
3. any director, executive officer, or general partner of the issuer;
4. any natural person who had individual income in excess of $200,000 in each of the two most recent years, or joint income with that person's spouse in excess of $300,000 in each of those years, and who has a reasonable expectation of reaching the same income level in the current year; and
5. any natural person whose individual net worth, or joint net worth with that person's spouse, at the time of the purchase exceeds $1 million.

Integration of Offerings In calculating the amount raised in a twelve-month period and the number of unaccredited investors, the SEC may combine *(integrate)* certain sales made within a limited period of time; that is, it may deem them to be part of a single sale. This is most likely to happen when the offerings (1) are part of a single plan of financing, (2) are made at or about the same time, (3) involve the same type of consideration and class of security, and (4) are made for the same purpose.

Rule 502(a) provides an integration safe harbor for regulation D offerings. Offers and sales made more than six months before the start of a regulation D offering or more than six months after its completion are not considered part of the regulation D offering, so long as there are no offers or sales of a similar class of securities during those six-month periods. Offerings to employees and others under rule 701 (discussed later) are not integrated with offerings under regulation D.

Rule 504: Offerings up to $1 Million in a Twelve-Month Period

Rule 504 exempts offerings of up to $1 million within a twelve-month period. It allows for an unlimited number of purchasers but prohibits public advertisements. Rule 504 is not available to issuers registered under the 1934 Act—known as public companies—or to investment companies such as mutual funds. It is also not available to *blank-check companies*—those that have no specific business except to locate and acquire a currently unknown business.

Because even unsophisticated purchasers can participate in a rule 504 offering, and there is no prescribed information disclosure requirement, rule 504 is the exemption most frequently relied on for the sale of securities to the founders and other investors in the initial round of financing. The issuer must file a notice on form D with the SEC within fifteen days of the first sale of securities.

Rule 505: Offerings up to $5 Million in a Twelve-Month Period

Rule 505 exempts offerings of up to $5 million within a twelve-month period and limits the number of unaccredited investors to no more than thirty-five. There is no limit on the number of accredited investors. General solicitations and advertising are not permitted in connection with a rule 505 offering, and the issuer must reasonably believe that there are not more than thirty-five unaccredited investors. Rule 505 is not available to investment companies. It requires that certain specified information be provided to all purchasers (unless all are accredited investors). This information is generally compiled in a private-placement memorandum, which should be prepared with the assistance of experienced securities counsel. Rule 505 also requires that purchasers have the opportunity to ask questions and receive answers concerning the terms of the offering. A notice on form D must be filed with the SEC within fifteen days of the first sale of securities.

Rule 506: Limited Number of Investors Who Understand Risks   Rule 506 exempts offerings of any amount to no more than thirty-five unaccredited investors, provided that the issuer reasonably believes immediately prior to making any sale that each investor, either alone or with his or her purchaser representative, has enough business experience to evaluate the merits and risks of the prospective investment. There can be an unlimited number of accredited investors. However, general solicitations and advertising are not permitted in connection with a rule 506 offering.

Like rule 505, rule 506 requires that certain specified information be provided to purchasers (unless all purchasers are accredited investors) and that purchasers have the opportunity to ask questions and receive answers concerning the terms of the offering. A notice on form D must be filed with the SEC within fifteen days of the first sale of securities.

Because rule 506 does not require a complicated offering document if sales are made only to accredited investors and permits sales in excess of $5 million, it is the exemption most commonly relied on in venture capital financings.

Intrastate Offerings

Section 3(a)(11) exempts securities offered and sold by an issuer if the issuer and the offerees and purchasers are residents of the same state. The issuer must be domiciled in and doing business in the state in which all of the offers and sales are made.

The issuer must place a legend on the stock certificate stating that the securities have not been registered and cannot be re-sold for nine months to a nonresident of the state. In addition, the issuer must obtain a written representation from each purchaser indicating his or her residence.

Regulation A

Under regulation A, a privately held U.S. or Canadian company may offer and sell up to $5 million in a twelve-month period; $1.5 million of the $5 million may be sold by selling security holders. Investment companies, blank check companies, companies issuing oil, gas, or mineral rights, and companies whose owners have violated the securities laws (designated "bad boys" under rule 262) cannot rely on regulation A. The issuer must file a disclosure document with the SEC and have it qualified before securities are sold.

A testing-the-waters provision permits issuers to solicit indications of interest before filing any required disclosure documents. The issuer need only file a solicitation-of-interest document with the SEC, along with copies of any written or broadcast media ads. There is no prohibition on general solicitation or advertising. Radio and television broadcasts and newspaper ads are permitted to determine investor interest in the offering.

However, no sales can be made or payment received during the testing-the-waters period until the company files form 1-A with the SEC and the offering statement is qualified by the SEC. Once the regulation A offering statement is filed, testing-the-waters activity must cease. In addition, a twenty-day waiting period from the time of the last solicitation of interest begins, during which no sales can be made.

Rule 701: Offerings to Employees

Rule 701 exempts offers and sales of securities by privately held companies (1) pursuant to a written compensatory benefit plan for employees, directors, general partners, trustees (if the issuer is a business trust), officers, consultants, or advisors; or (2) pursuant to a written contract relating to the compensation of such persons. If the benefit plan is for consultants or advisors, they must render bona fide services not connected with the offer and sale of securities in a capital-raising transaction. Exempt compensatory benefit plans include purchase, savings, option, bonus, stock appreciation, profit sharing, thrift incentive, and pension plans. The issuer must provide each plan participant with a copy of the plan and each contractor with a copy of his or her contract, but no other disclosure document is required by rule 701.

Rule 701 applies only to securities offered and sold in an amount not more than the greater of (1) $500,000, (2) 15% of the total assets of the issuer, or (3) 15% of the outstanding securities of the class being offered and sold. Moreover, the aggregate offering price of securities subject to outstanding offers made in reliance on rule 701 plus securities sold in the preceding twelve months in reliance on rule 701 may not exceed $5 million.

Rule 702T requires that a form 701 be filed not later than thirty days after the first sale that brings the aggregate sales under rule 701 above $100,000, and thereafter annually within thirty days following the end of the issuer's fiscal year.

Shares issued under rule 701 can be sold to the public without registration once the company goes public, without regard to the normal two-year holding period requirement of rule 144, provided that the seller is not an officer, director, or 10% shareholder of the company.

BLUE SKY LAWS

A company selling securities must comply not only with the federal securities laws but with the securities laws of all the states in which the securities are offered or sold. Fortunately, many states, the District of Columbia, and Puerto Rico have adopted the Uniform Securities Act, and thus there is some consistency among state laws. Other states, including California, have retained their own version of securities regulatory schemes.

Like the federal statutes, the Uniform Securities Act emphasizes disclosure as the primary means of protecting investors. However, some states authorize the securities administrator to deny a securities selling permit unless he or she finds that the issuer's plan of business and the proposed issuance of securities are fair, just, and equitable. Even if the state statute does not state this specifically, a state securities commissioner can usually deny registration until he or she is satisfied that the offering is fair. This process is referred to as *merit review*.

In late 1996 Congress passed a law designed in part to provide more uniformity between federal and state securities regulation. Under the new law, states are no longer permitted, in connection with transactions involving only accredited investors that are exempt pursuant to rule 506 under regulation D, to require more than the type of filing required by the SEC (including any amendments), a consent to service of process, and a filing fee. Accordingly, pre-offer and pre-sale notice filings and merit review requirements of the states have been preempted in connection with rule 506 offerings. The law similarly preempts state registration requirements and merit review in connection with most initial public offerings registered with the SEC. The new law also provides federal preemption for the issuance of securities to "qualified purchasers," a category of investors that will be defined by the SEC at a later time.

Exhibit 6.2 outlines some of the main limited-offering exemptions available to entrepreneurs in California, Connecticut, Massachusetts, New York, and Texas. Factors to consider with these exemptions include the number of offerees or purchasers, the type of persons who can be solicited, the time period of the offering, the manner of the offering, the aggregate amount of offering, the types of securities sold or excluded, notice requirements, and the exemption for offerings coordinated with regulation D of the Securities Act of 1933. Most of these exemptions are subject to many limitations and requirements, described at greater length in the Blue Sky statutes, regulations, statements of policy, advisories, and interpretations.

This information is current as of February 1, 1997. An issuer should consult with counsel before relying on any exemption.

FROM THE TRENCHES

In 1995, Spring Street Brewing Co., a New York-based microbrewer, raised $1.6 million in an offering of shares on the Internet, without incurring the investment banking fees that would normally be paid the underwriters in a public offering. The company relied on regulation A and qualified the offering in eighteen states and the District of Columbia. The company could not rely on regulation D because the posting of an offer to sell securities on the Internet is an advertisement, which is prohibited under regulation D.

Source: Constance E. Bagley and John Arledge, "SEC Could Ease Offering of Securities Via the Web," 19 National Law Journal B9 (Jan. 13, 1997).

Exhibit 6.1

Key Elements of Certain Federal Exemptions from Registration

Type of Exemption	Dollar Limit of the Offering	Limits on the Purchasers	Purchaser Qualifications	Issuer Qualifications
Section 4(2)	No limit	Generally limited to a small number of offerees able to understand and bear risk	Offerees and purchasers must have access to information and be sophisticated investors	No limitations
Regulation D[a]				
Rule 504[b]	$1 million in 12 months	No limit	No requirements	Not a 1934 Act public reporting company or an investment company
Rule 505[c]	$5 million in 12 months	No limit on the number of accredited investors but limited to 35 unaccredited investors	No requirements for unaccredited investors	Not an investment company
Rule 506[c]	No limit	No limit on the number of accredited investors but limited to 35 unaccredited investors	Unaccredited investors must have sufficient experience to evaluate the investment	No limitations

EXHIBIT 6.1 continued

Key Elements of Certain Federal Exemptions from Registration

TYPE OF EXEMPTION	DOLLAR LIMIT OF THE OFFERING	LIMITS ON THE PUR- CHASERS	PURCHASER QUALIFICA- TIONS	ISSUER QUALIFICA- TIONS
Regulation A	$5 million in 12 months, with a maximum of $1.5 million sold by selling security holders	No limit	No require- ments	A U.S. or Canadian company, but not a 1934 Act public reporting com- pany, an investment company, a blank check company, a company issu- ing oil/gas/ mineral rights, or a company disqualified under "bad boy" rule 262
Rule 701[d,e]	The greater of $500,000 or 15% of the total assets of the issuer or 15% of the outstanding securities of the same class, up to a limit of $5 million over 12 months	No limit on the number of employees, directors, officers, advisors, or consultants	Advisory and consulting ser- vices must not be connected with the offer and sale of securities in a capital-raising transaction	Not a 1934 Act public reporting com- pany or an investment company

Exhibit 6.1 continued

Key Elements of Certain Federal Exemptions from Registration

a. All issuers relying on these exemptions are required to file notice on form D with the SEC within fifteen days of the first sale of securities. In addition, solicitations, advertising, and the provision of information during such offerings are limited.
b. This exemption does not depend on the use of any type of disclosure document.
c. A disclosure document meeting the specified SEC requirements is mandatory if there are unaccredited investors.
d. All issuers relying on this exemption must file form 701 with the SEC within thirty days of the sale of more than $100,000 worth of securities, and annually thereafter.
e. Must be pursuant to written compensatory benefit plans or written contracts relating to compensation.

Adapted from Constance E. Bagley, Managers and the Legal Environment: Strategies for the 21st Century, 2nd ed. (St. Paul, Minn.: West, 1995), at 734–35. Used by permission.

EXHIBIT 6.2

Limited-Offering Exemptions Available in California,
Connecticut, Massachusetts, New York, and Texas

STATE	EXEMPTION	MAXIMUM NUMBER OF PURCHASERS AND/OR OFFEREES	EXEMPTION HIGHLIGHTS
CA	Limited offering exemption: small offers or sales of any security	Sales to no more than 35 persons, inside or outside California[a]	• All offerees must either have a pre-existing personal or business relationship with the offeror, or its partners, officers, directors, or promoters, or be persons who could be reasonably assumed to have the business and financial experience necessary to protect their own interests in connection with the transaction[b] • Offer or sale may not be accomplished by the publication of any advertisement[c] • Each purchaser must be purchasing for himself or herself, and not with a view to distributing the security • Certain individuals are excluded from the count: individuals whose net worth exceeds $1 million, whose joint income with their spouse exceeds $200,000 per year, or who purchased $150,000 or more of the securities offered in the transaction[d] • Other excluded categories: officers and directors of issuer, banks, and other financial institutions
CA	Offers or sales solely to qualified purchasers	No limit on number but can sell only to qualified purchasers (as defined)	• Issuer must be a California corporation (or a foreign corporation with more than half of its shares held by persons in California and its business centered in California)

EXHIBIT 6.2 continued

Limited-Offering Exemptions Available in California,
Connecticut, Massachusetts, New York, and Texas

STATE	EXEMPTION	MAXIMUM NUMBER OF PURCHASERS AND/OR OFFEREES	EXEMPTION HIGHLIGHTS
			• A written general announcement of a proposed offering may be published, but no securities may be sold to any natural persons until a disclosure statement meeting the requirements of regulation D is provided the prospective purchasers
			• Each purchaser must be purchasing for himself or herself, and not with a view to distributing the security
			• Requires filing of notice of transaction with the commissioner of corporations concurrently with the publication of a general announcement of a proposed offering or at the time of the initial offer of securities, whichever occurs first; failure to file the notice precludes one from using the exemption
CA	Offers or sales of voting common stock by a corporation	Sales to no more than 35 persons total[a]	• After sale and issuance, there can be only one class of the corporation's stock outstanding, which is owned beneficially by not more than 35 people
			• No promotional payments or selling expenses can be connected with the sale or offering[e]
			• Offer or sale may not be accomplished by publication of any advertisement[c]

EXHIBIT 6.2 continued

Limited-Offering Exemptions Available in California, Connecticut, Massachusetts, New York, and Texas

STATE	EXEMPTION	MAXIMUM NUMBER OF PURCHASERS AND/OR OFFEREES	EXEMPTION HIGHLIGHTS
CT	Connecticut uniform limited offering exemption: regulation D, rule 504[f]	Total of nonaccredited investors in Connecticut cannot exceed 35	If the transaction is exempt from federal registration in reliance on rule 504, it is exempted under Connecticut law provided that: • Each offeree is given a disclosure statement • Commission, discount, or other remuneration in connection with the sale[g] does not exceed 15% of the initial offering price
CT	Connecticut uniform limited offering exemption: regulation D, rule 505 or rule 506[f]	No limits on number of accredited investors, but no more than 35 nonaccredited investors	If the transaction is exempt from federal registration in reliance on rule 505 or rule 506, it is exempted under Connecticut law provided that: • If issuer sells to any nonaccredited investor, then the disclosure requirements in rule 502 apply to all purchasers in Connecticut regardless of their accreditation • Commission, discount, or other remuneration in connection with the sale[g] cannot exceed 15% of the initial offering price
MA	Limited offering exemption	25 non-excluded purchasers within a 12-month period[h]	• Excluded categories: officers and directors of issuer, banks, and other financial institutions • Only offers that are part of the same offering will be counted in the 25-purchaser total • Offer or sale may not be accomplished by the publication of any advertisement[c]

EXHIBIT 6.2 continued

Limited-Offering Exemptions Available in California,
Connecticut, Massachusetts, New York, and Texas

STATE	EXEMPTION	MAXIMUM NUMBER OF PURCHASERS AND/OR OFFEREES	EXEMPTION HIGHLIGHTS
			• The seller must reasonably believe that all buyers in Massachusetts are purchasing for investment purposes • Requires notice to the secretary of state if there is any commission or other remuneration involved in the solicitation of the transaction; failure to file the notice within 10 days may preclude one from using the exemption
NY	General limited offering exemption	No more than 40 offerees	
NY	Offerings exempt from federal provisions	No limit	• Transactions that are exempt from the federal provisions because they are New York intrastate offerings are excluded from this exemption
TX	General limited offering exemption: a sale of any security by the issuer	Total number of security holders cannot exceed 35 after sale	• No advertising may be published in connection with the transaction[c] • The issuer must reasonably believe purchasers are either sophisticated, well-informed investors who can protect themselves or well-informed investors who have a relationship with the issuer such that there is trust between the two parties[b]

Exhibit **6.2 continued**

Limited-Offering Exemptions Available in California, Connecticut, Massachusetts, New York, and Texas

STATE	EXEMPTION	MAXIMUM NUMBER OF PURCHASERS AND/OR OFFEREES	EXEMPTION HIGHLIGHTS
TX	General limited offering exemption: a sale of any security by the issuer	Sales cannot exceed 15 purchasers within a 12-month period, excluding purchasers who are purchasing securities under other exemptions	• No advertising may be published in connection with the transaction[c] • The issuer must reasonably believe purchasers are either sophisticated, well-informed investors who can protect themselves or well-informed investors who have a relationship with the issuer such that there is trust between the two parties[b] • Buyers must be purchasing securities for their own accounts and not with a view to distributing the security
TX	Intrastate limited offering exemption	Not more than 35 new security holders who became security holders during the 12-month period ending with the date of sale	• All offers and sales must be pursuant to an offering made and completed solely within the state of Texas • No advertising may be published in connection with the transaction[c] • The 35 new security holders must be either sophisticated, well-informed investors who can protect themselves or well-informed investors who have a relationship with the issuer such that there is trust between the two parties[b] • Sales may be made to other well-informed, accredited investors, bringing the total number of security holders beyond 35

a. For purposes of these totals, a husband and wife count as one person.
b. Keep in mind that the ultimate goal of the state in assessing business and personal relationships between issuers and purchasers is to ascertain the purchaser's ability to protect his or her interests in connection with the transaction. Factors

EXHIBIT 6.2 continued

Limited-Offering Exemptions Available in California,
Connecticut, Massachusetts, New York, and Texas

---

considered in determining the sophistication of an investor include financial capacity, total commitment in relation to net worth, and knowledge of finance and securities generally.

c. The states' prohibition on the use of advertising for purposes of these exemptions is very broad. Publication of any advertisement includes any written or printed communications (mailers, posters), any recorded and publicly broadcast communications (on television, radio, or otherwise), recorded phone messages, and even seminars or meetings that are publicly advertised. Most states encourage sellers to circulate disclosure materials only to individuals whom one believes to be interested in purchasing or to individuals who meet the purchaser requirements.

d. Individuals purchasing $150,000 or more of the securities may be excluded only if they have the capacity to protect their own interests, or they can bear the economic risk of the transaction, or the investment does not exceed 10% of the individual's net worth.

e. This means there must not be any payments incurred or made to individuals who organized or founded the enterprise or who helped bring about the sales of the security.

f. For the Connecticut, Massachusetts, and Texas Uniform Limited Offering Exemptions, a notice must be filed with the state commissioner/director, but failure to file on time does not necessarily preclude reliance on the exemption.

g. Not including legal or printing fees.

h. The number of offerees can be increased to the number of offerees to whom the offering was actually made if (1) the number of purchasers within Massachusetts is no greater than 10; (2) there is no discount, fee, or remuneration for the seller connected with the transaction; and (3) there was no general solicitation or advertisement connected with the sale.

Putting It into Practice

Once Alexandra and her cofounders decided to go forward with WebRunner, they needed to determine how to finance it. In choosing a finance structure, there were no hard-and-fast rules to follow, just guidelines. WebRunner's attorney, Michael Woo, outlined seven ways that Alexandra could finance her venture.

First, Alexandra could approach CSS and ask for financial support. Alexandra had already given CSS 15% of the equity in exchange for CSS transferring all of its rights in the IRRS technology to WebRunner. Alexandra could now approach the CSS management and discuss with them the possibility of getting funding to help her develop the product in exchange for more equity. Many mature companies, especially in the high-tech area, realize that some of their best and brightest employees have an entrepreneurial spirit. One way for a mature company to renew its own high-growth nature is to subsidize new ventures, typically by providing seed money. Alternatively, a corporate partnership could be set up.

Second, she could seek financing or a corporate partnership with a company other than CSS. She had the expertise and could offer an equity partnership in a business that could generate significant revenues. This method of financing had the advantage that it did not give one company (such as CSS) too much control over WebRunner. The downside, however, was that bringing in another company would require Alexandra to keep an additional major shareholder informed and happy. Also, CSS might object.

Third, Alexandra could approach family and friends. If Alexandra could get some short-term support from them, she could obtain the necessary capital to develop her business while still holding out for a higher valuation at a later stage.

Fourth, Alexandra could find an angel investor or a group of angel investors willing to make a significant investment in WebRunner in return for an equity stake. However, finding angel investors willing to invest at a reasonable price is often difficult.

Fifth, Alexandra could obtain venture capital funding. Venture capital funding is more prevalent in some parts of the country than in others, and more appropriate in some circumstances than in others. In deciding whether this was a viable funding method, Alexandra had first to decide

continued

continued

whether this was the type of business a venture capitalist would want to finance. To show a high enough rate of return to investors given the high risk of failure, a venture capitalist typically looks for a venture that will generate at least a 40% annual return on its investment in a period of three to five years.

Sixth, Alexandra could try to secure a bank loan. Because WebRunner did not yet have a product to ship and thus had no accounts receivable or inventory, a bank would not be willing to lend WebRunner any substantial amount of money, unless Alexandra could demonstrate personal wealth and personally guarantee the loan. In addition, it would be awhile before WebRunner generated cash flow, so it would have no way to pay interest and principal on a bank loan.

Seventh, Alexandra might be able to self-finance her company. This would allow her to continue to develop the business without diluting the equity share of the founders. Alexandra might, for example, be able to secure 50% prepayment from WebRunner's customers for certain orders. This would help cover the cost of materials. Typically, this would work if Alexandra had a client base from which she could find customers; ideally, these clients would have a prior relationship with her and the necessary confidence to prepay. This financing structure might be particularly beneficial to the customer as well, because, with an identified customer, the product could be better developed to suit the particular customer's need.

Alexandra decided not to approach CSS for funding, because she would have had to give CSS an even more significant share of the equity. If she allowed CSS to become a major shareholder, Alexandra could lose control or find herself pressured by CSS to take actions that were favorable to CSS.

Although going to another company in the industry would prevent one company from gaining too much influence, Alexandra and WebRunner would then have to answer to not one, but two corporate shareholders. In addition, Alexandra doubted that CSS would want a potential competitor to have an equity stake in WebRunner.

Alexandra knew that she wanted to get venture capital financing but planned to wait for the product to be further developed so she could get a higher valuation for the company. She decided to borrow a small sum of money from family and friends to start the business. Alexandra finished a detailed business plan that included five-year projections and the

continued

continued

assumptions underlying them. She then, with the help of Michael, found an angel investor named Kevin Jordan, a retired executive who was willing to contribute $50,000 in return for a 5% stake in WebRunner.

WebRunner sold Series A Preferred Stock to Kevin pursuant to rule 506 and the corresponding exemption in California. As Kevin was an accredited investor, WebRunner was not required to provide a disclosure document that went beyond Alexandra's business plan.

Alexandra hoped that these funds would be sufficient to support the business's operations for six months. She was now ready to focus her attention on product development.

Creditors' Rights and Bankruptcy

7

Although the entrepreneur hopes to raise sufficient capital to weather any financial difficulties, he or she is not always successful in doing so. Unanticipated events can result in the new company being unable to pay its bills in a timely manner. Unless the enterprise can access additional sources of funding in such a financial crisis, a company will need strategies for working with creditors and other constituencies. Bankruptcy is one of those strategies. To understand these strategies best, it is important to consider the types of creditors a company may have. In particular, founders should be familiar with the basics of secured lending, in which the lender is given the right to foreclose against company assets, because a secured lender is often at the center of a financial crisis.

The impact bankruptcy may have on the founders personally will be affected by the form of business entity selected for the enterprise and the extent to which the founders have personally guaranteed any of the enterprise's obligations. Although the bankruptcy of a corporation or LLC generally will not put at risk the personal assets of shareholders, a bankruptcy by a general partnership usually will expose each general partner's personal assets to liability for the partnership's debts. In addition, if an individual involved in a corporation or LLC has given a personal guaranty for any of the enterprise's debts, the creditor holding that guaranty may pursue the individual directly if the enterprise is unable to pay.

This chapter first describes the different types of loans available to an entrepreneur, then reviews issues raised in obtaining credit on a secured basis. It gives an overview of the types of creditors and others implicated in a financial crisis. The chapter explores various strategies for responding to a financial crisis, then goes on to discuss bankruptcy in more detail.

TYPES OF LOANS

A borrower may require funds to meet everyday working capital needs, to finance an acquisition of assets or a business, to finance a real estate construction project, or for a wide variety of other reasons. These reasons will dictate whether the loan should be a term loan or a revolving loan. Additionally, the borrower may also have to consider the implications of a secured loan.

Term Loans

Funds required for a specific purpose, such as an acquisition or a construction project, are generally borrowed in the form of a *term loan*. A specified amount is borrowed, either in a lump sum or in installments. It is to be repaid on a specified date—known as the *maturity date*—or *amortized,* that is, paid off over a period of time. For example, in an acquisition, the buyer may be required to pay the purchase price up front and thus will require a lump-sum loan. By contrast, the owner of a construction project will require a loan to be disbursed in installments as scheduled progress payments become due. Amounts repaid under a term loan cannot be reborrowed.

Revolving Loan

A borrower may project its working capital needs for a given period but desire flexibility as to the exact amount of money borrowed at any given time. A *revolving loan* or *revolving line of credit* allows the borrower to borrow whatever sums it requires, up to a specified maximum amount. The borrower may also reborrow amounts it has repaid (hence the term *revolving*). The lender will require a *commitment fee* as consideration for its promise to keep the commitment available, because it receives no interest on amounts not borrowed.

Secured Loans

Most start-ups are not able to qualify for a bank loan and instead rely on equity investments from the various sources described in chapter 6. However, understanding the basics of secured lending is critical. Not only will most young companies develop to a point at which a bank loan is sought for additional capital, but the many other funding sources that may be considered will often seek to invest on a secured note basis in addition to, or as an alternative to, equity.

In making a loan, the lender relies on the borrower's cash flow, the borrower's assets, or the proceeds of another loan as sources of repayment. If the lender relies solely on the borrower's promise to repay the loan, the lender's recourse for nonpayment is limited to suing the borrower. Moreover, even if the lender does sue the borrower, the lender stands in no better position than other *general creditors* of the borrower (those who have no special claim to any specific assets of the borrower as a source of repayment). Because of this risk, many lenders are often unwilling to make loans without something more than the borrower's promise of repayment. Lenders usually require *collateral,* that is, property belonging to the borrower that will become the lender's if the loan is not repaid. A loan backed up by collateral is known as a *secured loan.* Unsecured loans, if they are available at all, are priced at a higher rate to reflect the greater credit risk to the lender.

If the borrower fails to repay a secured loan, the lender, in addition to being able to sue for return of the monies lent, may *foreclose on* the collateral (that is, take possession of it) and either sell it to pay off the debt or keep it in satisfaction of the debt. However, under some *antideficiency* and *one form of action laws,* lenders seeking remedies against real property security may be restricted from suing the borrower personally. Furthermore, in cases in which a lender has recourse to the borrower or to other property of the borrower, and exercises such rights, the lender may be precluded from foreclosing on real estate mortgaged by the borrower. These laws, some of which date back to the Great Depression, are designed to protect borrowers from forfeiting their real estate to overzealous lenders.

LOAN AGREEMENTS

Given the variety of loans described above, the basic structure of loan agreements is surprisingly standard. Lenders are concerned about the administration of the loan, their ongoing relationship with the borrower, and the rights they have if the borrower breaches his or her promises. At times these concerns must be addressed in specially tailored documentation; however, banks generally use a collection of standard forms, which are distributed to loan officers along with instructions for their use. Loan agreements are discussed in greater detail in chapter 10.

SECURED TRANSACTIONS UNDER THE UCC

The mechanics of taking a security interest in personal property and *fixtures* (property attached to real property, such as light fixtures and built-in bookcases), and the consequences of taking such a security interest, are governed by article 9 of the Uniform Commercial Code (UCC), which has been adopted, with certain variations, in all states. Article 9 of the UCC provides a unified, comprehensive scheme for all types of *secured transactions,* that is, loans or other transactions secured by collateral put up by the borrower. Article 9 applies to any transaction (regardless of its form) that is intended to create a security interest in personal property or fixtures, including goods, documents, instruments, general intangibles, chattel paper, or accounts.

Article 9 of the UCC also sets forth the rights of the secured party as against other creditors of the debtor; the rules for *perfecting* a security interest, that is, making it valid as against other creditors of the debtor; and the remedies available to a secured party if a debtor defaults.

Terminology

The UCC uses the single term *security interest* to signify any interest in personal property or fixtures put up as collateral to secure payment or the performance of an obligation. The parties to a secured transaction are the debtor and the secured party. The *debtor* is the person who owes payment or performance of the obligation secured, whether or not that person owns or has rights in the collateral. The *secured party* is the lender, seller, or other person in whose favor there is a security interest. A *security agreement* is an agreement that creates or provides for a security interest.

Scope of Article 9

Article 9 provides a single source of reference for most consensual security interests, but some security interests are outside its scope. Article 9 does not apply to liens on real property. Various state and federal laws preempt the UCC in the areas of ship mortgages, mechanic's liens, and aircraft liens. Notices of security interests in trademarks and patents are commonly filed in the Patent and Trademark Office in addition to being perfected as general intangibles under the UCC. Article 9 does not apply to security subject to a landlord's lien, to a lien given by statute or other rule of law for services or materials, or to a contractual right to deduct the amount of damages from the amount of money otherwise due (a *right of setoff*). Security interests in stock and other securities are governed by article 8 of the UCC.

Formal Requisites

The UCC also prescribes the formal requisites for creating an enforceable security interest and describes the rights of the parties to a security agreement. If the secured party takes possession of the collateral, an oral agreement is sufficient to create a security interest; otherwise, a signed security agreement containing a description of the collateral is required. For a security interest to be enforceable, value must be given in exchange for it, and the debtor must have rights in the collateral. These requirements do not have to be fulfilled in any particular order. When all of the requirements have been met, a security interest is said to have *attached*.

SECURITY AGREEMENTS

A security agreement identifies the parties and the property to be used as collateral. It may also specify the debtor's obligations and the lender's remedies in case of default.

Parties

Security agreements typically use the UCC terminology to identify the parties. In a loan transaction the secured party is the lender. The debtor is the borrower if it owns the collateral or if the owner has authorized it to use the property for collateral. If the third-party owner acts as a guarantor of the borrower's obligation, he or she may also be referred to as the debtor.

Granting Clause

Unless the security interest is a possessory interest whereby the lender takes possession of the collateral (traditionally called a *pledge*), the security agreement must be signed by the debtor and must expressly grant a security interest in some specified property. The standard operative words are, "The debtor hereby grants to the secured party a security interest in. . . ." No precise form is required by the UCC; however, the collateral must be described.

Description of the Collateral

The description of the collateral need not be specific as long as it reasonably identifies it. Loans to finance the purchase of specific property, such as an equipment loan, will typically be secured by the property purchased, and the security agreement will contain a specific description of the property.

For example, a working capital loan may be secured by receivables and inventory. The inventory may be described as "any and all goods, merchandise, and other personal property, wherever located or in transit, that are held for sale or lease, furnished under any contract of service, or held as raw materials, work in process, supplies, or materials used or consumed in the debtor's business." Frequently, a secured party will take a security interest in all the assets of the debtor—not only fixed assets, inventory, and receivables, but also trademarks, trade names, patents, licenses, goodwill, books, and records. In such cases, the collateral may be described as "all tangible and intangible property which, taken together, is intended to preserve the value of the debtor as a going concern." Such a security interest is also known a *blanket security interest* because it covers all of the debtor's assets.

After-Acquired Property

After-acquired property is property that the debtor acquires after the execution of the security agreement. After-acquired assets may be specified in the security agreement either in addition to, or as replacements of, currently owned assets. A security interest in after-acquired collateral will attach when the debtor acquires rights in the collateral, assuming that the other prerequisites for attachment have previously been met. For example, a lender financing a car dealership's inventory would take a security interest in all cars currently owned by the dealership and all cars acquired later. When a car is sold and a new one purchased, the security interest automatically covers the new car.

FROM THE TRENCHES

When one software start-up was two months from a "cash cliff," it returned to its venture capital investors for a further round. The venture capitalists, unwilling to make another investment in return for equity, made the capital infusion in the form of a secured bridge loan. They required a blanket security interest, including a security interest in the venture's intellectual property, to secure repayment. The company used the much-needed cash to fund operations, continued to develop its business plan, and a year later paid off the bridge loan with proceeds from a further equity venture round, as a prelude to an initial public offering.

Proceeds

The UCC provides that, unless otherwise agreed, a security agreement gives the secured party a security interest in the *proceeds* if the collateral is sold, exchanged, collected, or otherwise disposed of. The security interest is equally effective against cash, accounts, or whatever else is received from the transaction. This feature makes a security interest created under article 9 a *floating lien*.

Debtor's Obligations

Under most secured loans, the debtor will be obligated to repay the debt and to pay interest and related fees, charges, and expenses. In addition, the debtor likely will have nonmonetary obligations such as obligations to maintain prescribed standards of financial well-being, measured by net worth, cash flow, and *debt coverage* (the ratio of debt to equity). These obligations are typically set forth in detail in a loan agreement or a promissory note, although occasionally they may be found in a security agreement.

Cross-Collateralization

The collateral for one loan may be used to secure obligations under another loan. This is done by means of a *cross-collateralization* provision—sometimes called a *dragnet clause*—in the security agreement. For example, a lender extending an inventory and receivables line of credit to a borrower may insist that the line be secured not only by inventory and receivables but by equipment owned by the borrower and already held by the lender as collateral for an equipment loan. Thus, if the lender *forecloses on* (sells) the equipment, any proceeds in excess of the amounts owed under the equipment loan will be available to pay down the inventory and receivables line of credit. Likewise, if the equipment loan is cross-collateralized with collateral for the inventory and receivables line of credit, any proceeds realized from foreclosure of the inventory and receivables in excess of what is owed under the inventory and receivables line of credit will be available to pay down the equipment loan.

Remedies for Default

The remedies described in a security agreement track the rights and procedures set forth in article 9. After default, the secured party has the right to take possession of the collateral, without judicial process if this can be done without breach of the peace. The secured party must then dispose of the collateral at a public or private sale, or propose to retain the collateral in satisfaction of the debt (sometimes called *strict foreclosure*). If there is a surplus from the sale of the collateral, the secured party is required to return it to the debtor. If there is a deficiency, the debtor remains liable for that amount. The proceeds from the sale must be applied in this order:

1. To the reasonable expenses of foreclosure and, if provided for in the agreement, reasonable attorneys' fees and legal expenses;
2. To the satisfaction of the obligations secured; and
3. To the satisfaction of any indebtedness secured by a subordinate security interest, if a written demand for satisfaction is received in a timely manner.

Although the UCC establishes a framework within which the lender may exercise its remedies, some details should be provided for by contract. For example, the parties may agree to apply the proceeds of a foreclosure sale to attorneys' fees and legal expenses. They may also agree that the debtor will assemble the collateral and make it available to the secured party at a designated place. All such provisions are subject to the requirement that the secured party's disposition of the collateral be *commercially reasonable*. This term is not defined in the UCC, but it is generally interpreted to require conformity with prevailing standards and to prevent one party from taking undue advantage of another. However, the secured party and the debtor are free to fashion a mutually acceptable standard of commercial reasonableness, and security agreements typically contain a description of such standards.

PERFECTING A SECURITY INTEREST

To protect its rights in the collateral, a lender must ensure that its security interest is *perfected,* that is, valid against other creditors of the debtor and against a trustee in bankruptcy of the debtor. The UCC does not define perfection; instead, it describes the situations in which an unperfected security interest will be *subordinated* to or put below the rights of third parties. For example, a security interest is subordinate to the rights of a person who becomes a lien creditor before the security interest is perfected. (A *lien creditor* is a creditor that has obtained a lien by prejudgment attachment or a levy on a judgment). Subordination to lien creditors essentially means that the security interest is not enforceable in bankruptcy.

Security interests can be perfected by possession of the collateral, by filing a financing statement, automatically, and (for certificated and uncertificated securities) through article 8.

By Possession

A security interest in letters of credit and advices of credit, instruments (other than certificated securities, which are covered by article 8 of the UCC), money, negotiable documents, or chattel paper is perfected by the secured party's taking possession of the collateral. A security interest in goods may be perfected either by possession or by filing a financing statement. For example, when a person goes to a pawnshop and surrenders possession of a wristwatch in exchange for a loan, the pawnshop acquires a perfected security interest in the wristwatch.

By Filing

For most other types of collateral, perfection is accomplished by filing a form known as a *UCC-1 Financing Statement*. Standard printed forms are widely available for this purpose.

Automatic Perfection

Some security interests require neither possession nor filing for perfection. For example, a *purchase-money security interest* (a security interest taken by the seller at the time of purchase) in consumer goods is automatically perfected. Under certain circumstances, a security interest in instruments or negotiable instruments is temporarily perfected without filing or possession. Automatic perfection is of limited duration, however, and must be followed by possession or filing if perfection is to survive for a longer period.

Certificated and Uncertificated Securities

Article 8 of the UCC, which governs investment securities, provides for the creation and perfection of security interests in certificated and uncertificated securities. Currently, these security interests are not governed by article 9 of the UCC.

FILING PROCEDURE

The fundamental concept behind perfection by filing is to provide notice to the world that assets of one person are subject to the security interest of another. When a security interest is not perfected by possession, the collateral remains in the debtor's possession and control. This happens, for example, when the collateral is intangible (such as accounts receivable) or when possession by the secured party is impractical (as in the case of inventory). A centralized system gives effective public notice that property in the possession and under the apparent control of the debtor is actually subject to the rights of another. The filing system enables a prospective creditor to determine whether, in claiming its rights to such assets, it will be competing with other creditors. It also enables a purchaser of goods to determine whether the seller's creditors have any claims against the goods. (It should be noted that, under certain circumstances, a purchaser of goods is protected from liens on such goods created by the seller; for example, consumers are protected from inventory liens on a seller's goods.)

Where to File

Generally, the proper place to file to perfect a security interest is in the office of the secretary of state in the state in which the property is located or, in the case of intangible property, where the debtor is located. A security interest in collateral closely associated with real property, such as fixtures, growing crops, timber, or minerals, must be filed in the office where a deed of trust or mortgage on the real estate would be recorded, usually the county recorder's office in the county where the property is located.

What to File

To perfect a security interest in personal property, a UCC-1 Financing Statement must be filed. The financing statement merely gives notice that a financing transaction is being or is about to be entered into, without describing the transaction. It need only contain the signatures of the parties to the transaction, their addresses, and a description of the kinds of collateral in which a security interest has been or may be granted. When a financing statement covers crops grown or to be grown, or goods that are or are to become fixtures, the UCC also requires a legal description of the land involved.

When to File

A financing statement may be filed in advance of the transaction or the signing of the security agreement. Timing is important because, under the UCC, a security interest is perfected when the statement is filed. Thus, the first secured party to file has priority over other parties with security interests in the same debtor's property, unless special priority rules apply, as in the case of purchase-money security interests.

TYPES OF CREDITORS AND THEIR RIGHTS

A lender with a security interest represents just one of several types of creditor. Other creditors of an entrepreneurial venture may include a bank, a venture capitalist acting as a lender, a seller of goods or services, an equipment lessor, a taxing authority, or an employee. The law gives certain creditors a priority position over other creditors, depending on the nature of the contract or relationship with the debtor. The number of creditors with priority positions, the amount of their claims, and the nature of their priority will affect the strategy selected by the company to deal with a financial crisis.

Secured Creditors

As discussed above, the secured party under a UCC security interest is known as a secured creditor. Generally, the first-to-perfect secured creditor has priority in payment over all other types of creditors, at least with respect to repayment from its collateral.

Equipment Lessors

Young companies often will need equipment, ranging from computers to manufacturing equipment to copy machines. Many companies prefer to rent or to finance the equipment, rather than use existing capital to purchase it. Although many dealers will offer to lease specific equipment, a separate segment of the financial industry has developed to provide equipment financing. Known as *equipment lessors,* these entities finance leases and provide extended financing for the lease or purchase of equipment.

In a true lease of equipment, the lessor retains ownership of the equipment. If the company defaults, the lessor is entitled to repossess the leased equipment and has an unsecured claim for the balance of the payments owed. In a bankruptcy, if the payments due under the lease equal the entire economic value of the equipment, the lease may be recharacterized as a financing arrangement, or *finance lease,* rather than a true lease, and the lessor treated as an unsecured creditor rather than as the owner of the equipment. To protect themselves against this outcome, equipment lessors commonly require a security interest in the equipment being leased and file a financing statement on the equipment. Then if the lease is recharacterized as a financing arrangement, the equipment lessor will at least be treated as a secured creditor in bankruptcy.

Taxing Authorities

The IRS and state taxing authorities have certain special creditors' rights. These include the right to place liens on a taxpayer's property for unpaid taxes and even to seize property. *Withholding taxes* (those taxes required to be withheld from employees' paychecks and paid to the IRS) are considered *trust fund taxes* and must be paid, or officers of a corporation may be personally liable for 100% of the unpaid taxes. Obviously, withheld funds should be paid in a timely manner to the taxing authorities and should not be used to pay other debts or operating expenses of the company.

Employees

An employee's claim for wages, salary, vacation, or sick leave pay is generally treated as an unsecured claim. However, in a bankruptcy, each employee is given a *priority claim* (entitling him or her to payment after secured creditors but before unsecured creditors) for up to $4,000 of compensation earned but unpaid in the ninety days prior to a bankruptcy filing. State law may give employers additional remedies. For example, in California, the labor commissioner can assist employees who have not been paid to collect their wages, and may issue fines or penalties against the employer for nonpayment of employees. In addition, an employee with an unsatisfied judgment for wages or salary can petition a court to require the employer to post a bond to pay the employee's wages or be ordered to cease doing business in California.

Unsecured Trade Creditors

Most of a new company's creditors will be unsecured creditors. *Unsecured creditors* have no security interest in any collateral but only a general claim against the company for payment. If debts remain unpaid, these creditors often first resort to telephone calls and letters to obtain payment. This is followed by turning over the claim to a collection agency or an attorney.

If an attorney becomes involved, he or she generally will file a lawsuit on behalf of the creditor and, in California and a few other states, may attempt to obtain a *prejudgment attachment* of the company's assets to secure payment for the claim. If an attachment is allowed before judgment, or if the creditor obtains a judgment against the company, the creditor then has the right to attempt *to levy* on the attachment or judgment. This involves seizing bank accounts and other assets of the company. A creditor that obtains an attachment or judgment also can file a lien similar to a UCC-1 Financing Statement against the company's equipment, inventory, and certain other types of non-real-estate assets, and can record an abstract of the judgment against any real estate the company owns. The more aggressive of these creditor actions often precipitate the kind of financial crisis that forces a company to pursue a workout strategy or to file a bankruptcy.

PERSONAL GUARANTIES

Some creditors, typically landlords and banks, may demand that an enterprise's founder or officers personally guarantee repayment of the credit extended. If given, a personal guaranty exposes the individual's home and other assets to the creditor's claim in the event the company does not pay the debt. Generally, a personal guaranty gives the creditor the right to sue the individual directly, regardless of whether the creditor has sued the company or whether the company is in bankruptcy. In addition, even though bankruptcy may provide the company with certain benefits (e.g., capping the extent of a landlord's damages from breach of a lease), those protections may not be available to an individual guarantor. For these reasons, an individual entrepreneur should obtain legal advice before giving a personal guaranty.

STRATEGIES FOR RESPONDING TO A FINANCIAL CRISIS

A young company's specific responses to a financial crisis will depend largely on the nature of the crisis, including the kinds of creditors involved and the amount and type of their claims. In almost every crisis, however, conserving cash and gaining additional time are critical. The company needs to be able to use its cash for essential business purposes and needs time to allow its business plan (or revised business plan) to develop. These objectives require methods for restructuring the company's liabilities. Although bankruptcy always remains an option, alternatives for restructuring or *working out* a company's debts short of bankruptcy can be less expensive and buy additional time, even if a bankruptcy is ultimately required. The discussion below provides only an overview of some of the alternative strategies. Because a financial crisis has many complexities, the company should obtain specific legal advice from an insolvency attorney.

General Considerations

As part of a workout strategy, the company may consider hiring a financial consultant or *turnaround expert,* who has experience in refocusing business plans, analyzing financial data, and preparing budgets and other reports helpful in persuading creditors that the venture can work its way out of the financial crisis. In some cases, the turnaround expert can serve as a management consultant or even as chief executive officer until the company has resolved the crisis. Retaining a turnaround expert can also help build credibility with creditors, an asset often in short supply as payment terms become stretched out or shifted to a cash-on-delivery (C.O.D.) basis.

If they desire, three or more creditors with claims aggregating $10,000 can file a petition to force the company into an involuntary bankruptcy. This threat is often used by trade creditors frustrated by a lack of payment. It can become a major distraction for management, especially because in some cases the threat can become real. However, because the Bankruptcy Code permits a company to recover damages against creditors that are unsuccessful in forcing it into an involuntary bankruptcy, creditors generally shy away from taking such a drastic step. Moreover, if an out-of-court workout is under way, and most creditors are observing a collection-action moratorium, the company may be able to persuade a bankruptcy court to abstain from hearing an involuntary bankruptcy filed by a few dissatisfied creditors. However, the possibility of involuntary bankruptcy only emphasizes the need to address aggressively a company's financial problems. (Involuntary bankruptcy is discussed more fully below.)

If the enterprise's founder has given a personal guaranty of any of the company's debts, the financial crisis may prompt the holder of the guaranty to demand payment on the personal guaranty and file a lawsuit to collect. Likewise, if the enterprise is a partnership, the individual general partners are personally liable for the partnership's debts and may face lawsuits for collection. Individual entrepreneurs in these situations should obtain personal legal advice about their own exposure caused by the enterprise's financial crisis.

In addition, as discussed below, when a company becomes *insolvent*— the sum of its debts exceeds the fair value of its assets—officers and directors of the company are generally held to owe expanded fiduciary duties, not just to shareholders but also to the creditors of the company. This expanded fiduciary duty means that officers and directors must take special care with the company's business so as to work in the interests of both shareholders and creditors, and not take steps that unduly favor shareholders at the expense of creditors.

Out-of-Court Reorganization

One workout method involves contacting creditors, individually or as a group, to request a payment moratorium or an agreement to some other payment terms the young company can afford. If a company has only a few large creditors, and they are willing to extend their payment terms, the immediate crisis may be avoided. If a company has many creditors, then a letter to creditors reporting on the company's difficulties and requesting new payment terms may be necessary. Although creditors have the legal right to ignore the request, most will assess the proposal to determine whether they will realize more from agreeing to new terms than they would if the company filed for bankruptcy. Because bankruptcy generally means no payments to unsecured creditors for months or years, if at all, an offer to pay creditors on terms more favorable than the bankruptcy alternative is often accepted.

Secured creditors may also be willing to work with a company in financial trouble and overlook defaults on *financial covenants* such as financial ratios, particularly if the company can keep current on its payments. Even if the company cannot, secured creditors often want to avoid the expense and likely financial loss associated with a foreclosure, or a potentially prolonged bankruptcy case, and will evaluate a serious restructuring proposal on its merits. If the secured creditors are venture capitalists, they may have even more flexibility to work with the company, although they may also demand a greater equity stake.

If the company has lost credibility with its creditors, often a result when honest promises to pay cannot be achieved, the workout may have a better chance of success if an intermediary is used. Credit associations like the Credit Managers Association of California (CMAC) facilitate workouts by organizing a meeting of creditors at which a creditors committee is formed to work with the company in trouble. The company and its creditors committee then enter into discussions in an attempt to negotiate a workout agreement. To convince the creditors to agree to a workout, the company will need to provide the creditors committee with financial reports and information on the company's current and projected performance. Confidentiality agreements can be entered into with the creditors committee members to protect the company's business information.

Once a workout agreement is reached, the credit intermediary will distribute the workout agreement with a consent form. The consent form asks each creditor for the amount of its claim and for an agreement to abide by the moratorium on collection actions generally provided for in each workout agreement. If signed, the creditor is contractually bound to honor the moratorium and will receive payments according to the workout agreement. Disputes over the amount of a claim must be worked out between the company and the creditor before the creditor receives any payment, enhancing the company's leverage in resolving the dispute. The workout agreement generally specifies a minimum percentage of creditors that must accept the terms of the agreement for it to become effective, although the percentage may be adjusted depending on the overall reaction of the creditors. The creditors committee will thereafter require financial reports from the company, to be discussed at periodic meetings, and reports on the company's progress.

To protect the creditors, the creditors committee usually will require the company to provide the credit intermediary, acting as a stakeholder on behalf of all of the creditors, with a security interest in all of the company's assets. The security interest also can protect the company from collection actions by creditors that refuse to agree to the moratorium, because any attachment or judgment lien obtained after the security interest is granted will be junior and subject to the security interest given to the credit intermediary on behalf of the other creditors. If a company has one or more senior secured creditors, it should disclose its intention to give the credit intermediary a junior security interest. Many secured creditors will permit the granting of such a security interest, although it generally violates the terms of their own security agreements, to enable the company to work out its overall financial problems. If not, the company may attempt to reach a workout agreement without granting the credit intermediary a security interest, or else may be forced to file bankruptcy.

Out-of-Court Liquidation

When a company's problems are more severe, especially if a nonrevenue-generating company cannot raise additional capital, liquidation of the company's assets may be required. Although filing for bankruptcy is one vehicle, a nonbankruptcy liquidation may result in higher payments to creditors. As with reorganizations outside of bankruptcy, these can be done by the company itself or with the help of outside organizations.

If the company is not faced with creditors levying on attachments or judgments, it generally can wind down its business operations over a period of time, liquidate its assets through sales of technology and other assets, close its doors, and distribute the proceeds on a pro rata basis according to the legal priorities of its creditors (secured creditors first, then unsecured creditors). If a company has long-term equipment or facilities leases, it may attempt to negotiate termination of those leases on terms that limit claims for the remaining years on the leases. Because bankruptcy offers the ability to cap a landlord's damages, the company often can use a threat of bankruptcy as leverage in these negotiations. Another complicating factor is the presence of agreements called *executory contracts* under which the company has continuing performance obligations other than or in addition to payment. The company may need to negotiate an assignment of these obligations to an asset purchaser or an amicable termination of the company's obligations.

When a liquidation is not feasible without an intermediary, two alternatives may be considered. The first involves hiring an organization such

> ### FROM THE TRENCHES
>
> When a start-up company's primary customer failed to place expected orders, the company found itself without sufficient cash to continue in business. It asked CMAC to organize a meeting of its trade creditors and granted CMAC a security interest in its assets. At the meeting, the creditors in attendance agreed to an interim collection-action moratorium and formed a creditors committee. Two months later, the company and its creditors committee reached a workout agreement, which continued the collection-action moratorium in return for the company's promise to repay its creditors over time. Many creditors returned consent forms agreeing to the workout agreement; others simply stopped calling the company for payment. When one aggressive creditor levied on one of the company's bank accounts to enforce a judgment, CMAC filed a third-party claim objecting to the levy and invoked its rights under the prior security interest the company granted CMAC. The funds were released back to the company, enabling the company to continue in business.

as CMAC, working at the direction of the company, to act as a liquidator. Much as with the reorganization effort described above, the intermediary will send a notice to creditors and organize a creditors meeting at which a collection-action moratorium will be requested and a creditors committee will be formed. The creditors committee, with or without its own counsel, will oversee the company's liquidation effort and help resolve disputes over creditors' claims. The fees of counsel for the creditors committee are paid by the company out of the liquidation proceeds.

If the company is willing to cede control over the liquidation to a liquidator it selects, a second alternative involves making a *general assignment for the benefit of creditors*. In this formal legal procedure the company appoints an individual to act as assignee and to take possession and control of the company's assets. The assignee then liquidates the assets and distributes the proceeds, much like a bankruptcy trustee does in a liquidation under chapter 7 of the United States Bankruptcy Code. Also, as with a bankruptcy trustee, the assignee can in some states (including California) sue creditors for recovery of preferential payments and fraudulent transfers. If insiders or other creditors have received substantial payments from the company on old debt, they may be subject to such preference lawsuits, explained more fully below. One major difference between bankruptcy and this form of liquidation arises if loans, leases, or other contracts provide for their automatic termination upon the making of an assignment for the benefit of creditors. Such provisions are unenforceable in bankruptcy, but they may be enforced if a general assignment for the benefit of creditors is made. In addition, many personal guaranties make a general assignment for the benefit of creditors by the company an event of default, triggering personal exposure for the guarantor. For these reasons, a careful legal review of the company's business is important before choosing this liquidation option.

Secured Creditors and Foreclosure

If the company has obtained financing by giving a security interest on some or all of its assets, consideration of reorganization and liquidation options must start with the secured creditor. If a liquidation is chosen, the secured creditor may simply prefer to repossess its collateral and foreclose, through a public or private sale or by retaining the collateral in lieu of the debt. If the secured creditor has a blanket security interest, this may result in disposal of all of the company's assets. Alternatively, the secured creditor may support a liquidation by the company itself, or a liquidation through an intermediary or by an general assignment for the benefit of creditors, with the secured creditor receiving a priority distribution of the proceeds. If an out-of-court reorganization is desired, some form of forbearance agreement or debt restructure must be reached with the secured creditor, as the secured creditor has the immediate right to foreclose on its collateral if the company defaults. If a forbearance agreement cannot be reached, a bankruptcy, with its automatic stay of foreclosure efforts, may be the only alternative.

BANKRUPTCY

Bankruptcy is a final alternative strategy for the young company in a financial crisis. A company choosing to file a *voluntary* bankruptcy gains an immediate breathing period from creditor actions, including foreclosure, by virtue of the automatic stay, discussed below. By filing under *chapter 11* of the United States Bankruptcy Code, a company can stay in possession of its assets, propose a plan to restructure its debts to creditors, and, in successful cases, emerge from bankruptcy in better financial shape.

Although bankruptcy gives a company the opportunity to reorganize in an orderly fashion, it also imposes many obligations. The company's finances become an open book, as a full schedule of assets and liabilities must be filed soon after the bankruptcy is filed, and a statement of the company's financial affairs must also be made. The company's officers are subject to questioning about every aspect of the company's business at deposition-style examinations, and bankruptcy-court approval is required for any business decision outside of the ordinary course of business. For these reasons, bankruptcy should be considered a last resort, although its unique benefits may make it the only viable strategy for solving the most severe of financial crises.

The following discussion assumes that the company has been organized as a corporation, the most common form of business organization, but should also apply generally to limited liability companies. Enterprises organized as partnerships can raise different issues, because individual general partners are liable for a partnership's debts.

Chapter 11 Reorganization versus Chapter 7 Liquidation

A chapter 11 reorganization bankruptcy offers a company the tools to propose a plan for restructuring its debts and emerging from bankruptcy as a going concern. When the financial problems become too severe, the company may file a *chapter 7* liquidation bankruptcy, also known as *straight bankruptcy*. In a chapter 7 bankruptcy, a bankruptcy trustee is automatically appointed to liquidate all of the company's assets for ultimate distribution to creditors. The company's management must turn over possession to the bankruptcy trustee, and no reorganization is attempted. A bankruptcy trustee is also under a fiduciary duty to pursue recovery of preferences and fraudulent transfers. Because the goal of most companies in a bankruptcy is to reorganize and maintain ownership of the enterprise, this chapter focuses primarily on chapter 11 bankruptcy.

Voluntary versus Involuntary Bankruptcy

When a company chooses to file for bankruptcy, it is known as *voluntary bankruptcy*. When three or more creditors holding claims totaling at least $10,000 jointly petition to force a company into bankruptcy, the result is *involuntary bankruptcy*. An involuntary bankruptcy is started by the filing of a petition, which is similar to a complaint in regular litigation. However, an involuntary bankruptcy petition seeks to have the bankruptcy court order that the company be placed into bankruptcy.

An involuntary bankruptcy can be filed as either a chapter 11 or a chapter 7 bankruptcy. An involuntary chapter 11 filing is often coupled with a request for appointment of a chapter 11 bankruptcy trustee. In a chapter 7 bankruptcy, appointment of a bankruptcy trustee is automatic. The company can respond to an involuntary bankruptcy petition by (1) objecting to the effort, in which case further litigation will ensue until the bankruptcy

Ladies and gentlemen, is there a bankruptcy attorney on board?

Drawing by Leo Cullum; © 1991 the New Yorker Magazine, Inc.

court makes its decision, or (2) consenting to the bankruptcy by filing its own voluntary chapter 11 or chapter 7 bankruptcy petition.

If the involuntary bankruptcy petition is successful, the company will officially be placed in bankruptcy with an *order for relief*. If the involuntary bankruptcy petition fails, then the involuntary case will be dismissed, and the company may be able to recover its costs and attorneys' fees from the petitioning creditors. In cases in which the petition was filed in bad faith, the company may even be awarded compensatory and punitive damages. The potential exposure to liability for damages inhibits many creditors from actually filing an involuntary bankruptcy petition. However, it does not stop creditors from threatening such a filing in an attempt to intimidate the company into paying their claims. An involuntary bankruptcy is more likely in those cases in which creditors suspect a company has engaged in fraudulent activity, is dissipating or concealing its assets, or has announced its inability to pay creditors but has failed to propose a credible workout plan.

THE CHAPTER 11 BANKRUPTCY PROCESS

Chapter 11 of the United States Bankruptcy Code is designed to permit a company to reorganize its business by changing the terms on which its debts must be paid. A reorganization is accomplished through a plan of reorganization, which is proposed by a debtor company and considered by the bankruptcy court according to specific substantive requirements set forth in the Bankruptcy Code. Chapter 11 can also preserve the *going-concern* economic value of an operating company, which is the enhanced value of the company's assets functioning together as an enterprise. This enhanced value is lost when the debtor company is liquidated piecemeal or torn apart by individual creditors foreclosing on security interests or levying on judgments. When a chapter 11 bankruptcy is filed, the debtor company, through its existing management, generally stays in possession and control of its assets. The company serves as a *debtor-in-possession* instead of a bankruptcy trustee being appointed to take control of the assets.

Automatic Stay

Immediately upon filing a bankruptcy petition, a company is protected by an *automatic stay* preventing its creditors from pursuing collection of debts. The automatic stay operates as a statutory injunction that prohibits a creditor from continuing litigation against the debtor (but not against others), sending dunning notices or taking other collection steps, or attempting to exercise control over the debtor's property (e.g., through repossession, foreclosure, or termination of contracts).

Although the automatic stay is one of the most powerful aspects of bankruptcy relief, it is subject to being lifted by the bankruptcy court. If the debtor does not have an equity in specific property over and above the claims of secured creditors and its reorganization prospects are doubtful, or if the court finds that other good cause exists to do so, it may terminate the automatic stay to permit certain creditor actions, including foreclosure.

Cost of Bankruptcy

Aside from the potential negative impact on customer or vendor confidence, and the possible stigma of having been associated with a company that filed bankruptcy, a very real cost of bankruptcy is attorneys' and other professional fees. A chapter 11 bankruptcy for a relatively small company can cost anywhere from $50,000 to $150,000 or more in attorneys' fees; in more complex cases, attorneys' fees can be substantially higher. In addition, given the company's financial condition, the majority of bankruptcy attorneys require these funds to be paid up-front as a prepayment retainer. When a creditors committee is active and retains its own attorneys, the company will be required to pay those fees as well. Similarly, if an investment banker, accountant, or other financial consultant is needed, these fees will also be charged to the company. Thus, although bankruptcy can offer significant relief, it also can be expensive.

Types of Creditor Claims in Bankruptcy

Every creditor of a company in bankruptcy has the right to file a proof of claim in the bankruptcy case. The *proof of claim* is the creditor's statement of its own claim. A deadline known as a *bar date* is established in the bankruptcy case, and all creditors (with some exceptions) must file their claims by that date or be barred from recovering anything in the bankruptcy. The debtor company must file a schedule of assets and liabilities which lists each creditor and the amount owed according to the company's books. The debtor company then, as appropriate, categorizes the creditors' claims. A claim is designated *disputed* if the company believes the claim is not valid; *contingent* if the company believes the claim will be valid only if some event does or does not occur; and *unliquidated* if the company believes the amount of the claim has not been established. If the company has designated a creditor's claim as disputed, contingent, and/or unliquidated, then a creditor must file a proof of claim. Otherwise, a creditor in a chapter 11 bankruptcy may rely on the statement of the claim shown in the company's schedules.

Payment Priority Creditor claims in a bankruptcy are paid in an order of priority established by the Bankruptcy Code. A secured creditor holds a *secured claim* to the extent of the value of that creditor's collateral. Thus, if, for example, a secured creditor is owed $100,000, and its collateral is worth $200,000, then that creditor is *fully secured*. However, if the same creditor's collateral is worth only $60,000, then the creditor is referred to as *undersecured,* with a secured claim to the extent of the $60,000 value of the collateral and an *unsecured claim* for the $40,000 balance. Secured creditors have the highest priority in a bankruptcy case and are entitled to certain specified, favorable treatment.

Creditors that are not secured by any collateral can file one of two types of claims, depending on their circumstances: priority claims or general unsecured claims. Certain claims are entitled to a priority over other unsecured creditors and are called *priority claims*. These may be claims relating to the expenses of administering the bankruptcy case (*administrative claims*), which receive first priority after secured creditors. Administrative claims include the claims of the debtor's attorneys and accountants, and postbankruptcy filing (known as *postpetition*) claims for business expenses, including wages and salaries for employees for work performed postpetition, postpetition raw material and office expenses, and postpetition payments for equipment and facilities leases (but only paid at a fair market value lease rate). Prebankruptcy *(prepetition)* claims of employees for unpaid salaries, wages, severance, vacation, and sick leave, earned within the ninety days prior to the bankruptcy filing, are entitled to a third priority to the extent of $4,000 per employee. (Claims of ordinary business creditors that arise between the filing of an involuntary bankruptcy petition and a decision putting a company in bankruptcy get the second priority.) Other common creditors with priority claims include consumer deposits for personal or household goods (sixth priority) and certain prepetition income and other taxes (eighth priority).

The claims of creditors that are not entitled to any priority are known as *general unsecured claims*. These claims include employee claims other than those claims entitled to the $4,000 priority, trade creditors, damage claims in litigation, and creditors whose executory contracts or leases have been rejected in the bankruptcy (discussed below). Exhibit 7.1 summarizes these payment-priority rules.

If a creditor files a proof of claim but the debtor company (or another party) believes the claim is invalid or in an improper amount, it can file an *objection* to the claim. If the creditor disputes the objection, it will file papers with the bankruptcy court so stating and requesting a hearing on its claim. Ultimately, the bankruptcy court will establish a procedure for resolving the objection to the claim, often by holding a short trial. If the

---

EXHIBIT 7.1

Payment Priority of Certain Claims

- Secured claims
- Administrative claims
- Claims of ordinary business creditors arising between involuntary bankruptcy filing and decision to put company in bankruptcy
- Prepetition claims of employers for unpaid salary and benefits up to $4,000 per employee
- Consumer deposits for personal and household goods
- Certain prepetition income and other taxes
- General unsecured claims (e.g., claims by trade creditors and creditors whose executory contracts have been rejected in bankruptcy)

court decides the claim is valid (or valid but in a different amount), it will *allow* the claim in the amount it finds appropriate, and the claim will be paid according to the terms of a plan of reorganization or the Bankruptcy Code. If the court decides the claim is not valid, the claim will be *disallowed* and will not be entitled to payment in the bankruptcy case.

Executory Contracts and Leases

An *executory contract* is an agreement in which both parties to the contract have continuing obligations to perform. Typical examples include joint development agreements, manufacturing agreements, and licenses in which each party has an ongoing, affirmative performance obligation. In bankruptcy, a debtor company has the right to terminate the active performance obligations in executory contracts by *rejecting* the executory contract. The debtor also has the right to terminate unfavorable leases for real property, including stores, facilities, and offices, by rejecting such leases. The rejection is treated as a breach of the contract and must be approved by the bankruptcy court. However, the court usually defers to management's business decision.

The other party to an executory contract or lease that has been rejected has the right to file a proof of claim for its damages caused by the breach, but the claim will be treated as an unsecured claim only. When a lease of real property is involved, the Bankruptcy Code gives the company another benefit, by capping the amount of the landlord's unsecured claim for unpaid rent under the lease to the greater of one year's rent or 15% of the total rent owed, not to exceed three years' worth of rent. This can be a major benefit to a company with a long-term lease at high rental rates. In some cases, a serious threat of bankruptcy can motivate a landlord to renegotiate lease terms.

The company also has the right to assume, or assume and assign, the executory contract or lease, generally regardless of whether the non-debtor party consents. When the company in bankruptcy *assumes* the executory contract or unexpired lease, it expressly agrees to continue to perform all of its obligations under the contract or lease. Before being permitted by the bankruptcy court to assume an executory contract or lease, the debtor must (1) cure any defaults; (2) compensate for any pecuniary losses suffered by the nondebtor party, which may include attorneys' fees incurred in responding to the bankruptcy case; and (3) provide the nondebtor party with adequate assurances of the debtor's ability to perform under the contract or lease in the future. When the debtor company seeks to *assume and assign* an executory contract or unexpired lease, these same three requirements must be met, although the party taking over the contract or lease from the debtor itself must provide adequate assurances of future performance. A few types of contracts, however, including nonexclusive patent licenses in which the debtor company is the licensee, and contracts for personal services, cannot be assigned to a third party without the nondebtor's consent.

Preference and Fraudulent Transfer Claims

The Bankruptcy Code provides that the debtor, a bankruptcy trustee if one is appointed, or in some cases a creditors committee may pursue recovery of preferential or fraudulent transfers made by the debtor prior to the bankruptcy. *Preferences* are transfers made by the debtor, when the debtor was insolvent, to or for the benefit of a creditor on account of preexisting debt in the ninety days prior to the filing of the bankruptcy petition. The ninety-day *reach-back period* means that potentially all payments made to a creditor during the ninety days prior to the bankruptcy filing may be recoverable. If such a transfer is made to an *insider* (such as an officer, director, or affiliate of the debtor company) within one year prior to the filing of the bankruptcy petition, it is also a recoverable preference.

The Bankruptcy Code provides creditors with certain defenses, including those for payments made in the ordinary course of business or for C.O.D. or other contemporaneous exchanges. In addition, creditors can offset against payments the amount of new value provided on an unsecured basis (credit or shipments) after each payment was received. Thus, despite the preference law, creditors may be able to keep certain payments.

Preference payments can be recovered not only from the recipient but also from those for whose benefit the payments were made. When an

FROM THE TRENCHES

A creditor of a company filed suit for collection of a past due account. The creditor sought and obtained a prejudgment attachment of the company's assets, and went so far as to post a sheriff's deputy in the company's offices. The company, unable to do business under these conditions, settled with the creditor by paying the creditor with a cashier's check. Approximately eighty days later, the company filed for bankruptcy. Some time later, it filed a preference lawsuit against the creditor, seeking return of the funds paid by cashier's check. The company ultimately negotiated a settlement with the creditor, recovering 75% of the money. Because of the extraordinary collection actions taken, the creditor had no ordinary course of business defense to the preference and agreed to settle on terms favorable to the debtor company.

officer or founder of a company gives a personal guaranty to a bank or other creditor, payments made that reduce the company's debt also reduce the individual's exposure on the guaranty. Thus, in a bankruptcy, the company (or more likely a bankruptcy trustee if one is appointed) may sue the guarantor to recover payments made by the company to the bank which indirectly benefited the guarantor. Because the guarantor is an insider, the reach-back period is one year, not ninety days. However, the company or bankruptcy trustee can recover the payments only once, and often will sue the recipient of the payments as well.

Fraudulent transfers include transfers made by the debtor with actual intent to hinder, delay, or defraud creditors. They also include transfers made by the debtor when financially impaired and for which the debtor did not receive reasonably equivalent value in return. Thus, if a company in need of cash sells a major line of its business for substantially less than its market value, the buyer may be subject to a lawsuit by the company, a bankruptcy trustee, or a creditors committee seeking to avoid the transfer or seeking damages for what is claimed to be the true value of the assets. Unlike the ninety-day rule for preferences, the reach-back period for fraudulent transfers generally extends back to transfers made four years before or even earlier in some circumstances.

Creditors Committee

The Bankruptcy Code provides for the appointment of a committee of unsecured creditors, generally including as members the debtor's largest unsecured creditors. In appropriate cases, committees also can be appointed for bondholders, equity security holders, or others. The United States Trustee, a division of the U.S. Justice Department overseeing bankruptcy cases, appoints the committee, usually in the first month after the case is filed. The committee may employ attorneys and financial advisors, whose fees and expenses are paid out of the debtor's assets *(estate)* as a priority administrative expense.

RUNNING A BUSINESS IN BANKRUPTCY

When a company is in bankruptcy, court approval is not necessary for transactions in the ordinary course of business. However, notice to parties in interest and court approval are required prior to, among other things, (1) using, leasing, or selling property of the estate outside the ordinary course of business; (2) borrowing money on a secured or superpriority basis; (3) rejecting or assuming prepetition contracts; or (4) entering into new contracts or settlement agreements that affect property of the estate.

The court will generally defer to the business judgment of the company's management with respect to affairs related to its everyday business operations, such as whether to assume or reject a contract or lease. However, business decisions become subject to closer judicial scrutiny as they begin to address core reorganization issues.

Cash Collateral

The company in bankruptcy must adequately protect any secured creditor whose collateral includes cash or cash proceeds of other collateral before its cash collateral may be used, absent its consent. If a debtor cannot provide the secured creditor with adequate protection or obtain the secured creditor's consent, then the debtor cannot use cash collateral. Generally, this means the debtor cannot spend any cash and may be forced to close its business. Although a secured creditor will have a security interest in the debtor's prepetition assets, the Bankruptcy Code generally provides that a secured creditor's security interest will not extend to *postpetition* assets, or those assets created after the bankruptcy petition is filed. Thus, adequately protecting a secured creditor often means giving the secured creditor a *replacement lien* on the same type of postpetition collateral that the secured creditor has in prepetition collateral. However, adequate protection can take a number of forms, including periodic cash payments, a replacement lien on additional types of assets, or both.

If the value of a secured creditor's collateral more than covers the outstanding debt owed, then the *equity cushion* of collateral value over debt generally will itself provide adequate protection. However, if the secured creditor is undersecured, with the outstanding debt exceeding the value of its collateral, some other form of adequate protection must be provided. This is particularly true for a *junior secured creditor* (a secured creditor whose priority position is behind one or more senior secured creditors), who may be undersecured given the outstanding debt owed a secured creditor with a higher priority security interest in the same collateral.

Postpetition Financing

In many chapter 11 cases, the debtor will need an additional credit line to continue operations. Under the Bankruptcy Code, a debtor may obtain *postpetition* or *debtor-in-possession financing* (often referred to as *DIP financing*) on such terms as the bankruptcy court approves. Generally, with DIP financing, the new, postpetition lender receives an administrative claim that is ahead of all other administrative expenses, including attorneys' and other professionals' fees (known as *superpriority administrative expense treatment*). Alternatively, the postpetition lender may receive a security interest in the debtor's postpetition assets. If the value of the debtor's assets is sufficiently high, the bankruptcy court can even approve a *priming* or *first priority lien,* which gives the DIP lender a first-position lien on all of the debtor's prepetition and postpetition assets, even ahead of a prepetition lender.

Effect of Bankruptcy on Director and Officer Litigation and Indemnification

Although the filing of a bankruptcy case immediately protects the debtor from further litigation on prepetition claims due to the automatic stay, there is no stay of litigation against anyone other than the debtor. For example, litigation against the debtor's directors and officers will not be stayed, even if it directly relates to the company's business. Under rare circumstances, a bankruptcy court can issue an injunction prohibiting further litigation against nondebtor officers or directors. This power is rarely used absent a compelling showing that the litigation would be so disruptive to management that, without an injunction, the debtor would not be able to reorganize.

Indemnification claims arising from prepetition services and based on a prepetition contract may be treated as prepetition unsecured claims even if the duty to indemnify arose postpetition. For example, if a director of the debtor company has a prepetition contractual right to be indemnified by the company for any liability arising out of board service, and the director is sued after the bankruptcy petition is filed, his or her claim for indemnification would be a prepetition unsecured claim. However, indemnification claims arising from prepetition services but based on an executory employment contract that the debtor has obtained bankruptcy court approval to assume should constitute postpetition administrative claims. If directors' and officers' *(D&O)* insurance policy proceeds are payable directly to the officer and director beneficiaries, the proceeds likely will not be deemed property of the bankruptcy estate and may be so paid. The automatic stay may prevent insurance companies from canceling a company's D&O policies after a bankruptcy is filed.

Officer and Director Liability and Governance Issues

When a company becomes insolvent, the fiduciary duty of its directors and officers extends beyond the shareholders to include the company's creditors as well. Accordingly, officers and directors must be careful not to approve of or take actions that favor shareholders at the expense of creditors. Management, officers, and directors have expanded fiduciary duties triggered by insolvency even if the company has not yet filed bankruptcy. They are required to act as trustees of the company's property for the benefit of creditors, shareholders, and other parties in interest, subject to the provisions of the Bankruptcy Code. If anything, a director's duty to shareholders after a bankruptcy is filed weakens in comparison with his or her duty to the creditors, because shareholders have a bottom-of-the-totem-pole status in bankruptcy. Balancing the interests of shareholders and creditors can be difficult. However, bankruptcy actually provides a forum conducive to resolution of conflicts among competing interests, because the contest is judicially supervised, and constituencies can form committees and seek to be represented at the expense of the company.

Continuation of prepetition management with prepetition levels of compensation ordinarily does not require court approval. Management and the board can continue to run the debtor company, and shareholders can continue to meet and vote their shares, absent intervention from the court.

CHAPTER 11 PLAN OF REORGANIZATION

When a debtor (or other party) proposes a plan of reorganization, the Bankruptcy Code provides for a procedure to determine whether the plan will be considered. Along with a plan, the plan proponent must file a disclosure statement. The *disclosure statement* functions much like a prospectus, informing creditors and equity security holders of material financial and business information to be used to evaluate the proposed plan of reorganization. The court must conclude that the disclosure statement contains adequate information before the plan itself can be considered. Once approved, the disclosure statement is sent to all creditors along with the plan and a ballot for voting on the plan. After the ballots are tabulated, the court holds a hearing on *confirmation* or approval of the proposed plan of reorganization.

Exclusivity Period

During the first 120 days after a bankruptcy petition is filed, the debtor has the exclusive right to propose a plan of reorganization, unless the bankruptcy court extends or reduces this period for cause. This precludes other parties in interest in the bankruptcy case (generally creditors) from proposing a plan that might dispossess the debtor and its management of control.

If *exclusivity* is terminated or expires, any creditor or party in interest in the bankruptcy case can file a proposed plan of reorganization. Sometimes creditors file plans to liquidate a debtor's assets, force a sale to a third party, or effect a corporate takeover. Thus, a creditor's plan can pose significant risks for a debtor's management, in addition to the potential litigation expense of opposing the plan.

Classification of Claims

Every plan of reorganization must classify creditors into classes. Usually, each secured creditor is placed in one class, and general unsecured creditors are placed in a separate class. Equity security holders are also placed in a separate class based on the type of securities held, and, depending on the circumstances, subordinated debenture holders can be placed in a separate class or grouped with unsecured creditors if they have no security interest in collateral.

Classes must be designated as impaired or unimpaired, depending on their treatment under the plan. If the plan provides that a particular class will not receive all of its state law rights (e.g., the plan provides that a secured creditor's loan is to be extended for two years), then the class will be deemed *impaired*. If the plan provides a class all of its state law rights (e.g., a secured creditor is to receive full payment pursuant to existing terms of a promissory note), then the class will be deemed *unimpaired*. Impaired classes are entitled to vote on a plan, but unimpaired classes do not vote and are deemed to have accepted the plan.

Unasserted, Contingent, and Unliquidated Claims

In many cases a debtor may have creditors or potential creditors whose claims are contingent or unliquidated, or may even not be asserted. If a creditor has a claim and learns of the bankruptcy (either through formal notice or otherwise) but fails to file a proof of claim, its claim can be barred from any recovery against the debtor and *discharged,* that is, deemed satisfied by the bankruptcy proceeding.

A debtor may have one or more creditors holding a contingent or unliquidated claim, the fixing or liquidation of which would unduly delay reorganization. In such an event, the debtor may seek intervention by the court to estimate the claim for purposes of the bankruptcy case. Thus, a creditor with an uncertain claim, which otherwise might take several years of litigation to establish, may have its claim estimated in a short evidentiary hearing or trial, and thereafter be limited to the amount of the estimated claim. This provides a debtor with the ability to reorganize even if faced with significant contingent or unliquidated claims.

FROM THE TRENCHES

A technology company had entered into a manufacturing agreement with a more established company to make products incorporating the technology company's key technology. When the technology company filed bankruptcy, it rejected the manufacturing agreement, which was an executory contract. The nondebtor party filed a proof of claim stating a multimillion-dollar claim, one that the debtor company could not have paid under its proposed plan of reorganization. Because the damages claimed were unliquidated, the debtor company filed a motion with the bankruptcy court to have the nondebtor party's claim estimated for all purposes, including for payment under the proposed plan. Even though a full trial of the claim ordinarily could have taken months outside of bankruptcy, the bankruptcy court scheduled only three days for the estimation hearing. The resulting pressure on the nondebtor party, which feared its claim might be estimated at an unrealistically low figure, led to a settlement of the claim prior to the estimation hearing, permitting the debtor to confirm its plan of reorganization.

Plan Voting Requirements

Under the Bankruptcy Code, certain voting requirements must be met before a plan of reorganization can be confirmed. Fundamentally, at least one impaired class must vote to accept the proposed plan of reorganization. If that happens, the plan proponent may attempt to *cram down* the plan on any classes of creditors or equity security holders that oppose it, seeking court confirmation of the plan without the consent of each of the classes. In contrast, if all impaired classes vote to accept the plan, confirmation is much more easily obtained. For voting purposes, the votes of insiders of the debtor (such as officers, directors, and controlling shareholders) are not counted.

For a class to vote to accept the plan, two thirds of the dollar amount of the claims actually voting on the plan, and a majority in number of the creditors actually voting on the plan, must vote to accept it. For example, assume a class of creditors has thirty members and $2,000,000 of claims. Only seventeen creditors voted, representing total claims of $1,000,000. In that case, at least nine of the seventeen creditors voting would have to vote in favor of the plan, and they would have to represent at least $666,666 in claims. If the class vote does not satisfy these requirements, the class will be deemed to have rejected the plan, and the plan proponent would have to attempt to cram down the plan on that nonaccepting class.

If the debtor files an objection to a creditor's proof of claim, absent further action, the creditor will not be permitted to vote. However, the creditor can file a motion seeking temporary allowance of its claim for purposes of voting only, with the actual allowance of its claim being subject to a later determination. The court will determine whether, or in what amount, the claim should be allowed for voting purposes.

Cramdown Issues and the Absolute Priority Rule

If a plan receives the acceptance of at least one impaired class of claims, but one or more other classes vote to reject it, the plan proponent can seek confirmation of its plan under the *cramdown* rules. These Bankruptcy Code provisions are designed to provide objecting classes with fair and equitable treatment. Although some variations exist, for a secured creditor, the plan must provide that the creditor retains its lien on its collateral and receives deferred cash payments (periodic cash payments over time with an appropriate discount rate of interest) equal to the allowed secured claim of the creditor (i.e., the value of the collateral or the amount of the claim, whichever is less).

For unsecured creditors to be crammed down, either they must be paid in full with interest, or all junior classes must be precluded from receiving any property on account of their claims. Generally, this means that equity security holders (preferred or common shareholders) may not receive anything by reason of their ownership of shares if unsecured creditors are not being paid in full with interest. Their shares would be canceled under such a plan. This requirement implements the *absolute priority rule* of bankruptcy, which provides that, absent consent, each senior class of creditors must be paid in full before any junior class of creditors may receive anything under a plan. Thus, if secured creditors are not being paid in full, unsecured creditors and equity security holders can receive nothing. Or, as discussed, if unsecured creditors are not being paid in full, equity security holders cannot retain their stock.

Some courts recognize what is known as a new value exception to this absolute priority rule. The *new value exception* permits a junior class, generally shareholders, to retain their shares if they contribute to the debtor substantial new value in the form of money or property that is essential to funding a reorganization. However, other courts do not recognize this exception, and even when the exception is recognized, satisfying its requirements remains difficult.

Instead of relying on the new value exception, equity holders usually work to negotiate a plan of reorganization in which all impaired classes vote in favor of the plan. If all impaired classes vote in favor of the plan, neither the cramdown rules nor the absolute priority rule applies, and equity holders may retain whatever percentage of ownership they are able to negotiate.

Considerations in the Negotiation and Proposal of a Chapter 11 Plan

A plan must adhere to the priority scheme of the Bankruptcy Code, including the requirement that the interests of shareholders become subordinated to those of creditors. During the first 120 days when the debtor has the exclusive right to propose a plan, a debtor's management and board must remember their fiduciary duty to all constituents, including creditors. When the venture's reorganization value is insufficient to pay all creditors in full, favoring equity over creditors can pose fiduciary duty problems for officers and directors.

The Bankruptcy Code also requires disclosure of which officers, directors, and other insiders will be employed or retained under the plan, and the nature of any compensation to be paid insiders by the reorganized debtor.

Discharge of Claims

A corporate debtor that successfully confirms a plan of reorganization and remains in business can receive a discharge of all of its debts. This means that creditors must accept as full satisfaction on their claims the property being distributed under the plan and cannot pursue the corporation thereafter on those claims. A discharge injunction, similar to the automatic stay, is issued to prevent creditors from taking action inconsistent with the confirmed plan of reorganization. As discussed above, equity holders either will have been able to negotiate a plan in which they retain ownership of some or all of the company's stock, will have successfully used the new value exception to the absolute priority rule to retain ownership even in a cramdown case, or will have been wiped out.

PREPACKAGED BANKRUPTCY AND PLANS OF REORGANIZATION

It often can take a debtor months or years to propose a plan, obtain approval for a disclosure statement, and finally confirm the plan. Consequently, the Bankruptcy Code permits a debtor to prepare and circulate to its creditors a disclosure statement and plan, and actually solicit and complete voting on the plan, prior to filing a bankruptcy petition. This process is known as a *prepackaged bankruptcy*. When a case has been prepackaged, the debtor typically files its disclosure statement, plan of reorganization, ballot, and ballot report on the day it files for bankruptcy. The debtor then seeks an expedited hearing both to approve the disclosure statement as having contained adequate information and to confirm the plan of reorganization. If the court finds that the disclosure statement was inadequate, a new one must be prepared and sent to creditors along with new ballots for voting. Because many companies filing bankruptcy hope for a quick (and successful) exit from bankruptcy, the notion of a prepackaged bankruptcy has become popular. However, it is very difficult to achieve, particularly for operating companies.

Assuming sufficient votes are received to permit the plan to be confirmed, a prepackaged bankruptcy can speed up a debtor's emergence from bankruptcy. An out-of-court workout can be structured as a prepackaged bankruptcy, with a disclosure statement and plan instead of simple notices and a workout agreement. If sufficient majorities support the workout for confirmation of a bankruptcy plan, but too many holdouts refuse to consent to the workout to make it practical without a bankruptcy, a prepackaged bankruptcy can be filed to bind the holdout creditors to the plan. The formality of the documentation required unfortunately adds to the cost of the out-of-court workout. In appropriate cases, however, this approach can be used.

A variant of the prepackaged bankruptcy is called the prenegotiated bankruptcy. In a *prenegotiated bankruptcy,* the debtor meets with its creditors and negotiates the terms of the plan of reorganization prior to filing bankruptcy but solicits votes only after the case is filed and the disclosure statement is approved. If the groundwork is laid with the creditor body, the prenegotiated plan can shorten a company's time in bankruptcy. Also, because a formal disclosure statement and plan are drafted only if a bankruptcy case is needed, it involves lower upfront costs.

Although a prenegotiated bankruptcy can be useful for some companies, a true prepackaged bankruptcy is most effective for corporations with large amounts of public bond or debenture debt that it seeks to restructure. This type of bankruptcy also works best for corporations with few or insignificant disputed, contingent, or unliquidated claims, and without major litigation pending.

> **FROM THE TRENCHES**
>
> Several years ago, when Southland Corporation, owner of the 7-Eleven convenience store chain, needed to restructure its high-yield public bond debt, it first solicited votes for a nonbankruptcy restructuring of the bonds. It placed advertisements in national newspapers and engaged in rounds of negotiations, all in an attempt to get bondholders to exchange their bonds for Southland stock and bonds at lower interest rates. In the end, Southland could get approval from only 80% of the bondholders, not the 95% it needed.
>
> However, because Southland used a disclosure statement and a plan of reorganization as part of its bond restructuring documents, it used the votes it did obtain (which were sufficient for bankruptcy plan confirmation) to file a chapter 11 bankruptcy case, along with the disclosure statement, plan, and ballots. Southland hoped to get bankruptcy court approval of its disclosure statement and confirmation of its plan based on those documents alone, but other creditors that were dissatisfied with the proposed plan objected to the disclosure statement and ballot process. The bankruptcy court ruled that defects in the process from a bankruptcy perspective meant that Southland had to redraft its disclosure statement and resolicit votes. Although this was done at considerable additional cost and delay, ultimately Southland did confirm a plan of reorganization restructuring its bond debt in far less time than would have been required if it had simply filed bankruptcy without any prepackaging.

BUSINESS COMBINATION THROUGH CHAPTER 11 BANKRUPTCY

It is possible to accomplish a merger between a debtor corporation and another corporation through a chapter 11 plan of reorganization. Similar to a plan of merger outside of bankruptcy, a chapter 11 plan may set forth the terms of a merger and provide that the stock of the debtor is to be sold to the acquiring corporation, or that a new corporation is to be formed into which the debtor and the acquiring corporation are merged, or that some other form of transaction is to be implemented.

The principal disadvantage of a stock merger with a debtor corporation is that the acquiring corporation generally will become liable for all debts of the debtor. It also may be very difficult to direct that the debtor's shareholders receive the proceeds of the merger, because the creditors have priority over the shareholders. If a plan proposes to pay the proceeds to the debtor's shareholders, it otherwise would have to meet the chapter 11 plan requirements, potentially including the cramdown and absolute priority rule of bankruptcy.

An alternative to a stock merger is a sale of a debtor company's assets, free and clear of liens, with the proceeds to be paid into the bankruptcy estate. Such a sale may be done either through a chapter 11 plan or as a separate asset sale after notice to creditors and court approval. The acquiring corporation purchases those assets free and clear of existing liens and debts but often assumes selected debts (usually those associated with the ongoing business). The purchase price is distributed in the debtor's bankruptcy pursuant to a chapter 11 plan or in a chapter 7 liquidation if the case is converted from chapter 11. If the debtor is insolvent, however, its shareholders would most likely not receive any of the proceeds.

LOSS OF CONTROL AND OTHER RISKS IN BANKRUPTCY

As discussed, in a typical chapter 11 case, a debtor company's management remains in possession and control, subject to replacement by the board of directors. However, creditors or others in a chapter 11 case can file a motion seeking appointment of an independent chapter 11 trustee to take possession of all of the debtor's assets. The most common grounds for such a motion are fraud or gross mismanagement by the debtor-in-possession. Accordingly, although a debtor's management generally will not be replaced by a chapter 11 trustee, replacement remains a risk of filing a bankruptcy.

Another risk of filing a chapter 11 case is that at some point the court may convert the case to a chapter 7 liquidation, with the accompanying automatic appointment of a chapter 7 trustee, or decide to dismiss the chapter 11 case altogether. Conversion or dismissal can be ordered for cause, including inability to effectuate a plan of reorganization, unreasonable delay prejudicial to creditors, failure to meet any court-imposed deadlines for filing a plan, or other failure to comply with court orders.

A decision to convert or dismiss is left to the discretion of the bankruptcy court. In most cases in which a chapter 11 case has failed, the court will convert the case rather than dismiss it, thereby permitting a chapter 7 trustee to evaluate the case for the protection of creditors.

BANKRUPTCY PROS AND CONS

Obviously, filing or not filing bankruptcy can be a life-or-death decision for a company. Although bankruptcy offers significant and often unique advantages, its disadvantages pose major risks. Exhibit 7.2 lists some of the major advantages and disadvantages of filing bankruptcy.

EXHIBIT 7.2
Pros and Cons of Filing Bankruptcy

ADVANTAGES	DISADVANTAGES
Automatic stay of creditor actions	Expensive
Power to reject unfavorable executory contracts and limit damages on leases	Court approval required for all decisions outside of the ordinary course of business
Power to force restructure of debts on nonconsenting creditors	Potential loss of customer or vendor relationships
Ability to recover preferences and fraudulent transfers	Possible loss of control through conversion to chapter 7 or appointment of trustee
Opportunity to preserve going concern value of company	Risk that shareholders' equity position will be wiped out in favor of creditors

Putting It into Practice

Although things started out well for WebRunner, the money raised from Kevin Jordan and family and friends proved insufficient to fund WebRunner's operations. Over the past three months the company had experienced an increasingly serious shortfall in cash. At first, Alexandra was able to pay the landlord and other operating expenses by delaying some payments to less critical vendors. As the cash flow problems became worse, payments to some more important creditors were delayed even further. Calls from creditors began to increase, with several threatening legal action if they were not paid. Alexandra paid the most vocal of the creditors, but cash was not available to pay all of them. Eventually, WebRunner was served with two complaints for breach of contract by vendors. She called Michael Woo for advice.

Michael involved his insolvency partner, David Rumon, who filed answers on WebRunner's behalf to the two complaints and asked Alexandra for a package of financial information on WebRunner. After reviewing it, David asked Alexandra for her most conservative projections of WebRunner's financial situation and an assessment of WebRunner's business plan in light of the current financial problems. David pressed Alexandra to be certain that these were realistic projections, and he warned that a failure to keep promises to creditors could seriously damage WebRunner's credibility if problems got worse. Mindful of her personal guaranty of the lease and the additional costs an unlawful detainer (eviction) action would involve, Alexandra made sure that funds were available to pay the landlord. After their discussions, however, Alexandra concluded that WebRunner needed the ability to stretch out payments to its creditors for another three months or so. If the creditors agreed, WebRunner probably could avoid a more formal workout effort.

Alexandra made a list of WebRunner's largest creditors, the amounts owed each, and how delinquent WebRunner was on payments. She then personally called each of the major creditors and explained WebRunner's financial condition. She asked that WebRunner be allowed to pay 20% of the normal payment for the next two months, at which point WebRunner projected it would be able to resume ordinary payment terms. She told these creditors that WebRunner would completely catch up on payments within six months.

continued

continued

Although several creditors refused these terms, most accepted Alexandra's proposal, with the proviso that WebRunner be caught up in five months. Building on the progress made with some of WebRunner's largest creditors, Alexandra again called the creditors that did not agree. She named some of WebRunner's creditors that had agreed to the terms and again asked for cooperation. After several more rounds of discussions, Alexandra finally was able to work out a less favorable, but still feasible, arrangement. Fortunately, the next few months proved to be close to Alexandra's projections, and WebRunner was able to work its way out of the immediate crisis. The litigation with the two vendors that filed suit continued during this period, and WebRunner later settled both cases by paying the full debt owed but without additional interest or attorneys' fees.

After several more months of successful operations, Alexandra felt it was time to seek additional financing. She decided to investigate venture capital financing.

8

Venture Capital

T he most common sources of capital for start-up enterprises are the entrepreneur and the entrepreneur's family and friends. For the most part, institutional investors have little interest in investing in start-up companies. One notable exception is the investment funds that comprise the venture capital industry. In the past forty years venture capitalists have grown some of the nation's leading companies, including Cisco, Netscape, Amgen, Genentech, Microsoft, and Sun Microsystems. Venture capitalists are making investments at a record pace. In 1996, the venture capital industry invested more than $10 billion in more than 1200 companies, according to VentureOne, a San Francisco firm that researches the industry. Venture funds raised $6.3 billion from investors in 1996, a new record. Venture capital money is available as never before to fund the dreams of entrepreneurs.

This chapter first discusses the pros and cons of seeking venture capital, then outlines strategies for finding it, and provides tips for preparing business plans to present to venture capitalists. It then highlights factors to consider when selecting a venture capitalist. Next follows a discussion of how the parties reach agreement on a valuation for the company, and thus the percentage of the equity the venture capitalists will receive in exchange for their investment. The chapter then analyzes the rights and protections normally given venture capitalists buying preferred stock. These include the liquidation preference, the dividend preference, redemption rights, conversion rights, antidilution provisions (including preemptive rights and price-protection provisions), voting rights, registration rights, information rights, and co-sale rights. The chapter concludes with a brief description of the vesting requirements normally imposed by venture capitalists, and their expectations with respect to the granting of employee stock options.

Certain aspects of the topics covered in this chapter were introduced in previous chapters. This chapter will build on those discussions and further develop them in the context of an entrepreneur seeking venture capital.

DECIDING WHETHER TO SEEK VENTURE CAPITAL

The first question the entrepreneur should consider in deciding whether to pursue venture capital is whether the new venture will meet the criteria used by most venture capitalists (often referred to as *VCs*). Generally, a venture capitalist will want to invest a substantial amount of money, usually more than $500,000 and often more than $1,000,000. However, a few funds will do seed investing for a new start-up at a lower level. Venture capitalists are usually looking for an enterprise that has the potential to grow to a significant size quickly and to generate an annual return on investment in excess of 40%. Venture capitalists need to target that rate of return to realize the compounded returns of at least 20% per annum expected by their investors.

For the most part, venture capitalists have focused on the information-technology industry, which includes computer hardware and software, scientific instruments, telecommunications, multimedia, and, most recently, cyberspace. Venture-backed public companies include Netscape, Yahoo!, and Apple Computer. The second largest concentration of venture capital investing has been in life science companies, including those focusing on biotechnology, medical devices, diagnostics, and therapeutics. Genentech and Amgen were both venture-backed. Although venture capital investment remains most concentrated in these two fields, venture capitalists are financial investors seeking an optimal rate of return, and they have invested successfully in other areas such as retail, consumer products, new materials, health services, and environmental technology. For example, Odwalla, a fresh-juice producer based in Half Moon Bay, California, relied on venture capital to grow before going public in 1993.

As discussed briefly in chapter 6, venture capital financing can be an attractive funding source for a number of reasons. Venture capital may allow the entrepreneur to raise all of the capital from one source, or from a lead investor who can attract other venture funds. Venture capitalists have experience with the challenges of start-ups and know how to grow a company to an initial public offering, sale of the business, or other liquidity event. Experienced venture capitalists have a large network of contacts who can help the company succeed. Venture capitalists are often able to provide valuable assistance in recruiting other members of the management team. Being venture-backed gives an enterprise a certain cachet, which can open doors to other financing and resources.

Most venture capitalists look for companies that can provide liquidity in three to five years. If an entrepreneur is looking for a longer time horizon—a factor that should be discussed with any investor—the enterprise may not be suitable for venture capital. Other reasons to avoid using venture capital funding include these: (1) Venture investors are more sophisticated and may drive a harder bargain on pricing their investment than friends or family; (2) venture investors may be more likely to assert their power in molding the enterprise than more passive investors; and (3) venture investors may be more interested than passive investors in taking control of the enterprise if the entrepreneur stumbles.

Most commonly, an entrepreneur's choice will be between raising the funds from family and friends and obtaining venture capital financing. Family and friends may be willing to invest at a lower price (i.e., to accept a higher valuation of the company at the time they invest) but often bring little else to the table. Venture capitalists may demand a lower valuation but will almost always bring many intangibles that can assist the company to grow faster and to be more successful. Often this decision is referred to as the choice between "dumb money" and "smart money."

FINDING VENTURE CAPITAL

Sending unsolicited business plans to a venture capital firm is almost certainly a formula for failure. Venture capitalists receive dozens of unsolicited plans each week. Very few of these plans are read thoroughly, if at all, and even fewer lead to financing.

A good way to get a venture capitalist's attention is to arrange an introduction by someone who knows the venture capitalist. If the entrepreneur has friends who have obtained venture capital financing, they may be able to provide the introduction. Similarly, personnel at universities, government labs, and other entities that license technology to venture-backed companies may have connections worth pursuing. Accountants and bankers who do business with venture-backed companies also are good sources for introductions, as are money managers at pension funds, insurance companies, universities, and other institutions that invest in venture funds.

Perhaps the best way to find venture money is to engage a lawyer who works primarily in the venture capital field as a business attorney. Although many lawyers may have done a venture capital deal, fewer than a dozen law firms nationwide truly specialize in representing venture-backed companies. More than half of these law firms are located in or near northern California's Silicon Valley.

In choosing a law firm, an entrepreneur should ask for information about the venture funds that the law firm has formed, the number and identity of venture funds the firm has represented in investments, and the venture-backed companies the firm represents. A law firm that specializes in this area will have lists of these clients readily available. Less experienced firms may speak in generalities.

A firm that specializes in this area will also have lawyers with the experience to give information and advice, and to ensure that negotiations with the venture capitalists go smoothly. Although deal-making in the venture capital industry is not rocket science, it is a bit clubby, and it helps to have an attorney who knows the club rules.

Because it is a small club, it is likely that the entrepreneur's lawyer may have represented, or is currently representing, the venture capitalist. The legal code of ethics requires that the attorney disclose his or her involvement in other transactions to both parties and obtain appropriate consents. An entrepreneur may wish to explore with the attorney his or her relationships with the venture capitalists to whom the entrepreneur is being introduced.

Because attorneys in this industry work with a large number of venture capitalists, they should be able to introduce the entrepreneur to those venture capitalists who would be most interested in this particular deal. Most venture capitalists specialize in particular industries; thus, it does not make much sense to present an Internet deal to a venture capitalist who specializes in medical device companies. Venture capitalists also tend to prefer to invest at a particular stage of development: *seed* (raw start-up); *early stage* (product in beta testing or just being shipped); *later stage* (product is fully developed or is being sold and generating revenue); or *mezzanine* (the financing round before the anticipated initial public offering).

There are a number of sources of printed and electronic information on the venture industry. An entrepreneur may wish to consult published guides such as *Pratt's Guide to Venture Capital* and *West Coast Venture Capital*; magazines that cover the industry such as *Upside* and *The Red Herring*; and reports from information-gathering organizations such as VentureOne Corporation, Venture Economics, and Securities Data Corporation. An entrepreneur may also want to use Nexis or a similar on-line service to cull news articles on particular companies or venture capitalists. Some information also may be available on the World Wide Web.

SELECTING A VENTURE CAPITALIST

Generally, an entrepreneur begins the process of seeking venture capital by preparing a business plan, although many deals have been done without a plan. (The preparation of business plans and offering memoranda is discussed generally in chapter 6.) However, plans prepared for venture capitalists should be more concise and less legalistic than plans prepared for other investors. Venture capitalists are very sophisticated and do not need, or expect, the type of disclosure mandated by federal and state securities laws for sales to less experienced investors.

The business plan prepared for circulation to venture capitalists usually describes the product or service concept and the opportunity for investors. Typically, the plan includes sections describing the industry, the market, the means for producing the product or delivering the service, the competition, the superiority of this product or service over existing products or services, the marketing plan, the barriers to entry, and the strengths of the management team. Projections and the assumptions on which they are based are generally included. The entrepreneur should prepare an executive summary, keeping in mind that many venture capitalists will not read beyond the first paragraph of that summary. Therefore, the compelling reason to make the investment should appear at the top of the executive summary and should be borne out by the remainder of the plan. An experienced lawyer can assist in editing the business plan.

Most venture capitalists will focus on the viability of the concept, the size of the opportunity, and the quality of the management team. To the extent that there are holes in the team (e.g., the team has technicians but no experienced managers, or the team lacks a strong CFO or VP of Marketing), these weaknesses should be acknowledged in discussions with venture capitalists, and the venture capitalists should be asked for assistance in finding the right people. More than one venture capitalist has said that the three most important factors in making an investment are "people, people, and people." The right team can fix a flawed concept, but a flawed team cannot get a brilliant concept to market.

Venture capitalists comment that certain weaknesses appear again and again in the plans they review. The following are some common pitfalls:

- **The plan is too long.** Most venture capitalists will have little tolerance for reading more than fifteen or twenty pages. Details such as projections, financials, press clips, detailed biographies, detailed schematics, and detailed market analysis can be shortened, eliminated (for now, but presented later to those really interested), or moved into appendices for the most interested reader.

- **The executive summary is too long.** The executive summary should be one page and should concisely describe (1) the market; (2) the unmet need in the market; (3) the compelling solution offered by the entrepreneur; (4) the strategy for connecting the need, the solution, and the customers; (5) the technology or other proprietary aspects of the solution that will give this venture an edge over the competition; and (6) the experience of the team that demonstrates that the plan can be implemented.

- **The opportunity is too small.** There are many good business opportunities that are too small for venture investors because of their need to earn a high return on investment. Although other investors might be willing to put up $2 million to grow a company into a $25 million business with net income of 10% of sales in five years, these returns are too low to interest most venture capitalists.

- **The plan is poorly organized.** A poorly organized plan suggests that the team may be incapable of taking on the larger task of organizing a company. There is no set formula, but a plan should have a logical progression and should not be overly focused on one area at the expense of others. For example, many plans drafted by engineers devote substantial pages to explaining the technology in minute detail but fail to adequately describe the market, the competition, or the strategy for connecting customers and the product.

- **The plan lacks focus.** Many plans call for a company to pursue multiple opportunities simultaneously in multiple markets. The more complex the story, the harder it is to sell to venture capitalists. Great opportunities are conveyed in few words (e.g., remember "plastics" from the movie *The Graduate*). Focus on the greatest opportunity. The other opportunities can be discussed later or handled in a very brief section toward the back of the plan.

Once introductions are made, venture capitalists will follow up with meetings if they are interested in investing. This begins a courtship process that typically takes two to three months. For this reason, it is a good idea to engage a number of venture capitalists in discussions simultaneously, rather than serially. Generally, venture capitalists will be quick to let a company know if they are interested. Follow-up meetings are an expression of interest, and many venture capital funds hold weekly internal meetings to discuss the status of various prospects.

As a part of this courtship, the venture capitalists will perform due diligence. *Due diligence* is the process through which venture capitalists will examine a company's concept, product, potential market, financial health, and legal situation. Due diligence is typically conducted by venture capitalists or consultants with financial and technical expertise and by lawyers. This means they often will send in a technical or industry expert to meet with the entrepreneur and take a close look at the technology or concept. Also, the venture capitalist may talk with potential customers to help understand the size of the potential market for the product.

Similarly, as the courtship continues, the entrepreneur should perform due diligence on the venture capitalist. Much information can be gathered conversationally. Appropriate questions include these:

- What other companies within this industry has the venture fund invested in?
- What deals has this particular venture capitalist done?
- On what boards does the venture capitalist sit?
- How many more years are there to run in the fund that will be making the investment?
- Will the venture capitalist be willing and able to participate in the next round of financing?
- Are there other venture capital firms that the venture capitalist thinks should be invited into the deal?
- Would the venture capitalist be willing to work alongside other venture capitalists with whom the entrepreneur is in discussions?
- How has the venture capitalist handled management changes in the past?
- Are there any founders who were pushed aside or pushed out?

- What is the time horizon for this investment?
- What if there is no exit event providing liquidity by that date?
- What kind of return does the venture capitalist need to make on this investment?

The venture capitalist should be asked to provide introductions to other founders of companies in which he or she has invested, and those founders should be contacted to provide insight on the kind of partner the venture capitalist is likely to be.

If it is possible to attract and accommodate more than one venture capitalist in a round, it can be to the company's advantage to do so. Although it may be a bit more complicated to work with more than one venture investor, it does increase the network of resources available to the company. In addition, another venture capitalist may be able to serve as a counterbalance if the entrepreneur and the first venture capitalist end up at loggerheads on some issue. Such venture capitalists are often excellent partners. However, some venture capitalists will not participate in a deal unless they are the only investor or the only lead investor.

In raising money during the next round of venture capital, the company will want to be able to tell new investors that the prior-round investors are stepping up to invest more. Often the lead venture capitalist in the prior round will allow the new investor(s) to take the lead in negotiating with the company the price of the stock in the subsequent round. Once price is set, the lead investors from the prior round will indicate how much stock they will buy. If there is more than one venture capitalist in the initial round, the company will stand a better chance of having at least one of the existing investors invest in the next round. Also, if the company underperforms, the entrepreneur is more likely to have an ally who can coax further investment from the group if there are several venture investors in the initial round.

DETERMINING THE VALUATION

Eventually, a venture capitalist will indicate that he or she is ready to make the investment, and the discussion will turn to valuation. In

---

FROM THE TRENCHES

Polly President, the founder of a multimedia company, bootstrapped her company into a leader in its nascent industry. The company had been financed by family and friends, plus modest earnings. With the advent of cyberspace, Polly decided to raise $2.5 million in venture capital to move into the new medium. By chance, she was introduced to Joe Venture, a venture capitalist who had just set up a new fund for cyberspace investing. Polly had little time to devote to fund-raising, and because the discussions with Joe were going so well, she decided not to seek introductions to any other venture capitalists. After weeks of discussion, Joe and Polly agreed on a valuation, and Joe sent over a term sheet. Unbeknownst to Polly, Joe's prior employment had been in the banking industry, and he had only recently moved into the bank's venture fund, which did only mezzanine investing (the financing round before an anticipated public offering). The term sheet Joe presented looked more like a complex loan deal than a venture deal, due both to his background in banking and the focus of mezzanine-round investors on protecting against the downside (due to the limited upside of a mezzanine deal). It took more than five months to conclude a deal with Joe, and the ultimate deal contained highly unusual downside protection for Joe's fund. Although Joe had the right industry focus for Polly's company, an inquiry about his experience would have revealed that he was the wrong investor for this stage of investment.

Comment: Had Polly pursued multiple investors and selected a more appropriate venture capitalist, she would have saved time and been able to negotiate a less onerous deal.

---

essence, this is a discussion of price: How much will the venture capitalist pay for what percentage of the company?

The venture capitalist's offer is often communicated in an arcane shorthand that is unfathomable to the uninitiated. For example, a venture capitalist might say,

- "I'll put in $2 million based on three pre-money."
- "I'm thinking two-thirds based on three pre-; that will get you to five post."
- "I'm looking for two-fifths of the company post-money, and for that I'll put up the two."

- "It's worth $3 million pre-money, and I want to own 40% of it after we close."

What does all this mean? This is exactly the question the entrepreneur needs to ask to make sure that there is no misunderstanding about the price being offered.

Each of the above statements is a different way of expressing exactly the same proposal. The venture capitalist is willing to invest $2 million in the company. The terms *pre-money* and *post-money* refer to what valuation is put on the company before and after the investment. The venture capitalist is proposing that the company is worth $3 million before the investment of $2 million and is therefore worth $5 million immediately after the investment. The amount of ownership being requested is an amount equivalent to 66⅔% of the equity based on the pre-money number (i.e., $2 million/$3 million), which is 40% of the company measured immediately after the closing of the deal (i.e., $2 million/$5 million). It is a very good idea to ask what dollar amount is to be invested and what the percentages of the equity are that translate into pre- and post-money.

If the investor knows the number of shares the company has outstanding, he or she may give the entrepreneur a per-share price. It is relatively easy to translate valuations based on share prices into pre- and post-money company valuations, and vice versa. For example, if 6 million shares were outstanding, 4 million shares would need to be issued at $0.50 per share for a venture capitalist to invest $2 million and end up owning 40% of the company.

If one knows what percentage the investor wants to own after the deal closes, one can back into the number of shares that will need to be issued through the following two equations:

(1) Shares outstanding post-money = Shares outstanding pre-money divided by 1 minus the percentage to be owned by investor post-money

(2) Shares to be issued = Shares outstanding post-money minus shares outstanding pre-money

Accordingly, if 6 million shares are outstanding pre-money and the venture capitalist wants to end up owning 40% of the company, then

6 million divided by 60% (i.e., 1 minus .40) tells us that 10 million shares need to be outstanding after the offering. Therefore, the company will need to issue 4 million new shares.

Often there is some negotiation during pricing discussions. A venture capitalist may ask what valuation the company is seeking or may volunteer a ballpark figure for pricing. Valuing a company is never easy. It is especially difficult with a start-up, which has no operating history. Venture capitalists will often base their valuations on management's own projections and on other deals done in the industry by other companies. Obtaining information on comparable companies that have received venture financing can help the entrepreneur establish the right valuation.

The entrepreneur should press the venture capitalist on how the reservation of shares for future stock issuances to employees will work or, alternatively, propose to the venture capitalist how it will work. For example, if the venture capitalist's offer of $2 million is for 40% of the company *including* the reservation of 1 million shares for options, then he or she is saying that there are in effect 7 million shares outstanding or reserved (not 6 million). Therefore, under the formulas set forth above, the venture capitalist would be entitled to 4.667 million shares (not 4 million) for the $2 million investment. Applying the formulas:

$$11.667 \text{ million} = \frac{7 \text{ million}}{60\%}$$

$$4.667 \text{ million} = 11.667 \text{ million} - 7 \text{ million}$$

If this is not what the entrepreneur has in mind, the company should propose that the 1 million reserved shares should *not* be taken into account in the valuation. If they are not, then the venture capitalist will be issued 4 million shares, as we saw above. In that case, the holders of the 6 million old shares and the venture capitalist holding the 4 million new shares will jointly bear the dilution for the 1 million reserved shares in a ratio of 60/40, rather than having the holders of the 6 million old shares bear all of the dilution.

When the entrepreneur is confident that an offer is about to be made, or immediately after an offer is made, he or she will want to inform the other potential venture capitalists and ask any that remain interested for their offers. Provided that they have had a chance to do some due diligence and to discuss the investment with their colleagues within the fund, other venture capitalists who are interested in the deal will generally put their valuation offers on the table fairly quickly. These valuations may differ substantially, and the entrepreneur may attempt to use the higher offers to persuade others to pay a higher price.

The venture capitalist willing to pay the highest price is not necessarily the person whom the entrepreneur will want most in the deal. Another venture capitalist who is not willing to pay quite as much may be a better partner in growing the business. Due diligence in the form of reference checks should be undertaken by the entrepreneur to determine who the best partners might be. An entrepreneur who has more than one offer should be pleased and move quickly to choose the investors and finalize the deal. Indeed, if the entrepreneur is extremely comfortable with the venture capitalist with whom he or she has been primarily negotiating, the entrepreneur may decide not to shop the offer to other venture capitalists after reviewing the initial offer but may simply proceed to a closing.

Although it may seem like a good idea just to get all the suitors into a room to negotiate the price, this approach should be resisted. There is little incentive for those offering the higher valuation to talk the lower offerors into offering more, and the lower offerors may convince those willing to pay a higher price that they are paying too much.

The final price will depend on whom the entrepreneur wants to have in the deal and how much money needs to be raised. For tax reasons and for fairness, generally there is just one price paid for the stock in a round. Once the valuation is agreed upon, it is unusual to revisit the issue, unless there is a material adverse change in the business before the closing, or material adverse information is discovered. Although most venture capitalists will not attempt to renegotiate the price absent those kinds of developments, there are always some who feel that all items are negotiable before the deal is closed. To avoid these types of partners, the entrepreneur should find out all he or she can about each venture capitalist.

By far the most important issue in these negotiations will be price. Nonetheless, some of the most time-consuming and difficult negotiations may still lie ahead—determining the other terms and conditions of the investment.

Rights of Preferred Stock

As explained in chapter 4, for tax reasons, most venture funds are precluded by their pension-fund limited partners from investing in a tax pass-through vehicle such as an S corporation, a limited partnership, a general partnership, or a limited liability company. Therefore, when venture capitalists make an investment, it is almost always in preferred stock of a C corporation.

Traditional preferred stock issued by large, publicly traded companies carries a preference on liquidation, pays a higher dividend than common stock, and is often set up to be redeemed at a certain date. It is usually not convertible into common stock and is often nonvoting. In many ways, it functions like debt.

Venture capital preferred stock is a very different beast. It does have a preference on liquidation. It also has a dividend preference but typically only if and when the directors declare dividends; everyone's expectation is that none will be declared. If all goes well, the preferred stock will almost certainly be converted into common stock (upon an initial public offering or upon a successful sale of the company). The preferred stock is convertible at any time at the election of the holder and automatically converts on certain events. It votes on an as-if-converted-to-common basis and may have special voting rights with respect to certain events and the election of directors. It often has no mandated redemption provision, which would require the company to buy back the stock at a set price on a given date in the future. Even if it does have a redemption provision, the ability of a start-up company to make the redemption is far from certain.

Over the years a number of bells and whistles have been added to the preferred stock issued to venture capitalists. At first this was done to differentiate it from the common stock and to bolster the argument that it has a higher value for tax purposes. As explained in chapter 5, this allows the common stock to be sold to the founders and employees at a much lower price than the preferred stock. Later, many features were added to increase the rights and protections provided to the preferred investors in the event that the company ran into difficulty.

Many seasoned venture capitalists will tell you that no investor has ever made any significant money off of these downside protection features, and they receive far too much attention in the negotiation of a venture deal. Under this line of reasoning (which an entrepreneur should embrace in the negotiations), once the valuation is set, the preferred stock only needs to have a liquidation preference and a dividend preference (if declared); the preferred stock should otherwise function as common stock so that all investors are on essentially the same terms going forward. By having all shareholders aligned in this manner, the entrepreneur and the outside investors will focus only on what will create value for the company, rather than on special circumstances that may afford one or the other greater leverage or returns. If the preferred stock gets special rights and downside protection, the stock begins to look like debt rather than equity. If it functions like debt, the argument goes, it should have a fixed return (like a loan) rather than the unlimited upside of equity in a high-growth venture.

Other venture capitalists will argue that the special rights of preferred stock are necessary because the investors are putting up most of the cash for the enterprise and will not be managing company affairs on a day-to-day basis. They will argue that if there are difficulties down the road, the preferred investors may need to assert certain rights to protect their investment from mismanagement or abuse by the founders, who hold common stock. This debate over what rights the preferred stock requires and whether these rights will create misalignment in the shareholders' incentives as the company goes forward often arises as the various terms of the investment are discussed and negotiated.

Most of the terms of the deal will relate to rights that attach to the preferred stock. These rights will be spelled out in the company's certificate of incorporation. Certain other rights will not be contained in the company's charter but will be established in one or more contracts.

The next sections of this chapter review the typical rights sought by venture capitalists investing in preferred stock. The discussion begins with the simplest type of deal and then proceeds with an outline of the different bells and whistles that may be added and the reasons raised for and against such additions.

Entrepreneurs should bear in mind that most venture capitalists have completed far more venture investment deals than have the entrepreneurs with whom they negotiate. It helps to have an advisor who has seen dozens of these transactions from different perspectives. An entrepreneur should also be skeptical about any term that is described as "standard." What is "standard" for one venture fund may be unusual for another.

Another very important issue for entrepreneurs to remember is that there are likely to be subsequent rounds of financing for the company. In deciding what rights to give investors in the first round, the company must also consider the effect that giving rights to this group of investors will have on negotiations with investors in subsequent rounds. It is highly unusual for investors in a subsequent round to accept fewer rights than were granted in a prior round.

Each round of investors is likely to receive a slightly different type of preferred stock (usually differentiated at least by price). Each round typically receives what is called a different *series* of preferred stock. By convention, the first round purchases a security called "Series A Preferred Stock"; each subsequent series follows alphabetically: "Series B Preferred," "Series C Preferred," and so on.

Liquidation Preference

Simply put, the *liquidation preference* provides that upon a liquidation or dissolution of the company, the preferred shareholders must be paid some amount of money before the common shareholders are paid anything. The definition of a liquidation is typically broad enough to include any sale of the business or sale of substantially all of the company's assets. In the simplest case, the preference amount typically is an amount equal to the amount initially paid for the stock.

For example, if the Series A Preferred is sold to the investors at a price of $.50 per share, it would be given a liquidation preference of $.50 per share. This means that if the preferred shareholders invested $2 million for

---

FROM THE TRENCHES

The first-round investor's rights in an investment in a telecommunications company included the right to put the stock back to the company if the company did not make its projections, the right to add directors and control the board if milestones were missed, a full-ratchet antidilution provision, and a right to buy all of any future issuance. Extending these rights to additional investors would have created misaligned incentives and created rivalry within the investor group.

When the company lined up its second-round investors, it went back to the first-round investor and explained that it had investors ready to put in $4 million. The company also explained that if these rights stayed in place, the new investors would either seek the same rights or would want a deep discount on the true value of the company. The first-round investor agreed to carve back its rights to those found in a conventional deal so that the company could have the greatest opportunity for success.

Comment: This entrepreneur was fortunate in being able to convince subsequent investors to take lesser rights and to restructure the rights of the earlier round to be less onerous. The better practice is to consider carefully the rights to be given to a round of investors on the assumption that investors in follow-up rounds will expect rights that are at least as great.

40% of the company, then the first $2 million to be distributed to shareholders would go to the preferred shareholders. The remainder would then go to the common shareholders. If the company were to be liquidated for more than $5 million, it would make sense for the holders of the preferred stock to convert to common stock immediately prior to the liquidation. For example, if the company is to be liquidated for $9 million, the preferred shareholders would be better off converting to common stock and abandoning their liquidation preference (since 40% of $9 million is $3.6 million as opposed to the $2 million liquidation preference).

Often the liquidation preference will add to the original purchase price any accrued and unpaid dividends. Because most venture-backed companies do not expect to pay dividends, this language normally has little effect. However, in some deals (as discussed below), there will be a mandatory annual dividend that, if not paid, will cumulate (a *cumulative dividend*). Usually, the sole purpose of this cumulation is to build up the liquidation preference over time. Everyone expects that the dividend will never be paid if the company does well and the preferred stock converts (on a public offering or a high-priced sale of the company), but it will be there to ensure that the preferred investors receive some rate of return on the investment ahead of the common shareholders if the company does not do well. Sometimes, rather than having dividends cumulate (which may require an accounting footnote of explanation), the same objective is achieved by having the liquidation preference increase annually by some rate (often 6%, 7%, or 8%, sometimes higher).

The venture capitalist who seeks either a cumulative dividend or an increasing liquidation preference will argue that the hard-money investors are entitled to receive at least a money market rate of return before the common shareholders are paid on their very cheaply priced common stock. The entrepreneur may want to resist this concept by pointing out that this transaction is not a loan deal with a guaranteed rate of return and no other upside. Instead, the entrepreneur will argue that each of the investors should be focused on what brings the greatest value for the company, rather than creating a situation in which some investors may push to sell the company because a particular deal provides a better return on their series of stock than available alternatives. The entrepreneur will also argue that while the common stock may have been sold cheaply, it is as "hard dollar" as the preferred stock when the value of the "sweat equity" of the entrepreneur is taken into account.

Another twist on the liquidation preference concept is called participating preferred. If an investor holds *participating preferred stock*, then after the preferred stock is paid its liquidation preference, it also, in addition, receives its pro rata share of what remains as though the preferred stock had converted to common stock. If the preferred shareholder is not participating, all proceeds in excess of the liquidation preference go to the common shareholders.

The investor's argument here is similar. If the founders have paid only pennies for their stock (as is typically the case) and the preferred investors have paid hard dollars, then there are prices for the company at which the preferred stock would sensibly convert to common stock but would still earn only a relatively modest internal rate of return on the investment. In contrast, the common shareholders who paid little for their stock would earn huge internal rates of return. For example, if the company is sold after five years for $8 million and the preferred stock converts into common stock to get its $3.2 million return (40% of $8 million) on its $2-million investment, the internal rate of return is only about 11%, which is a disappointment in a venture portfolio; the founder team, on the other hand, which may have paid less than $100,000 for its common stock, is able to split the remaining $4.8 million for a large return. So, the argument goes, the preferred shareholders should both receive their preference (commonly referred to as *getting the bait back*) and be allowed to participate in the common stock share. The entrepreneur can argue that the preferred shareholder is trying to double-dip and should either take its preference or convert. Founders can be quite emotional about the issue because holders of the common stock have invested not just their cash but also years of sweat equity in building the company. If the preferred shareholder is to participate, one could argue, then the founders should receive back pay at the market rate.

When a subsequent series of preferred stock is issued, one matter that will need to be addressed is whether one series comes before the other in

---

FROM THE TRENCHES

An entrepreneur and a venture capitalist had agreed on a $10-million post-money valuation for a storage device company but were at loggerheads over the issue of whether the venture capitalist's preferred stock should be participating. The entrepreneur appreciated the venture capitalist's point that if the company were only modestly successful (often referred to as a *sideways deal*), the venture capitalist's return on its investment would be quite small. However, the entrepreneur could not understand why, in a successful deal, the venture capitalist ought not only to share in the upside enjoyed by the common shareholders, but also to receive a return of its capital. To solve the impasse, the venture capitalist proposed that the preferred stock be participating if, at exit, the company was worth less than $30 million; at any greater valuation, the participating feature would be inoperative. The entrepreneur agreed, and the deal was struck.

a liquidation, or the series are all treated equally (in legal terms, *pari passu*) with a pro rata allocation based on what is available to satisfy the liquidation preferences of the preferred stock prior to any distribution to the common stock. The new money has the greatest negotiating leverage for being paid out first (otherwise it may not invest), but to maintain good relations among preferred investors (and to set the precedent for the next round), the new investors may consent to having payouts to the preferred be pari passu.

Dividend Preference

Typically, the preferred stock is to earn a dividend at some modest rate (6% to 8%) when and if declared by the board of directors of the company. As noted above, the venture capitalist does not expect the dividend to be declared; this provision is included primarily to bolster the argument for tax purposes that the preferred stock is worth more than the common stock purchased by the founders at a lower price.

Also, as noted above, some deals provide for cumulative dividends, used primarily to push up the value of the liquidation preference over time.

Redemption Rights

Some venture investors will ask for the right to force the company to repurchase (i.e., *redeem*) its own stock at some point in the future (a *voluntary redemption right*). The investors may argue that they are minority shareholders and need some mechanism to ensure that they will have some exit from the investment in the future. In asking for a redemption right, the venture capitalist is concerned that if the company does not perform well enough to be a public offering or acquisition candidate, there may be no effective way to achieve any liquidity.

Although redemption requests seem reasonable on their face, and are increasingly granted, they can cause difficulties for companies both in raising future rounds of capital and in meeting redemption requirements. If a redemption right is granted, the next round of investors may be legitimately concerned that the money they are putting into the company may be used to redeem the earlier-round investors rather than to grow the company. Also, once a redemption right is granted, it is likely that future investors will want one as well.

The company can argue that no redemption rights should be given and that the investors should rely on the judgment of the board of directors on liquidity matters. The board will seek a liquidity opportunity for all investors but should not be forced into making a poorly timed decision because of a looming redemption deadline. Another strong argument against redemption rights is that they may turn out to be meaningless if the company has no money. Of course, a counterargument is that if they are so meaningless, there is no harm in granting them.

Another tactic in resisting redemption rights is to suggest that if the investor is to have what is in essence a *put* on the stock (i.e., the right to sell the stock back to the company at a set price by a given date in the future), then it is only fair that the company should have a right to *call* the stock (the right to force the investors to sell the stock back to the company at a set price by a given date in the future). However, this strategy is of little benefit to the company. In reality, a fast-growing company is probably not going to want to use its limited cash to exercise the call. In addition, the put-and-call approach could end up pitting different investor groups against one another, as their own interests are no longer aligned with what creates the most value for the company as a whole.

If redemption rights must be granted, they should be pushed as far into the future as possible. Redemption rights that are seven years out are not as threatening as those that kick in after five years. Similarly, it might be worthwhile to specify that the actual payment of the redemption price be spread over two or three years in order to have as little impact as possible on the company's cash flow. The period in which redemption can be requested should be quite limited so that the threat to cash flow is not an ongoing concern. Any redemption rights should terminate upon an initial public offering.

The redemption price is another matter for negotiation. Often, venture capitalists will want the stock redeemed at its liquidation preference plus any accumulated but unpaid dividends. However, if the sole purpose is to give the investor liquidity, an argument can be made that the redemption price should be based on the fair market value of the company's stock at the time (which may be less than the investment plus unpaid dividends). If not agreed upon by the company and the investors, the fair market value may be determined by an appraisal process that should apply appropriate discounts for any lack of liquidity of the stock and the lesser value of a minority interest.

Conversion Rights

Right to Convert Holders of preferred stock in venture deals normally have the right to convert their preferred stock into common stock at any time. The ratio at which preferred stock is converted into common stock is typically determined by dividing the initial purchase price of the preferred stock by a number called the *conversion price*, which is adjusted upon certain events. Initially, the conversion price is equal to the purchase

---

FROM THE TRENCHES

One San Francisco Bay Area venture fund is particularly fond of redemption rights and insists on them in every deal. The fund does a fair amount of investing outside the technology industry, where it is less likely to run into companies with advisors who are knowledgeable about typical venture deals. In one such deal, the venture capitalists requested a redemption right that kicked in after three years at a price equal to twice the initial investment. The venture capitalists explained that, without the redemption right, they would receive less than a 25% internal rate of return, which would be deemed a bad investment in the venture industry. In addition, they argued that the company should be willing to honor their request because their management's own projections had shown a much higher rate of return. The management responded that it had no doubt that the company was a good long-term investment but that it could not accurately predict every bump in the road toward success. The company could not take the risk of being caught in a cash-short position if the venture capitalist exercised the redemption right at an inopportune time. After much haggling, the parties agreed to a redemption right at any point after the seventh year for the then fair-market value of the stock as determined by an appraiser.

price of the preferred stock, so the preferred stock converts into common stock on a one-to-one basis.

Automatic Conversion The preferred stock usually is automatically converted into common stock upon certain events. Typically, these events are the vote of some specified percentage of the preferred stock or an initial public offering that meets certain criteria. The company would like the preferred stock to convert as soon as possible to eliminate its special rights and to clean up the balance sheet for the initial public offering.

Often an affirmative vote of a majority or a supermajority of the preferred stock is required to force an automatic conversion of all of the preferred stock. A high threshold requirement ensures that no one investor controls the preferred stock. The entrepreneur should favor a simple majority or as small a supermajority as possible, and should resist any language that gives one investor the right to block a conversion if the other investors believe it is in the company's best interest. If there are only a few investors in the deal, or if one investor holds a majority of the preferred stock, it may be difficult to avoid having an investor with a blocking right.

The criteria for automatic conversion on an initial public offering generally include the following: (1) The offering must be firmly underwritten (i.e., the underwriters must have committed to placing the entire offering, rather than adopting the best efforts approach common in penny stock offerings); (2) the offering must raise a certain amount of money for the company; and (3) (often) the offering price must be at a certain minimum (e.g., four times the conversion price of the preferred stock).

Upon any conversion of the preferred stock, the rights associated with it (i.e., liquidation preference, dividend preference, antidilution protection, special voting rights, and redemption provisions) cease to exist. Some contractual rights, such as *registration rights* (the right to force the company to register the holder's stock), usually survive, although others, such as *information rights* (the right to certain ongoing financial information about the company) and *preemptive rights* (the right to buy stock issued by the company), often will terminate upon an initial public offering.

Antidilution Provisions

Structural Antidilution Any equity issuance to another person can be considered a dilutive issuance to existing shareholders, because it reduces their percentage ownership stake. All shareholders are customarily entitled to protection against the dilution caused by certain issuances. For example, when common stock is issued as a stock dividend, a pro rata dividend is given to each common shareholder, not just to some of them.

Preferred stock is also customarily given antidilution protection against stock dividends, stock splits, reverse splits, and similar recapitalizations. The conversion price is adjusted to ensure that the number of shares of common stock issuable upon conversion of the preferred stock represents the same percentage of ownership (on a converted-to-common basis) as existed prior to the stock dividend, stock split, reverse split, or recapitalization. For example, if there is a five-to-one stock split, the conversion price would be reduced to one fifth of its prior amount. If the conversion price was $1.25 prior to the split, it would be $0.25 after the split. In this way, the number of shares of common stock issuable upon the conversion of the preferred stock would increase proportionately with the effect of the split.

This type of *structural antidilution protection* from stock dividends, stock splits, and reverse splits is the most basic kind of antidilution provision and is nearly always included in venture capital financings. When venture capitalists say they want protection against dilution, they may be referring to this basic type of protection, or they may have in mind some of the more complex provisions discussed below.

Preemptive Right and Right of First Refusal Another type of antidilution provision is called a right of first refusal or preemptive right. A *right of first refusal* or *preemptive right* entitles any shareholder to purchase his or her pro rata share in any subsequent issuance to ensure that the shareholder maintains his or her percentage ownership. In venture deals, this type of provision, if adopted, usually is a contractual right that terminates upon an initial public offering. It can, however, be made a right attached to the preferred stock if it is included in the certificate of incorporation. In its most extreme form, a preemptive right can require the company to first offer all shares of subsequent offerings to the venture group, not merely sufficient shares to maintain their pro rata ownership interest.

Although a pro rata preemptive right appears reasonable on its face, there are many circumstances in which a company may want to sell stock to a particular investor without being required to first offer it to every current investor. For that reason, if this right is included, it usually exempts stock issued to employees, directors, consultants, strategic partners, those providing leases or loans to the company, and acquisition targets.

Waiting for a right-of-first-refusal time period to expire (or soliciting waivers of such rights) can be time-consuming and can interfere with consummating a deal. An entrepreneur may want to avoid giving up the company's flexibility to choose to whom it sells stock in the future. For example, the company may want to bring in a new venture capitalist or corporate investor but may find that, due to the exercise of preemptive rights, there is not enough stock to meet the new investor's minimum investment criteria. Also, if there is no such right, investors who want to be invited to buy in future rounds have an incentive to remain on good terms with the company. Finally, a preemptive right, if exercised by a large shareholder, may force other investors either to buy into the offering or to risk losing control of the company.

Price Protection   One could argue that the two types of antidilution provisions discussed above (protection from stock splits and the like, and the right to participate in future offerings) should be sufficient protection for an investor. However, most venture deals feature a third type of antidilution protection known as price protection. *Price protection* gives the venture capitalist some protection from subsequent financing rounds in which stock is issued at a lower share price than the investor paid.

The theory behind price protection is that the valuation of a company at the time a venture capitalist purchases stock is open to debate, and the investor is entitled to a price adjustment if it turns out that the company was overvalued. As it is impractical to give back a portion of the venture capitalist's money, more shares are issued to the investor to make the investor whole.

Full Ratchet The simplest form of price protection (although by no means the fairest) is called full ratchet antidilution protection. If the venture capitalist has *full ratchet antidilution protection*, then if stock is sold at a lower price per share in a subsequent round, the ratio for converting preferred stock to common stock is adjusted so that an investor in a higher-priced earlier round gets the same deal as he or she would have gotten had the purchase been made in a later lower-priced round. The mechanics of the adjustment are straightforward: The conversion price of the prior round is adjusted to the purchase price of the new round.

Consider this example:

Acorn Enterprises issues Series A Preferred Stock based on a pre-money valuation of $9,000,000. Acorn issues shares resulting in a 25% ownership interest to investors for $3,000,000 (i.e., post-money valuation of $12,000,000). Assuming that there are 4,500,000 shares of common stock outstanding (which founders may have bought in the early days of the company for pennies a share or more recently for 20 cents a share), the Series A investors will purchase 1,500,000 shares at $2.00 per share. The shares convert into common stock based on the original price, so $3,000,000 of preferred stock at $2.00 per share will convert into 1,500,000 shares of common stock. It is said to initially convert on a one-to-one basis.

Business does not go according to plan, and when Acorn tries to raise another $2,000,000, it finds it can obtain a pre-money valuation of only $10,000,000. It may seem counterintuitive that the second round could have a valuation lower than the post-money valuation of the first round, but it does happen. Typically, this occurs either because the earlier round was overvalued or because the business has not met the projections in its plan.

The second-round Series B venture capitalists buy their preferred stock at $1.67 per share (i.e., the $10,000,000 pre-money valuation divided by the 6,000,000 total shares already outstanding). At this valuation, the second-round investors will receive 1,200,000 shares of Series B Preferred Stock for the $2,000,000 second-round investment. After the first and second rounds the capitalization would be as follows:

	No. of Shares	% of Company
FIRST ROUND		
Common	4,500,000	75.00
Series A	1,500,000	25.00
SECOND ROUND (with no adjustment for dilution)		
Common	4,500,000	62.50
Series A	1,500,000	20.83
Series B	1,200,000	16.67

The Series A venture capitalists will be none too pleased about over-paying for their Series A stock compared to the Series B investors. If the Series A investors have full ratchet antidilution protection, their conversion price will be reset to the lower sale price of the Series B stock. It is as though the Series A investors were able to purchase at the most recent price. The $3,000,000 Series A investors would now be able to convert into 1,800,000 shares of common stock. As a result of the lower-priced dilutive issuance, additional stock would be issued to the Series A upon conversion of their preferred stock, and the capitalization would be as follows:

SECOND ROUND (with full ratchet protection)		
	No. of Shares	% of Company
Common	4,500,000	60.00
Series A	1,800,000	24.00
Series B	1,200,000	16.00

Full ratchet appears simple and fair on its face, but it is rarely used because it is widely viewed as unfair. Most of the dilution is pushed onto the common shareholders, and in an anomaly, the Series B ends up buying less of the company than it bargained for (which can push down its price even further). Perhaps most unfairly, all of the Series A stock is repriced regardless of the size of the issuance of Series B stock.

Although the ratchet formula is used much less often than the weighted average formula discussed next, a ratchet may be appropriate under some limited circumstances. For example, if a venture capitalist uncovers a fact in due diligence that suggests that the company is overvalued and may need a cash infusion sooner than was anticipated, a company might agree to a ratchet for six or twelve months to give the investors some assurance that there will not need to be a subsequent financing at a lower price per share than the price paid in the previous financing (a *down-priced financing*). Similarly, if some event may occur within the next year that will have a dramatic effect on valuation (such as the issuance of a patent), the venture capitalist may seek ratchet protection to protect him or her if the event does not occur and more money must be raised. Also, investors in a mezzanine round might be concerned about the company being over-valued and about a down-priced financing if the public market window closes. They too might seek a ratchet for a limited period. In such cases, typically when the ratchet period expires, the weighted average method becomes applicable.

Weighted Average Today almost all venture deals use a weighted aver-age antidilution formula, which attempts to calibrate the repricing based on the size and price of the dilutive round. *Weighted average antidilution* sets the new conversion price of the outstanding preferred stock as the product of (a) the old conversion price multiplied by (b) a fraction in which (1) the numerator is the sum of (x) the number of shares out-standing before the issuance plus (y) the quotient of the amount of money invested in this round divided by the old conversion price, and (2) the denominator is the sum of (x) the shares outstanding before this round and (y) the shares issued in this round. Algebraically,

$$NCP = OCP \times \frac{OB + \frac{MI}{OCP}}{OB + SI}$$

where *NCP* is the new conversion price, *OCP* is the old conversion price, *OB* is the number of shares outstanding before the issuance, *MI* is the amount of money invested in the current round, and *SI* is the number of shares issued in the current round.

The weighted average formula provides a result that adjusts the con-version price based on the relative amount of the company that is being sold at the lower price.

Applying this formula to the example set forth above, one calculates the new conversion price as follows:

$$NCP = 2.00 \times \frac{6,000,000 + \frac{2,000,000}{2.00}}{6,000,000 + 1,200,000}$$

$$NCP = \$1.944$$

Under weighted average antidilution, the capitalization table would be as follows:

SECOND ROUND (with weighted average protection)

	No. of Shares	% of Company
Common	4,500,000	62.13
Series A	1,542,860	21.30
Series B	1,200,000	16.57

No longer does the Series A stock convert on a one-to-one basis; each share of Series A stock now converts into 1.029 shares of common ($2.00/1.944) based on the new conversion price.

The weighted average formula is fairly standard in venture capital financings, but there are some variations. The most common variation involves how options are counted—whether as issued or unissued common stock. Although counting the options would add the same amount to both the denominator and the numerator in the weighted average formula, the effect of including them is that the broader base absorbs more dilution and keeps the conversion price from falling as quickly. Often, shares reserved for options already granted are counted, but those reserved for future grants are not. This issue is a minor negotiating point, as it tends to have a negligible effect unless the option pool is unusually large.

Certain issuances will often be carved out from the price-protection antidilution provisions. For example, it is usually anticipated that additional members of the management team will have to be hired and that it will be necessary to offer those employees stock options or low-priced common stock. Over time, other members of management may need to have their incentives revitalized (following dilutive venture rounds) with additional stock options. For this reason, options to be granted under stock option plans and other equity arrangements with employees are generally excluded from the price-protection formula. Often, there is a cap on the aggregate amount of stock that a board can allocate under this carve-out (typically between 10% and 30% of the stock for equity incentive programs) without obtaining the approval of the investors. Similarly, any outstanding rights to purchase shares at a lower price that were granted prior to the issuance of the preferred stock are usually excluded. Shares of common stock issued upon conversion of preferred stock into common stock are also excluded.

Pay to Play Some venture capitalists like to add a pay-to-play provision. With a *pay-to-play provision*, a holder of preferred stock gets the benefit of price protection antidilution only if it buys its pro rata share of any subsequent down-priced round. An investor who does not participate at least pro rata in a down-priced round is automatically converted into a different series of preferred stock that is identical to the original series in all respects, except that there is no price protection. This provision is intended to encourage all investors to step up and help the company in difficult times, and is therefore generally favored by entrepreneurs as well as by some venture capitalists. Although prominent in discussions of types of antidilution provisions, in practice, pay-to-play provisions are atypical.

Voting Rights

The preferred stock issued to the venture capitalist votes on most matters on an as-converted-to-common basis (i.e., one vote for each common share into which the preferred can be converted). On most matters the preferred and common shareholders vote together.

Protective Provisions There may be certain matters for which the company must obtain the approval of the preferred stock voting as a class. These matters generally include any change in the certificate of incorporation that would adversely affect the rights, preferences, and privileges of the preferred shareholders. For example, the liquidation preference cannot be changed without the consent of the preferred shareholders. There is often a separate prohibition on the issuance of any security senior to (or even on par with) the existing preferred stock, as well as separate provisions prohibiting changes in the liquidation preference, dividend rights, conversion rights, voting rights, or redemption rights of the preferred shareholders (even though all of these rights might be considered to fall within the general prohibition on adverse change to the preferred shareholders).

Some investors will want these *protective provisions* to require the approval of holders of each series of preferred stock, with each series voting separately, because these investors control a larger percentage of a particular series than of the preferred stock as a whole. It is in the company's best interest to avoid a series vote in order to give the company greater flexibility and to lessen the likelihood that any single investor will have blocking power. Even if some investors end up with blocking power, the fewer who have this power, the better for the company.

Another common protective provision is a prohibition on the redemption of stock, other than redemptions provided for in the certificate of incorporation and repurchases from departed employees, consultants, and directors pursuant to the contractual arrangements made when stock was sold to such persons (but often still subject to some cap on the number of shares that can be redeemed). There may be a prohibition on any sale of substantially all of the assets of the company or merger in which the surviving entity is not controlled by shareholders of the company prior to the merger. Any increase in the authorized number of shares of stock may be prohibited. If there is an agreement on how the board is to be elected, changes in the number of directors or the designation of who elects a stated number of directors may also require approval by the preferred shareholders.

Some preferred investors may try to expand the number of items requiring their approval to include the types of matters often found in bank loan covenants, such as (1) investing in any other enterprise; (2) establishing subsidiaries; (3) incurring certain levels of indebtedness; (4) making loans to others; and (5) exceeding certain levels for capital expenditures. Generally, such provisions should be vigorously resisted by the company. The investors should rely on the board of directors of the company to do what is prudent, rather than forcing such matters to be delayed by a shareholder vote.

Board Elections   As discussed in chapter 5, the board of directors is charged with the management of the company's business affairs, and it appoints the officers to carry out board policies and handle day-to-day operations. In America's version of shareholder democracy, as reflected in the corporation laws of the fifty states, the shareholders elect the board to run the company; at the same time, the shareholders are permitted to vote on a limited number of matters (e.g., amendments to the certificate of incorporation, decisions about selling the business, certain merger transactions, and dissolution). Control of the company is determined by the persons with the power to elect the board of directors, along with the directors themselves.

Generally, the lead venture capitalist in a round will expect a board seat. Sometimes, each venture capitalist would like a board seat. As the number of venture investors increases over time, the board can become too large and may find itself completely dominated by financial investors.

At the time of the first venture round, it is likely that the founders will retain a majority of the company and will be permitted to elect a majority of the board. If there is only one venture fund in the round, it is not unusual for it to request two board seats.

Usually, the founders and the investors will enter into a voting agreement or will designate in the certificate of incorporation that a certain number of seats are to be elected by the common shareholders, another number of seats are to be elected by the preferred shareholders, and perhaps the balance elected by the shareholders at large. Keep in mind that control of the board is likely to shift over time as subsequent financings occur.

An entrepreneur may wish to establish from the outset that he or she wants to be able to look to the board as a repository of business experience and advice. To this end, the founder group may decide to limit itself to just two founders on the board, with one or two seats reserved for venture investors, and two or three seats reserved for industry leaders who are respected by the venture capitalists and founders. With this type of board composition, no one group controls the board, and the board can focus on what is in the best interest of the company rather than on what is in the best interest of any particular group. (Chapter 9 further discusses board composition issues.)

Milestones

Sometimes venture capitalists will require the company to achieve certain goals (*milestones*) within a specified time. These milestones might include reaching certain points in product development, or attaining certain sales or profitability levels. The rationale for milestones is that they protect the venture capitalist from overvaluing the company to a greater degree than price antidilution provisions. Sometimes the achievement of milestones will trigger an obligation by the venture capitalist to make a follow-on investment in the company at a previously determined price per share. In some cases, failure to meet the milestones will permit the investor to purchase shares at a much lower price. In other cases, the conversion price of the venture capitalist's preferred stock may be adjusted downward, with the effect of increasing the venture capitalist's ownership of the company. In still other cases, an investor will suggest that control of the board should shift to the investors if the management team fails to achieve the milestones.

The company should resist any milestones that would result in a change of control. Business is filled with risks, and the unexpected can occur. When that happens, all shareholders in the company need to pull together, rather than splitting into groups of shareholders trying to use the company's difficulty to their own advantage. Although milestones associated with subsequent rounds of investment are not quite as onerous, they too may cause misalignment of incentives among shareholders. For example, some may want the company to fall short, in order to be relieved of a further investment obligation (or, more likely, to be in a position to purchase stock cheaply or to renegotiate the deal). Milestones that trigger ownership adjustments similarly put the venture capitalist and the founders on different sides of the table, which is hardly where the parties should or want to be. Finally, milestones of any kind in a deal may distort the behavior of the entrepreneur, whose focus may be too much on the milestone and not enough on what actions or expenditures are in the best interest of the business. For these reasons, many venture capitalists avoid using milestones.

Registration Rights

The parties will devote a fair amount of discussion to the subject of registration rights. A *registration right* is the right to force the company to register the holder's stock with the Securities and Exchange Commission (SEC) so that it can be sold in the public markets. Often when a company goes public, the underwriters are unwilling to permit existing shareholders to sell in the offering, as such sales will adversely affect the marketing of the new issuance of stock being sold by the company to raise capital. If the shareholder has held the stock for more than one year and the company is public, the holder may be able to sell a limited amount of stock (up to the greater of 1% of the outstanding stock and the average weekly trading volume in the preceding four weeks) in any three-month period under rule 144. But if the holder wishes to sell more than that amount or is unable to sell under rule 144 (for example, because it has held the shares for less than one year or because it is an *affiliate* [officer, director, or owner of more than 5% to 10% of the outstanding shares] of a private company), it may need to register the shares to exit from the investment.

There are three types of registration rights that venture investors are likely to request: demand rights, S-3 rights, and piggyback rights.

A *demand right* is a right to demand that the company file a registration statement on form S-1 to sell the holder's stock. This is the form the company uses for an initial public offering (IPO); it requires a prospectus with extensive information about the company and the offering. (Initial public offerings are discussed further in chapter 15.) A company generally will want to limit this right as it can be expensive and time-consuming, and can adversely affect the company's own capital-raising plans. Generally, the investor group will receive only one or two demand rights, with limits on when they can be exercised. The company will resist granting demand rights that can be used to force the company to go public. The argument is that one cannot force a management team to find underwriters, to do the road show required for the offering, and to make the offering successful if the company is not yet ready. (During the *road show*, the company's managers and investment bankers travel around the country and make presentations to potential investors.) The investors will seek such a right, arguing that an IPO may be their only path to liquidity.

An S-3 right is actually another type of demand right. An *S-3 right* allows the investor to force the company to register the investor's stock on form S-3. This form is part of a simpler procedure that can be used by most companies with a *public float* (market value of securities held by nonaffiliates) of at least $75 million twelve months after they have gone public. The S-3 form permits the registration statement to incorporate by reference information already on file with the SEC, so the preparation of the registration statement is simpler, less time-consuming, and cheaper than the preparation of a form S-1 registration statement. S-3 rights granted to venture capitalists tend to be unlimited in quantity but are available only once or twice per year and may expire at some point.

A *piggyback right* is the right to participate in an offering initiated by the company. Piggyback rights are generally subject to a cutback or elimination by the offering's underwriter, who may determine, based on market conditions, that a sale by shareholders will adversely affect the company's capital-raising effort. The venture capitalist will seek rights that may not be completely cut back except in connection with the company's initial public offering. Piggyback rights granted to venture capitalists are generally unlimited in number but often expire five to seven years after the company's initial public offering or after a certain percentage of the venture investors have sold their shares. Unless the rights expire, the company must notify all holders of rights every time the company has a public offering and perhaps include a portion of the holder's shares in the offering.

Information Rights

Holders of significant blocks of preferred stock may be granted the rights to certain information, such as monthly financial statements, annual audited financial statements, and the annual budget approved by the board. These rights should expire upon an initial public offering, when the investors will be able to rely on SEC filings.

Some investors may seek more expanded rights, such as review of the auditor's letter to management concerning the audit of the financial statements and any weaknesses in internal controls, prepared by the

---

FROM THE TRENCHES

One venture fund was quite thankful that it had obtained a demand registration right exercisable five years after it invested in a consumer products company, that became very successful. The founder decided that he liked running a profitable private company and had no desire to take it public. He was also unwilling to sell the company or to find some other path to liquidity at a high enough valuation to satisfy the investor. The investor insisted on a public offering and threatened to exercise its demand right. Because the company had a well-known brand and was not a development-stage technology company, it appeared that a fairly successful offering could be consummated even without an enthusiastic management team. Faced with the investor's threat, the founder and management agreed that the company should go public and completed a successful offering, which gave the investors liquidity.

---

company's accountants; the right to make on-site inspections and inquiries of officers or employees; and the right to observe board meetings. Generally, these additional information rights should be resisted. They can be disruptive to the company's operation and conflict with the board's performance of its duties. Investors who maintain good relations with the company will be able to obtain sufficient information to monitor their investment without placing undue burdens on the start-up enterprise.

Co-Sale Rights

Venture capitalists will often ask for a co-sale right. Typically, a *co-sale right* binds some of the key founders of the company and gives the investor a contractual right to sell some of the investor's stock alongside the founder's stock if the founder elects to sell stock to a third party. A co-sale right protects the investor from a situation in which the founder transfers control of the company by selling his or her stock to another person. In such a circumstance, the investor is looking for the opportunity to consider exiting as well. Mechanically, a co-sale right usually gives the investor the right to replace a portion of the stock the founder planned to sell with the investor's stock. The portion is usually the pro rata share of the investor's total holdings compared with the founder's total holdings.

It is reasonable for a founder to resist a co-sale right except in those circumstances in which a substantial portion of the stock held by all founders is being sold. Founders may insist on exceptions to permit a sale of some of their stock for liquidity purposes (e.g., to cover a house down payment or private-school tuition) and carve-outs for dispositions upon death or upon termination of employment. Founders may also ask for a reciprocal co-sale right so that they can obtain some liquidity if the venture capitalist seeks to sell its shares. This reciprocal right is not usually given.

OTHER PROTECTIVE ARRANGEMENTS

Vesting

The venture investors may request that the founders subject their stock, and all other common stock to be sold to employees, to a vesting schedule

---

FROM THE TRENCHES

One venture fund learned the hard way the merits of a co-sale right. The fund led a $2 million financing of a toy-and-video-game distribution company. The key founder resisted any effort to put vesting on his shares, arguing that the company was more than two and a half years old and he had earned his shares. He also argued successfully that a co-sale right was not needed, because he had no reason to transfer his shares as the company could not make it without him and the shares represented most of his net worth. He also persuaded the venture capitalist that it was fundamentally unfair to put restrictions on his right to transfer his shares. Within twelve months of the closing, the entrepreneur transferred his shares to a competitor for more than $1 million and left the company. The company was unable to compete effectively without the entrepreneur, and the venture capitalist's investment became virtually worthless.

if they have not already done so. As explained in chapter 5, the vesting schedule is usually four years, with cliff vesting for the first year, then monthly vesting for the next three years. If the vesting schedule is not put in place until the venture round closes, the founders may want to commence the vesting period on an earlier date, such as the day founders first acquired stock or joined the company.

Employees whose stock is subject to repurchase will likely want to file a *section 83(b) election* with the IRS. As explained in chapter 5, this election allows the stock to be taxed at the time it is acquired (when there is no tax, assuming the employee paid fair market value) rather than on the date the vesting is complete (when it may have increased dramatically in value over the original purchase price). The 83(b) election must be filed within thirty days of the commencement of the vesting arrangement. It is extremely important that this filing be made on time; a missed or late filing can result in a very large tax bill at a time when the shareholder has no money because the stock is not liquid.

Options

As discussed in chapter 5, common stock is typically issued to founders at the earliest stages of a company. However, soon thereafter, many companies set up stock option plans as additional equity incentives for employees. The venture capitalist understands well the need for such programs and is a supporter of them as long as they are not excessively generous.

Options provide employees with an opportunity to share in the equity upside of the business without having to invest any of their own money until a future date. Incentive stock options (ISOs) are particularly popular because they permit an employee to purchase cheap common stock at a future date without triggering a taxable event. After a company goes public, ISOs become less important because there is liquidity in the stock, and an option holder can buy the stock and then sell enough to pay taxes on the gain within the same tax period.

An entrepreneur will want to reserve (at least mentally) a certain percentage of the company for future equity incentives to new and existing employees. Generally, somewhere between 10% and 30% of the stock postventure financing is reserved for this purpose. A generous plan will dilute the holders of the common stock and the preferred stock alike, so such options should be granted with some care. Nonetheless, a healthy pool of options will likely be advisable so that the young company can attract the talent necessary for success. Options generally vest over four or five years (although credit is sometimes given in the initial grant for prior service to the company). Unlike stock, which vests by the repurchase right lapsing, options vest by the exercise right extending to a greater proportion of the grant over time.

The entrepreneur should reach agreement with the venture capitalist on the scope of any option plan prior to the closing of the financing. If the company later wishes to exceed this scope, the entrepreneur may be required to obtain the written approval of the investors. Alternatively, the investors may agree that the scope can be exceeded so long as their representatives on the board vote in favor of the option grants.

Putting It into Practice

Alexandra talked with Michael Woo about venture capital funding. Because WebRunner had successfully validated the technology and had modest overhead needs, Alexandra figured that WebRunner was worth about $1,200,000 and would need only about $600,000 in an initial round. This would result in one-third ownership by the venture capitalists. Michael suggested bumping that figure up to $800,000 to reflect unanticipated delays and expenses, and to allow a venture capitalist to buy 40% of the company. Alexandra agreed, particularly in light of her earlier miscalculation of cash needs. Also, she hoped some of the extra money could be used to buy out Kevin Jordan, who had become dissatisfied with his $50,000 investment during WebRunner's earlier financial crisis. Michael liked this idea, because it meant that the new investors would be able to purchase Series A Preferred Stock rather than a Series B, thus simplifying the capital structure.

Alexandra had already prepared a business plan for Michael's review. She worked with Josh Austin to pull together all of the company's material agreements and information on its technology, so that once an investor was selected, the investor could proceed quickly with its due diligence investigation.

Michael suggested approaching Centaur Partners, a venture capital group looking for Internet opportunities, which he thought would be a good investor. Michael told Alexandra that he was obligated to disclose that his firm had represented Centaur Partners in the past and would continue to do so in the future. He said that he personally always represented the issuer in venture capital financings and that his firm would not represent Centaur in any business relating to WebRunner. Michael told Alexandra, however, that he would understand if she wanted to seek other representation for the transaction. Alexandra said she was comfortable with Michael continuing to represent WebRunner, and asked Michael to contact Centaur on her behalf.

Michael set up an initial meeting between Alexandra and Centaur's managing partner. That meeting went well, and Alexandra used the opportunity to discuss her thoughts on valuation and to sound out Centaur on such issues as their vision for the company, their willingness and ability to step up for other rounds, their view on the company's weaknesses, and their capabilities in assisting the company in addressing those weaknesses. Alexandra also performed her own due diligence investigation of Centaur, keeping in mind that Centaur was not just a source of needed capital but was about to become her partner in one of the most important undertakings of her life.

continued

continued

After several more successful meetings, including meetings involving all three Centaur general partners and the Eagles, Centaur agreed to invest in WebRunner, pending a satisfactory due diligence review. Alexandra, along with Michael and Josh, met with Centaur and its counsel to hammer out a term sheet.

After much negotiation, the two parties agreed on a term sheet that reflected the $1,200,000 pre-money valuation that Alexandra was seeking. (A sample venture capital term sheet is set forth in "Getting It in Writing" at the end of this chapter.) Centaur agreed to use $60,000 of its investment to purchase Kevin Jordan's 50,000 shares, which would then be folded into the new Series A Preferred Stock to be issued by WebRunner.

Michael negotiated a provision that would permit WebRunner to bring in another venture firm for up to $200,000 of the $800,000 financing, with Centaur's permission. After the meeting, Michael suggested gently to Alexandra that she might want to talk to a few other firms and to select one to be another voice in the investor group. However, Alexandra was comfortable with Centaur being the only investor because of the rapport she had established with the Centaur partners and the smoothness with which negotiations had occurred. Michael pointed out that other venture funds could be part of the next round, as Centaur had agreed to a limited preemptive right of 50% of future financings.

Alexandra instructed Michael to immediately draft and circulate documents for closing the transaction. Although the attorneys for Centaur, Michael, and the principals were able to reach agreement on the documents within three weeks, Centaur did not complete its due diligence until a month after the principals had agreed to the term sheet. As no problems were found, Centaur proceeded to invest $800,000.

Having locked up sufficient funding for at least the next year, Alexandra focused on forming a board that would provide her with sound business advice and expertise. She asked the Centaur partners for help in finding additional board members. She also began to work closely with Centaur's board representative to make sure he was kept in the loop on activities at the company. Alexandra planned to brief Centaur's representative prior to board meetings so that board discussions could be as thoughtful as possible and surprises could be kept to a minimum. Centaur would play a critical role in helping the company raise money in subsequent rounds, and her relationship with the Centaur board representative was central to the success of their partnership.

G E T T I N G   I T   I N   W R I T I N G

SAMPLE VENTURE CAPITAL TERM SHEET

WEBRUNNER INC.
SALE OF SERIES A PREFERRED STOCK
SUMMARY OF TERMS

Issuer: WebRunner Inc. (the "Company").

Amount of Financing: $800,000.

Type of Security: 666,667 shares of Series A Convertible Preferred Stock (the "Series A Preferred"), initially convertible into an equal number of shares of the Company's Common Stock (the "Common Stock").

Price: $1.20 per share (the "Original Purchase Price").

Resulting
Capitalization: The Original Purchase Price represents a post-financing valuation of $2 million, based on fully diluted outstanding common stock of 1,666,667 shares as of the Closing.

Purchaser(s):   Centaur Partners, L.P. as lead investor will purchase at least $600,000 and up to $800,000 of Series A Preferred. The Company may seek other investors (together with the lead investor, the "Investors") to invest up to $200,000, subject to the approval of the lead investor.

Anticipated Closing
Date (the "Closing"): March 5, 1997.

TERMS OF SERIES A
PREFERRED STOCK

Dividends: The holders of the Series A Preferred shall be entitled to receive cumulative dividends in preference to any dividend on the Common Stock at the rate of 7% of the Original Purchase Price per annum, when and as declared by the Board of Directors. The Series A Preferred will participate pro rata in dividends paid on the Common Stock.

Liquidation
Preference: In the event of any liquidation or winding up of the Company, the holders of the Series A Preferred shall be

continued

entitled to receive in preference to the holders of the Common Stock an amount equal to the Original Purchase Price plus any unpaid cumulative dividends (the "Liquidation Preference"). After the payment of the Liquidation Preference to the holders of the Series A Preferred, the remaining assets shall be distributed ratably to the holders of the Common Stock and the Series A Preferred until the Series A Preferred holders have received three times their original investment. All remaining assets shall be distributed ratably to the Common Stock. A merger, acquisition, or sale of substantially all of the assets of the Company in which the shareholders of the Company do not own a majority of the outstanding shares of the surviving corporation shall be deemed to be a liquidation.

Conversion:

The holders of the Series A Preferred shall have the right to convert the Series A Preferred, at any time, into shares of Common Stock. The initial conversion rate shall be 1:1, subject to adjustment as provided below.

Automatic
Conversion:

The Series A Preferred shall be automatically converted into Common Stock, at the then applicable conversion price, (i) in the event that the holders of at least 50% of the outstanding Series A Preferred consent to such conversion, or (ii) upon the closing of a firmly underwritten public offering of shares of Common Stock of the Company at a per share price not less than $3.60 per share (as presently constituted) and for a total offering of not less than $10,000,000 (before deduction of underwriters' commissions and expenses).

Antidilution
Provisions:

The conversion price of the Series A Preferred will be subject to a weighted average adjustment to reduce dilution in the event that the Company issues additional equity securities (other than employee, director, and consultant shares approved by the Board of Directors) at a purchase price less than the applicable conversion price. The conversion price will also be subject to proportional adjustment for stock splits, stock dividends, recapitalizations, and the like.

continued

Redemption at
Option of Investors: Commencing on the fifth anniversary of the Closing, at the election of the holders of at least 50% of the Series A Preferred, the Company shall redeem the outstanding Series A Preferred in three equal annual installments. Such redemption shall be at the Original Purchase Price plus any unpaid cumulative dividends.

Voting Rights: The Series A Preferred will vote together with the Common Stock and not as a separate class except as specifically provided herein or as otherwise required by law. Each share of Series A Preferred shall have a number of votes equal to the number of shares of Common Stock then issuable upon conversion of such share of Series A Preferred.

Board of
Directors: The size of the Company's Board of Directors shall be changed to five. The holders of the Series A Preferred, voting as a separate class, shall be entitled to elect two members of the Company's Board of Directors. The holders of the Common Stock shall be entitled to elect two directors. The fifth director must be approved by both the Common Stock and Preferred Series A holders, voting separately.

Protective
Provisions: For so long as at least 300,000 shares of Series A Preferred remain outstanding, consent of the holders of at least 50% of the Series A Preferred shall be required for any action which (i) alters or changes the rights, preferences, or privileges of the Series A Preferred, (ii) increases or decreases the authorized number of shares of Series A Preferred, (iii) creates (by reclassification or otherwise) any new class or series of shares having rights, preferences, or privileges senior to or on a parity with the Series A Preferred, (iv) results in the redemption of any shares of Common Stock (other than pursuant to employee agreements), or (v) results in any merger, other corporate reorganization, sale of control, or any transaction in which all or substantially all of the assets of the Company are sold.

continued

Information Rights:
So long as an Investor continues to hold shares of Series A Preferred or Common Stock issued upon conversion of the Series A Preferred, the Company shall deliver to the Investor audited annual and unaudited quarterly financial statements. So long as an Investor holds not less than 120,000 shares of Series A Preferred, the Company will furnish the Investor with monthly financial statements and will provide a copy of the Company's annual operating plan within thirty (30) days prior to the beginning of the fiscal year. Each Investor shall also be entitled to standard inspection and visitation rights. These provisions shall terminate upon a registered public offering of the Company's Common Stock.

Registration Rights:
Demand Rights: If Investors holding at least 50% of the outstanding shares of Series A Preferred, including Common Stock issued on conversion of Series A Preferred ("Registrable Securities"), request that the Company file a Registration Statement for at least 30% of the Registrable Securities having an aggregate offering price to the public of not less than $5,000,000, the Company will use its best efforts to cause such shares to be registered; provided, however, that the Company shall not be obligated to effect any such registration prior to the third anniversary of the Closing. The Company shall have the right to delay such registration under certain circumstances for two periods not in excess of ninety (90) days each in any twelve (12) month period.

The Company shall not be obligated to effect more than two (2) registrations under these demand right provisions, and shall not be obligated to effect a registration (i) during the ninety (90) day period commencing with the date of the Company's initial public offering, or (ii) if it delivers notice to the holders of the Registrable Securities within thirty (30) days of any registration request of its intent to file a registration statement for such initial public offering within 90 days.

Company Registration: The Investors shall be entitled to "piggyback" registration rights on all registrations of the Company or on any demand registrations of any

continued

other investor subject to the right, however, of the Company and its underwriters to reduce the number of shares proposed to be registered pro rata in view of market conditions. If the Investors are so limited, however, no party shall sell shares in such registration other than the Company or the Investor, if any, invoking the demand registration. No shareholder of the Company shall be granted piggyback registration rights that would reduce the number of shares includable by the holders of the Registrable Securities in such registration without the consent of the holders of 50% of the Registrable Securities.

S-3 Rights: Investors shall be entitled to two (2) demand registrations on Form S-3 per year (if available to the Company) so long as such registered offerings are not less than $500,000.

Expenses: The Company shall bear registration expenses (exclusive of underwriting discounts and commissions) of all such demands, piggybacks, and S-3 registrations (including the expense of a single counsel to the selling shareholders, which counsel shall also be counsel to the Company unless there is a conflict of interest with respect to the representation of any selling shareholder or the underwriters otherwise object).

Transfer of Rights: The registration rights may be transferred to (i) any partner or retired partner of any holder that is a partnership, (ii) any family member or trust for the benefit of any individual holder, or (iii) any transferee who acquires at least 100,000 shares of Registrable Securities; provided the Company is given written notice thereof.

Termination of Rights: The registration rights shall terminate on the date five years after the Company's initial public offering.

Other Provisions: Other provisions shall be contained in the Stock Purchase Agreement with respect to registration rights as are reasonable, including cross-indemnification, the period of time in which the Registration Statement shall be kept effective, and underwriting arrangements.

continued

Right of
First Refusal: The Investors shall have the right in the event the Company proposes to offer equity securities to any person (other than securities issued to employees, directors, or consultants, or pursuant to acquisitions, etc.) to purchase up to 50% of such shares (on a pro rata basis among the Investors). Such right of first refusal will terminate upon an underwritten public offering of shares of the Company.

Purchase
Agreement: The investment shall be made pursuant to a Stock Purchase Agreement reasonably acceptable to the Company and the Investors, which agreement shall contain, among other things, appropriate representations and warranties of the Company, covenants of the Company reflecting the provisions set forth herein, and appropriate conditions of closing, including an opinion of counsel for the Company. The Stock Purchase Agreement shall provide that it may only be amended and any waivers thereunder shall only be made with the approval of the holders of 50% of the Series A Preferred. Registration rights provisions may be amended or waived solely with the consent of the holders of 50% of the Registrable Securities.

EMPLOYEE MATTERS

Stock Vesting: Unless otherwise determined by the Board of Directors, all stock and stock equivalents issued after the Closing to employees, directors, and consultants will be subject to vesting in accordance with the vesting provisions currently in place under the Company's stock option plan.

Proprietary
Information and
Inventions Agreements: Each officer and employee of the Company shall enter into acceptable agreements governing nondisclosure of proprietary information and assignment of inventions to the Company.

Co-Sale Agreement: The shares of the Company's securities held by Alexandra Scott, Paul Eagle, and Sheryl Eagle shall be made subject to a co-sale agreement (with certain

continued

reasonable exceptions) with the holders of the Series A Preferred such that they may not sell, transfer, or exchange their stock unless each holder of Series A Preferred has an opportunity to participate in the sale on a pro rata basis. This right of co-sale shall not apply to and shall terminate upon the Company's initial public offering. In addition, such co-sale agreement will contain a right of first refusal such that Scott, Eagle, and Eagle may not sell, transfer, or exchange their stock without first offering to the Company and then to each holder of Series A Preferred the opportunity to purchase such stock on the same terms and conditions as those of the proposed sale.

Key-Person Insurance: As soon as reasonably possible after the Closing, the Company shall procure key-person life insurance policies for each of Alexandra Scott, Paul Eagle, and Sheryl Eagle in the amount of $1,000,000 each, naming the Company as beneficiary.

OTHER MATTERS

Finders: The Company and the Investors shall each indemnify the other for any finder's fees for which either is responsible.

Legal Fees and
Expenses: The Company shall pay the reasonable fees, not to exceed $15,000, and expenses of one special counsel to the Investors.

Forming the Board

9

A corporation is legally required to have a board of directors to protect the interests of the corporation and its equity holders. But there are other reasons to have an active board. A board of directors that brings together people with a variety of strengths and skills can be a valuable asset to a young company and contribute to its success by functioning as a strategic sounding board. The most effective boards are those that give independent, informed advice to management, and challenge the CEO, rather than acting as a rubber stamp.

When asked to list the most difficult things about starting a business, many entrepreneurs respond that they never realized how many details they needed to be mindful of and how difficult it would be to do so many things simultaneously. It is a challenge to keep an eye on the big picture of the business while being continually concerned with day-to-day operational issues. In the midst of trying to solve countless problems, entrepreneurs often turn to the directors for answers and advice.

This chapter examines the benefits of having an independent and active board of directors, and the factors to consider in selecting board members. It also summarizes directors' legal responsibilities, which include a duty of loyalty and a duty of care. The chapter discusses board compensation, outlines the types of information that should be provided to directors, and suggests ways to make effective use of directors' time.[1]

THE BENEFITS OF HAVING AN INDEPENDENT BOARD

Many corporations, large and small, have filled the positions of directors with agreeable family members or personal friends, rather than selecting an active, outside, and truly independent board. Small-company CEOs and entrepreneurs may be reluctant to have an active, outside board for a variety of reasons. Many CEOs are hesitant to give up any control of the company that they created. The entrepreneur may not feel sufficiently organized to deal with a board. Many entrepreneurs dislike criticism and tend to minimize its sources. The entrepreneur may be reluctant to reveal confidential information, financial or otherwise. CEOs of family businesses may be even more reluctant to invite outsiders in when traditionally only family members have been involved in the enterprise. In addition, many CEOs think that outsiders will not understand their business as well as they do. They may feel that their business is unique, and that no one else can assist effectively in long-range planning and development of strategy.

However, the benefits of an independent board greatly outweigh the drawbacks. A CEO can better assist the company in achieving its full potential when he or she is able to benefit from what often amounts to decades of other people's experience and wisdom. As Clayton Mathile, CEO of the IAMS pet food company, explained,

> *Your outside board can be your inside sparring partner who tests your strengths and weaknesses before you get to the main arena—the marketplace. Where else can a business owner go to find help from someone he trusts, who is unbiased, and who will help him do the job?*[2]

The reasons for creating an active, outside board are numerous. Board members can bring perspective and experience to the table, and provide a set of complementary skills for the CEO. If the prospective directors have been entrepreneurs and CEOs in their own right, they are able to provide vision and insight that insiders cannot supply. The board can help top management recognize the need for long-term planning and can assist the CEO in developing long-range strategies. Boards can provide a framework for control and discipline, and give the CEO someone to answer to. Directors can be challenging and objective critics. Securing financial information as well as other information needed by the board can become an internal check for the CEO. Directors can fill the CEO's need for a mentor. One CEO of a small company explained, "I need a person on the board with whom I can talk very frankly and not be fearful—someone on the board I can tell, 'I don't know.'"[3] Boards can give the CEO the emotional support needed for difficult decision making.

The presence of experienced businesspersons on the board of directors will lend an air of credibility to the venture that it would not otherwise have. This credibility is particularly important when the enterprise is trying to raise funds. Valuable business connections and introductions can be made through the board. In the case of family corporations, a board of directors with some outside perspective and independence from family politics can ease the often difficult generational transitions.

FROM THE TRENCHES

An entrepreneur founded a company to produce sophisticated software designed to "read" or extract information from form documents, such as insurance claim forms, and to store it digitally. He initially financed the company with money from his father. His board of directors consisted of himself and an industry consultant. After five beta tests proved successful, he decided to seek venture capital funding for the company at a $5-million pre-money valuation. Before starting this process, however, he added two individuals to his board. Both had been venture capitalists before cofounding a company that, after obtaining venture capital financing, had recently gone public. The founder wanted someone at his side who could not only access the venture capital community but could "walk the walk and talk the talk" when it came to negotiating a deal. The founder reasoned that his new directors also would be able to help him deal with the myriad issues that would face his company, as they had very recent start-up experience.

THE SIZE OF THE BOARD

The board of directors should be small enough to be accountable and to act as a deliberative body, but large enough to carry out the necessary responsibilities. Most CEOs find that between five and ten directors is a good, manageable size. Many venture-backed companies have five directors.

The outsiders should outnumber the insiders in order to reap the benefit of independent directors. If a board of ten directors is desired, seven outsiders and three insiders might be appropriate.

FREQUENCY OF BOARD MEETINGS

In deciding the frequency of formal board meetings, the CEO must consider how he or she envisions the role of the board. If the board is very hands-on, a meeting every month may be appropriate. But if the board meets formally only to discuss major issues, less frequent meetings may be sufficient. Typically, the CEO should be in touch with each board member between the meetings.

The length of the meetings and the location are also important strategic decisions. Some boards meet for several hours at a time, or for an entire day, with a break for lunch, which facilitates informal discussions among members. The ideal meeting lasts between three and five hours, which is long enough to accomplish the necessary work but not so long that the board members cannot continue to give their full attention. Sometimes, the board members will get together for several days at a time so they can concentrate on strategic issues without being distracted by the day-to-day aspects of the business. For example, one company has a three-day off-site meeting every six months. Although off-site meetings can be very valuable, some companies will find it impossible to schedule them because many directors have full-time jobs, such as running their own companies, and cannot afford to be away from them for so long.

FROM THE TRENCHES

An entrepreneur who started a bicycle helmet business had a board of directors to satisfy the legal requirements, but it was composed of only himself and two other insiders. For advice, he turned to a business school professor and two retired executives. Every few years, the entrepreneur gathered this unofficial board for a freewheeling discussion of the business and its strategies. Between these infrequent meetings, the entrepreneur called these advisors when he wanted to discuss a problem or an idea. Even as the company grew, the entrepreneur never felt the need to form a board with outsiders, and instead continued to use his unofficial board. This practice continued until recently, when he sold his business to a large competitor.

   Comment: The ideal situation is to have outside advisors as members of the board of directors. If that is not possible due to liability concerns or time constraints, the next best alternative is to have outside advisors who can augment the official board of directors.

TYPE OF REPRESENTATION DESIRED

There are at least two major aspects to consider in building an independent and active board. The first is the combination of functional skills needed to keep the business running smoothly and to bring it to the next level of growth. The second is the mix of personalities. Combining these components, both of which are very important to the successful running of the company, is more an art than a science.

Before selecting board members, the CEO must anticipate the needs of the corporation for the next few years and ask such questions as:

- What is the competitive advantage of the company?
- What are the demands on the company and the likely changes in the next few years?
- What are the factors that would contribute to the success of the company?
- What role does marketing play? Research and development? Customer service?
- What is the company's access to financial sources?

By inventorying the resources and anticipating the needs of the company, the CEO will be better equipped to choose a board that will unlock the company's inherent possibilities.

The Needed Skills

The goal in putting together the board is to compile a complete combination of abilities. The entrepreneur should assess his or her own weaknesses and strengths, and supplement them with complementary talents. These talents should include industry experience, financial expertise, marketing experience, start-up experience, and technical know-how. Although the ideal board member will be familiar with the product, market, and any technologies that may be involved, the entrepreneur should strive to promote breadth on the board. Certainly, if the company is contemplating international expansion, it should consider seeking directors who have had such experience.

In assembling a successful board, one might also want to consider the age, gender, and cultural background of each director. It may be a good idea, especially in a family business, to have at least one director who is of the same generation as the likely successor to the CEO, so that when the transition takes place he or she will have a peer on the board. Many CEOs are choosing directors whose gender and culture are similar to the spectrum of employees and customers of the company. For example, in a specialty boutique selling women's clothes, it is important to have a woman on the board who understands the market.

Although outside representation is important to bring new insights to the company and maintain a truly independent board, the potential benefits of having company insiders on the board are many. Directorships provide a tangible incentive for employees, and insiders often provide invaluable expertise and perspective in a specific area of management.[4]

The entrepreneur should be wary of filling the board with people whose interests may not be aligned with the company's or to whom the company already has access. For example, the interests of the company's commercial banker may not be consistent with the best strategic planning for the company. Although it is common in a family business to have corporate counsel or the founder's personal counsel on the board, the result may be the inadvertent waiver of the attorney-client privilege. Consultants of all kinds should be considered carefully. People who already work for the CEO may not be the most appropriate people to challenge him or her.

For companies with venture capital funding, the financing agreement will usually give the investors the right to elect one or more directors. Venture capitalists tend to be very involved and effective board members. They can also be a good source of introductions to other potential board members.

Personality Mix

It is important that the board function cohesively as a group, which means that the board members' personalities must be compatible. Board members need to respect each other; no one person should so dominate the meetings as to preclude others from voicing their opinions. The board's chairperson should be alert to such an exertion of power, including his or her own. Although a diverse board is ideal, it is important to avoid creating a board that acts like a legislature, with each director focused on championing his or her own constituency.

In selecting board members, the entrepreneur should consider the need for a board that is willing to take a hands-on approach to its job. Board members should be selected to include those with practical experience and business savvy, and not just theoretical or technical expertise. At the same time, the board as a whole must understand the difference between a meddling relationship with the company's management and a healthy one. The goal is to have a board that will be actively involved in the formulation of long-range planning, will scrutinize the budget, and will question assumptions.

THE RESPONSIBILITIES OF THE BOARD

Legally, the directors of a corporation owe two major responsibilities to a corporation and the shareholders: a duty of loyalty and a duty of care.[5]

A breach of either of these duties can lead to multimillion-dollar liability. For example, the directors of Trans Union corporation were held liable for $23.5 million ($13.5 million in excess of their directors' and officers' liability insurance) because they approved the sale of company stock at $55 a share without first informing themselves of the stock's intrinsic value, which the court decided was higher.[6]

Although shareholder suits involving privately held companies are less common than public company suits, they do occur, particularly in the context of a majority shareholder allegedly violating the rights of the minority shareholders. For example, one case involved United Savings and Loan Association, which did not have actively traded shares. The majority shareholders of the association transferred their shares to a new holding company, the United Financial Corporation. The majority shareholders continued to control the association through the holding company. The association's minority shareholders were not permitted to exchange their association shares for holding-company shares. The holding company went public and active trading commenced. In contrast, trading in the association's shares dried up. The minority shareholders of the association successfully sued the majority shareholders and the individuals who set up the holding company for breach of fiduciary duty. The transaction was not fair because the defendants had misappropriated to themselves the going-public value of the association, to the detriment of the minority shareholders.[7]

Duty of Loyalty

As a fiduciary of the corporation, a director must act in the best interest of the corporation. Personal interests, financial and professional, must be subjugated to the interests of the corporation during decision making. Directors should avoid any hint of self-dealing.

Upholding this duty of loyalty applies to decisions that concern the day-to-day operations of the company, such as executive compensation, as well as strategic decisions, such as a merger. Executive compensation should be determined by those directors with no personal interest in the decision. As well, a director must not usurp an opportunity that is in the

> **FROM THE TRENCHES**
>
> Digidyne was a venture-backed company founded in the early 1980s to produce minicomputers to emulate a line of Data General products. The founder's family owned approximately 50% of the company after the initial round of venture financing at $3.00 per share. However, the company fell on hard times. To keep Digidyne alive, the venture capitalists, who controlled the board of directors, invested in several rounds of financing at ever-lower prices per share. The prices were set by the board of directors. The lowest round was at $0.25 per share. The founder's family had the right to participate in the subsequent rounds but didn't because they did not have the money. Eventually the founder's family's interest was diluted down to approximately 2% of the company. Digidyne thereafter won a lawsuit that resulted in a favorable return to all shareholders. The founder's family then sued the venture capitalists, alleging in part that they had violated their fiduciary duty to the minority shareholders by selling themselves stock at too low a price, which had the effect of unfairly diluting the ownership interests of the original shareholders.
>
> The judge, after hearing the evidence, granted a verdict for the defendants, not permitting the case to be tried by the jury. Although there was no reported opinion, it appeared that the judge was influenced by the fact that at every round of financing, the venture capitalists had offered all shareholders the right to purchase their proportionate share (based on existing ownership percentages) of the stock being offered. Accordingly, all shareholders were treated equally, the venture capitalists did not favor themselves at the expense of the other shareholders, and no breach of fiduciary duty was found.

corporation's line of business for himself or herself without first disclosing the corporate opportunity to the other board members and obtaining the board's permission to pursue it.[8]

In determining whether a board of directors is sufficiently disinterested, a relevant factor in some jurisdictions is whether a majority of the board members are outside directors. The fact that outside directors receive directors' fees but not salaries is viewed as heightening the likelihood that the directors will not be motivated by personal interest when making decisions affecting the company.

Sometimes it is impossible to have a disinterested vote of the directors. When that happens, all the board can do is to try its best to ensure that the directors are informed and that the transaction is fair to the company and all shareholders. If there is a challenge to a transaction approved only by interested directors, the burden of proof is on them to prove that the transaction was fair.

Duty of Care

A board member must act with the level of care that a reasonably prudent person would use under similar circumstances. To that end, the board member must make a reasonable effort to make informed decisions. In most jurisdictions, the general corporation law authorizes directors to rely on reports prepared by officers of the corporation or outside experts such as investment bankers and consultants. However, passive reliance on these reports without further inquiry when the situation warrants can lead to an insufficiently informed decision.

Limitations on Liability and Indemnification As noted in chapter 5, many states, including California and Delaware, have adopted legislation that permits shareholders to amend the certificate of incorporation to limit or abolish a director's liability for a breach of duty of care, except for clear cases of willful misconduct or fraud. This can provide a partial substitute for directors' and officers' liability insurance *(D&O insurance),* which is often too costly for private companies. It is appropriate to reduce the potential liability a director faces by amending the corporate charter and entering into agreements that would provide for the advancing of legal fees should a director be sued. If it is ultimately found that indemnification is not warranted, the director would be required to reimburse the company for the monies advanced. A sample indemnity agreement is set forth in "Getting It in Writing" at the end of this chapter.

BUSINESS JUDGMENT RULE

Challenges made to the decisions of a corporation's directors are reviewed using the *business judgment rule,* which protects directors from having their business decisions second-guessed. If the directors are disinterested and informed, the business judgment rule requires the plaintiff to prove that the directors were grossly negligent or acted in bad faith before liability will attach. This high burden of proof protects directors from being liable for merely poor decisions.

The business judgment rule recognizes that all business decisions have inherent risk, and often reasonable decisions can have poor results. Protection under the business judgment rule allows those who might otherwise be deterred from serving on boards to serve without undue fear of being held personally liable for decisions made in good faith.

COMPENSATION OF BOARD MEMBERS

Directors receive both tangible and intangible compensation. A person does not usually serve on a board of directors for a private company for the monetary compensation alone, as it is normally not very large. Most directors agree to serve on boards because they enjoy the advisory process and like to keep in touch with what is going on in their industry. Successful entrepreneurs enjoy advising start-ups and sharing their experience.

Intangible Compensation for Directors

Bob Burnett, the former CEO of a large publishing company, has served on the boards of numerous companies, large and small, as well as on the boards of universities and other public institutions. He believes that most CEOs sit on other companies' boards in the hope of benefiting from the cross-fertilization of ideas, learning, and gaining personal fulfillment.

The intangible benefits of board service include the opportunity to learn, through exposure to another company's operations and experiences, strategies or techniques that may prove valuable to the director's own business. Board service provides the opportunity to work collaboratively with colleagues. There is often prestige associated with sitting on the boards of various ventures. Many directors find it satisfying to advise and contribute to a new company. Especially at the early stages, the director can significantly shape the financial and marketing strategy of the business.

Tangible Compensation for Directors

Typically, the company will pay some if not all of the expenses related to the directors' attendance at meetings, including travel and meals. It is also a good idea for the entrepreneur to compensate the directors monetarily for their time and effort. This monetary compensation is more a token of appreciation and acknowledgment than a payment to the directors for their time, which many small companies could not afford anyway.

In addition to attending the actual meetings, most effective directors spend at least half a day examining materials sent to them by the CEO to prepare for the board meeting. Also, the directors usually participate in informal discussions with the CEO for a few hours each quarter. They may also meet in committees. Assuming a schedule of quarterly meetings, board work would comprise about eight days of a director's year.[9] As a reflection of time commitment alone, board honoraria could be calculated at 2% to 3% of a CEO's annual salary.

According to one survey, most private companies pay their directors about $1,000 per meeting. If one assumes a board size of six members and a schedule of quarterly meetings, directors' fees alone would be $24,000. Adding expenses to this amount would bring the total up to about $35,000. If the company has D&O insurance, the annual cost of a board this size would be roughly $60,000 to $65,000. (For a private company, $2 million of D&O insurance should cost between $25,000 and $30,000.)

Many companies compensate directors with equity in the company, such as stock options or restricted stock grants. This form of compensation is effective because it helps to align the directors' incentives with those of the shareholders. Sometimes, directors already own shares of the company and view their involvement on the board as a way to protect their financial investment.

In the more informal advisory board setting, monetary compensation may not even be discussed. Although this approach may be appropriate initially, the entrepreneur is risking the possibility of future contention with the advisors, who may be anticipating some monetary or other compensation.

TYPE OF INFORMATION DIRECTORS NEED

Before the board meeting, the company should supply the directors with an agenda of what will be discussed at the next meeting so that the directors can prepare effectively. Included in this information packet should be some general statistics on how the company is doing so that the directors can keep abreast of the company in general and alert management to any potential problems. A sample agenda for a board meeting is shown in Exhibit 9.1.

Attorney Martin Lipton and Harvard Business School Professor Jay W. Lorsch have suggested that directors be given more information about the longer-term trends of the company. This would include not

"Well, that makes it four 'aye's' two 'nay's' and one 'hey, no problem'."

Drawing by Joe Mirachi; ©1989 the New Yorker Magazine, Inc.

EXHIBIT 9.1

Agenda

ALTAIR, INC.
BOARD MEETING
THURSDAY, MARCH 6, 1997 @ 2:00 P.M.

Agenda

I. Review of February 5 Board Minutes

II. Engineering Update

III. Executive Search

IV. FDA

- Strategy

- Time Lines

V. Business Development

- Company X

- Company Y

- University Z

VI. Financials Review

- Current Financials

- Preliminary Budget – 1998

VII. Financing Plans

- Action Items to Be Completed

- Lease Line

VIII. Patent Strategy Review

IX. Competitive Update

X. Approval of Option Grants

just information of a financial nature but also information regarding the company's competitive position and organizational health.[10] Efforts should be made to quantify the plans of the company regarding research and development, and to set goals for the future.

The types of information that directors need is presented in Exhibit 9.2, arranged by update guidelines.

EXHIBIT 9.2

Information to Be Provided to Directors

PERMANENT INFORMATION

The Vision: Core Values and Purpose of the Corporation[11]
Mission of the Corporation
Strategy of the Corporation
Certificate of Incorporation
Bylaws of the Corporation
Directors Curricula Vitae
Any Director Indemnification Agreements

INFORMATION TO BE UPDATED ANNUALLY

Current Year Budget
Top Competitors
Top 20 Customers
Distribution Channels
Top 10 Vendors
Five-/Ten-Year Balance Sheets
History of Financial Information
Any Changes in Accounting Policy
Insurance Coverage, including D&O Coverage
Employee Benefits, including Stock Options
Corporate Charitable Contributions
Organizational Chart
List of Officers, Directors, and Key Advisors
Listing of Individuals Who Own More Than 1% of Stock
Biographies of Key Executives
Summary of Contractual Obligations That Exceed One Year:
      Union Contracts
      Patents/Intellectual Property Rights
      Employment Agreements
      Customer and Supplier Agreements

EXHIBIT 9.2

Information to Be Provided to Directors (cont.)

Summary of Real Estate:
    Long-Term Leases
    Owned Properties

INFORMATION TO BE UPDATED MONTHLY

Current Results with Variance Reports Against Plan and Last Year's
(for both month and year-to-date numbers and management's current view of what they
will look like at year's end) for:
    Income Statement
    Statement of Cash Flow *
    Balance Sheet
Summary of Financial and Operating Statistics:
    Return on Investment
    Return on Assets
    Return on Sales
    Inventory Turns
    Days of Receivables
    Return on Assets
    Gross Margin
    Sales per Employee
    Other Relevant Statistics for a Particular Industry
Any Changes in Key Personnel
Any Changes in Key Competitors, Customers, and Distributors
Summary of Expected or Pending Litigation
List of Possible Negative Occurrences (Changes in Assumptions in Budget, Contracts,
etc.)

HOW TO MAKE THE MOST EFFECTIVE USE OF THE BOARD

It is widely believed that most boards do not operate at their maximum
effectiveness and, in fact, often function poorly. Management expert
Peter Drucker once called the board of directors "an impotent ceremonial
and legal fiction."[12] But although Drucker and others may express hope-
lessness at the workings of some boards, many academics and practitioners believe that the focus of criticism should be on individuals and

circumstance, rather than the inherent nature of the system. In other words, the formation of a board of directors need not automatically convert a talented group of dedicated individuals into an inefficient bureaucratic body.

So then how does one best use a board of directors? Perhaps by revisiting the most important functions of a board, one can examine and refine the board's priorities. If the board is spending considerable time on company-related activities that do not fall into one of these categories, perhaps the CEO should take a closer look at that activity and ask, How was it delegated to the board? Is it a task that could be more economically handled by management?

The Business Roundtable suggests the following relationship between the CEO and the board:

> *The relation between board and chief executive officer should be challenging yet supportive and positive. It should be at arm's length, but not adversary. The Board should stimulate management to perform at the peak of its capacity, not by carping, but by setting high standards and providing level-headed encouragement.*[13]

Although the Business Roundtable was referring to the large public corporation in this description, the suggestions are equally relevant to small, private companies. The relationship between the board and the chief executive officer can often be fraught with tension. On the one hand, the board of directors lends support to the CEO. (The CEO is most often the chairman as well, although the wisdom of this dual role has been questioned in recent years and is not usually the case in Britain.[14]) At the same time, it is the board's responsibility to oversee the CEO and ensure that his or her performance is satisfactory.

Robert Stempel, former CEO and chairman of General Motors Corporation, resigned after a firestorm of speculation about his departure and very public problems with the board. Stempel explained, "I think I had good support in some quarters, but you don't run this business on the basis of 50 or 60%. Any CEO needs the full support of the board."[15]

> **FROM THE TRENCHES**
>
> A lighting-manufacturing company was in poor financial shape after competitive pressures had squeezed its margins. It misjudged the market, requiring it to incur large inventory write-downs. The best solution was to consolidate its product line and lay off part of the workforce. The CEO hesitated to make dramatic changes, but the board pushed him to take the necessary steps. The measures were successful, and three years later the company was sold for a good price.
>
> The board of directors was successful in turning the company around because of the relationship the directors had with the CEO. The key directors were friends of the CEO and had worked with him at another company. Because of their relationship, the CEO respected the directors' business acumen and knew that they were acting in the company's best interest.

The board should perform an annual review of the performance of the CEO. The resulting action taken will vary with ownership. For example, the Dayton Hudson Corporation is well known for its board's annual review of the CEO because it includes a report card of scores, broken down by area. Although it is unlikely that the CEO entrepreneur will oust himself in the same manner as Stempel did in leaving General Motors, the function is the same. In all things, the CEO must remain accountable to the board.

Eugene Zuckert, an experienced senior U.S. government official who sat on numerous boards, once said,

> *In the case of boards of directors, our expectations are so extravagant with such high potential for conflict that disappointment is inevitable. For example, we sometimes say that we want a strong board that really runs the business. If pressed, we say that we don't really want the board to run the business because that's a full-time job, and we don't expect the board to operate full time or anything like it. And besides, if we had a board that was too powerful, we probably could not get the strong CEO that we needed.*[16]

However, both CEOs and boards can operate effectively, through cooperation with one another. Consultant John Carver succinctly points out that the board has only one employee, the CEO. All other employees are those of the CEO.[17] By considering the activities of the board and CEO in this light, some of the tension is resolved.

The board is charged with outlining long-term planning and the purpose, mission, and outlook for the future of the corporation. At the same time, it monitors the CEO's performance in light of the long-term strategy. If the board is indeed functioning effectively, a CEO will have a clear set of goals to work toward in the management of the company, and the freedom and autonomy to achieve these goals. In sum, the board is looking toward the future, freeing the CEO to deal with the present.

One of the most important functions of the board is to engage in strategic planning. In shorthand, John Ward has suggested that directors focus on "big picture" questions such as these:

- Is this company meeting its potential? Why or why not?
- Which is our priority, growth or profit? How do we attain this objective?
- What are we learning as an organization? How can we learn more?
- What risks are we currently taking? Do they serve our mission well?
- Are we prepared for political and economic changes that may come suddenly?
- How are we positioned for the next two decades? Can we adapt to a changing world?
- Are we responsible corporate citizens? How can we become more responsible?[18]

Putting It into Practice

During negotiations with Centaur Partners, the venture capitalists investing in WebRunner, all parties agreed that the board would consist of five directors. The stock purchase agreement specified that the holders of the Series A Preferred Stock (the investors), voting as a class, would elect two directors. The holders of the common stock (the founders) would also elect two directors, one of whom would be Alexandra. The second management director was to be chosen by a vote of the common shareholders. The fifth seat was to be filled by an independent director, preferably someone with significant experience in the computer industry. The stock purchase agreement specified that the fifth director had to be approved by both the common and the preferred shareholders, with each class holding a veto.

Alexandra's first decision was whom to select to fill the second management seat. Although she knew that she had the votes to get whomever she wanted elected, Alexandra realized that it was important to have Paul and Sheryl Eagle agree with her choice. After some thought, Alexandra decided to invite her personal attorney, Patria Stein, who was an early supporter of her concept, to serve on the board. She discussed the idea with the Eagles, who reluctantly agreed with her decision. She then called Patria, invited her to join, and upon her agreeing, welcomed her to the board.

In selecting an independent director to fill the fifth board seat, Alexandra decided to turn to Michael Woo, WebRunner's attorney, for advice. Michael explained that, if chosen carefully, the fifth director could bring several benefits to the board, including industry connections, technical expertise, years of business experience, assistance in predicting future market trends, and, most important, a different perspective from that of the other directors.

Michael pointed out that the venture capitalist directors would bring their business experience and connections to the table. Therefore, Michael suggested, the ideal fifth director should be someone who has had direct experience with an Internet business, has connections in the industry, and possesses technical expertise and sound judgment. Unfortunately, Alexandra did not know anyone who fit those criteria. Centaur Partners had suggested a person who met most of those criteria, but Alexandra

continued

continued

hesitated to go with their choice because he had been the CEO of a company that had been funded by the same venture capital group. She questioned the proposed director's independence and was concerned that the former CEO might side with Centaur Partners based on his prior relationship.

Alexandra asked Michael if he had any suggestions. Michael thought about it, then suggested Elizabeth Khanna, the head of a research team that had written an important protocol for the Internet. Elizabeth had shrewdly persuaded some of the biggest players in the computer industry to adopt her protocol, and within months, it had become the standard in the field. Elizabeth subsequently left the Fortune 500 company for whom she had worked to start her own company. Elizabeth's new business was selling data compression software for content providers on the Web. Michael said that his firm had been involved in the initial incorporation of Elizabeth's venture but was no longer active in it. Alexandra thought about Michael's suggestion and decided to set up a meeting with Elizabeth.

Before meeting Elizabeth, Alexandra wanted to finalize with Michael the compensation that the directors would receive for their service. Michael suggested, and Alexandra agreed, that nonemployee directors who were not affiliated with Centaur Partners should receive stock options for each year of service and be paid $500 for each board meeting attended. In addition, the company would purchase a D&O liability insurance policy with $1 million of coverage. WebRunner's charter already limited directors' liability and provided mandatory indemnification and advancement of expenses to the maximum extent the law allowed.

Alexandra then met with Elizabeth, whom she liked right away. Elizabeth was friendly but not afraid to speak her mind. Alexandra realized that Elizabeth's prior and current experience uniquely positioned her to predict the direction of the Internet industry. In addition, Elizabeth's contacts in the industry, particularly with the larger players, would be invaluable. Alexandra told Elizabeth that the venture capitalists had to approve the fifth director. Alexandra then explained the directors' compensation structure and asked Elizabeth if she would be willing to serve as a director. Elizabeth said she would be honored.

continued

continued

Immediately after the meeting, Alexandra called Centaur Partners. The partners at Centaur had also heard good things about Elizabeth from the venture capitalists that had funded her start-up, and they quickly agreed to the selection. Alexandra consulted with the Eagles, who concurred, and then called Elizabeth with the good news.

Having filled the board, Alexandra turned her attention to her next project—negotiating and signing the leases, licenses, and other contracts that WebRunner needed to gear up its operations.

GETTING IT IN WRITING

SAMPLE INDEMNITY AGREEMENT

THIS AGREEMENT is made and entered into as of January 31, 1997 by and between [COMPANY X], a Delaware corporation (the "Corporation"), and [OFFICER] ("Agent").

RECITALS

WHEREAS, Agent performs a valuable service to the Corporation in the capacity as Vice President, [FINANCE] of the Corporation;

WHEREAS, the stockholders of the Corporation have adopted bylaws (the "Bylaws") providing for the indemnification of the directors, officers, employees, and other agents of the Corporation, including persons serving at the request of the Corporation in such capacities with other corporations or enterprises, as authorized by the Delaware General Corporation Law, as amended (the "Code");

WHEREAS, the Bylaws and the Code, by their nonexclusive nature, permit contracts between the Corporation and its agents, officers, employees, and other agents with respect to indemnification of such persons; and

WHEREAS, in order to induce Agent to continue to serve as Vice President, [FINANCE] of the Corporation, the Corporation has determined and agreed to enter into this Agreement with Agent;

NOW, THEREFORE, in consideration of Agent's continued service as Vice President, [FINANCE] of the Corporation after the date hereof, the parties hereto agree as follows:

AGREEMENT

1.   **Services to the Corporation.** Agent will serve, at the will of the Corporation or under separate contract, if any such contract exists, as Vice President, [FINANCE] of the Corporation or as a director, officer, or other fiduciary of an affiliate of the Corporation faithfully and to the best of Agent's ability so long as Agent is duly elected and qualified in accordance with the provisions of the Bylaws or other applicable charter documents of the Corporation or such affiliate; provided, however, that Agent may at any time and for any reason resign from such position (subject to any contractual

continued

continued

obligation that Agent may have assumed apart from this Agreement) and that the Corporation or any affiliate shall have no obligation under this Agreement to continue Agent in any such position.

2.   **Indemnity of Agent.** The Corporation hereby agrees to hold harmless and indemnify Agent to the fullest extent authorized or permitted by the provisions of the Bylaws and the Code, as the same may be amended from time to time (but, only to the extent that such amendment permits the Corporation to provide broader indemnification rights than the Bylaws or the Code permitted prior to adoption of such amendment).

3.   **Additional Indemnity.** In addition to and not in limitation of the indemnification otherwise provided for herein, and subject only to the exclusions set forth in Section 4 hereof, the Corporation hereby further agrees to hold harmless and indemnify Agent:

(a) against any and all expenses (including attorneys' fees), witness fees, damages, judgments, fines and amounts paid in settlement, and any other amounts that Agent becomes legally obligated to pay because of any claim or claims made against or by Agent in connection with any threatened, pending, or completed action, suit, or proceeding, whether civil, criminal, arbitrational, administrative, or investigative (including an action by or in the right of the Corporation) to which Agent is, was, or at any time becomes a party, or is threatened to be made a party, by reason of the fact that Agent is, was, or at any time becomes a director, officer, employee, or other agent of Corporation, or is or was serving or at any time serves at the request of the Corporation as a director, officer, employee, or other agent of another corporation, partnership, joint venture, trust, employee benefit plan, or other enterprise; and

(b) otherwise to the fullest extent as may be provided to Agent by the Corporation under the nonexclusivity provisions of the Code and Section 43 of the Bylaws.

4.   **Limitations on Additional Indemnity.** No indemnity pursuant to Section 3 hereof shall be paid by the Corporation:

(a)   on account of any claim against Agent for an accounting of profits made from the purchase or sale by Agent of securities of the Corporation pursuant to the provisions of Section 16(b) of the Securities Exchange Act of 1934 and amendments thereto or similar provisions of any federal, state, or local statutory law;

(b)   on account of Agent's conduct that was knowingly fraudulent or deliberately dishonest or that constituted willful misconduct;

continued

continued

(c) on account of Agent's conduct that constituted a breach of Agent's duty of loyalty to the Corporation or resulted in any personal profit or advantage to which Agent was not legally entitled;

(d) for which payment is actually made to Agent under a valid and collectible insurance policy or under a valid and enforceable indemnity clause, bylaw, or agreement, except in respect of any excess beyond payment under such insurance, clause, bylaw, or agreement;

(e) if indemnification is not lawful (and, in this respect, both the Corporation and Agent have been advised that the Securities and Exchange Commission believes that indemnification for liabilities arising under the federal securities laws is against public policy and is, therefore, unenforceable and that claims for indemnification should be submitted to appropriate courts for adjudication); or

(f) in connection with any proceeding (or part thereof) initiated by Agent, or any proceeding by Agent against the Corporation or its directors, officers, employees, or other agents, unless (i) such indemnification is expressly required to be made by law, (ii) the proceeding was authorized by the Board of Directors of the Corporation, (iii) such indemnification is provided by the Corporation, in its sole discretion, pursuant to the powers vested in the Corporation under the Code, or (iv) the proceeding is initiated pursuant to Section 9 hereof.

5.   **Continuation of Indemnity.** All agreements and obligations of the Corporation contained herein shall continue during the period Agent is a director, officer, employee, or other agent of the Corporation (or is or was serving at the request of the Corporation as a director, officer, employee, or other agent of another corporation, partnership, joint venture, trust, employee benefit plan, or other enterprise) and shall continue thereafter so long as Agent shall be subject to any possible claim or threatened, pending, or completed action, suit, or proceeding, whether civil, criminal, arbitrational, administrative, or investigative, by reason of the fact that Agent was serving in the capacity referred to herein.

6.   **Partial Indemnification.** Agent shall be entitled under this Agreement to indemnification by the Corporation for a portion of the expenses (including attorneys' fees), witness fees, damages, judgments, fines and amounts paid in settlement, and any other amounts that Agent becomes legally obligated to pay in connection with any action, suit, or proceeding referred to in Section 3 hereof even if not entitled hereunder to indemnification for the total amount thereof, and the Corporation shall indemnify Agent for the portion thereof to which Agent is entitled.

continued

continued

7.   Notification and Defense of Claim. Not later than thirty (30) days after receipt by Agent of notice of the commencement of any action, suit, or proceeding, Agent will, if a claim in respect thereof is to be made against the Corporation under this Agreement, notify the Corporation of the commencement thereof; but the omission so to notify the Corporation will not relieve it from any liability which it may have to Agent otherwise than under this Agreement. With respect to any such action, suit, or proceeding as to which Agent notifies the Corporation of the commencement thereof:

(a) the Corporation will be entitled to participate therein at its own expense;

(b) except as otherwise provided below, the Corporation may, at its option and jointly with any other indemnifying party similarly notified and electing to assume such defense, assume the defense thereof, with counsel reasonably satisfactory to Agent. After notice from the Corporation to Agent of its election to assume the defense thereof, the Corporation will not be liable to Agent under this Agreement for any legal or other expenses subsequently incurred by Agent in connection with the defense thereof except for reasonable costs of investigation or otherwise as provided below. Agent shall have the right to employ separate counsel in such action, suit, or proceeding, but the fees and expenses of such counsel incurred after notice from the Corporation of its assumption of the defense thereof shall be at the expense of Agent unless (i) the employment of counsel by Agent has been authorized by the Corporation, (ii) Agent shall have reasonably concluded that there may be a conflict of interest between the Corporation and Agent in the conduct of the defense of such action, or (iii) the Corporation shall not in fact have employed counsel to assume the defense of such action, in each of which cases the fees and expenses of Agent's separate counsel shall be at the expense of the Corporation. The Corporation shall not be entitled to assume the defense of any action, suit, or proceeding brought by or on behalf of the Corporation or as to which Agent shall have made the conclusion provided for in clause (ii) above; and

(c) the Corporation shall not be liable to indemnify Agent under this Agreement for any amounts paid in settlement of any action or claim effected without the Corporation's written consent, which shall not be unreasonably withheld. The Corporation shall be permitted to settle any action except that it shall not settle any action or claim in any manner which would impose any penalty or limitation on Agent without Agent's written consent, which may be given or withheld in Agent's sole discretion.

continued

continued

8.   Expenses. The Corporation shall advance, prior to the final disposition of any proceeding, promptly following request therefor, all expenses incurred by Agent in connection with such proceeding upon receipt of an undertaking by or on behalf of Agent to repay said amounts if it shall be determined ultimately that Agent is not entitled to be indemnified under the provisions of this Agreement, the Bylaws, the Code or otherwise.

9.   Enforcement. Any right to indemnification or advances granted by this Agreement to Agent shall be enforceable by or on behalf of Agent in any court of competent jurisdiction if (i) the claim for indemnification or advances is denied, in whole or in part, or (ii) no disposition of such claim is made within ninety (90) days of request therefor. Agent, in such enforcement action, if successful in whole or in part, shall be entitled to be paid also the expense of prosecuting Agent's claim. It shall be a defense to any action for which a claim for indemnification is made under Section 3 hereof (other than an action brought to enforce a claim for expenses pursuant to Section 8 hereof, provided that the required undertaking has been tendered to the Corporation) that Agent is not entitled to indemnification because of the limitations set forth in Section 4 hereof. Neither the failure of the Corporation (including its Board of Directors or its shareholders) to have made a determination prior to the commencement of such enforcement action that indemnification of Agent is proper in the circumstances nor an actual determination by the Corporation (including its Board of Directors or its shareholders) that such indemnification is improper shall be a defense to the action or create a presumption that Agent is not entitled to indemnification under this Agreement or otherwise.

10.   Subrogation. In the event of payment under this Agreement, the Corporation shall be subrogated to the extent of such payment to all of the rights of recovery of Agent, who shall execute all documents required and shall do all acts that may be necessary to secure such rights and to enable the Corporation effectively to bring suit to enforce such rights.

11.   Nonexclusivity of Rights. The rights conferred on Agent by this Agreement shall not be exclusive of any other right which Agent may have or hereafter acquire under any statute, provision of the Corporation's Certificate of Incorporation or Bylaws, agreement, vote of shareholders or directors, or otherwise, both as to action in Agent's official capacity and as to action in another capacity while holding office.

12.   Survival of Rights.

(a) The rights conferred on Agent by this Agreement shall continue after Agent has ceased to be a director, officer, employee, or other agent of the

continued

continued

Corporation or to serve at the request of the Corporation as a director, officer, employee, or other agent of another corporation, partnership, joint venture, trust, employee benefit plan, or other enterprise and shall inure to the benefit of Agent's heirs, executors, and administrators.

(b) The Corporation shall require any successor (whether direct or indirect, by purchase, merger, consolidation, or otherwise) to all or substantially all of the business or assets of the Corporation, expressly to assume and agree to perform this Agreement in the same manner and to the same extent that the Corporation would be required to perform if no such succession had taken place.

13.   **Separability.** Each of the provisions of this Agreement is a separate and distinct agreement and independent of the others, so that if any provision hereof shall be held to be invalid for any reason, such invalidity or unenforceability shall not affect the validity or enforceability of the other provisions hereof. Furthermore, if this Agreement shall be invalidated in its entirety on any ground, then the Corporation shall nevertheless indemnify Agent to the fullest extent provided by the Bylaws, the Code, or any other applicable law.

14.   **Governing Law.** This Agreement shall be interpreted and enforced in accordance with the laws of the State of Delaware.

15.   **Amendment and Termination**. No amendment, modification, termination, or cancellation of this Agreement shall be effective unless in writing signed by both parties hereto.

16.   **Identical Counterparts.** This Agreement may be executed in one or more counterparts, each of which shall for all purposes be deemed to be an original but all of which together shall constitute but one and the same Agreement. Only one such counterpart need be produced to evidence the existence of this Agreement.

17.   **Headings.** The headings of the sections of this Agreement are inserted for convenience only and shall not be deemed to constitute part of this Agreement or to affect the construction hereof.

18.   **Notices.** All notices, requests, demands, and other communications hereunder shall be in writing and shall be deemed to have been duly given (i) upon delivery if delivered by hand to the party to whom such communication was directed or (ii) upon the third business day after the date on which such communication was mailed if mailed by certified or registered mail with postage prepaid:

continued

continued

(a) If to Agent, at the address indicated on the signature page hereof.

(b) If to the Corporation, to

[COMPANY X]

_____

_____

or to such other address as may have been furnished to Agent by the Corporation.

IN WITNESS WHEREOF, the parties hereto have executed this Indemnity Agreement on and as of the day and year first above written.

[COMPANY X]

By: _____

Title: _____

AGENT

_____

(Signature)

Print Name and Address of Agent:

_____

_____

_____

NOTES

1. This chapter is based on an unpublished manuscript entitled "Effective Boards of Directors" by William C. Lazier, Constance E. Bagley, and Christy A. Haubegger. Professor Lazier is the Nancy and Charles Munger Professor of Business at Stanford Law School. He received his A.B. from Grinnell College and his M.B.A. from Stanford University. He is a certified public accountant. Ms. Haubegger is President of Latina Publications, L.L.C., publishers of *Latina* magazine. She received her B.A. from the University of Texas (Austin) and her J.D. from Stanford Law School, where she was a senior editor of the *Stanford Law Review*. Copyright ©1996 by William C. Lazier. *Used by permission.*

2. John L. Ward, *Creating Effective Boards for Private Enterprises* (San Francisco, Calif.: Jossey-Bass, 1991), at 4.

3. *Quoted in* Robert Stobaugh, "Voices of Experience: Part One—How Boards Add Value in Small Companies," *Director's Monthly*, Feb. 1996, at 3.

4. *See* Myles L. Mace, *Directors: Myth and Reality* (Boston, Mass.: Harvard Graduate School of Business Administration, Division of Research, 1986), at 112–15.

5. Directors' duties are discussed in more detail in Constance E. Bagley, *Managers and the Legal Environment: Strategies for the 21st Century,* 2nd ed. (St. Paul, Minn.: West, 1995), at 672–74.

6. *Smith v. Van Gorkom,* 488 A.2d 858 (Del. 1985).

7. *Jones v. H.F. Ahmanson & Co.,* 460 P.2d 464 (Cal. 1969).

8. *See* Bagley, *supra* note 5, at 694–95.

9. J. L. Ward and J. L. Handy, "Survey of Board Practices," 1 *Family Business Review* 289–308 (1988).

10. *See* Martin Lipton and Jay Lorsch, "A Modest Proposal for Improved Corporate Governance," 48 *Business Lawyer* 59, 71 (1992).

11. For a complete and informative discussion of vision, core values, purpose, mission, and strategy for companies, *see* James C. Collins and William C. Lazier, *Beyond Entrepreneurship: Turning Your Business into an Enduring Great Company* (Englewood Cliffs, N.J.: Prentice Hall, 1992).

12. Peter Drucker, *in* Charles A. Anderson and Robert N. Anthony, *The New Corporate Directors* (New York: John Wiley & Sons, 1986), at 1.

13. The Business Roundtable, *The Role and Composition of the Board of Directors of the Large Publicly Owned Corporation* (New York: Business Roundtable, 1978).

14. For a recent article advocating a split between the CEO and chairman roles or the appointment of a lead director, *see* Constance E. Bagley and Richard H. Koppes, "Leader of the Pack: A Proposal for Disclosure of Board Leadership Structure," forthcoming in volume 34 of the *San Diego Law Review* in May 1997.

15. "Ex-GM Chairman Fires Back," *Chicago Tribune,* Dec. 3, 1992, at 1.

16. Eugene Zuckert, *in* Anderson and Anthony, *supra* note 12, at 2.

17. John Carver, *Boards That Make a Difference* (San Francisco, Calif.: Jossey-Bass, 1990).

18. Ward, *supra* note 2.

IO

Contracts

A *contract* is a legally enforceable promise. Without contract law, entrepreneurs would find themselves filling orders and merely hoping to get paid for them. Banks would not lend them money because their promise to repay would not be enforceable. Investors would be reluctant to invest without an enforceable stock purchase agreement. An entrepreneur might find that the storefront on which he or she made a deposit is occupied by a new tenant who is an old friend of the landlord. An understanding of the principles of contract law permits the entrepreneur to read intelligently the agreements drafted by others, and, in some cases, to create the first drafts of his or her own agreements.

The strength of contract law lies in carefully drafted contracts. By using clear, specific language to state the understandings of the parties, the parties are often able to avoid misunderstandings later. But precise contracts do not come without costs. An entrepreneur must balance the time and expense of having a lawyer draft or review an agreement against the costs of litigating the problems that can stem from a poorly drafted contract and the value of the benefits that might not be attained if the contract does not accurately reflect the entrepreneur's needs.

This chapter first explains some of the basic concepts of contract law, including the three elements necessary to form a contract: offer, acceptance, and consideration. Next, the chapter deals with the different ways to form a contract. Contracts can be written, oral, or implied. Although most contracts are enforceable even if they are not in writing, the statute of frauds requires certain types of contracts to be in writing to be enforceable.

An *implied contract* is a contract that is not explicitly articulated and is held to exist based on certain circumstances or on the conduct of the parties. An entrepreneur is most likely to encounter an implied contract in connection with employees who argue that they were promised that they would not be terminated without cause. Implied employment contracts are discussed in chapter 13.

Included in this chapter is an explanation of the remedies that may be available if a contract is breached. Remedies can be monetary, and in situations in which money may not be adequate, a court might order someone to do what that person agreed to do under the contract (i.e., order specific performance).

The chapter concludes with a description of four types of contracts the entrepreneur is likely to see and their special characteristics: leases, contracts for the purchase of real property, loan agreements, and contracts for the sale or acquisition of a business. Employment agreements are discussed in chapter 13 and licensing agreements are discussed in chapter 14.

The Main Principles of Contract Law

There are two sources of contract law: common law and the Uniform Commercial Code (UCC). Most contracts, such as those involving the rendering of services or the purchase of real estate, are governed by common law, rather than by statute. Common law is law developed by judges in court cases. The UCC is a body of statutes, enacted in some form in every state, designed to codify certain aspects of the common law applicable to commercial contracts and to release those engaging in commercial transactions from some of the requirements of the common law. Article 2 of the UCC governs the sale of goods, such as computers, automobiles, and sacks of flour.

Unless otherwise specified, the principles of contract law presented in this chapter are generally accepted common-law principles. Note, however, that each individual state has its own governing body of law that will be used in determining whether a contract existed, and, if so, what the terms were, whether a breach occurred, and what remedies are available.

A written contract will often include a *choice-of-law provision*, which specifies which state's law is to govern the contract. In the absence of such a provision, the governing law will be the law of the state that has the strongest relationship with the substance of the contract and the parties and the greatest governmental interest in having its law apply.

Elements of a Contract

For a contract to exist there must be (1) an offer, (2) acceptance, and (3) consideration. An *offer* is a statement by a person (the *offeror*) that indicates a willingness to enter into a bargain on the terms stated. *Acceptance* occurs when the person to whom the offer was addressed (the *offeree*) indicates a willingness to accept the offeror's proposed bargain. *Consideration* is anything of value that is exchanged by the parties. It can be money, property, a promise to do something a person is not otherwise legally required to do, or a promise to refrain from doing something a person would otherwise be legally entitled to do.

For example, assume Angela owns a software consulting company. Zany, a friend who is starting her own travel business, asks Angela to design a software package to keep track of clients for her. Angela (the offeror) says she would be willing to design the software for $2,000. Zany (the offeree), familiar with the high quality of Angela's work, immediately agrees to pay her $2,000 for the software. The agreement, casual though it may seem, incorporates all the basic requirements of a contract: (1) an offer to design the software for a certain price, (2) acceptance, which includes a promise to pay for the work done, and (3) consideration—the exchange of promises by each party to contribute something of value, one to design the software and the other to pay. The acceptance must be the mirror image of what is being offered; otherwise, there is no meeting of the minds.

If the offeror proposes that something be done, but the offeree does not accept the proposal, then there is no contract. For example, in one case, a person with insurance requested his insurance agent to increase the coverage limits on his existing policies. The agent, who had no authority to bind the insurers, wrote the insurers, asking whether they would be willing to increase coverage in the specified amounts. He received no answer. Because there was no express or implied acceptance by the insurance companies of the insured's offer to buy increased coverage, the court found that there was no meeting of the minds between the insured and the insurer, and thus no additional coverage.[1]

Although the Uniform Commercial Code's requirements of offer, acceptance, and consideration parallel the common-law requirements, the code is more liberal in some respects. For example, the UCC presumes the existence of a contract if the parties act as if there is one, such as when a seller has shipped goods and the buyer has paid for them. To determine the exact terms of the contract, a court will examine whatever writings existed between the parties, identify the provisions on which the writings agree, and fill in the rest of the terms based on the circumstances, industry practice, and certain rules set forth in article 2 (called *gap fillers*).

Unless specifically agreed on, an offer is usually considered open for acceptance for a reasonable time, unless it is revoked or becomes void. What is considered reasonable depends on the circumstances and practices in the industry. If the offeree waits beyond a reasonable time to accept an offer, no contract will result. To keep an offer open for a longer length of time, parties can enter into a separate agreement, called an *option contract*, that requires the offeree to pay something to the offeror for the privilege of having the offer left open. Option contracts are often used when real estate or businesses are sold. Without a separate option contract, the offer would no longer stand if the offeror revoked it before the offeree had accepted or relied upon it. The UCC permits merchants to enter into enforceable option contracts for the sale of goods without the payment of consideration. However, the option cannot be in effect for more than three months.

Counteroffer

If the offeree does not accept the terms specified in the offer, but instead offers different terms, that would be a *counteroffer*, not an acceptance. No contract is formed unless the initial offeror accepts the different terms proposed by the offeree. In other words, the offer and acceptance must be

---

FROM THE TRENCHES

Irwin Schiff, a tax protester, appeared on the CBS News program *Nightwatch* in 1983. Schiff offered a $100,000 reward to anyone calling the show who could cite a section of the Internal Revenue Code that required an individual to file a tax return. No one called in with the code section during the show, but the next morning CBS replayed a two-minute segment which included Schiff's $100,000 reward offer. John Newman then called CBS and cited the relevant code provisions; he also sent a letter to CBS repeating the citations. Schiff refused to pay the $100,000 reward, and Newman filed suit for breach of contract.

   The court ruled that Schiff's statement that he would pay a $100,000 reward constituted a valid offer, and that if anyone had called in during the original broadcast with the correct code sections, then a contract would have been formed and Schiff would have been obligated to pay the reward. However, the court held that Schiff's offer had expired at the end of the *Nightwatch* show and that the morning newscast's rebroadcast of the segment did not renew or extend the offer. Therefore, although there was an offer, there was no acceptance while the offer was open, and thus no contract was formed.

Source: Newman v. Schiff, 778 F.2d 460 (8th Cir. 1985).

---

mirror images of each other. A counteroffer extinguishes the original offer, so if the counteroffer is rejected, the person making the counteroffer cannot go back and accept the initial offer. Many business negotiations involve several rounds of counteroffers before a contract is formed.

The UCC is not as strict as the common law. Under the UCC, the offer and acceptance do not have to be mirror images of each other. If an offer to sell goods under certain terms is accepted by the buyer with a minor modification in the contract terms, a contract has been formed, even though the offer and acceptance are not mirror images of each other. Examples of minor modifications include a change in the delivery date, a shifting of responsibility for insuring merchandise during shipping, or a small change in price or quantity.

Whether the modifications become part of the contract depends on whether both of the parties to the agreement are merchants. A *merchant* is a person in the business of selling goods of the type involved in the transaction. If one or more parties is not a merchant, the modifications are not considered part of the contract unless they are expressly approved by both parties. That means that the contract terms are those contained in the offer unless the offeror expressly agrees to modify them. However, if both parties are merchants, the modifications are automatically considered part of the contract, unless (1) either of the parties expressly objects to them; (2) they are considered to be major alterations (e.g., the substitution of a different product); or (3) the original offer contains a clause expressly barring any such modifications. If an offeree wants to make a counteroffer under the UCC, rather than accepting the offer presented with proposed modifications, the offeree should state unambiguously that acceptance of the offer is conditional upon the offeror's assent to the modified or additional terms.

Consideration

Consideration is a legal concept that means a bargained-for exchange. This requirement is met when one party gives up something of value in exchange for the other party's giving up something of value. Value has many meanings and can include the exchange of things with monetary worth, as is found in money or property, or the exchange of things with intrinsic worth, as is found in the performing of a service or the making of a promise to do something or to refrain from doing something. Even if the value exchanged is small, there will still be consideration. Hence the adage that even a peppercorn is adequate consideration.

The relative value of the promises exchanged is irrelevant to the issue of whether a contract has been formed. For example, in our software example, had Angela offered to design the software for a fee of $10, and Zany accepted that offer, a contract would have been formed, despite the wide disparity between the value of the fee and the work done.

Any time there is a modification to the original contract, additional consideration must be provided for the modification to be enforceable. This requirement is sometimes an issue when an employer asks a current employee to sign and agree to be bound by a personnel manual that provides that the employee's employment is at-will and can be terminated by the employer at any time, with or without cause. If the employer had previously made representations or given assurances giving rise to an implied contract that the employee would not be fired absent just cause, then even if the employer later persuaded the employee to sign and agree to be bound by a new personnel manual providing for at-will employment, the new agreement would not be enforceable unless the employer gave the employee something of value—other than just continued employment—as consideration. In cases of at-will employment with no implied contract not to terminate without just cause, courts in many states have held that a promise given in exchange for continued employment is adequate consideration. But for continued employment to count as consideration, it must be for a substantial period. Although the court typically does not inquire into the adequacy of the consideration, in one case seven months was not considered a substantial period, and the covenant not to compete the employee had signed was struck down. In contrast, in a case involving a salesman employed at-will for eight years after signing a covenant not to compete, the court held that the covenant was supported by adequate consideration, as the salesman was essentially granted eight more years of employment by signing the covenant.[2]

FROM THE TRENCHES

Shortly before he died, Elvis Presley was engaged to be married to Ginger Alden. Presley offered to give Alden's mother, Jo Laverne Alden, $40,000 to pay off the mortgage on the Alden home. Presley died several months later without paying off Alden's mortgage. Presley's estate informed Alden that it would not assume the liability for her mortgage, and Alden sued to enforce Presley's promise.

The court held that Presley's promise was not supported by consideration and therefore was not binding. The court refused to apply the doctrine of promissory estoppel because Alden failed to show that her reliance on Presley's promise was reasonably justified.

Source: Alden v. Presley, 637 S.W.2d 862 (Tenn. 1982).

Illusory Promises

An *illusory promise* does not result in a contract; it occurs when one party fails to provide anything of value. In a classic example of a supplier and a distributor, a coal company agreed to sell coal to a lumber company for a certain price regardless of the amount ordered. The lumber company, in contrast, was obligated only to pay for the amount it ordered. The court found the agreement to be an illusory promise lacking consideration because the lumber company had the option to order nothing and thus had not bound itself to any promise.[3]

Had the lumber company agreed to order all of the coal it needed from the coal company, then even if it wound up needing no coal at all, there would have been adequate consideration because the lumber company would have agreed to refrain from buying coal from anyone else. A buyer's agreement to purchase all of a specified commodity it needs from a particular seller is called a *requirements contract*. A seller's agreement to sell all of its output to a particular buyer is an *output contract*.

Unilateral Contract

The examples discussed above are considered *bilateral contracts*, meaning that in each case one promise is exchanged for another promise. Another, equally valid, type of contract is the *unilateral contract*, in which a promise is exchanged for the performance of a certain act. Acceptance of a unilateral contract takes place when one party has completed the required act.

To illustrate, a pharmaceuticals company offered to provide a one-year free supply of an experimental drug to patients who participated in the drug's clinical trials, which included submission to intrusive and necessarily uncomfortable testing for one year. Patients were free to drop out of the study before the end of the trials, but if they did so, they were not eligible to receive the one-year posttrial free supply. When the patients who stayed the course through the end of the trials requested their free supply, the pharmaceuticals company refused to provide it, arguing that the patients had given no consideration as they could have voluntarily dropped out of the study. The court disagreed, holding that this was a classic example of a unilateral contract, which the patients accepted when they remained in the study until the end.[4]

WRITTEN CONTRACTS VERSUS ORAL CONTRACTS

Most types of contracts are enforceable even if they are oral and not set forth in writing. The law that requires a writing for certain types of contracts—called the statute of frauds—is discussed below.

Oral Contracts and the Statute of Frauds

Sometimes an entrepreneur will not want to spend the time or money needed to reduce a deal to writing, and will instead decide to rely on an oral exchange of promises. Before moving ahead with an oral contract, it is important to make sure that it will be enforceable in a court of law. Individual states have adopted a type of legislation—called a *statute of frauds*—that requires parties to put certain types of contracts in writing. Although the exact requirements vary from state to state, the following types of business contracts are usually subject to the statute: (1) contracts that cannot be performed within one year; (2) contracts that involve the transfer of interests in real property; (3) contracts by which someone agrees to assume another person's debt; (4) prenuptial contracts whereby a man and woman who are going to be married agree how assets are to be allocated if they divorce; and (5) contracts for the sale of goods for $500 or more (which are governed by the UCC's statute of frauds). Failure to put a contract in writing in accordance with the statute will not invalidate the contract made but will render it unenforceable in court if the other party asserts that the contract should have been in writing.

Even if a contract does not by its terms make it clear that it cannot be performed in one year, a court may still hold that the contract is subject to the statute of frauds. For example, in a case that involved a partnership agreement to purchase and develop properties throughout the country, the court held that because the agreement was not intended to be performed within a year, it was subject to the statute of frauds. In deciding that the contract would take longer than a year to complete, the court looked at the intent of the parties, as inferred from surrounding circumstances and the goal of the contract.[5] To avoid the possibility of having an agreement ruled unenforceable, the parties should put in writing any contract that might take more than a year to perform.

The writing must be signed by the party against whom enforcement is sought. For example, a purchase order between a steel manufacturer and an intermediary, which was not signed by the manufacturer, and a separate purchase order between the intermediary and the final purchaser, did not together constitute a writing sufficient to evidence a contract between the manufacturer and the purchaser under the UCC statute of frauds. The manufacturer could get out of the contract because the manufacturer never signed anything.[6]

The agreement does not have to be very formal to satisfy the requirements of the statute of frauds. In general, all that is required is a signed writing setting forth the essential terms, as determined from the overall context of the agreement. Initialed notes on the back of an envelope or on a napkin will suffice.

The UCC, whose statute of frauds governs contracts for the sale of goods over $500, requires only three elements to be in writing: a *statement* recognizing that an agreement exists, the *signature* of the party against whom enforcement is sought, and an indication of the *quantity of goods* being sold. If the contract is between merchants, then the contract can still be enforced against the party who has not signed it if the other party sent a written confirmation that the first party did not respond to within ten days. If a party goes to court to enforce a contract that specifies quantity but has other terms missing, the court will fill in the rest of the terms (including price) based on general tradition and practice within the particular industry.

For example, in a suit between a vending machine manufacturer and a buyer, the court held that a series of nine documents (including internal correspondence, minutes from a board meeting, and purchase orders) supported the manufacturer's claim that he had a contract to sell 15,260 vending machines and satisfied the statute of frauds. The court stated that a writing could be deemed "signed" if it bore any authentication that identified the party to be charged.[7]

The drafters of the UCC have proposed amendments to article 2 to facilitate commerce in cyberspace. The amendments would allow parties to meet the writing requirements by exchanging electronic messages on the Internet with a verifiable digital signature.

ADVANTAGES OF PUTTING A CONTRACT IN WRITING

Even if the oral contract in question does not come within the statute of frauds, the entrepreneur should still be wary. Oral agreements, by their nature, are difficult to enforce. For this reason, even if a writing is not legally required, it is advantageous to put the terms of the deal on paper. Putting a contract in writing helps prevent later misunderstandings by forcing the parties to articulate their intentions and desires. A clearly drafted contract provides a written record of the terms agreed to and is more reliable evidence of the parties' intentions than the faded memories of what was said. The act of signing an agreement reinforces the fact that a contract gives rise to legal rights and duties. The drafting process sometimes identifies misunderstandings or unclear points that might otherwise come to the surface only in the event of a later dispute that could lead to an expensive lawsuit.

In situations in which negotiations have been drawn out or are complicated, the parties can avoid ambiguity about what the parties finally agreed to by including a clause to the effect that "this agreement constitutes the entire agreement of the parties and supersedes all prior and contemporaneous agreements, representations, and understandings of the parties." This is called an *integration* or *merger clause*. The parties can prevent ambiguities with regard to discussions taking place after the contract has been signed simply by providing that "no supplement, modification, or amendment of this agreement shall be binding unless executed in writing by both parties."

Despite the advantages of having a written contract that clearly sets forth the parties' respective rights and obligations, many businesspersons

> **FROM THE TRENCHES**
>
> Twenty-seven years after the release of the 1969 hippie-biker film *Easy Rider* (which made famous the Steppenwolf song *Born to Be Wild*, played while a group of long hairs on motorcycles roared side by side cross-country), the two lead actors, Dennis Hopper and Peter Fonda, were involved in a lawsuit over how the profits should be divided and who should get credit for creating the now-classic film. In keeping with the hippie themes of free love and drugs, the actors never wrote down the terms of their profit-sharing agreement. While Peter Fonda told *The Wall Street Journal* that he has "an extraordinarily accurate memory," the lawsuit could have been avoided entirely if Hopper and Fonda had put down on paper the agreed-upon split and credits.
>
> *Source: "Hey, Man, See You in Court: 'Easy Rider' Gets a New Epilogue," The Wall Street Journal, Feb. 9, 1996, at A1.*

find themselves relying on a handshake or signing contracts that are riddled with ambiguities or otherwise do not protect their interests. Many entrepreneurs, after working cooperatively with another party to reach a mutually advantageous agreement, find it awkward and sometimes even impolite to ask the other party to put it in writing. Ironically, this seemingly cooperative approach to doing business may actually hinder the formation of a clearly understood agreement between the parties. Studies have shown that people tend to be unrealistically optimistic about the future of their personal relationships. Because the parties believe it is unlikely that misunderstandings will arise, they spend little time addressing them in the process of drafting a carefully worded contract. Also, many businesspersons tend to overestimate the strength of memory. During negotiations, some issues may seem so obvious that one does not even think to include them in the contract. However, as time passes and memories fade, the parties to the contract may find themselves differing as to what they thought they had originally agreed on.

A careful entrepreneur will be wary of rushing to sign an incomplete or poorly worded contract. The pressure of a deadline is often used as a stratagem by the other party when negotiating a contract. The entrepreneur may feel compelled to sign a contract that he or she does not

---

FROM THE TRENCHES

Two struggling semiconductor capital equipment manufacturers merged in search of synergy. Company A, an established but somewhat anemic venture-backed firm, was looking for a chief executive officer. Company B, a start-up, had a CEO and potential new technology but no access to venture capital. The merger agreement referred to and incorporated by reference a business plan for the merged company, created by Company B's CEO. The business plan stated the intention of the merged company to raise "up to $1 million, a large portion of which has been committed by the current venture capital investor." When the merged company was unable to attract new financing or to build its new product, it failed. The Company B investors then sued the venture backers of Company A for breach of contract and fraud.

The lawsuit resulted in a six-week jury trial. After two days of deliberation, the jury found the venture capitalists not liable. The jury concluded that the business plan and merger documents did not constitute an enforceable promise to supply funding but rather signaled an intent to assist the merged company in obtaining financing—an intent that was frustrated by problems of the merged company's own making.

Comment: Although the venture capitalists were vindicated, the case highlights the importance of communicating funding expectations in clear and unambiguous language, and ensuring that the expectations of all parties to a deal are clearly understood and put in writing.

---

understand or with which he or she may not be in complete agreement. It is important to resist these pressures.

WRITTEN CONTRACTS: THE FORM AND TERMS TO INCLUDE

Written contracts do not need to be in a particular form or use stylized language such as "party of the first part." All that is required is a writing containing information such as the identities of the parties, the subject matter of the agreement, and the basic (what is *basic* depends on the particular situation) terms and conditions, signed by all parties.

Contractual wording is very literal. "All" means everything; "shall" means it must be done; and "may" means it is permitted but not required.

The term "and/or" should be avoided, as it tends to be ambiguous. "And" means that both elements must be satisfied, whereas "or" means that satisfying either element is sufficient.

The contract should set forth all aspects of the relationship or agreement that the entrepreneur believes are truly important to the needs of the business. For example, a new cafe owner preparing to negotiate a lease in a strip mall might decide that having adequate parking for her customers and a restriction on other cafes in the strip mall are considerations worth paying a higher rent to obtain. By carefully considering her priorities in advance, she minimizes the chances that something important will be excluded in the final agreement.

The Form

Letters of Agreement   One format often used to organize a simple agreement between parties is the *letter of agreement.* Typically, one of the parties drafts this letter. The drafter first includes a statement to the effect that the letter constitutes a contract between the parties and will legally bind them, then lists all of the important terms and conditions of the agreement. The end of the letter invites the recipient to indicate his or her approval of the terms by signing his or her name, inserting the date after the word "Accepted" typed at the bottom of the page, and returning the letter to the drafter. Official acceptance takes place when the letter is mailed or otherwise sent by the offeree to the drafter-offeror.

Standard Form Contracts   Another commonly used format is a generic printed form (a *standard form contract*). Standard form contracts can be used for many business purposes. If the entrepreneur decides to use one, he or she should obtain an industry-specific sample. Because it will be used frequently, the entrepreneur should have an attorney review it. Even with a preprinted contract, many of the terms and conditions remain negotiable. The wise entrepreneur will assess his or her needs and rank them, rather than settling for a cursory review of a preprinted contract. Any changes, modifications, additions, and deletions (which can be handwritten in the margin, if necessary) should be signed or initialed and dated by both parties, so that neither party can later claim that one party made the changes without the assent of the other party.

The law generally holds those entering contractual relationships responsible for reading and understanding the contracts they sign. This is known as the *duty to read*. Nevertheless, people sometimes claim that they should not be bound by the promises they made in a contract because they were not aware of what they signed. Small print or a crowded format can lend credence to this claim. Besides writing clearly and using a readable type size, the entrepreneur can take other steps to counter this problem. For example, if some of the terms and conditions are printed on the reverse side of the page, the drafter can state in bold letters: "This contract is subject to terms and conditions on the reverse side hereof." Leaving a blank for the signer's initials next to certain terms or conditions can also help to prove later that the signer was aware of those terms.

A good standard form contract enhances rather than obscures the understanding between the parties. Therefore, the drafter should write clearly and concisely, using simple language and short sentences.

Attachments Attachments may also be used to supplement an agreement. Attachments are ideal when the additional terms are too extensive to note in the margins of the agreement. For example, Kay, a caterer, uses a general form contract for her customers that contains not only printed terms and conditions but blank spaces in which she can fill in such information as the quantity of hors d'oeuvres required, the date of the function, and the price. Additional issues not covered in the form contract can be addressed in a simple attachment that both parties sign and date at the same time they sign the main document. To ensure that the attachment is treated as part of the contractual agreement (in other words, that the meeting of the minds incorporates both documents), the drafter should name the attachment (e.g., "Attachment A") and include a clause in the main contract clearly stating that the main agreement and the named attachment are incorporated into one contract.

Addenda Like attachments, *addenda* provide a way for the parties to modify the main agreement. However, while attachments are used at the time the main contract is approved by both parties, addenda are used *after* the main contract has been approved by both parties. Typically, the parties note changes to an already approved contract by crossing out words and writing in new ones, then initialing the revisions. However, if the modifications are extensive, an addendum may be drawn up instead.

Each addendum should include an explicit reference to the main contract. For example, "This is an addendum to the contract dated May 17, 1997, between Karen Wells and Juliet Tyler for the purchase of . . . ." The addendum should also spell out the relevant changes and state clearly that, if the terms of the original agreement and the addendum conflict, the addendum's terms should prevail. It is also wise to note that "the parties agree to the above changes and additions to the original contract" and "in all other respects, the terms of the original contract remain in full effect."

General Contract Terms to Consider

Exactly what should be included in a written contract varies from situation to situation, but what should without question be included in any contract are certain provisions that establish the existence of a contractual relationship and verify the intent of the parties to be bound by a contract. Other provisions more specifically address the important terms of the agreement, timing, and allocation of risk.

Establishing Intent to Enter into a Contract The following items are found in almost all contracts and serve primarily to verify that a contractual relationship exists.

Existence of an Agreement/Intent of the Parties Some disputes over contractual relationships center on the question of original intent, or even the very existence of a contract. Because an arbitrator or court might later have to determine the parties' intentions, it is useful to have an explicit preamble or statement summarizing the parties' intentions (called the *recitals*) drafted at the time the parties enter into the agreement.

Identification Contracts should explicitly state the names and addresses of the parties. Corporations, partnerships, and other entities should be identified as such.

Date It is important to establish when the meeting of the minds took place. If the parties all sign the agreement on the same date and want it to be effective immediately upon signing, then the agreement should provide: "This Agreement is executed and entered into on [date]." If the parties sign on different days, then the agreement might provide that it is "made and entered into as of the later of the two dates on the signature page." If the agreement is to be effective as of a date other than the date it is signed, then the agreement should provide: "This Agreement is executed and entered into as of [date]."

Signatures A contract that is subject to the statute of frauds can be enforced only against the party or parties who have signed it.

Sole proprietors may sign on their own behalf, making them personally responsible for fulfilling the terms of the agreement. A general partner should sign on behalf of a general or limited partnership. This is done by setting forth the name of the partnership and then on a separate line writing:

By _____
[name of person signing]

Its _____
[title]

By making it clear that the contract is being entered into by the partnership, the general partner can require the other party to exhaust the partnership's assets first before going against the general partner's personal assets.

The officer of a corporation is not personally responsible for the obligations of the corporation so long as the officer makes it clear that he or she is signing only in a representative capacity. This is done by setting forth the name of the corporation and then on a separate line writing:

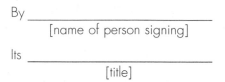

By _____
   [name of person signing]

Its _____
   [title]

Ideally, the parties should produce two identical copies of the agreement and sign both copies, so that each party may retain an original. However, duplicate photocopies, facsimiles, or photographs may be substituted for the original in court unless (1) a genuine question is raised as to the authenticity of the original, or (2) circumstances suggest that it would be unfair to admit the duplicate in place of the original. If possible, all parties should sign on the same signature page. If this is not possible (e.g., if one party is located out of town), then the agreement should expressly provide for the signing of counterparts. When using *counterparts*, each party signs a copy of the signature page, and all signature pages taken together are deemed to be one original.

Authority When a contract is entered into with an entity, such as a partnership, limited liability company, or corporation, it is important to make sure that the person who signs the agreement has the authority to do so. Normally, a general partner would have the authority to bind a partnership, as would the managing member of a limited liability company. However, in the case of an LLC, some major transactions might have to be approved by the members.

A contract with a corporation must be signed by a duly authorized officer. The president of the corporation has the authority to enter into most contracts relating to the operation of the business, but contracts for the issuance of stock must be authorized by the board of directors. Thus, an agreement granting stock options must be authorized by the board of directors. When dealing with persons besides the president, it is prudent to verify their authorization, perhaps by requiring a copy of the board of directors' resolution on the subject or the section of the corporation's bylaws that spells out the authority of different officers. Some contracts, like an agreement to sell substantially all of the corporation's assets, must be approved by both the board and the shareholders.

In situations in which goods or services are being purchased on credit through a sales representative, the seller may afford itself some flexibility by including an approval clause in the sales order specifying that the order, although signed by the sales representative, is not a valid contract until it has been approved, either by the home office or by a corporate officer above a specified level. In this way, the sales representative is free to take orders without unknowingly binding the company to an unauthorized buyer.

Special care should be used when entering into a contract with a governmental body to ensure that the contract is authorized under state or other applicable law and is signed by the proper official. In addition, it is important to determine whether the governmental entity can be sued if it breaches the contract, or if it has contractual immunity.

Terms of the Agreement The following types of provisions are the heart of the agreement and determine the parties' contractual obligations to one another.

Representations and Warranties Any key assumptions or understandings upon which the agreement rests should be explicitly stated as representations and warranties. For example, "Party A represents and warrants that the hardware when installed meets the specifications on Schedule A for use in the production of computer chips." If such a representation were not included in the contract, Party A could later claim that it was under the impression that the equipment was to be installed under less stringent specifications or for a different use.

Representations and warranties are also used to contractually guarantee that certain facts are true. For example, an investor will want assurance that the company owns all of its intellectual property and that it is not violating any other person's rights. The investors can sue for breach of contract if it later turns out that someone else—such as a prior employer of the founder or a university where the founder was a graduate student—owns key technology.

Sellers of goods should be very careful about how they represent the qualities of their products. If a seller has made a representation about the product's qualities that is then relied on by the buyer in choosing to purchase that product, the buyer can sue for breach of express warranty if the product does not live up to that representation. The wording "AS IS, WITH ALL FAULTS" should be used in an agreement for the sale of a substandard item. Warranties in connection with the sale of goods are discussed further in chapter 11.

Conditions The fulfillment of some contractual obligations may be conditioned on the occurrence of certain events, such as the approval of a loan application by a third party, or on the other party's performance of a particular obligation, such as the procurement of insurance. Normally a party's obligation to perform under a contract is conditional on the representations and warranties being true and correct in all material respects.

The only restriction on the use of conditions is that one party's obligation may not be made conditional upon some occurrence exclusively within the control of that same party. If one party to an agreement had complete control over the occurrence of a condition, it would effectively negate that party's obligation, reducing an otherwise valid contract to an illusory promise.

The condition should be stated clearly, using simple, straightforward language such as "if," "only if," "unless and until," or "provided that." For example, a stock purchase agreement will usually include language to this effect: "The investors shall have no obligation to purchase the shares and to pay the purchase price unless all conditions set forth in Section 4 are satisfied."

Logistical Considerations Such details as performance requirements, delivery and installation instructions, risk allocation, and the procurement of insurance should be discussed in advance and included in the written agreement.

Payment Terms Payment terms should specify both when and in what form payment must be made. If payment is to be made in installments, the seller can attempt to deter a buyer from missing payments by including an acceleration clause in the written agreement. An *acceleration clause* specifies that all remaining installments (and interest, if applicable) become immediately due and payable if the buyer is late in the payment of any installment. Some acceleration clauses take effect automatically upon default, but in many contracts (especially when long-term relationships are a factor), it may be preferable to make the exercise of the acceleration clause optional at the creditor's discretion.

Notice and Opportunity to Cure Especially when the evaluation of performance is subjective, it is helpful to include a provision requiring the giving of written notice of a failure to comply with the contract and some opportunity to cure the default.

Timing Issues The parties should agree in advance on such crucial questions as the duration, termination, and renewal of the contract, as well as specifying when their obligations to each other must be fulfilled.

Duration and Notice of Termination Regardless of the original intent of the parties, contracts lacking a specific duration may be construed later as terminable at-will by either party. It is better to avoid this ambiguity by including a clause stating that the contract is terminable at-will or indicating its duration.

Furthermore, a contract terminable at-will should be drafted so as to avoid providing either party with an absolute right of termination, which might cause a court to find an illusory promise and thus no contract. For example, the drafter can stipulate that a party or parties must give notice of intent to terminate the contract a set amount of time before actual termination. It is also wise to outline specific rules as to how proper notice shall be effected.

When Performance Must Be Completed Special deadlines or time requirements should be stated explicitly. For example, if *time is of the essence* (performance being completed on time is especially important), that fact should be noted in the contract. The entrepreneur may want to reserve the right to terminate the contract in the event the other party fails to perform on time. This would be appropriate, for example, if a computer manufacturer ordered a certain number of boards from a vendor in anticipation of filling an order; boards delivered a week late would be of no use to the manufacturer, who would have had to find another source.

Another method of discouraging tardiness is to build in a specific amount that one party will pay the other party if it does not perform its obligations by the deadline. In drafting such a *liquidated damages* clause, the drafter must take care not to build the wrong incentives into the contract. He or she must ensure that finishing the job safely and properly is not subordinated to finishing it on time. To realign performance with proper values such as safety and quality, the drafter may want to include a separate clause that, for example, requires a third party's approval of the completed performance before payment is due. This arrangement is often used in construction contracts. In addition, determining a proper amount to be paid as liquidated damages may be difficult. The amount should reflect the parties' best estimate of the actual damage that would result from the delay in performance. Moreover, the amount should be high enough to influence the party's behavior, but not so high as to constitute a penalty. Courts generally are unwilling to enforce penalties.

Renewability of the Contract The contract may be automatically renewable, meaning that the contract is automatically extended for a certain period unless one of the parties gives notice of its intention not to renew within a stated period of time before expiration of the contract. Or the contract may be renewable dependent on prior notice of intention to renew. Either way, the drafter should take care to leave an out, so that the contract cannot be construed as perpetual.

Addressing Risk The parties to a contract should decide what events would relieve one or more parties of their obligations under the contract. For example, the occurrence of certain natural disasters (known as *acts of God*), such as an earthquake, fire, or flood, that make performance impossible or commercially impracticable may release the parties from their contractual obligations. Similarly, unanticipated governmental action (such as an international embargo) or *force majeure* (literally translated as *superior force* but used to designate problems beyond the reasonable control of a party) may excuse the parties from performance if they make performance impossible or commercially impracticable.

Courts are very reluctant to find *commercial impracticability*. The event must have been both unforeseen and unforeseeable, and the party asserting impracticability must not have expressly or implicitly assumed the risk of the occurrence. It is not enough that performance becomes unprofitable or more costly. For example, most shipping companies that incurred substantial losses when political turmoil in the Middle East resulted in the closing of the Suez Canal in 1967, requiring them to detour around the Cape of Good Hope, were unsuccessful in nullifying the contracts entered into before the Suez Canal was closed. However, in one case, under the UCC, a tenfold to twelvefold increase in cost was considered sufficient to excuse performance. But then, in another, the court observed that it knew of no case that had found less than a 100% cost increase sufficient to find impracticability.

It is often advisable to draft an exculpatory clause that designates each of the many potentially disastrous events that could prevent the party or parties from fulfilling their obligations under the contract. For example,

> *Party A will not be liable for any loss, including, without limitation, the loss of Party B's prospective profits, resulting from events outside of Party A's control. Examples of occurrences outside of Party A's control include, but are not limited to, strikes, lockouts, fires, floods, mud slides, earthquakes, machine breakdowns, lack of shipping space, carrier delays, governmental actions, and inability to procure goods or raw materials.*

Although it may be challenging to persuade another party to accept such a wide-ranging exculpatory clause, it is worth the effort to include as many potential problems as possible. Despite the wording "but not limited to," any events that are not listed in the clause may be subjects of dispute in an action for breach of contract. Also, it should be noted that the inclusion of such a clause in the contract does not automatically release the party from liability under the circumstances listed; if a court concludes that a contingency could have been reasonably guarded against, it may decide not to excuse the party from liability for the resulting loss.

In some instances, the parties might consciously want to shift the risk of certain events occurring to one party. For example, a customer might want its supplier to insure against certain risks, such as fire, that might make delivery impossible or commercially impracticable. If this is the parties' intent, then the contract should expressly state that occurrence of the specified events shall not excuse nonperformance.

Arbitration and Mediation Despite the best intentions of both parties, misunderstandings and disputes do arise. One way to avoid the expense, tension, delay, and publicity of litigation, and the vagaries of a jury trial, is to address the issue through arbitration. In *arbitration*, the parties take their dispute to one or more persons with the power to make a final decision that binds the parties. However, unless the parties agree in advance to employ arbitration for conflicts that arise, it is likely that they will wind up in litigation in the event of a dispute. Often, once a dispute has arisen, one of the parties feels he or she has a strong case against the other party and is unwilling to concede that advantage by seeking an equitable solution through arbitration.

"I still say you never can tell which way a jury will go."

Drawing by Modell; © 1989 the New Yorker Magazine, Inc.

The American Arbitration Association (AAA) suggests inserting a clause similar to this:

Any controversy or claim arising out of or relating to this contract, or the breach thereof, shall be settled by arbitration in accordance with the Commercial Rules of the American Arbitration Association, and judgment upon the award rendered by the Arbitrator(s) may be entered in any court having jurisdiction thereof.

One may want to specify which arbitration service will be used. Some industries have special arbitration agencies that perform this service for members of their trade; some do not, forcing parties to rely instead on a private arbitration firm or a branch of the AAA itself. The parties may also wish to spell out in which jurisdiction the case should be arbitrated, and who will pay the resulting fees. If the two parties will be doing business with each other on a continual basis, the clause can be drafted to cover all their dealings.

Sometimes the parties are not willing to submit disputes to arbitration. In such cases, it is helpful to include a *mandatory mediation clause*. Such a clause requires the parties to discuss their claims with a mediator before filing a lawsuit. The mediator, who is often a lawyer, does not have the power to make a final decision. Rather, a mediator facilitates the settlement discussions and works with the parties to craft a mutually acceptable resolution. If the mediation fails to result in a binding settlement agreement, the parties are free to go to court.

The American Mediation Council, LLC (AMC), a national organization studying mediation standards and providing mediators for business disputes, suggests inserting into a contract a clause similar to this: "Any controversy or claim arising out of or relating to this agreement shall be submitted to American Mediation Council, LLC, under its Mediation Rules, before the parties resort to arbitration, litigation or some other dispute resolution procedure." The AMC Mediation Rules, which are virtually the same as those written by the Center for Public Resource Institute for Dispute Resolution, do not require the parties to use an AMC mediator.

Choice of Law and Forum The contract should specify where disputes are to be adjudicated and which jurisdiction's law is to be applied. It is almost always advantageous to require that litigation be commenced in the city and county where the entrepreneur does business. This gives the entrepreneur the home-court advantage and increases the likelihood of finding a sympathetic jury. If local law governs the contract, the entrepreneur's lawyers will not have to learn another jurisdiction's law or hire counsel in the other state. Traveling expenses are also minimized. The contract should expressly state that all parties submit to the jurisdiction of the courts in the designated locale.

Attorneys' Fees If there is no clause in the contract requiring the loser to pay the winner's attorneys' fees, then each party must pay its own. Typically a clause will be added specifying that the losing party shall pay the prevailing party's reasonable attorneys' fees and court costs.

CHECKLIST FOR CONTRACT ANALYSIS

Below is a checklist of questions to consider when drafting a contract, signing a contract, and assessing claims that a contract has been breached or that performance is excused.

- Is this contract void because it is illegal or violates public policy? A contract to do something illegal or immoral is void.
- Is this contract being entered into freely? Unlawful explicit or veiled threats to induce a party to enter an agreement (referred to as *duress*) make it unenforceable.
- Is this contract so one-sided that it would be grossly unfair to enforce it in accordance with its terms? Such a contract is *unconscionable*, meaning that it would shock the conscience of the court to enforce it. Sometimes, a contract is unconscionable because onerous terms (such as a limitation of liability or release of claims) are buried in fine print, thereby creating an element of surprise. Other times a party may be aware of the terms, but because of a lack of bargaining power, agree to

a totally unfair exchange. For example, in one case, the court refused to enforce a contract for the purchase on credit by a welfare recipient of a freezer worth $300 for a total purchase price of $1,234.80 (including time credit charges, credit life insurance, credit property insurance, and sales tax).[8]

- Has performance become impossible or commercially impracticable? If so, then nonperformance will be excused unless the event making performance impossible or impracticable was foreseeable or one party assumed the risk of its occurrence.

- Is the contract clearly worded and structured to prevent ambiguity? If a contract is worded in a way that makes it subject to different interpretations of its terms, it may be voidable by the party that would be hurt by the use of a particular interpretation. This is true only when both interpretations would be reasonable, and either both parties or neither party knew of both interpretations when they contracted with each other. However, if one (but not both) of the parties knew of the existence of differing interpretations, a court would find in favor of the party who was unaware of the ambiguity. Some courts will resolve any ambiguity by finding against the person who drafted the contract.

- Was there a mutual mistake of fact that rendered this contract voidable? To determine whether a mistake of fact calls for the undoing of the contract, courts consider three things: (1) whether the mistake had a material effect on one or both of the parties; (2) whether either party allocated the risks of such a mistake to itself; and (3) whether the party alleging mistake did so promptly after discovering it. A classic case involved a contract for the purchase of 125 bales of cotton to be brought by the seller from India to England on a ship named *Peerless*. There were, however, two ships named *Peerless* sailing out of Bombay that year. The buyer meant the one sailing in October, while the seller meant the one sailing in December. When the cotton arrived on the later ship, the buyer refused to complete the purchase. The seller then sued for breach of contract. The court found for the buyer, holding that this was a case of mutual mistake of fact so there was no meeting of the minds and thus no contract.[9]

- A *mistake of fact* occurs when the parties make a mistake about the actual facts of the transaction. In determining whether there was a mutual mistake of fact, the courts will often look at the recitals in the beginning of the agreement to determine the intent of the parties.

  Unlike a mistake of fact, a *mistake of judgment* is not grounds for undoing a contract. A mistake of judgment differs from a mistake of fact in that a mistake of judgment occurs when the parties make an erroneous assessment about some aspect of what is bargained for. For example, if Agnes buys an apartment building with the assumption that housing values in that location will soon skyrocket, but two years later prices have not risen, the contract is still valid. Agnes's mistake was in her own judgment, not in the character of the subject of the bargain, the apartment building. Similarly, a court held that a contract to sell a stone for $1 was enforceable when neither party knew at the time that the stone was in fact a diamond.[10]

  It should be noted that much of the time, the distinction between mistakes of fact and mistakes of judgment is very difficult to determine.

FROM THE TRENCHES

Spokane Computer Systems was planning to purchase a surge protector to protect its computers from damage caused by electrical surges. The employee in charge of investigating the various products found several units priced between $50 and $200. The employee also contacted Konic International Corp., whose salesman quoted a price of "fifty-six twenty." The salesman meant $5,620, but the Spokane employee thought he meant $56.20.

The discrepancy was not discovered until after the equipment was installed and the invoice was received. Spokane asked Konic to remove the equipment, but Konic refused and sued Spokane for nonpayment.

The court ruled that because both parties attributed a different meaning to the same ambiguous term "fifty-six twenty" there was no meeting of the minds and thus no valid contract was formed. The court relieved Spokane of its debt.

Source: Konic Int'l. Corp. v. Spokane Computer Servs. Inc., 708 P.2d 932 (Idaho Ct. App. 1985).

- Was there a breach of contract by one party that resulted in damages to the other party? Breaches of contract are usually not punished in and of themselves. Some substantial damage to the other party must result for a court to provide a remedy for breach of contract.
- Did the party claiming injury mitigate the damages? When a breach of contract has taken place that causes injury to one party, that party has a common-law duty to ensure that the injury does not become worse, or in some cases, to attempt to lessen the injury. If the party does not mitigate its damages, a court may order the defendant to pay only the damages that would have occurred had the plaintiff used reasonable efforts to limit the damage resulting from the defendant's breach.

EFFECT OF BANKRUPTCY

The entrepreneur should understand what happens if a party to a contract goes into voluntary or involuntary bankruptcy. As was explained in chapter 7, when a party enters bankruptcy, the law provides for an *automatic stay*, which means that creditors are barred from taking any legal action to enforce the contract or to collect money owing under it. A company that has a contract with the bankrupt party (the *debtor*) may neither foreclose on collateral nor stop performing its obligations under the contract without first receiving permission from the bankruptcy court. A provision in a contract that purports to give a party the right to terminate the contract if the other party goes into bankruptcy (a *bankruptcy clause*) is not enforceable.

The penalty for willful violation of an automatic stay is stiff. The debtor may recover lost profits and punitive damages (discussed in chapter 12).

In addition to obtaining the automatic stay, a debtor may also choose which contracts it wishes to maintain and which it wants to reject. If the debtor rejects a contract, then the other party becomes an unsecured creditor of the debtor for an amount equal to the damage caused by the breach of contract. This often means that the non-breaching party either receives cents on the dollar or nothing at all if all of the debtor's assets are mortgaged or otherwise have been used as collateral for secured loans. On the other hand, if the debtor chooses to affirm a contract (as would happen with a lease with a below-market rent or a favorable supply contract in a tight market), then the other party must continue to perform it in accordance with its terms.

An entrepreneur who has a contract with a party in bankruptcy, or in danger of entering bankruptcy, should consult with a lawyer before taking any action to enforce or terminate the contract.

REMEDIES

In cases involving a contract breach, remedies can be monetary or, in cases in which monetary compensation would not be adequate, take the form of specific performance or an injunction. In some cases in which there is no contract, the courts may grant limited relief under the theory of promissory estoppel, or provide compensation for the services rendered under the doctrine of quantum meruit, both of which are discussed later in this chapter.

Monetary Damages

If a party breaches its contract with another, the nonbreaching party is usually entitled to monetary damages. Damages can take one of three forms: expectation damages, reliance damages, and restitution. Sometimes more than one remedy is appropriate, in which case the plaintiff may ask for remedies measured by each of the three types of damages. In some cases, consequential and liquidated damages may also be avoidable.

Expectation Damages *Expectation damages* compensate the plaintiff for the amount he or she lost as the result of the defendant's breach of contract; in other words, it puts the plaintiff in the position he or she would have been in if the contract had not been breached. For example, suppose that Angela had agreed to design Zany's software for $2,000 (payable on delivery) and that Zany had a contract to resell it for $3,000, which would net her $1,000. If Angela fails to deliver the software, then subject to the duty to mitigate damages discussed below, she would be liable for expectation damages in the amount of $1,000. This is the amount required to put Zany in the position she would have been in had Angela completed the job.

Mitigation The nonbreaching party is required to make reasonable efforts to minimize damages in the event of a breach. This is called *mitigation of damages*.

Thus, if the supplier fails to deliver goods in accordance with the contract, the buyer must try to procure them elsewhere. For example, if a farmer fails to deliver oranges to a buyer operating a fresh-fruit juice business and the market price of oranges is increasing, the buyer must try to buy them from another supplier before the market price goes up even further.

Suppose that Christina's company has a contract to sell 10,000 microchips to a computer-game manufacturer on a certain schedule. If she doesn't meet her obligations under this contract, she will lose a great deal of money, plus the possibility of future contracts with that company. Christina has a contract with Trevor's company for production and delivery of certain chemicals used in the production of microchips. Two weeks before she must deliver her first installment of microchips, Trevor informs Christina that his regular shipment of chemicals will be late, which Christina knows will delay her shipment unacceptably. In this case, Christina has a duty to mitigate the damages caused by Trevor's breach, perhaps by calling other suppliers or by substituting another chemical. She may not simply sit back, lose her contract with the computer-game manufacturer, and then sue Trevor for the loss of her profit on the contract.

Similarly, if an employee is fired in violation of an employment agreement, the employee must try to find comparable work. If the employee fails to take a comparable job elsewhere, then he or she will be able to recover only the difference between what he or she would have been paid under the employment agreement and what he or she could have earned at the comparable job.

Using our software example, when Zany learns that Angela will be unable to fulfill the contract, Zany is required to try to get someone else

---

FROM THE TRENCHES

Actress Shirley MacLaine and Twentieth Century-Fox Film Corp. signed a contract for MacLaine to appear in the musical motion picture *Bloomer Girl* in 1966. Before production began, the studio decided not to produce *Bloomer Girl* and instead offered MacLaine a role in a dramatic Western called *Big Country*. MacLaine declined the offer and sued the studio for the compensation due under the contract. The studio conceded that there was a valid contract and a breach of the contract, but contended that MacLaine had failed to properly mitigate damages by unreasonably refusing to accept the studio's offer of the leading role in *Big Country*.

The court ruled for MacLaine, finding that the *Big Country* lead was both different from and inferior to the role in *Bloomer Girl*. The court reasoned that *Bloomer Girl* was a musical to be produced in Los Angeles that would have called upon MacLaine's talents as a dancer and an actress. *Big Country*, on the other hand, was a Western requiring a straight dramatic role and was to be filmed in Australia. The court said that the role of dramatic actress in a Western is not equivalent or substantially equivalent to the lead in a song-and-dance production, and therefore MacLaine was not obligated to accept the role as mitigation.

Source: Parker v. Twentieth Century-Fox Film Corp., 474 P.2d 689 (Cal. 1970).

---

to provide the software. If Zany were able to hire another programmer to write the software at the cost of $2,200, then Angela would be liable for only $200, the additional amount Zany was required to pay to get the software written. If Zany could have hired someone else but didn't, then a court probably would award Zany only $200, which is the additional amount she would have paid had she properly mitigated her damages.

Reliance Damages   A second measurement of damages is *reliance*, which compensates the plaintiff for any expenditures he or she made in reliance on a contract that was subsequently breached. Instead of giving the plaintiff the benefit of the bargain (expectation damages), reliance damages return the plaintiff to the position that he or she was in before the contract was formed. For example, suppose Jim agrees to sell Frank a mainframe computer system, and Frank invests in renovating a room to allow for proper ventilation and cooling of the computer. If Jim then sells the computer to someone else, Jim will be required to reimburse Frank for the renovation expenses.

Restitution   Restitution is similar to reliance damages, but while reliance damages look at what the plaintiff has lost, restitution looks at what both parties have gained from the transaction. *Restitution* puts both parties back in the same position they were in before the contract was formed. For example, if Zany had paid Angela $2,000 when she commissioned the programming, and Angela never wrote the program, Angela has benefited by receiving the $2,000. Thus, Zany's restitution damages are $2,000.

Consequential Damages and Liquidated Damages   *Consequential damages* are damages that the plaintiff is entitled to as compensation for losses that occur as a foreseeable result of a breach. Consequential damages can include harm resulting from the loss of future business. For example, if Zany loses a future contract worth $5,000 because of Angela's failure to deliver the software on time, Zany may be entitled to consequential damages of $5,000. To be recoverable, the damages must be reasonably foreseeable. Consequential damages will be awarded only if the breaching party knew, or should have known, that the loss would result from a breach of contract. In our software example, Zany will be entitled to consequential damages only if Angela knew or should have known that the successful delivery of the software would allow Zany to receive a future contract worth $5,000. Angela will not be liable for consequential damages if Zany mitigates and receives the future contract, or fails to properly mitigate and as a result loses the contract. But if Zany tries to mitigate but cannot find another programmer to write the software, then Angela would be liable for the damages that were reasonably foreseeable.

The nonbreaching party is entitled to receive consequential damages based on lost future profit only if he or she can demonstrate that he or she would have earned the profit had the other party not breached the contract. This requirement can be a problem for entrepreneurs who seek to recover lost profits for a business that either never got started or ran for only a short time.

One way to address this problem is to provide for liquidated damages in the contract. Such a provision, agreed on ahead of time, would specify a set figure that the breaching party would pay the injured party in the event of breach. The figure should be the parties' best estimate of what their expectation damages would be. If the specified amount exceeds this reasonable estimate, the court may consider it a form of punishment, which is not permissible under contract law, and refuse to enforce the liquidated damages provision.

Nonmonetary Remedies

Specific Performance and Injunctions Sometimes granting monetary damages to a plaintiff is neither appropriate nor suitable compensation for the defendant's contract breach. In such cases, the court may grant *specific performance*, that is, order the defendant to do exactly what he or she promised. Specific performance is used if (1) the item involved in the contract was unique (e.g., a sculpture); (2) the contract involved real property; or (3) the calculation of monetary damages would likely be difficult to do accurately, making it unfair to do so.

Injunctions are court orders to do something or to refrain from doing something. For example, although specific performance by an employee may never be required in a case for breach of an employment contract (individuals may not be forced to work), courts can enjoin the employee from working for the injured party's competitor. Sometimes a court will issue a *temporary restraining order (TRO)* or *preliminary injunction* before the case goes to trial to preserve the status quo. Courts will usually not issue a TRO or preliminary injunction unless the plaintiff proves that it would be irreparably damaged if certain conduct by the defendant (e.g., disclosure of trade secrets) was not halted.

Rescission In some situations, such as mistake or misrepresentation, in which enforcing the contract would be unfair, a court may decide to *rescind* (cancel) a contract and order restitution. For example, Geert, an importer, paid $7,500 for a very rare desk that turned out to be a reproduction worth only $2,000. If the seller misled the importer and told him that the desk was genuine when he knew it to be a reproduction, then the court could rescind the contract, and each party would return the benefit it received up until that point. Geert would return the desk in exchange for the return of his $7,500.

PROMISSORY ESTOPPEL

Under certain circumstances a court will use a doctrine called *promissory estoppel* to give limited relief to a person who relied, to his or her detriment, on the promises of another. This is most likely to occur when a person relies on promises made in the course of negotiations that break down before there is a meeting of the minds on all essential terms.

A party may recover under promissory estoppel only if four conditions are met: (1) there must be a *promise*; (2) *reliance* on the promise must be *genuine* and *justifiable*; (3) the actions taken in reliance must be *reasonably foreseeable* to the person making the promise; and (4) grave *injustice* must result if no relief is given. If all four requirements are met, then the court will require the person who made the promise to pay to the person who relied to his or her detriment damages in an amount equal to the out-of-pocket loss the plaintiff suffered by relying on the promise.

For example, in a landmark case, Hoffman had been negotiating with Red Owl Stores for two years, trying to secure a franchise for a Red Owl grocery store. During the two-year period, Hoffman relied on the promise Red Owl had made that he could get a franchise for a stated price. In reliance on that and other promises, he moved, bought a small grocery store to gain experience, sold a bakery that he had previously owned, and borrowed money from his family. Negotiations broke down when the chain insisted that Hoffman's father-in-law sign a document stating that the money he was advancing was an outright gift. Hoffman sued Red Owl for damages based on its failure to keep promises that had induced Hoffman to act to his detriment. The court held that the doctrine of promissory estoppel applied, and awarded Hoffman reliance damages equal to the amount he was out-of-pocket because of his reliance on Red Owl's promises.[11]

FROM THE TRENCHES

Michigan passed several statutes allowing municipalities to provide tax exemptions for businesses to encourage the creation and maintenance of jobs. In 1988 General Motors Corporation (GM) announced that it would build a new vehicle, the Chevrolet Caprice, at its Willow Run, Michigan, plant. GM applied for and received a twelve-year, 50% reduction in its property taxes for its $75-million project. In 1991, after suffering record losses, GM announced its intention to close its Willow Run manufacturing plant in Michigan and instead build its Chevrolet Caprice models exclusively at its Arlington, Texas, plant.

Michigan and the county and township in which the plant was located sued GM to prevent it from closing the Willow Run plant. The plaintiffs claimed that GM had breached a contract created by the tax abatement, and that even if a contract did not exist, GM should be prevented from closing the plant under the doctrine of promissory estoppel.

The trial court ruled that although there was no contract, GM was bound by promissory estoppel to continue operations at the Willow Run plant so long as the company continued to manufacture the Caprice model. The trial court stated that the citizens of the surrounding area had given up millions of tax dollars, which could have been used for education and government services, in return for the plant. Therefore, the trial court reasoned, it would be a gross inequity and patent unfairness to allow GM to close the plant and lay off 4,500 workers just because it thought it could make the same cars more cheaply somewhere else.

The appellate court, however, overturned the trial court decision, holding that promissory estoppel did not apply. GM had merely taken advantage of a statutory opportunity, and GM's abatement application did not constitute a promise or an assurance of continued employment.

Source: Charter Township of Ypsilanti v. General Motors Corp., 506 N.W.2d 556 (Mich. Ct. App. 1993).

QUANTUM MERUIT

Quantum meruit can be used to recover the value of products or services provided in the absence of a contract in a situation in which it was clear that the products or services were needed but the party receiving the benefit could not agree to purchase them. For example, if Fiona is unconscious on the side of the road, and paramedics pick her up and take her to the emergency room, then Fiona will be required to pay the paramedics, the hospital, and the physician treating her the value of the services provided, even though she did not ask for them and did not agree to pay for them.

Similarly, suppose that an entrepreneur asked his or her advertising agency to place an advertisement. The advertising agency contracts with an industry publication to place the advertisement but fails to pay for it. The advertising agency's default on payment for the advertisement would render the entrepreneur liable to the publication, under the doctrine of quantum meruit, for the value of the benefit the entrepreneur received (the advertisement). The entrepreneur must pay the publication even though there was no contract between the entrepreneur and the publication.

SPECIAL TYPES OF CONTRACTS AND THEIR CHARACTERISTICS

Entrepreneurs are likely to encounter a variety of contracts, including leases, contracts for the purchase of real property, loan agreements, and contracts for the sale or acquisition of a business. These four types of contracts are discussed below.

Leases

The entrepreneur who does not work out of his or her home may need to lease a place in which to conduct the business. A *lease* is a contract between a landlord (also called a *lessor*) and tenant (also called a *lessee*). Usually, the landlord presents a preprinted contract with language favoring his or her interests. It is then up to the tenant to try to negotiate better terms.

The best way for a potential tenant to approach a lease negotiation is to determine what issues are important and rank them. By systematically considering all options in advance, the tenant minimizes the possibility that important interests will be overlooked.

For example, when negotiating a lease for a restaurant, the key is to secure a good location. It is more important for Bruce's rotisserie chicken restaurant to be located in the vacant slot next to the anchor tenant, a well-known video rental store, than to pay $300 per month less in rent for a vacant space located at the far end of the mall. Without carefully considering his business's ultimate needs, Bruce might have bargained away thousands of dollars of income each month just to save $300.

A tenant should carefully think through all of the aspects of what he or she wants in a lease. For example, in rental negotiations for the restaurant space, Bruce might seek a provision by which the landlord promises not to rent space to another take-out restaurant in the same half of the mall. Other issues to consider include the landlord's provision of janitorial services; trash removal; maintenance of plumbing and electrical systems; repair, maintenance, or even remodeling of the interior of the rental property; snow removal; payment of utilities and property taxes; guarantees against environmental hazards; indemnification provisions; and maintenance of the building's common areas (such as lobbies and hallways). If the lessee is a start-up, it is not uncommon for the lessor to demand a personal guarantee by the major shareholder.

It is also important to make sure that the lessee's contemplated use of the property does not interfere with anyone else's property rights. In one situation, the entrepreneurs' neighbors threatened to sue them for using the alleyway; they said that the entrepreneurs were violating their

---

FROM THE TRENCHES

When they started renovating, several entrepreneurs found asbestos in the building they were leasing. The lease did not specify who was responsible for remedying preexisting environmental problems. The tenants had to negotiate with the landlord after the fact to establish who was responsible for removing the asbestos.

easement. The entrepreneurs ended up buying some of the neighbors' space to appease them.

Two main elements that appear in almost any commercial lease merit some discussion: (1) the rental charge, and (2) restrictions on subleasing the space or assigning the lease to a third party. Often, the rental charge is a flat monthly or yearly rate. Sometimes, however, the landlord may require some percentage of the tenant's gross sales, in addition to the flat rate. For example, Bruce might be charged a $3,000 flat rate, plus 7% of his gross sales above $100,000 each year, not to exceed $20,000 per year. In such a situation, Bruce would be wise to clearly define what is meant by *gross sales*, carefully excluding such things as sales tax, which are not really a part of his income.

Subleasing and assignment of a lease to a third party are very important issues to an entrepreneur setting up a new business. Should he find himself in an unprofitable location or even on the verge of going out of business, he will not want to be responsible for the entire duration of the lease. A landlord may agree to permit the tenant to sublet the space to a responsible third party, if necessary, with the tenant still ultimately responsible for the payment of the rent. However, the landlord may not agree to a tenant's request for the right to assign the remainder of the lease to a third party, because an assignment would eliminate the original tenant's involvement completely and potentially leave the landlord in the position of trying to extract rent from an uncooperative or insolvent new tenant. In fact, the landlord may attempt to forestall the possibility of subletting or lease assignment completely by allowing the tenant to sublet the space or assign the lease only with the landlord's prior written consent. In practice, requiring the landlord's consent means that the tenant has no such right. Tenants can even the playing field a bit by negotiating a sentence into the contract that states, "The landlord's consent shall not unreasonably be withheld."

Contracts for the Purchase of Real Property

The laws governing the acquisition of real property, such as an empty lot or a building, are highly technical and vary markedly from one state to another. An entrepreneur should never enter into a contract to buy real property without first consulting an experienced real-property lawyer in the state where the property is located.

One particularly dangerous trap for the unwary is liability for the cleanup of hazardous waste. Under the Comprehensive Environmental Response, Compensation, and Liability Act (CERCLA), the current owner or operator of real property can be liable for the cleanup of all hazardous waste on the property even if it was dumped there by a previous owner. To avoid liability, the purchaser must be able to prove that it acquired the facility after the hazardous substances were disposed of and without any knowledge or reason to know that hazardous substances had previously been disposed of at the facility. To establish that the purchaser had no reason to know that hazardous substances were disposed of at the facility, the purchaser must show that, prior to the sale, it undertook all appropriate inquiry into the previous ownership and uses of the property consistent with good commercial or customary practice in an effort to minimize liability. This can be very difficult to prove, and counsel experienced in environmental law should be consulted to help devise an appropriate environmental audit.

Loan Agreements

Loan agreements are usually long, standardized agreements, carefully designed to ensure that the lender's money will be repaid (to the extent it is possible to ensure such a thing). Loan agreements are also characterized

---

FROM THE TRENCHES

A partnership that ran a local newspaper planned to buy a small building. Before doing so, one of the partners consulted with an experienced lawyer, who suggested that they hire an environmental auditing firm to obtain and analyze soil and water samples. The audit revealed the existence of hazardous waste underground. Armed with their report, the partners were able to negotiate a more favorable purchase price.

by many technical clauses regarding calculation of interest, interest rates, special repayment terms, and so forth. As with all contracts, the parties have a duty to read, and therefore be responsible for, the agreement. However, this duty is especially important with loan agreements, which may contain substantial obligations for the borrower that are buried in technical language.

Four particular loan agreement provisions require the borrower's special scrutiny:

1. *Logistical details of receiving the loan*, such as whether the money will be wired or sent by check, and whether the amount will be transferred in full or in installments.
2. *Conditions precedent*, which are all the conditions that must be met by the borrower (or in some cases a third party) before the loan may be funded.
3. *Covenants*, which are promises made by the borrower to the lender that, if breached, will result in an event of default and a termination of the loan, usually thereby accelerating payment of all amounts due.
4. *Repayment terms*, including any rights to cure an event of default due to a late or missed payment.

In addition, if the loan is secured by a mortgage or deed of trust on real property or by a security interest in other collateral, it is critical that the borrower understand what happens to the collateral if there is an event of default and whether the creditor has recourse to all assets of the borrower or only the collateral. (Secured lending is discussed in chapter 7.)

An entrepreneur should not sign a loan agreement without first consulting with counsel.

Contracts for the Sale or Acquisition of a Business

There may come a time when the entrepreneur wishes to expand the company's business through the acquisition of another entity. Alternatively, the entrepreneur may wish to sell the business to a third party as a means of liquefying the value that has been built in the enterprise. In fact, for most entrepreneurs, sale of the business to achieve liquidity is much more likely than a public offering of the company's shares. But whether the entrepreneur is selling the business or acquiring another business, a contract spelling out the terms of the acquisition (an *acquisition contract*) will be necessary to protect the interests of the buyer and the seller.

The acquisition of a business (the business being acquired being the *target*) can be structured as a purchase of the assets of the target, a purchase of the stock of the target, or a merger of the target into the buyer. In an assets deal, the buyer acquires only those assets enumerated in the acquisition contract. The buyer may agree to assume no liabilities, only certain liabilities, or all liabilities. The target corporation will continue as a legal entity unless its shareholders liquidate it. In a stock deal, the buyer acquires the stock held by the target's shareholders, and thus acquires all of the assets and all of the liabilities of the acquired business, with the target becoming a subsidiary of the buyer. In a merger of the target into the buyer, the buyer acquires all of the assets and all of the liabilities of the acquired business, and the target ceases to exist.

Tax considerations often dictate the form of an acquisition. An acquisition can be structured as a taxable assets purchase, a taxable stock purchase, a taxable merger, or a tax-free reorganization in which tax is not payable upon the acquisition by either the target or the target's shareholders.

In a *taxable assets purchase*, the selling entity must pay tax on the difference between the tax basis of the assets sold (their value for tax purposes, roughly, cost less depreciation) and the consideration (e.g., cash) paid by the buyer for the assets plus the amount of any assumed liabilities. Thus, if, for example, the target sold all of its assets, which had a tax basis of $6 million, for $8 million cash plus the assumption by the buyer of target liabilities of $2 million, then the target would have to pay tax on the $4 million gain [($8 million + $2 million) minus $6 million]. However, the buyer is able to *step-up* (increase) the tax basis of the assets acquired (the value attributable to the assets for tax purposes) to equal the cash and other consideration paid and liabilities assumed. This permits the depreciation of assets after the acquisition to be based on the higher, stepped-up value, thereby increasing the depreciation deductions. For example, if the buyer paid $10 million for a target whose assets had been depreciated to $6 million for tax purposes, the buyer would be permitted to take depreciation deductions of $10 million. However, the target's net operating losses and other tax attributes cannot be transferred to the purchaser. A *taxable merger* of the target into the buyer is taxed the same as an asset sale.

In a *taxable stock purchase*, no tax is paid by the target but capital gains tax is paid by the shareholders on the difference between the basis for their stock (often its cost) and the consideration paid by the buyer for that stock. In a taxable stock purchase, the tax attributes of the target, such as net operating losses and tax credit carryovers, are generally preserved, but the basis in the assets remains the same as it was in the seller's hands (i.e., no step-up). In the example cited above, the buyer would be able to depreciate only $6 million of asset value. In certain circumstances, a *section 338 election* can be made to permit the purchaser in a taxable stock sale to achieve a step-up in basis.

The interplay of these factors will determine the buyer's choice of structure from a tax perspective. From the seller's viewpoint, the preference for a taxable assets or a taxable stock sale will turn on which alternative will produce the largest after-tax return. Gains on asset sales are generally taxed twice, first to the target and second to its shareholders when the sale proceeds are distributed. This double level of taxation (contrasted with a sale of stock that involves no entity-level tax) causes most taxable sales to be structured as stock sales, absent other factors. Exceptions to this general rule include sales by S corporations (which pay no corporate tax); sales by corporations with operating losses, which can shelter the corporate tax; and transactions in which nontax considerations are particularly important, as described below. The facts and circumstances of each situation and the objectives of each party must be examined to determine the optimal structure of a particular transaction from a tax perspective.

In addition to taxable sales of assets or stock and taxable mergers, an acquisition transaction can be structured as a tax-free reorganization. (The term is a misnomer; tax is not forgiven, but merely postponed.) In a *tax-free reorganization*, stock of the acquiring company is exchanged for the stock or assets of the target. Generally speaking, the gain or loss to the selling shareholders will not be recognized until the stock received is sold. In certain types of tax-free reorganizations, consideration in addition to stock may be received by the sellers, with taxes being due immediately on the nonstock portion of the total consideration received. This taxable portion is called *boot*.

The types of tax-free reorganizations include the following:

1. a statutory merger under state law in which the target disappears [a so-called *A reorganization* because it is described in section 368(a)(1)(A) of the Internal Revenue Code (the Code)];
2. an exchange of stock of the purchaser for all of the stock of the target [a *B reorganization,* described in section 368(a)(1)(B) of the Code];
3. an exchange of stock of the purchaser for the assets of the target, followed by the liquidation of the target corporation and distribution of the purchaser's stock to the target corporation's shareholders [a *C reorganization,* described in section 368(a)(1)(C) of the Code];
4. a *forward triangular merger* in which the target is merged into a subsidiary of the purchaser in exchange for stock of the purchaser [a *D reorganization,* described in section 368(a)(2)(D) of the Code]; and
5. a *reverse triangular merger* in which a subsidiary of the purchaser is merged into the target in exchange for stock of the purchaser [an *E reorganization,* described in section 368(a)(2)(E) of the Code].

Although tax consequences are critical in determining the structure of an acquisition transaction (including, most importantly, whether the transaction will be tax-free to the seller), other factors come into play as well. The buyer may be unwilling to issue its stock in the transaction because of the dilutive effect on its ownership. On the other hand, the buyer may be unable to borrow money or otherwise finance the transaction, so its stock may be its only currency. Certain key contracts of the target may not be assignable, thus preventing an assets sale. Alternatively, the buyer may be unwilling to assume certain liabilities of the target, thus precluding the acquisition of the target's stock. Or perhaps the buyer is willing to take on these liabilities only in a subsidiary. In addition, the buyer may have significantly more favorable financial accounting reporting if it acquires the target with the buyer's own stock. Of course, the seller may be unwilling to accept the risk in taking the buyer's stock, rather than cash. In any event, such issues must enter the mix with tax considerations when the parties are negotiating the structure of the acquisition transaction.

Once the structure of the acquisition has been agreed to, and sometimes before, the parties and their lawyers will negotiate the acquisition contract. After the contract is signed, the buyer will commit resources to conduct its *due diligence* or investigation of the target's business. The acquisition will not close until the due diligence is completed and the buyer is satisfied with all aspects of the business.

Regardless of the form of the acquisition transaction, certain key elements will be found in most acquisition contracts. These are:

- *Representations and warranties of the target and its shareholders about the business and, if target stock is to be transferred, about title to the sellers' shares.* Matters normally covered by the representations and warranties about the business include its proper organization as a corporation (or other entity such as a partnership or limited liability company), the accuracy of its financial statements, title to its assets (including intellectual property), the absence of liabilities not otherwise disclosed to the buyer, the absence of legal proceedings not otherwise

---

FROM THE TRENCHES

An entrepreneur had built a Southern California fastener (nuts and bolts) distribution business into a company with more than forty employees and $11 million in annual revenue. He knew that the business was well positioned for additional growth, particularly if the company continued to expand out of state and began to acquire other available fastener businesses. But he also knew that a growth strategy involved financing and execution risks. The entrepreneur decided to sell the business based on the value he had achieved to date, and to sell for cash so that his return would not be subject to market risk associated with a potential buyer's stock. He engaged a business broker to find a buyer, and the business was sold for $12 million to a corporation planning an aggressive growth strategy.

disclosed to the buyer, its compliance with all laws (including tax laws and environmental laws), its compliance with all contractual obligations by which it is bound, and, in addition, its full disclosure to the buyer of all facts necessary to make the other representations and warranties made not misleading.

* *Representations and warranties by the buyer about its business if the buyer's stock is to be the acquisition currency.*
* *Covenants (promises) of the target*, including promises to permit access to the business to enable the buyer to conduct its due diligence, to not take certain actions out of the ordinary course of business during the due diligence phase without the buyer's consent, and to not solicit or respond to other offers for the purchase of the business.
* *Covenants of both the target and the buyer* to take certain actions necessary to permit the transaction to occur, including obtaining any necessary consents of third parties.
* *Conditions to closing of the acquisition* (closing conditions), including completion of the buyer's due diligence, the obtaining of necessary consents, the delivery of legal opinions, and the absence of any material adverse change to the target's business.
* *Procedures governing termination of the acquisition contract* before the closing.
* *Indemnification provisions* to govern the liabilities of the parties for breach of the representations, warranties, and covenants contained in the acquisition contract.

Two aspects of the acquisition contract deserve special mention: (1) the representations and warranties made about the target's business, and (2) the indemnification provisions. The representations and warranties can be absolute, such as "The Target is not a party to any litigation." If it turns out that a lawsuit was filed against the target the day before the closing, but legal notice of the suit was not delivered until after the closing, the selling shareholders, even though they were unaware of the suit, would be liable to the buyer for any damages arising out of the undisclosed lawsuit. On the other hand, if the representation and warranty had been modified by a *knowledge qualifier* (e.g., "to the best of Selling Shareholders' knowledge, the Target is not a party to any litigation"), the selling shareholders would not be liable for damages suffered by the buyer. Because knowledge qualifiers shift the risk that a representation and warranty may be innocently untrue, the selling shareholders will seek to have as many knowledge qualifiers as possible inserted into the contract. The buyer naturally will resist because the resulting harm to the buyer is the same regardless of whether the seller knew of the problem. The parties often spend a great deal of time arguing over these issues. Experienced counsel can provide the entrepreneur and the other selling shareholders with advice regarding which representations and warranties are most commonly qualified and where the use of qualifiers is most important.

A critical aspect of the representations and warranties about the target business is the Disclosure Schedule, also known as the *Schedule of Exceptions*. The *Disclosure Schedule* is an exhibit to the acquisition contract in which the sellers are permitted to disclose any exceptions to the representations and warranties made in the acquisition contract, which are often stated in absolute terms. For example, if there is known litigation, the sellers would list it on the Disclosure Schedule, because the contract representation on litigation is likely to be that there is none except as set forth on the Disclosure Schedule. Similarly, the acquisition contract is likely to contain a representation that all material contracts of the target are listed on the Disclosure Schedule. It is very important for the sellers to review carefully every representation and warranty with counsel to ensure that the Disclosure Schedule is complete. In fact, sellers often include trivial facts about their business on the Disclosure Schedule because the buyer, once it signs the acquisition contract, is agreeing to purchase the business subject to all that is stated on the Disclosure Schedule.

Sellers will want the acquisition contract to allow them to update the Disclosure Schedule before the closing to account for events occurring after the acquisition contract is signed, subject to the buyer's right to withdraw from the transaction prior to closing if the changes sought to be added are material. Buyers will resist such a provision because it may force them to walk from a favorable acquisition after a binding acquisition agreement is entered into or to close and buy damaged goods with no remedy against the seller.

The indemnification provisions of the acquisition contract govern the duration and scope of the sellers' liability for breaches of the representations and warranties. The sellers have an interest in limiting the time during which a claim can be made, and will argue that after a certain period of time the buyer, as the operator of the business, should have discovered any misstatements. The buyer will argue that certain matters, such as environmental liabilities or liability under previously filed tax returns, may not surface for several years. The sellers will be particularly interested in limiting the time for making a claim if all or a portion of the purchase price (whether in cash or shares of the buyer's stock) has been placed in *escrow* (held by an independent third party) to secure payment of any indemnification claim. (Such an arrangement is called a *cash* or *stock holdback*.) The release of assets from escrow is usually tied to the expiration of the claims period. Often the parties compromise on the claims period by agreeing to different periods for different representations and warranties (typically one, three, or five years).

As for scope of liability, the sellers often seek to limit their exposure to some percentage of the total purchase price. The sellers will argue that if the entire purchase price can be taken back as damages for a breach of the representations and warranties, they would be better off retaining the business and running it themselves, so they can control exposure to breaches. The buyer, of course, wishes to be protected from any damages, arguing that monies paid by the buyer because of a breach of a representation or warranty are in effect an addition to the purchase price for which the buyer should not be responsible. If an escrow of a portion of the purchase price is sought by the buyer, the sellers, as a condition to accepting the escrow, may seek to limit their total exposure to the amount of the escrow.

If the target is owned by more than one shareholder, the issue of joint versus several liability needs to be addressed. Can the buyer sue any target owner for the full amount of its damages, or is it limited to a pro rata share from each owner? Finally, the sellers will seek to have a *basket* or a minimum amount of damages that must arise before a claim can be made, arguing that the buyer should be discouraged from "nickeling and dimeing" the seller for every trivial occurrence. The buyer will often agree to a basket but will insist that once the basket threshold is exceeded, the buyer can go back and claim all of its damages. For example, in a recent contract for the sale of a distribution company for $50 million, the contract provided for a $500,000 basket, but once the claims exceeded $500,000, the buyer was permitted to recover every dollar of claims, not just claims above the initial $500,000.

Additional information relating to acquisition contracts, including sample provisions and explanations of their use, is provided in *Model Stock Purchase Agreement with Commentary*, Committee on Negotiated Acquisitions of the Section of Business Law of the American Bar Association (1995), and *Drafting Agreements for the Sale of Businesses*, California Continuing Education of the Bar (1988; Supplement 1995).

Sales of Goods

Although this chapter has touched on some of the main differences between common-law contract law and article 2 of the Uniform Commercial Code (which governs the sale of goods), it does not by any means cover all of the important provisions contained in the UCC. The UCC contains numerous provisions on such topics as the delivery of goods, inspection of goods, return of defective goods, specification of a price, methods of payment, risk of loss, breach of contract, and available remedies. Implied and express warranties under the UCC are discussed in chapter 11.

Like a typical contract, a supply agreement details who the parties are and the general terms of the relationship. If the supplier is doing something new and innovative for the entrepreneur, the entrepreneur needs to ensure that he or she protects this privilege, especially if the two parties have worked together in developing the product.

FROM THE TRENCHES

Two entrepreneurs collaborated with their supplier to develop a uniquely flavored tortilla. They didn't realize what a success it would be and later had to negotiate with the supplier to ensure that the supplier would not start selling the tortilla to others. They stated, "We worked long and hard with our supplier to develop a special recipe for a flavored tortilla. Ideally you make sure you agree in advance with the supplier that he can't go off and distribute the product to the competitor."

Putting It into Practice

Alexandra knew that she needed to negotiate and sign several contracts to keep WebRunner on the fast track. WebRunner had outgrown its original space, so the first order of business was renting new, expanded office space. After a week of searching for an appropriate location, Alexandra found one that both met WebRunner's needs and was affordable. The landlord, however, refused to lease the premises to WebRunner unless Alexandra personally guaranteed the payments due under the lease. At first Alexandra balked at doing this, but after she checked around, she discovered that a personal guarantee by the key shareholder was customary when start-ups rented space. She wanted to limit her exposure, though, so she negotiated a two-year lease, with three one-year options.

After reading the proposed lease and going over it with Josh Austin, Alexandra had some other concerns as well. The first issue was employee parking. Because the proposed space was downtown, parking would be both scarce and expensive. She knew that the landlord owned an adjacent parking lot and proposed that WebRunner be given five free spaces. The landlord balked and countered with an offer of one free space and the guaranteed right to rent an additional space at the lowest available market rate. After some haggling, Alexandra and the landlord agreed that the lease would provide for two free spaces and the right to rent an additional two spaces at the lowest rate charged any other person.

The second issue was outside lighting. Alexandra and the other programmers were likely to work late many nights, and she was concerned about the lack of lighting in the area. She raised the issue with the landlord, who said that he too had been unhappy with the street lighting. The landlord agreed to install several external lights.

The final lease issue was a provision prohibiting an assignment of the lease or the subleasing of the space. The landlord explained that he prohibited lease assignments because the party assuming the lease may not be creditworthy, and he was very selective about the type of tenants he allowed. After some discussion, Alexandra agreed to the no-assignment provision in exchange for the right to sublease. However, in the event of a sublease, Alexandra and WebRunner would be liable for

continued

continued

the rental payments if the sublessee failed to make them, and any remaining one-year options would be extinguished.

The second major contract that needed to be negotiated was a license agreement with Full Action Sports Telecast (FAST), a major sports broadcaster and content provider. Alexandra had met Curtis Hall, FAST's president, at a local trade show, and Curtis had expressed interest in WebRunner's technology. He mentioned the possibility of licensing FAST's content to WebRunner in return for royalty payments and user-access fees, and invited Alexandra to meet with him at his office to discuss it.

After Alexandra discussed the idea with the other directors, they decided to try to design a WebRunner applet around FAST's content. The applet would provide up-to-the-minute scores and highlights, and would allow users to create their own tailored sports-highlights shows.

Going into a meeting with Curtis, Alexandra felt that the most important objective was to lock in an exclusive long-term license of FAST's content. Alexandra did not want to put the time and money into making the sports applet a success only to have FAST turn around and license its content to someone else.

Within an hour, Alexandra and Curtis had agreed on the basic outline of a five-year deal. Curtis, however, wanted the license to be nonexclusive to preserve FAST's future business opportunities. Alexandra explained that any deal would have to provide an exclusive license for use of FAST's content on the Internet. Curtis countered that FAST could agree to an exclusivity clause only if WebRunner agreed that the license could not be sublicensed, would be nontransferable, and would revert back to FAST if WebRunner were acquired by another company. Curtis was concerned that if WebRunner were acquired by one of FAST's competitors, that competitor could lock FAST out of cyberspace by no longer allowing users to access FAST's content. Alexandra had no intention of sublicensing or transferring the rights to FAST's content to anyone else. However, including the reversion provision would effectively eliminate WebRunner's ability to be sold at a good price; its only remaining exit strategy would be an initial public offering. Although Alexandra planned to take WebRunner public, she certainly did not want to limit its options, especially this early in its existence. After some further negotiating,

continued

> *continued*
>
> Alexandra was able to persuade Curtis to accept a provision that would have the license revert to FAST only if WebRunner were acquired by one of the competitors listed on an appendix to the agreement.
>
> With the lease and license agreement in hand, Alexandra and the Eagles worked furiously to finish the product in preparation for its upcoming launch.

NOTES

1. *Engleman v. General Accident, Fire & Life Assurance Corp.*, 250 F.2d 202 (9th Cir. 1957).
2. *Curtis 1000, Inc. v. Suess*, 24 F.3d 941 (7th Cir. 1994).
3. *Wickham & Burton Coal Co. v. Farmers' Lumber Co.*, 179 N.W. 417 (Iowa 1920).
4. *Dahl v. HEM Pharmaceuticals Corp.*, 7 F.3d 1399 (9th Cir. 1993).
5. *Dwight v. Tobin*, 947 F.2d 455 (11th Cir. 1991).
6. *Nucor Corporation v. Aceros y Maquilas de Occidente*, 28 F.3d 572 (7th Cir. 1994).
7. *Roboserve, Ltd. v. Tom's Foods, Inc.*, 940 F.2d 1441 (11th Cir. 1991).
8. *Jones v. Star Credit Corp.*, 298 N.Y.S. 2d 264, 6 UCC Rep. Serv. (Callaghan) 76 (N.Y. Sup. Ct. 1969).
9. *Raffles v. Wichelhaus*, 159 Eng. Rep. 375 (Exch. 1864).
10. *Wood v. Boynton*, 25 N.W. 42 (Wis. 1885).
11. *Hoffman v. Red Owl Stores, Inc.*, 133 N.W.2d 267 (Wis. 1965).

II

Product Liability, Warranties, and Advertising

Many entrepreneurs are in the business of selling goods. Entrepreneurs operating service businesses will almost certainly buy goods as part of that business. Sometimes goods delivered pursuant to a contract do not live up to the buyer's expectations. The buyer may sue the seller for breaching an express or implied warranty that the goods sold would have certain qualities or would perform in a certain way. Alternatively, if the product has a defect or did not contain proper warnings, the plaintiff may sue in tort for strict product liability, which imposes liability regardless of the seller's fault. Often product advertisements will include claims about a product's performance. False or misleading advertising is illegal.

This chapter discusses express and implied warranties, product liability, and the regulation of advertising.

WARRANTIES

There are three types of warranties under article 2 of the Uniform Commercial Code (UCC): an express warranty, an implied warranty of merchantability, and an implied warranty of fitness for a particular purpose.

Express Warranty

An *express warranty* is an explicit guarantee by the seller that the goods will have certain qualities. Two requirements must be met for the creation of an express warranty. First, the seller must make a statement or promise relating to the goods, provide a description of the goods, or furnish a sample or model of the goods. Second, the buyer must have relied on the seller's statement, promise, or sample in making the purchase decision. The seller has the burden of proving that the buyer did not rely on the representations. A warranty may be found even though the seller never uses the word "warranty" or "guarantee" and has no intention of making a warranty. For example, the statement "this printer prints seven color pages per minute" is an express warranty.

Puffing   If a seller is merely *puffing*, that is, expressing an opinion about the quality of the goods, then he has not made a warranty. For example, a statement that "this is a top-notch car" is puffing, whereas a factual statement such as "this car gets 25 miles to the gallon" is an express warranty.

Unfortunately, the line between opinion and fact is difficult to draw. Much turns on the circumstances surrounding the representation, including the identities and relative knowledge of the parties involved.

If the seller asserts a fact of which the buyer was ignorant, the assertion is more likely to be a warranty. But if the seller merely states a view on something about which the buyer could be expected to have formed his or her own opinion, and the buyer can judge the validity of the seller's statement, then the seller's statement is an opinion.

Implied Warranty of Merchantability

The *implied warranty of merchantability* guarantees that the goods are reasonably fit for the general purpose for which they are sold, and that they are properly packaged and labeled. The warranty applies to all goods sold by merchants in the normal course of business. This warranty is implied even if the seller makes no statements and furnishes no sample

FROM THE TRENCHES

A man wishing to buy his wife a diamond bracelet for Christmas consulted a jeweler, who offered to sell a specific bracelet for $15,000. The jeweler described the diamonds as "nice," but his appraisal letter, enclosed for insurance purposes, described the diamonds as "v.v.s. grade," which is one of the highest ratings in the quality classification system used by jewelers and gemologists. The customer purchased the bracelet and gave it to his wife.

Four months later, another jeweler looking at the bracelet informed the customer that the diamonds were not v.v.s. quality. The customer asked the original jeweler to replace the bracelet with one containing v.v.s. diamonds. The merchant refused but offered to refund the $15,000 purchase price in exchange for the return of the bracelet. Because the price of diamonds had appreciated during the four-month period, the customer rejected the offer and filed suit against the dealer.

The court found that the diamonds were substantially less than v.v.s. grade. The jeweler, however, contended that the appraisal letter was intended for insurance purposes only and that, in any case, it was merely an opinion. The court ruled that only the appraised value listed in the letter was for insurance purposes, and that the description of the bracelet in the letter should be treated like any other statement that the jeweler made about the bracelet. The court also ruled that the jeweler's writing that the diamonds were v.v.s. quality was more than a mere opinion. When a person with superior knowledge makes a statement about goods and does not qualify the statement as a mere opinion, the statement will be treated as a statement of fact. Therefore, the jeweler's letter constituted an express warranty that the diamonds were v.v.s. quality. Accordingly, the court ordered the jeweler to pay damages to the customer.

Source: Daughtrey v. Ashe, 413 S.E. 2d 336 (Va. 1992).

or model. To be considered a *merchant*, a seller must regularly deal in or sell the goods. A casual seller is not considered a merchant.

To be merchantable, the goods must (1) pass without objection in the trade under the contract description; (2) be fit for the ordinary purpose for which such goods are used; (3) be within the variations permitted by the agreement; (4) be of even kind, quality, and quantity within each unit and among all units involved; (5) be adequately contained, packaged, and labeled as the agreement may require; and (6) conform to the promises or affirmations of fact made on the container or label, if any.

The key issue in determining merchantability is whether the goods do what a reasonable person would expect of them. The contract description is crucial. Goods considered merchantable under one contract may be considered not to be merchantable under another. For example, a bicycle with a cracked frame and bent wheels is not fit for the ordinary purpose for which bicycles are used, but will pass under a contract for the sale of scrap metal.

FROM THE TRENCHES

A hotel operator building a new hotel purchased blue carpet for its single rooms and mauve carpet for its double-occupancy rooms. Although the rate of occupancy in the blue-carpeted rooms had exceeded that of the mauve-carpeted rooms, within ninety days the mauve carpet was so badly worn that it was unsightly and needed to be replaced. On the other hand, the blue carpet had maintained its original appearance.

An agent of the carpet manufacturer looked at the carpet and agreed that the mauve carpet needed to be replaced. Nevertheless, the carpet manufacturer did not replace the carpet. The hotel operator filed suit, claiming that the carpet maker had breached an implied warranty of merchantability.

The carpet manufacturer defended by claiming that the carpet damage was due to excessive cleaning by the hotel operator and also misuse because the carpet was classified as "residential." The court ruled for the hotel operator because the mauve carpet had been put on the same cleaning schedule as the blue carpet. In terms of the second defense, the court found that even though the carpet had been classified as residential, it had not been subjected to particularly heavy use during the period. In addition, the blue carpet had also been classified as residential, but had not lost its original condition. The court held that the mauve carpet was not fit for any of its ordinary uses at the time of delivery, and thus the carpet manufacturer had breached the implied warranty of merchantability. The court awarded the hotel operator damages for the cost of replacement and interest from the date of the carpet's failure.

Source: Meldco, Inc. v. Hollytex Carpet Mills, Inc., 796 P. 2d 142 (Idaho. App. Ct. 1990).

Implied Warranty of Fitness for a Particular Purpose

The *implied warranty of fitness for a particular purpose* guarantees that the goods are fit for the particular purpose for which the seller recommended them. Unlike the implied warranty of merchantability, this warranty does not arise in every sale of goods by a merchant. It will be implied only if four elements are present: (1) the buyer had a particular purpose for the goods; (2) the seller knew or had reason to know of that purpose; (3) the buyer relied on the seller's expertise; and (4) the seller knew or had reason to know of the buyer's reliance. Although a warranty for a particular purpose can be created by any seller, typically the seller must be a merchant, because the seller must purport to be an expert regarding the goods, and the buyer must have relied on the seller's expertise.

A seller may prove that a buyer did not rely on the seller's expertise by showing that (1) the buyer's expertise was equal to or superior to the seller's; (2) the buyer relied on the skill and judgment of persons hired by the buyer; or (3) the buyer supplied the seller with detailed specifications or designs that the seller was to follow.

Limiting Liability

Subject to certain federal and state law restrictions, the seller can limit its liability under any of these warranties. First, the seller need not make any express warranties. This may be difficult to do, however, because even a simple description of the goods may constitute a warranty. Second, a seller may disclaim any warranties of quality if it follows specifically delineated rules in the UCC designed to ensure that the buyer is aware of, and assents to, the disclaimers. A seller can exclude all implied warranties by using expressions such as "AS IS" or "WITH ALL FAULTS," or other language that in common understanding calls the buyer's attention to the exclusion of warranties and makes plain that there is no implied warranty. (Capital letters are used to fulfill the UCC's requirement that waivers of warranties be prominently displayed.) If this language is used, the buyer assumes the entire risk as to the quality of the goods involved. To avoid creating a warranty of fitness for a particular purpose, the seller can refrain from professing expertise with respect to the goods, and can leave the selection to the buyer.

More commonly, the seller limits responsibility for the quality of the goods by limiting the remedies available to the buyer in the event of breach. A typical method is the inclusion of a provision limiting the seller's responsibility for defective goods to repair or replacement.

It should be noted that some state laws limit the ability of sellers to disclaim warranties and to limit remedies in consumer contracts.

MAGNUSON-MOSS WARRANTY ACT

The Magnuson-Moss Warranty Act is a federal law that protects consumers against deception in warranties. The act provides that if a seller makes an express warranty to a buyer, the seller may not disclaim the warranties of merchantability and fitness for a particular purpose.

Although no seller is required to make a written warranty under this act, if the seller does make a written promise or affirmation of fact, then it must also state whether, for example, the warranty is a full or a limited warranty. A *full warranty* has to satisfy three requirements. First, it must give the consumer the right to free repair of the product within a reasonable time period or, after a reasonable number of failed attempts to fix the product, permit the customer to elect a full refund or replacement of a defective product. Second, the warrantor may not impose any time limit on the warranty's duration. Third, the warrantor may not exclude or limit damages for breach of warranty unless such exclusions are conspicuous on the face of the warranty. Any warranty that does not meet these minimum federal standards must be designated as *limited*.

LIABILITY FOR DEFECTIVE PRODUCTS

Even if the seller makes no warranties, it may still be liable to the buyer if the goods are defective under the theory of strict product liability. Liability extends to anyone in the business of selling the goods, or in the chain of distribution.

Most states have adopted strict product liability, whereby an injured person does not need to show that the manufacturer was negligent or otherwise at fault, or that a contractual relationship existed between the manufacturer and the injured person. The injured person merely needs to show that the product was sold in a defective or dangerous condition, and that the defect caused the injury. For example, a person who is injured by a product purchased from a retail store can sue the original manufacturer.

In those jurisdictions that do not impose strict liability, a plaintiff can sue for negligence if he or she can prove that the defendant failed to use reasonable care; if the defendant made a warranty, the plaintiff could sue for breach of warranty. Proving negligence by the defendant allows the plaintiff to receive punitive damages, whereas a plaintiff can receive only compensatory damages for breach of warranty or strict product liability. Negligence and punitive damages are discussed further in chapter 12.

Defective Product

An essential element for recovery in strict liability is proof of a defect in the product. The injured party must show that the product was defective

---

FROM THE TRENCHES

A plaintiff sued a bottling company for the physical and emotional distress he suffered when he consumed part of a bottled soda containing a decomposed mouse. An appellate court found that a toxicologist's testimony that mouse feces on the bottom of the bottle must have been there when the soda was added was sufficient evidence to find that the mouse was in the bottled beverage when it was bottled. The Nevada Supreme Court affirmed a $2,500 jury verdict because public policy demands that a manufacturer who markets a bottled beverage in a dangerous condition be strictly liable for injuries resulting from its use regardless of whether the seller exercised reasonable care.

Source: Shoshone Coca-Cola Bottling Co. v. Dolinski, 420 P. 2d 855 (Nev. 1966).

when it left the hands of the manufacturer or seller, and that the defect made the product unreasonably dangerous. Typically, a product is dangerous if it does not meet the consumer's expectations as to its characteristics. For example, a consumer expects a stepladder not to break when someone stands on the bottom step. A product may be dangerous because of a manufacturing defect, a design defect, or inadequate warnings, labeling, or instructions.

Certain laws and regulations set minimum safety standards for products. Compliance with a regulatory scheme is not an automatic defense. The regulatory standards are often considered minimal requirements, and compliance with them will not shield a manufacturer from liability in all circumstances.

Manufacturing Defect   A *manufacturing defect* is a flaw in the product that occurs during production, such as a failure to meet the design specifications. A product with a manufacturing defect is not like the others rolling off the production line. For example, suppose the driver's seat in an automobile was designed to be bolted to the frame. If the worker forgot to tighten the bolts, the loose seat would be a manufacturing defect.

Design Defect   A *design defect* occurs if, even though the product is manufactured according to specifications, its inadequate design or poor choice of materials makes it dangerous to users. Typically, there is a finding of defective design if the product is not safe for its intended or reasonably foreseeable use. A highly publicized example was the Ford Pinto, which a jury found to be defectively designed because the car's fuel tank was too close to the rear axle, causing the tank to rupture when the car was struck from behind.

Failure to Warn   A product must carry adequate warnings of the risks involved in normal use. For example, the manufacturer of a ladder must warn the user not to stand on the top step. A product must also include instructions on its safe use. For example, sellers have been found liable for failing to provide adequate instructions about the proper use and capacity of a hook, and the assembly and use of a telescope and sun filter.

A warning will not shield a manufacturer from liability for a defectively manufactured or designed product. For example, an automobile manufacturer cannot escape liability for defectively designed brakes merely by warning that "Under certain conditions this car's brakes may fail." On the other hand, a plaintiff can win a suit for *failure to warn* even if there was no manufacturing or design defect.

Who May Be Liable?

In theory, each party in the chain of distribution may be liable: manufacturers, distributors, wholesalers, and retailers. Manufacturers of component parts are frequently sued as well.

FROM THE TRENCHES

The plaintiffs were mushroom enthusiasts who purchased a reference book published by the defendant entitled *The Encyclopedia of Mushrooms*. Relying on the descriptions in the book to determine which wild mushrooms were safe to eat, the plaintiffs picked and ate some deadly species of mushrooms, became critically ill, and required liver transplants. The plaintiffs alleged that the book contained erroneous and misleading information, and they sued the book manufacturer under, among other things, a theory of product liability and negligence.

The U.S. Court of Appeals held that product liability law focuses on and is limited to tangible items, and does not take into consideration ideas and expressions. The court disposed of the negligence claim by ruling that the publisher had no duty to investigate the accuracy of the books it published and had no duty to warn the consumer that the information in the book was not complete and should not be completely relied upon.

Source: Winter v. G.P. Putnam's Sons, 938 F. 2d 1033 (9th Cir. 1991).

A manufacturer will be held strictly liable for its defective products regardless of how remote it is from the final user of the product. The one requirement is that the manufacturer be in the business of selling the injury-causing product. Thus, occasional sellers, such as a typesetting company selling an unused computer, are not strictly liable. The manufacturer may be held liable even when it is the distributor who makes final inspections, corrections, and adjustments of the product. Wholesalers are usually held strictly liable for defects in the products they sell. However, in some jurisdictions, a wholesaler is not liable for latent or hidden defects if the wholesaler sells the products in exactly the same condition that it received them.

A retailer may also be held strictly liable. For example, in the automobile industry, retailers have a duty to inspect and care for their products. Several jurisdictions, however, will not hold a retailer liable if it did not contribute to the defect and played no part in the manufacturing process.

Sellers of used goods are usually not held strictly liable because they are not within the original chain of distribution of the product. In addition, the custom in the used-goods market is that there are no warranties or expectations relating to the quality of the products (although some jurisdictions have adopted rules requiring warranties for used cars). However, a seller of used goods is strictly liable for any defective repairs or replacements that he or she makes.

A maker of component parts to manufacturers' specifications is not liable if the specifications for the entire product are questioned, as this is considered a design defect. For example, the maker of a car's fuel injection system would not be liable if the automaker's specifications for the fuel injection system are defective because the engine provides insufficient power to change lanes safely on a freeway. However, makers of component parts are liable for manufacturing defects.

There is no strict liability in the service industries, only liability for negligence. In some cases it is unclear whether an injury was caused by a defective product or a negligently performed service. For example, a person may be injured by a needle used by a dentist, or the hair solution used by a beautician. Some courts apply strict liability in these situations. Other courts will not go so far down the chain of distribution.

Successor Liability

A corporation purchasing or acquiring the assets of another is liable for its debts if there is (1) a consolidation or merger of the two corporations; or (2) an express or implied agreement to assume such obligations. Even if a transaction is structured as a sale of assets, there will still be successor liability if (1) the purchasing corporation is merely a continuation of the selling corporation; or (2) the transaction was entered into to escape liability. Thus, the acquiring corporation can be liable to a party injured by a defect in the transferor corporation's product.[1]

Defenses

The defendant in a product liability case may raise the traditional tort defenses of assumption of risk and, in some jurisdictions, a variation of comparative negligence known as comparative fault. In addition, there are defenses that apply only to product liability cases, such as the state-of-the-art defense available in some jurisdictions. Acceptance of the following defenses varies from state to state.

Comparative Fault Contributory negligence by the plaintiff is not a defense in a strict liability action. However, the damages may be reduced by the degree to which the plaintiff's own negligence contributed to the injury. This doctrine is known as *comparative fault*.

Assumption of Risk When a person voluntarily and unreasonably assumes the risk of a known danger, the manufacturer is not liable for any resulting injury. For example, if a toaster bears a conspicuous warning not to insert metal objects in it while it is plugged in, and a person sticks a metal fork in it anyway and is electrocuted, the toaster manufacturer will not be liable. Similarly, if a person goes to a baseball game and is injured by a foul ball, the baseball club will not be liable.

Courts are reluctant to find assumption of risk. For example, one court found no assumption of risk when a grinding disc exploded and hit a person in the eye.[2] The court reasoned that, although the injured person should have been wearing goggles, he could not have anticipated that a hidden defect in the disc would cause it to explode. By not wearing goggles, the injured person assumed only the risk of dust or small particles of wood or metal lodging in his eyes.

Obviousness of the Risk   If the use of a product carries an obvious risk, the manufacturer will not be held liable for injuries that result from ignoring the risk. For example, a Volkswagen microbus was held not defective even though the shortened front end resulted in more serious injuries in a collision.

Misuse of the Product   A manufacturer or seller is entitled to assume that its product will be used in a normal manner. The manufacturer or seller will not be held liable for injuries resulting from abnormal use of its product. However, an unusual use that is reasonably foreseeable may be considered a normal use. For example, operating a lawn mower with the grass bag removed was held to be a foreseeable use, and the manufacturer was liable to a bystander injured by an object that shot out of the unguarded mower.[3]

State-of-the-Art Defense   This defense is based on a manufacturer's compliance with the best available technology (which may or may not be synonymous with the custom and practice of the industry). The *state-of-the-art defense* shields a manufacturer from liability if no safer product design is generally recognized as being possible. For example, an Indiana statute provides: "It is a defense that the design, manufacture, inspection, packaging, warning, or labeling of the product was in conformity with the generally recognized state of the art at the time the product was designed, manufactured, packaged, and labeled."[4] A Missouri statute provides that, if the defendant can prove that the dangerous nature of the product was not known and could not reasonably be discovered at the time the product was placed in the stream of commerce, then the defendant will not be held liable for failure to warn.[5]

ADVERTISING

Sellers of goods will usually want to advertise. Three main bodies of law regulate advertising, with the purpose of each being protection of consumers against false or deceptive advertising.

Common Law

A traditional common-law approach provides two remedies for a consumer who has been misled by false advertising. First, a consumer may be able to sue for breach of contract. In this instance, however, it may be difficult to prove the existence of a contract, because advertisements are usually considered by the courts to be only an offer to deal. A consumer might also sue for the tort of deceit. Deceit requires the proof of several elements, including knowledge by the seller that the misrepresentation is false. Here, however, the misrepresentation must be one of fact and not opinion, a difficult distinction to make in the context of advertising. (Deceit, also called fraudulent misrepresentation, and other business torts are discussed in chapter 12.)

Statutory Law

The UCC and the Lanham Act are two statutes that may protect consumers from false advertising. As explained above, under the UCC, any statement, sample, or model may constitute an express warranty if it is part of the basis of the bargain. Sometimes, advertisement of a product may be construed as an express warranty. If so, the buyer can recover for breach of warranty under the UCC.

A federal law called the Lanham Act forbids the use of any false "description or representation" in connection with any goods or services, and provides a claim for any competitor (rather than consumer) who might be injured by any other competitor's false claims. The purpose of the act is to ensure truthfulness in advertising and eliminate misrepresentations of quality regarding one's own product or the product of a competitor.

For example, the Coca-Cola Company, maker of Minute Maid orange juice, sued Tropicana Products, Inc., in the early 1980s under the Lanham Act. At issue was a television commercial in which athlete Bruce Jenner squeezed an orange while saying, "It's pure, pasteurized juice as it comes from the orange," and then pouring the juice into a Tropicana carton. Coca-Cola claimed that the commercial was false because it represented that Tropicana contains unprocessed, fresh-squeezed juice when in fact the juice is heated (pasteurized) and sometimes frozen before packaging. The court agreed that the representation was false because it suggested that pasteurized juice comes directly from oranges. The court granted an injunction to prevent Tropicana from continuing to use the advertisement.[6]

Revlon sued rival Procter & Gamble in 1995 over ads that suggested that Revlon's ColorStay lipstick "kisses off," contrary to Revlon's claim that it stays on. Revlon withdrew the case while the parties tried to resolve their claims privately. The maker of antacid Tagamet HB sued the maker of Pepcid AC in 1995, arguing that the maker of Pepcid AC engaged in deceptive advertising when it claimed that its product relieved heartburn for nine hours. The makers of Tagamet asserted that Pepcid AC takes two hours to work and thus relieves heartburn for only seven hours. The case is still pending.[7]

Roughly sixteen states permit consumers to bring suits for deceptive trade practices. For example, purchasers of Kenner Corp.'s Easy Bake Oven brought a class action under California law. The plaintiffs alleged that it took children twenty-nine to thirty-four minutes to bake a treat, not the less than ten minutes claimed by Kenner Corp. The case was settled under a confidentiality agreement in 1995.[8]

Both companies and consumers can handle disputes privately and more cheaply by turning to a private court run by the National Advertising Division of the Council of Better Business Bureaus. This option is particularly attractive to growing companies that are cash constrained.

Regulatory Law: The FTC

Unfair or deceptive acts or trade practices, including false advertising, are illegal. Congress has given the Federal Trade Commission (FTC) the authority to prevent unfair and deceptive trade practices. Among the areas the FTC has addressed are deceptive price and quality claims, false testimonials, and mock-ups.

Deceptive Price   Deceptive pricing is any practice that tends to mislead or deceive consumers about the price they are paying for a good or service. One example of deceptive pricing practices involves car rental companies. Collision damage waivers (CDW), which release renters from liability for damage to the car, can add up to $14 to the advertised daily rental price of a car. Consumers are enticed by advertisements offering low daily rates but are then often pressured into buying the additional CDW. At least one state has prohibited the use of CDWs as a way to maintain an artificially low daily rental price.

Deceptive pricing practices also include offers of free merchandise with a purchase, or two-for-one deals in which the advertiser recovers the cost of the free merchandise by charging more than the regular price for the merchandise bought. Another example of deceptive pricing, *bait and switch advertising*, is regulated by the FTC. An advertiser violates FTC rules if it refuses to show an advertised item, fails to have a reasonable quantity of the item in stock, fails to promise to deliver the item within a reasonable time, or discourages employees from selling the advertised item.

Quality Claims   Advertisements often include quality claims. These claims imply that the advertiser has some reasonable basis for making the claim. Under the FTC's general view, quality claims made without any substantiation are deceptive. On the other hand, obvious exaggerations and vague generalities are considered puffing, and are not considered deceptive because they are unlikely to mislead consumers. To determine whether an advertiser has made a deceptive quality claim, the FTC must first identify the claim and then determine whether the claim is substantiated.

False Testimonials and Mock-ups   Testimonials and endorsements in which the person endorsing a product does not, in fact, use or prefer it are deceptive and violate the law. Additionally, it is deceptive for the endorser to imply falsely that he or she has superior knowledge or experience of the product. It is also illegal to show an advertisement that purports to be an actual product demonstration but in fact is a mock-up or simulation.

For example, television and print ads from an October 1990 ad campaign showed a Volvo automobile withstanding the impact of a giant-tired "monster truck" named Bear Foot that flattened the rest of a line of cars. What was not readily apparent from the advertisement was that the Volvo's roof had been reinforced, and some of the other vehicles' supports had been weakened. In response, the Federal Trade Commission required, for the first time, the advertising firm (and not just the advertiser) to pay a fine for the deceptive ad. Thus, the carmaker and its New York advertising firm each agreed to pay a $150,000 penalty, though neither admitted violating laws against false advertising.[9]

FROM THE TRENCHES

Colgate-Palmolive Company ran three one-minute television commercials designed to show that its Rapid Shave shaving cream outperformed other brands. Each commercial contained the same sandpaper test, in which the announcer informed the audience that "To prove Rapid Shave's super moisturizing power, we put it right from the can onto this tough, dry sandpaper. It was apply. . . soak. . . and off in a stroke." While the announcer was speaking, Rapid Shave was applied to a substance that appeared to be sandpaper, and immediately thereafter a razor was shown shaving the substance clean.

The Federal Trade Commission (FTC) issued a complaint charging that the commercials were false and deceptive. Evidence disclosed that sandpaper of the type depicted in the commercials could not be shaved immediately following the application of Rapid Shave but required a soaking period of approximately eighty minutes. The evidence also showed that the substance resembling sandpaper was in fact a simulated prop, or mock-up, made of plexiglass to which sand had been applied.

The FTC found that Colgate-Palmolive had misrepresented Rapid Shave's moisturizing power and issued an order prohibiting Colgate-Palmolive from presenting advertisements that depicted a test, experiment, or demonstration as actual proof of a product claim, when, in fact, there was the undisclosed use of a prop or mock-up.

The Supreme Court agreed with the FTC that the undisclosed use of plexiglass in the commercials was a material deceptive practice and that advertisers should either inform viewers that they are not seeing an actual test, experiment, or demonstration, or should show simulated demonstrations in a truthful manner. If neither option is possible, advertisers should refrain from showing such demonstrations on television.

Source: Federal Trade Comm'n. v. Colgate-Palmolive Co., 380 U.S. 374 (1965).

Putting It into Practice

With its products ready for launch, WebRunner enlisted the aid of an advertising agency to create a marketing campaign. The agency produced several thirty-second commercials showing WebRunner's products in action. Alexandra liked the commercials but sensed that something wasn't quite right with the product demonstrations. Although the IRRS would allow information to be obtained in a matter of seconds, the programs in the commercial were retrieving information almost instantaneously.

She asked the ad's designer about it. "Oh yeah, we filmed the program and sped up the tape by a factor of three," the designer replied. "We thought it looked better accelerated." Alexandra nodded her head but knew she would have to check with Michael Woo to see whether this was all right.

"I'm glad you thought to ask," said Michael. "The ad must either show the program at its normal speed or have a disclaimer flashed on the screen telling viewers that the demonstration has been accelerated. Otherwise WebRunner could be guilty of false advertising and subject to FTC sanctions."

Alexandra discussed the alternatives with the Eagles. After some deliberation, they decided that the ad program should be shown in real time and that the several-second lag could easily be filled with conversation between the actors.

Alexandra was also concerned that buyers might use WebRunner's products for purposes for which they were not intended. For example, one of WebRunner's applets quickly retrieves sports scores, highlights, and predictions. Alexandra was concerned that buyers in states permitting gambling might use the applet to compile statistics that they would rely on in placing bets.

She discussed the matter with Michael, who suggested that the IRRS software include a feature whereby a buyer could not purchase and download an applet unless the buyer first scrolled through a software license agreement and checked a box on the screen indicating that the buyer agreed to be bound by the terms and conditions of the software license agreement. Michael said that the license should explicitly waive all UCC warranties and should indicate that the product is intended for recreational purposes only.

Michael and Josh Austin prepared the following license agreement:

1. **License.** This WebRunner License Agreement grants you the non-exclusive right to use one copy of the enclosed software and enclosed

continued

continued

documentation on a single computer for recreational purposes only. You may use the software on a different computer only if you first delete the software from all previous computers.

2. **Limited Warranty.** WebRunner warrants that the software will be free from defects for a period of ninety days from the date of purchase. If defects are present, WebRunner's entire liability and your exclusive remedy shall be limited to the replacement of the defective software or, at WebRunner's option, refund of the purchase price.

3. **No Other Warranties.** To the maximum extent permitted by applicable law, WebRunner expressly disclaims all warranties, both express and implied, including but not limited to implied warranties of merchantability and fitness for a particular purpose, with respect to the software and documentation. This product is sold AS IS. WebRunner does not warrant that the software will meet your needs or that operation of the software will be uninterrupted or error free.

4. **Limitation of Liability.** To the maximum extent permitted by applicable law, neither WebRunner nor its content providers shall under any circumstances, including negligence, be liable for any incidental, special, or consequential damages that result from the operation of or inability to use the software or documentation, even if WebRunner has been advised of the possibility of such damages.

Alexandra then scheduled a meeting with Michael to discuss ways of minimizing WebRunner's likelihood of becoming embroiled in a lawsuit claiming a business tort.

Notes

1. *See, e.g., Ray v. Alad Corp.*, 560 P.2d 3 (Cal. 1977) (successor that continues to manufacture the same product line as the predecessor, under the same name, with no outward indication of any change of ownership of the business could be held liable for product liability claims resulting from products manufactured by the predecessor). *See also Turner v. Bituminous Casualty Co.*, 244 N.W.2d 873 (Mich. 1976).
2. *Haugen v. Minnesota Mining and Mfg. Co.*, 550 P.2d 72 (Wash. Ct. App. 1976).
3. *LaPaglia v. Sears, Roebuck & Co.*, 531 N.Y.S.2d 623 (N.Y. App. Div. 1988).
4. Ind. Code Ann. section 33-1-1.5-4.
5. Mo. Rev. Stat. section 537.764.
6. *Coca-Cola Co. v. Tropicana Products, Inc.*, 690 F.2d 312 (2d Cir. 1982).
7. *See* Jeff Barge, "Advertising Wars Heating Up," *ABA Journal*, April 1996, at 32.
8. *Id.* at 32–33.
9. "F.T.C. Accord on Volvo Ads," *The New York Times,* Aug. 22, 1991, at D19.

Business Torts

A *tort* is a wrong that injures a person, property, or certain economic interests and business relationships. The injured party is entitled to recover damages from the responsible party. A company is always liable for the torts it commits. In addition, companies are vicariously liable for torts committed by employees acting within the scope of their employment.

It is important for the entrepreneur to understand a company's potential tort exposure so as to minimize the potential risk. Tort liability and its ensuing litigation can threaten a new business venture's viability. The risk of tort liability is a major reason for incorporating or otherwise properly structuring a company to shield the owners from personal liability. (Forms of business organizations offering limited liability are discussed in chapter 4.)

The chapter first introduces the tort of negligence, its elements, and its defenses. It then covers intentional torts that protect people, property, and certain economic interests and business relationships. The chapter next describes strict liability for ultrahazardous activities. The chapter continues with a discussion of the means by which a company may be liable for torts committed by its employees, then concludes with suggested methods by which an entrepreneur may reduce tort risks.

ELEMENTS OF NEGLIGENCE

Negligence is conduct that involves an unreasonably great risk of causing injury to another person or damage to property. To establish liability under a negligence theory, the plaintiff must show that (1) the defendant owed a duty to the plaintiff to act reasonably under the circumstances; (2) the defendant breached that duty by failing to use the care that a reasonably prudent person would have used; (3) there is a reasonably close causal connection between the defendant's breach and the plaintiff's injury; and (4) the plaintiff suffered an actual loss or injury.

Duty

A person with a legal duty to another is required to act reasonably under the circumstances to avoid harming the other person. Duty exists in a variety of contexts, including the two discussed below.

Duty of Landowner or Tenant A possessor of land (such as a tenant) or its owner has a legal duty to keep the property reasonably safe. Such a person can be liable for injury that occurs outside, as well as on, his or her premises. For example, a person may be liable for harm caused if water from his cooling tower floods the highway, or if sparks from improperly maintained machinery start a fire on adjacent property.

Generally, landowners are not liable for harm caused by natural conditions on their property, such as uncut weeds that obstruct a driver's view, the natural flow of surface water, or falling rocks. However, the landowner may be liable if he or she has altered the natural state of the land, for example, by building a dam that floods a highway, or erecting a sign or planting trees that obstruct a motorist's view.

In a few jurisdictions, landowners have a duty to maintain sidewalks immediately adjacent to their property. In all jurisdictions, a landowner has a general duty to inspect a building on his or her land and keep it in repair, and may be liable if a showroom window, a downspout, a screen, or a loose sign falls and injures someone.

Landowners have varying duties to persons on their land, depending on the person's reasons for being on the property. The duty owed to individuals ranges from almost no duty to someone who is a trespasser to an affirmative duty to protect a person who enters the premises for business purposes (an *invitee*). A customer is clearly an invitee and is accordingly owed a higher duty of care than a mere social guest (called a *licensee*).

Duties of Employer to Third Parties Under certain circumstances, employers have a legal duty to protect strangers from injuries caused by their employees. For example, an employer was held potentially liable for an automobile accident in which an intoxicated employee sent home by his employer killed someone while driving home.[1] An employer may also be responsible for the safe passage home of an employee who is not intoxicated but is tired from working too many consecutive hours.[2] In addition, as discussed later in this chapter, an employer is liable for any torts committed by employees acting within the scope of their employment.

Standard of Conduct

A person is required to act as a reasonable person of ordinary prudence would act under the circumstances. The standard of care is not graduated to include the reasonably slow person, the reasonably forgetful person, or the reasonable person of low intelligence. On the other hand, a person who is specially trained to participate in a profession or trade will be held to the higher standard of care of a reasonably skilled member of that profession or trade. For example, the professional conduct of a doctor, architect, pilot, attorney, or accountant will be measured against the standard of the profession. The fact that one complied with a law is not a defense if a reasonably prudent person would have done more than the law required. Thus, for example, a tugboat operator that did not have a radio could still be found negligent even though a radio was not legally required, if prudent tugboat operators would have installed one.

DEFENSES TO NEGLIGENCE

In some jurisdictions, the defendant may absolve itself of part or all of the liability for negligence by proving that the plaintiff was also negligent.

Contributory Negligence

Under the doctrine of *contributory negligence*, if the plaintiff was also negligent in any manner, he or she cannot recover any damages from the defendant. Thus, if a plaintiff was 5% negligent and the defendant was 95% negligent, the plaintiff's injury would go unredressed. Most courts have replaced the doctrine of contributory negligence with that of comparative negligence.

"To answer your question. Yes. If you shoot an arrow into the air and it falls to earth you know not where, you could be liable for any damage it may cause."

Drawing by Maslin; © 1990 the New Yorker Magazine, Inc.

Comparative Negligence

Comparative negligence allows the plaintiff to recover the proportion of his or her loss attributable to the defendant's negligence. For example, if the plaintiff was 5% negligent and the defendant was 95% negligent, the plaintiff can recover 95% of the loss. Some jurisdictions allow plaintiffs to recover for the percentage the defendant is at fault only if the plaintiff is responsible for less than 50% of his or her own injuries. Thus, in these jurisdictions, if the plaintiff is found 51% negligent and the defendant 49% negligent, the plaintiff cannot recover at all.

INTENTIONAL TORTS

A number of business torts require an intent to harm the plaintiff, the plaintiff's property, or certain economic interests and business relationships. A person is automatically liable for intentional torts without regard to duty.

Torts to Protect Persons

Several business torts are designed to protect individuals from physical and mental harm. These include false imprisonment, intentional infliction of emotional distress, defamation, and appropriation of another's likeness. A single set of facts may give rise to claims under more than one theory.

False Imprisonment *False imprisonment* is intentional restraint of movement, imposed against someone's will by physical barriers, physical force, or threats of force. False imprisonment has also been found when the plaintiff's freedom of movement was restricted because of force applied to the plaintiff's valuable property. For example, a court found false imprisonment when a store's clerk confiscated a shopper's purchase after the shopper had paid for it.[3] Most states have legislation exempting shopkeepers from false imprisonment claims if it can be shown that the shopkeeper acted in good faith and the detention was made in a reasonable manner, for a reasonable time, and was based on reasonable cause.

FROM THE TRENCHES

A customer in a supermarket was stopped by a store security guard and accused of taking a bottle of aspirin which he had in the top pocket of his sweater. The guard told the customer that he had been under surveillance and had been seen taking the bottle of aspirin. The customer explained that he had bought the aspirin elsewhere and was just comparing prices.

The security guard notified the store manager that he had apprehended a shoplifter. While the manager called police, the security guard took the customer to a stockroom in the rear of the store, searched him, and handcuffed him to a large metal container.

The man protested his innocence to the security guard, to the store manager, and to the police who arrived to arrest him. The customer suggested that if they counted the aspirin, they would find that he had already taken two, and if they went to the drugstore where he had bought the aspirin, they would find the box for the aspirin in a trash can in front of the store. Neither the security guard nor the manager complied with the customer's request. After the police left with the customer, the store manager searched the supermarket unsuccessfully for the aspirin box that the guard claimed that the customer had ditched.

The customer filed suit against the corporation owning the supermarket, alleging false imprisonment and several other intentional torts. A jury awarded the customer $400 in actual damages and $175,000 in punitive damages. The appellate court upheld the actual and punitive awards on the grounds that the store manager's conscious indifference and refusal to attempt to ascertain the truth as to whether or not the aspirin had been purchased elsewhere justified the award by the jury.

Source: Colonial Stores, Inc. v. Fishel, 288 S.E. 2d 21 (Ga. App. 1981).

Intentional Infliction of Emotional Distress The tort of *intentional infliction of emotional distress* protects the right to peace of mind. In most jurisdictions, to prove intentional infliction of emotional distress, a plaintiff must show that (1) the defendant's conduct was outrageous; (2) the defendant intended to cause emotional distress; and (3) the defendant's actions caused severe emotional suffering.

The plaintiff's emotional distress must be foreseeable and the defendant's acts must have been outrageous or intolerable for the tort to arise. Insulting, abusive, profane, or annoying conduct is not in itself a tort.

Everyone is expected to be hardened to a certain amount of abuse. In determining outrageousness, courts will consider the context of the tort, as well as the relationship of the parties. For example, in the workplace, the plaintiff can expect to be subjected to evaluation and criticism, and neither criticism nor discharge is in itself outrageous.

The entrepreneur is most likely to encounter claims of intentional infliction of emotional distress in situations in which an employee complains to a supervisor about sexual harassment and the employer fails to investigate the claim and take appropriate remedial action.

Defamation *Defamation* is the communication (often termed *publication*) to a third party of an untrue statement of fact that injures the plaintiff's reputation. *Libel* is written defamation, and *slander* is spoken defamation.

Claims of defamation in the business context often arise out of adverse comments about a former employee's performance. Fear of such claims causes many employers to refuse to act as references for former employees other than to confirm dates of employment, title, and salary.

Appropriation of Another's Likeness *Appropriation of a person's name or likeness* may be an invasion of privacy. Often this tort is committed for financial gain. For example, using a fictitious testimonial in an advertisement, or using a person's picture in an advertisement or article with which he or she has no connection, would be a tort.

Torts to Protect Interests in Property

A number of torts are designed to protect interests in property. These include trespass to land, nuisance, conversion, and trespass to personal property.

Trespass to Land *Trespass to land* is an intentional invasion of real property without the consent of the owner. For example, a person driving a truck onto land belonging to another person commits trespass even if the land is not injured. The intent required is the intent to enter the property, not the intent to trespass. Thus, a person would still be liable for trespass

FROM THE TRENCHES

Leta Fay Ford won a suit against cosmetics manufacturer Revlon, Inc. for intentional infliction of emotional distress after company officials failed to stop ongoing harassment by her supervisor, Karl Braun.

The harassment began in April 1980 after Braun invited her to dinner, supposedly to discuss business. However, at the end of the evening, when Ford tried to leave, Braun told her to stay because he planned to spend the night with her. When she rejected his advances, he told her, "You will regret this." This was only the first of several incidents in which Braun harassed Ford, including one a month later at a company picnic at which Braun held Ford in a choke hold, fondled her, and made lewd comments to her.

Although Ford had not reported the first incident to Revlon management, after the company picnic incident she initiated a series of meetings with several members of Revlon management to report her complaints. She told them that she was afraid of Braun, that she wanted help, and that the strain of dealing with Braun and his advances was making her sick.

The harassment continued throughout 1980 with Braun threatening to destroy Ford and promising her that as long as she worked for him she was never going to go anywhere. When no action had been taken by Revlon management by December 1980, Ford contacted a manager to whom she had complained earlier. The manager told Ford that the situation was too hot to handle, and that Ford should put the matter in the back of her mind and try to forget about it. During the time of the harassment, Ford developed high blood pressure, a nervous tic in her left eye, chest pains, rapid breathing, and other symptoms of emotional distress.

In February 1981, Ford requested a job transfer and met with a personnel representative to try to resolve her grievance. Not until three months later did the personnel representative submit a report on Ford's complaint to a Revlon vice president. The report confirmed Ford's charge of sexual assault and recommended that Braun be censured. In May 1981, a full year and a month after Braun's initial act of harassment, Braun was issued a letter of censure from Revlon.

In October 1981, Ford attempted suicide. Later that month Revlon fired Braun. In April 1982, Ford sued both Braun and Revlon for assault and battery, and for intentional infliction of emotional distress.

The Arizona Supreme Court upheld a jury verdict against Revlon, holding that Revlon's conduct in ignoring Ford's situation for months was outrageous and extreme, and thus fulfilled the requirements for intentional infliction of emotional distress.

Source: Ford v. Revlon Inc., 734 P. 2d 580 (Ariz. 1987).

FROM THE TRENCHES

Samsung Electronics America, Inc. ran a series of print advertisements, each of which depicted an item from popular culture along with a Samsung electronics product. Each ad was set in the twenty-first century and conveyed the message that the Samsung product would still be in use at that time.

One advertisement for Samsung videocassette recorders (VCRs) depicted a robot, dressed in a wig, gown, and jewelry, that Samsung had intentionally selected to resemble Vanna White, the hostess of *Wheel of Fortune*. The ad contained the caption "Longest-running game show. 2012 A.D." Vanna White, unlike the other celebrities depicted in the ads, neither consented to the depiction nor was paid.

White sued Samsung for unlawfully appropriating her image, among other things. The trial court ruled in favor of the defendants without letting a jury decide the case. The appellate court reversed and ordered a jury trial.

Source: White v. Samsung Electronics America, Inc., 971 F. 2d 1395 (9th Cir. 1992).

---

if he intentionally stood on land he believed was owned by a friend who had given consent that was in fact owned by someone who had not given consent; the mistake as to ownership is irrelevant.

Trespass may occur both below the land's surface and in the airspace above it. Throwing something, such as trash, onto the land or shooting bullets over it may be trespasses, even though the perpetrator was not standing on the plaintiff's land.

Refusing to move something that at one time the plaintiff permitted the defendant to place on the land may be a trespass. For example, if the plaintiff gave the defendant permission to leave a forklift on the plaintiff's land for one month, and it was left for two, the defendant may be liable for trespass.

Nuisance *Nuisance* is a nontrespassory interference with the use and enjoyment of real property, for example, by an annoying odor or noise.

Public nuisance is unreasonable and substantial interference with the public health, safety, peace, comfort, convenience, or utilization of land. A public nuisance action is usually brought by the government. It may also be brought by a private citizen who experiences special harm different from that of the general public.

Private nuisance is unreasonable and substantial interference with an individual's use and enjoyment of his or her land. Discharge of noxious fumes into the air, the pollution of a stream, or playing loud music late at night in a residential neighborhood can constitute a private nuisance.

To determine whether the defendant's conduct is unreasonable, the court will balance the utility of the activity creating the harm and the burden of preventing it against the nature and the gravity of the harm. For example, hammering noise during the remodeling of a house may be easier to justify than playing loud music purely for recreation.

Conversion *Conversion* is the exercise of dominion and control over the personal property, rather than the real property, of another. This tort protects the right to have personal property left alone. It prevents the defendant from treating the plaintiff's property as if it were his or her own. It is the tort claim a plaintiff would assert to recover the value of property stolen, destroyed, or substantially altered by the defendant.

The intent element for conversion does not include a wrongful motive. It merely requires the intent to exercise dominion or control over goods, inconsistent with the plaintiff's rights. The defendant need not know that the goods belonged to the plaintiff. If someone takes a box of computer hardware from the back of the store without paying for it, puts it in his car, and drives away, that is conversion.

Trespass to Personal Property If personal property is interfered with but not converted there is a *trespass to personal property* (sometimes referred to as *trespass to chattels*). No wrongful motive need be shown. The intent required is the intent to exercise control over the plaintiff's personal property. For example, an employer who took an employee's car on a short errand without the employee's permission would be liable for trespass to personal property. However, if the employer damaged the car or drove it for several thousand miles, thereby lowering its value, he or she would be liable for conversion.

Torts that Protect Certain Economic Interests and Business Relationships

This section will conclude with torts designed to protect certain economic interests and business relationships, namely, fraudulent misrepresentation, interference with contractual relations, interference with prospective business advantage, and unfair competition.

Fraudulent Misrepresentation   The tort of *fraudulent misrepresentation*, also called *fraud* or *deceit*, protects economic interests and the right to be treated fairly and honestly. Fraud requires proof that the defendant intentionally misled the plaintiff by making a material misrepresentation of fact on which the plaintiff relied. It also requires that the plaintiff suffer injury as a result of the reliance. For example, if an entrepreneur told an investor that she had developed certain key technology and owned all rights to it when in fact she knew that it belonged to her former employer, that would be fraudulent misrepresentation.

Fraud can also be based on the defendant's omission of a material fact when he or she has a duty to speak because of a special relationship with the plaintiff. For example, in one case, the plaintiff owned an auto dealership and had relied on a bank for several years for financial advice. The plaintiff contacted the bank about purchasing a second dealership and was advised to purchase a certain dealership; the bank did not tell the plaintiff that the other dealership was losing money and owed the bank money. The plaintiff took the bank's advice and bought the troubled dealership. The plaintiff suffered great financial hardship and eventually lost both dealerships after the bank refused to extend financing. The plaintiff sued the bank for fraudulent misrepresentation and won a $4.5 million verdict.

Interference with Contractual Relations   The tort of *interference with contractual relations* protects the right to enjoy the benefits of legally binding agreements. It provides a remedy when the defendant intentionally induces another person to breach a contract with the plaintiff.

Interference with contractual relations requires that the defendant know there is a contract.

Perhaps the most famous case involving tortious interference with a contract was *Pennzoil v. Texaco*. A jury assessed Texaco $10.5 billion in damages for interfering with Pennzoil's contract to buy Getty Oil. Texaco offered Getty Oil a better price and agreed to indemnify Getty Oil if sued by Pennzoil for breach of contract.[4] The case was ultimately settled for $3 billion.

In some jurisdictions, interference with contractual relations also requires an unacceptable purpose; if good grounds exist for the interference, the defendant is not liable. For example, if a manager of a corporation is incompetent, a shareholder of a corporation may be able to induce breach of the employment agreement between the manager and the corporation. The shareholder's motive would be to protect his or her investment. On the other hand, a defendant may not interfere with another person's contract in order to attract customers or employees away from that person.

Interference with Prospective Business Advantage   Courts are less willing to award damages for interference with prospective contracts than they are to protect existing contracts. A party still engaged in negotiating a contract has fewer rights not to have his or her deal disturbed than a party that has already entered into a contract.

To prove *interference with prospective business advantage*, the plaintiff must prove that the defendant unjustifiably interfered with a relationship the plaintiff sought to develop and that the interference caused the plaintiff's loss. The interference must be intentional. However, in rare cases, courts have permitted recovery if the defendant was merely negligent.

Interference with prospective business advantage is usually committed by a competitor, or at least by one who stands to benefit from the interference. However, it is not a tort to compete fairly. Most jurisdictions recognize a privilege to act for one's own financial gain.

Unfair Competition   Courts are willing to find certain kinds of anticompetitive behavior actionable if the activities complained of seem egregious to the court. These cases fall under the rubric of *unfair competition*, which is defined in California, for example, to include "unlawful, unfair or deceptive business practices."[5] The improper use of trade secrets and customer information of prior employers often is found to constitute unfair competition. Also, destroying a business by hiring away all of its employees has been deemed unfair competition.

FROM THE TRENCHES

The general manager and the chief engineer, respectively, of two divisions of AMCOA left the company to join a competitor. Prior to leaving, one had prepared a list showing all jobs bid by AMCOA that totaled more than $10,000. He also had prepared a list of recently completed jobs, showing customers, type of materials, and dollar amount. During the two days immediately following the resignations, the two former employees called virtually all of the sales representatives of AMCOA throughout the country to inform them of their resignation and to tell them that either the competitor would buy AMCOA or the two former employees would start their own company. Sales representatives were informed that a majority of the representatives were canceling their contracts with AMCOA and signing on with the competitor. The competing firm placed bids on jobs on which the former employees had prepared preliminary specifications for AMCOA. Additionally, the former employees contacted key personnel of AMCOA on behalf of the competitor. The former employees informed the key personnel that AMCOA was a sinking ship and would not be in business long, and expressed the belief that they would be able to hire away AMCOA's entire sales force for the competitor.

AMCOA sued the competitor and the two former employees. The court held that the destruction or substantial injury of a business, by means of attracting away all or a large percentage of the personnel on whom the business depended, is unfair competition and compensable, even in the case of at-will employees, especially if other circumstances, such as misrepresentation of the plaintiff's solvency to the plaintiff's employees or customers or misappropriation of confidential information, are involved.

Source: Architectural Manufacturing Co. v. Airotec, Inc., 166 S.E. 2d 744 (Ga. App. 1969).

STRICT LIABILITY

Strict liability is liability without fault, that is, without negligence or intent. Strict liability is imposed in product liability cases and for ultra-hazardous activities. (Strict liability for defective products is discussed in chapter 11.)

Ultrahazardous Activities

If the defendant's activity is *ultrahazardous*, that is, so dangerous that no amount of care could protect others from the risk of harm, the defendant is strictly liable for any injuries that result from his or her activity. Courts have found the following activities ultrahazardous: (1) storing flammable liquids in quantity in an urban area; (2) pile driving; (3) blasting; (4) crop dusting; (5) fumigation with cyanide gas; (6) emission of noxious fumes by a manufacturing plant located in a settled area; (7) locating oil wells or refineries in populated communities; and (8) test-firing solid-fuel rocket motors. However, courts have considered parachuting, drunk driving, maintaining power lines, and letting water escape from an irrigation ditch not to be ultrahazardous. A court is more likely to consider a dangerous activity ultrahazardous when it is inappropriate to the particular location.

Under strict liability, once the court determines that the activity is abnormally dangerous, it is irrelevant that the defendant observed a high standard of care. For example, if the defendant's blasting injured the plaintiff, it is irrelevant that the defendant took every precaution available. Although evidence of such precautions might prevent the plaintiff from recovering under a theory of negligence, it does not affect strict liability. Strict liability for ultrahazardous activities makes liability insurance particularly important.

TOXIC TORTS

Since the 1970s tort law has been evolving in response to sustained social and political concern over toxic substances and their potential for personal injury and environmental and property damage. A *toxic tort* is a wrongful act that causes injury by exposure to a harmful, hazardous, or poisonous substance. Modern industrial and consumer society uses these substances in a variety of ways, creating countless opportunities for toxic tort claims.

Potential toxic tort defendants include the following kinds of manufacturers: (1) those that use substances that may injure an employee, a consumer, or a bystander; (2) those whose processes emit hazardous by-products into the air or discharge them into a river; (3) those whose waste material goes to a disposal site if it could migrate to the groundwater and contaminate nearby wells; and (4) those whose products contain or create substances that can injure. However, liability is not limited to manufacturers. Everyday activities of governmental agencies, distribution services, and consumers may provide a basis for toxic tort claims. Some substances once thought safe, such as asbestos, have resulted in ruinous litigation when it was later established that they were harmful. Even financial institutions can be caught in the toxic tort net by becoming involved in the operations of a company handling hazardous materials or by foreclosing on contaminated land held as collateral.

Open-ended claims for punitive damages are commonplace in toxic tort cases. Thus, plaintiffs typically allege intentional torts such as trespass, intentional infliction of emotional distress, and outrageous or despicable conduct in pursuing a toxic tort claim.

VICARIOUS LIABILITY AND RESPONDEAT SUPERIOR

It is possible for a company to be held liable for the negligent, or in some cases the intentional, conduct of its employees. Under the doctrine of *respondeat superior*—"let the master answer"—an employer is vicariously liable for the torts of an employee acting within the scope of his or her employment. The employer is liable even if the employer had no knowledge of the actions or had instructed the employee not to do the wrongful act. For example, a pizza company would be liable if its delivery person hit someone while speeding to deliver a pizza on time, even if the manger had instructed the employee not to speed.

Activities within the scope of employment are activities closely connected to what the employee is employed to do or reasonably incidental to it. Generally, an employee's conduct is considered within the scope of employment if it (1) is of the nature that he or she was employed to perform; (2) is within the time and space limitations normally authorized by the employer; and (3) furthers, at least in part, the purpose of the employer. On the other hand, an employer is not vicariously liable if an employee commits a tort while engaged in an activity solely for his or her own benefit. However, it is often unclear whether the employee's act was entirely outside the employer's purpose.

The law draws a distinction between a frolic and a detour. A *frolic* occurs when an employee goes off and does something unrelated to the employer's business for himself or herself. A *detour* occurs when an employee temporarily interrupts his or her work to do something for himself or herself. Although the law holds an employer responsible for an employee's torts occurring during a detour, an employer is not responsible for a frolic. For example, if an employee leaves work to run a personal errand and in the process hits someone with his or her car, it is a frolic. If, however, the employer sends the employee to drive and pick something up and the employee runs a personal errand along the way, then it is a detour, and the employer would be liable for any torts committed by the employee, including those committed during the portion of the trip relating to the personal matter.

If an employee intentionally causes injury to the plaintiff or the plaintiff's property, an employer may still be liable if the wrongful act in any way furthered the employer's purpose, however misguided the manner of furthering that purpose. For example, if an employee of a financially troubled company misrepresented the company's financial condition to obtain a bank loan needed for working capital, the employer would be liable for fraud.

REMEDIES

Tort damages are intended to compensate the plaintiff for the harm caused by the defendant. Tort damages may include punitive as well as compensatory damages. In addition, if monetary damages are not sufficient, a court may impose equitable relief.

Actual Damages

Actual damages, also known as *compensatory damages*, measure the cost to repair or replace an item, or the decrease in market value caused by the tortious conduct. Actual damages may also include compensation for medical expenses, lost wages, and pain and suffering.

Punitive Damages

Punitive damages (also called *exemplary damages*) may be awarded to punish the defendant and deter others from engaging in similar conduct. Punitive damages are awarded only in cases of outrageous misconduct. The amount of punitive damages may properly be based on the defendant's

---

FROM THE TRENCHES

In a well-publicized case that has become the poster child for tort reform, an 82-year-old woman was awarded almost $2.9 million by a jury for the third-degree burns she suffered after spilling her McDonald's coffee in her lap while a passenger in a car stopped at a McDonald's drive-thru window. The verdict consisted of $160,000 of compensatory damages and $2.7 million in punitive damages. The trial judge subsequently reduced punitive damages to $480,000.

McDonald's served its coffee at between 180 and 190 degrees on the advice of a coffee consultant, who said that it tastes best at that temperature. Coffee brewed at home, however, is typically between 135 and 140 degrees. McDonald's acknowledged receiving 700 complaints of scalding. The parties reached an out-of-court settlement for an undisclosed amount. McDonald's lowered the temperature of its coffee.

Source: "Coffee Spill Burns Woman; Jury Awards $2.9 Million," The Wall Street Journal, Aug. 19, 1994, at B3; "Coffee Case a Hot Topic; Facts Cool Debate," Hartford Courant, April 10, 1995, at A5.

wealth and, in most jurisdictions, must be proportional to the actual damages. Several states have limited punitive damage awards to situations in which the plaintiff can prove by clear and convincing evidence that the defendant was guilty of oppression, fraud, or malice.

Equitable Relief

If a money award cannot adequately compensate for the plaintiff's loss, courts may apply *equitable relief*. For example, the court may issue an *injunction*, that is, a court order, prohibiting the defendant from continuing in a certain course of activity. This remedy is particularly appropriate for torts such as trespass or nuisance, when the plaintiff wants the defendant to stop doing something. The court may also issue an injunction ordering the defendant to do something. For example, a newspaper could be ordered to publish a retraction.

LIABILITY OF MULTIPLE DEFENDANTS

The plaintiff may name numerous defendants in a liability action. In some cases, the defendants may ask the court to *join*, or add, other defendants. As a result, when a court determines what liability exists, it must grapple with the problem of allocating the losses among multiple defendants.

Joint and Several Liability

Under the doctrine of *joint and several liability*, multiple defendants are jointly (i.e., collectively) liable and also severally (i.e., individually) liable. This means that once the court determines that multiple defendants are at fault, the plaintiff may collect the entire judgment from any one of them, regardless of the degree of that defendant's fault. Thus, it is possible that a defendant who played a minor role in causing the plaintiff's injury might be required to pay all the damages. This is particularly likely when only one defendant has the money to pay the damages.

Joint and several liability often is imposed in toxic tort cases when a number of companies might have contributed to the contaminated site, such as a landfill or a river, yet it is the company with deep pockets that ends up having to pay for all the harm done the plaintiff. Some states have adopted statutes to limit the doctrine of joint and several liability.

Contribution and Indemnification

The doctrines of contribution and indemnification can mitigate the harsh effects of joint and several liability. *Contribution* distributes the loss among several defendants by requiring each to pay its proportionate share to the defendant that discharged their joint liability. *Indemnification* allows a defendant to shift some of its individual loss to other defendants whose relative blame is greater. These other defendants can be ordered to reimburse the one that has discharged a joint liability.

However, the right to contribution and the right to indemnification are worthless to a defendant if all the other defendants are insolvent or lack sufficient assets to contribute their share. In such a case, the defendant with money must still pay the plaintiff the full amount of damages awarded even though other defendants will not be able to pay the solvent defendant back for their share of the damages.

REDUCING TORT RISKS

The entrepreneur should implement ongoing programs of education and monitoring to reduce the risks of tort liability. Because torts can be committed in numerous ways, the programs should cover all possible sources of liability. For example, the management of a company that does not respond satisfactorily to an allegation of racial discrimination may be liable for intentional infliction of emotional distress. False statements made by representatives of a company about a competitor can constitute defamation.

In addition to preventing intentional torts such as these, employers should work to prevent their employees from committing acts of negligence, which can lead to large damage awards against the company. Any tort prevention program must recognize that, under the principle of respondeat superior, employers will be held liable for any torts their employees commit within the scope of their employment. It is crucial, therefore, to define the scope of employment clearly.

The entrepreneur should use care to avoid committing torts that are related to contractual relations and competition with other firms. For example, a company may be held liable for interference with contractual relations if a court finds that the company intentionally tried to induce a party to breach a contract. Also, while competition itself is permissible, intentionally seeking to sabotage the efforts of another firm is not. Employers may need to consult counsel when they are unsure whether their activity has crossed the line from permissible competition to tortious interference with a prospective business advantage.

In the toxic torts area, employers should adopt a long-term policy to protect employees, customers, and the environment from excess toxic exposure. They should identify any hazardous toxic substances used in their business activities or products, or released into the environment. When appropriate, employers should test and monitor to determine levels of exposure. Often, it is necessary to obtain an expert assessment of the hazards of toxicity of these substances.

A program of overall risk management and reduction is essential to reduce the potential of tort liability. It is often desirable to designate one person to be in charge of risk management. That person would keep track of all claims and determine what areas of company activity merit special attention. The head of risk management should be free to report incidents and problems to the chief executive officer and the board of directors, in much the same way as an internal auditor reports directly to the independent directors on the audit committee. This protocol enhances independence and reduces the fear of reprisals if the risk manager blows the whistle on high-ranking managers.

The entrepreneur should make certain that the company's insurance broker adequately understands the risks associated with the business and has put in place insurance sufficient to cover those risks.

Putting It into Practice

Alexandra was sitting in her office feeling pleased with the success of the product launch. Her thoughts were interrupted by a knock on her open door. She turned and saw Shawn Gersich, one of WebRunner's licensing representatives, poke his head into her office. "Do you have a minute to talk?" Shawn asked.

"Sure, what's up?" Alexandra replied. She watched Shawn, a former football lineman, sheepishly walk into her office and settle into a chair.

"I messed up," Shawn said. "And now someone is threatening to sue me and the company."

"Uh-oh," Alexandra muttered. "Start from the beginning, and tell me everything."

Shawn explained that he had been meeting with James Ward, an employee from Avatar Communications, which owned several major newspapers and television stations. WebRunner had been interested in licensing Avatar's content for an applet that would allow users to create personalized and up-to-date virtual newspapers and newscasts. The negotiations had been difficult, but Shawn and James had finally reached an agreement, at which point James offered to write up a term sheet. However, when James gave the term sheet to Shawn, Shawn saw that James had incorporated all of WebRunner's concessions but none of Avatar's. Enraged, Shawn ripped the term sheet in half and hurled it at James, striking him in the face. James rose to leave, but Shawn moved quickly to block his exit.

"No, you don't," Shawn said. "Neither of us is leaving until we write up a term sheet that reflects our agreement." After two hours, both Shawn and James were satisfied, and James left without saying a word.

The next day Shawn received a phone call from an attorney representing James, threatening to sue him and WebRunner for assault, battery, and false imprisonment. It was at this point that Shawn had gone to talk with Alexandra.

As Shawn finished the story, Alexandra shook her head and sighed. "Well, thank you for telling me about this," she said. "Let me look into it and we'll talk about this later."

The moment Shawn left her office, Alexandra picked up the phone, called Michael Woo, and said, "Michael, I have a problem." After

continued

continued

hearing her story, Michael replied, "You're right, Alexandra, you do." Michael explained that under the doctrine of *respondeat superior*, WebRunner is liable for the actions of its employees so long as they are within the scope of employment or further the employer's goals. Shawn's actions, although out of line, were within the scope of employment because they occurred while Shawn was working on WebRunner's behalf. Michael said that WebRunner was probably liable for battery (a harmful or offensive contact) and false imprisonment, and that the damages could easily reach $100,000.

Although Alexandra had purchased a liability policy for WebRunner that would cover the damages, she didn't want to use it because she knew the premiums would then go up. At the same time, WebRunner didn't have $100,000 or the thousands of dollars that would be spent in legal fees. Michael suggested that Alexandra call James and invite him to discuss the matter to see if there was some alternative to litigation.

Alexandra called James and invited him to meet with her the following day. After listening carefully to his story, Alexandra agreed with James that what Shawn had done was wrong, and she apologized for his actions. Alexandra assured James that she would sternly warn Shawn about his behavior and put a memorandum describing the incident in his personnel file. She also said that she would assign a different licensing representative to deal with Avatar in the future. James appreciated being heard, and told Alexandra that he was satisfied with her handling of the situation and would drop the matter.

Relieved that one potential crisis was averted, Alexandra decided to focus on human resources to prevent such an incident from ever occurring again.

NOTES

1. *Otis Engineering Corp. v. Clark*, 668 S.W. 2d 307 (Tex. 1983).
2. *Robertson v. LeMaster*, 301 S.E. 2d 563 (W.Va. 1983).
3. *Burrow v. K-Mart Corp.*, 304 S.E. 2d 460 (Ga. App. 1983).
4. *Texaco, Inc. v. Pennzoil Co.*, 729 S.W. 2d 768 (Tex. App. 1987).
5. Cal. Bus. & Prof. Code section 17200.

Human Resources

13

Employers must devote significant attention and resources to complying with a sometimes bewildering array of overlapping state and federal statutes, regulations, and common-law principles that govern their relations with their employees. This chapter addresses some of the more prevalent laws, with an emphasis on federal statutes of nationwide application.

For example, title VII of the Civil Rights Act of 1964 is one of the most important employment statutes, prohibiting employment discrimination based on race, color, religion, sex, or national origin. The Age Discrimination in Employment Act guards against age-discriminating employment practices. The Americans with Disabilities Act prohibits discrimination against individuals with disabilities. The Family and Medical Leave Act gives certain employees a right to up to twelve weeks of unpaid medical or family leave per year. The Fair Labor Standards Act regulates the minimum wage, overtime pay, and use of child labor. The Occupational Safety and Health Act was designed to reduce workplace hazards and improve safety and health programs for workers. The National Labor Relations Act gives employees the right to organize unions. In addition to these federal laws, state laws may impose additional employment requirements.

A company may decide to hire a worker as an independent contractor rather than as an employee. A worker, such as a painter, who provides unsupervised, specialized work that is needed only sporadically is the most clear-cut example of an independent contractor. How a worker should be classified, however, is often unclear. Many times, the worker is trying to claim the status of an employee to qualify for the legal protections afforded employees at the same time the employer is classifying him or her as an independent contractor. Often, the Internal Revenue Service (IRS) asserts that a person is an employee to recover Social Security payments (plus penalties) from the employer, and to force the employer to withhold income taxes from the worker's pay. Misclassification can create serious legal problems, including audits of the entire workforce.

Because the application of many employment statutes hinges on this distinction, this chapter begins with a discussion of what differentiates an employee from an independent contractor. The chapter continues with a summary of certain key employment legislation, then a discussion of employment at-will and wrongful discharge. It concludes with an outline of what should be contained in certain key employment agreements, including stock option agreements.

EMPLOYEES VERSUS INDEPENDENT CONTRACTORS

Although workers may perform identical duties for the company, it is possible for them to be classified into two legal categories: employee and independent contractor. The distinction between them is crucial. From the employer's standpoint, considerable money can be saved by classifying a worker as an independent contractor. An employer who hires a worker as an independent contractor, rather than as an employee, does not have to provide workers' compensation insurance and unemployment compensation, or provide job benefits (such as health insurance and a retirement savings plan). More important, when an independent contractor is hired, the employer is not required to pay any portion of his or her Social Security and Medicare taxes. Because the IRS prefers to have a worker classified as an employee for tax revenue purposes, the penalties for misclassification can be severe.

Although IRS guidelines and various employment statutes differ as to who is granted employee status, two primary criteria distinguish independent contractors from employees. First, independent contractors control the outcome of a piece of work and the means and manner of achieving the outcome. Second, independent contractors offer services to the public at large, not just to one business.

The following criteria have been used by various courts in determining whether an employment relationship existed:

1. the extent to which the services in question are an integral part of the employer's business;
2. the amount of the worker's investment in facilities and equipment;
3. the kind of occupation;
4. the nature and degree of control or supervision retained or exercised by the employer;
5. the worker's opportunities for profit or loss;
6. the method for calculating the payment for the work (by time worked or by the job);
7. the skill, initiative, and judgment required for the independent enterprise to succeed;
8. the permanence and duration of the work relationship;
9. whether annual or sick leave is given;
10. whether the worker accumulates retirement benefits or is given medical benefits;
11. whether the employer pays Social Security taxes; and
12. the intention of the parties, including any written agreement between the parties, regarding independent contractor or employee status.

Employee status is more likely to be found for workers who are lower paid, lower skilled, lack bargaining power, and have a high degree of economic dependence on their employer.

Misclassification of a worker can result in very serious consequences for an employer. Every attempt should be made to determine proper status prior to the commencement of the work relationship. An employer who wishes to hire an independent contractor must ensure that this status will be upheld in case of a dispute. Although a provision in a written agreement between the two parties specifying the worker's status is given significant weight, it is not determinative. For the finding of independent contractor status to withstand challenge, the worker must be hired as a separate company, perform tasks not central to the employer's primary business, and retain sufficient control over the manner and means of his or her performance.

For example, a court recently concluded that a group of Microsoft software testers and writers of technical manuals were employees for purposes of participation in Microsoft's benefit plans, even though their contracts specified that they were independent contractors responsible for their own federal taxes and benefits. The court was particularly influenced by the fact that some workers had worked exclusively for Microsoft for years doing work that was supervised by the same Microsoft supervisors who supervised employees doing the same kind of work in the same offices.[1]

Even though an employer can never guarantee that a worker will not qualify for employee status, the employer can take certain steps to help establish nonemployee status.

A written contract spelling out the intent of the parties and detailing the worker's duties and the terms and conditions of his or her service will provide some support for the finding of the independent contractor status. The agreement should clearly lay out the responsibilities of the contractor, describing the services to be performed, the time frame in which they will be completed, and the payment that will be given in consideration for these services. The contract should specify what is expected of the contractor (e.g., the contractor will supply all necessary tools, equipment, and supplies). Unless all work must be done by the contractor alone, the contract should give the contractor the right to hire any assistants, at his or her own expense. The contractor should be responsible for carrying his or her own liability and workers' compensation insurance, and for paying his or her own taxes and benefits.

The more the employer can establish the independent economic viability of the worker, the better. Thus, a file should be kept containing, for example, the worker's business card, references, and stationery samples. When feasible, it is best to retain contractors who are incorporated, and have their own business offices and equipment. That way, more of the work can be completed off the employer's premises. It is also important to make it clear that the independent contractor is free to offer services to other businesses as well.

An example of an agreement between a company and an independent contractor is set forth in "Getting It in Writing" at the end of this chapter.

(Before using any form, the entrepreneur should consult with legal counsel to ensure that the form agreement complies with all legal requirements and meets all of the entrepreneur's needs.)

The existence of an independent contractor agreement is essential from an entrepreneur's standpoint, but it may not be dispositive. When the interests of relatively low-paid workers are weighed by state agencies or courts against those of employers, in close cases the workers' interests usually prevail.

FROM THE TRENCHES

A transportation engineering firm obtained a contract from a city to measure ridership on the city's bus routes. The firm needed a large number of short-term workers to ride buses and count passengers. The firm entered into independent contractor agreements providing for minimum wages with more than fifty persons (most of whom were unemployed at the time) who responded to a newspaper advertisement. The firm provided the forms that each worker was required to fill out, pens, clipboards, and manual counters to aid in filling out the forms, and gave each worker a schedule of routes to ride.

Each worker rode the buses alone, receiving no supervision. The firm carefully explained to each worker the nature of the independent contractor agreement, which specified that no workers' compensation or unemployment benefits were included. Upon completion of the project, the firm informed each worker that the agreement was terminated. Thereafter, several of the workers filed claims for unemployment benefits with the state unemployment department.

Notwithstanding the written agreements, the state unemployment department awarded the workers benefits, which were charged to the firm's account. The state unemployment department reasoned that the firm exercised control over the workers by specifying the form to be filled out and by providing the tools to complete the forms. The state unemployment department, which also had responsibility to ensure that employers withheld amounts for state income tax, issued an assessment against the firm requiring it to pay the amounts that should have been withheld for all fifty-plus workers, plus penalties. The firm unsuccessfully appealed these rulings and was ultimately required to pay unemployment benefits to the relatively small number of workers who filed claims, and to pay withholding for all fifty-plus workers.

MAJOR EMPLOYMENT LEGISLATION

Title VII of the Civil Rights Act of 1964

All businesses, public and private, with fifteen or more employees are covered by title VII of the Civil Rights Act of 1964. Title VII protects employees from discrimination based on race, color, religion, sex, or national origin. Congress later amended title VII to expand the coverage of sex discrimination to include discrimination on the basis of pregnancy, childbirth, or related medical conditions. Of all the civil rights legislation, title VII has had the greatest impact on the recruitment, hiring, and other employment practices of American businesses. Many states have adopted comparable legislation that, in some states, applies regardless of the number of employees employed by the business. Title VII does not apply to independent contractors, and because of this, a worker's status can be a contentious point in title VII litigation.

Before the enactment of the Civil Rights Act of 1991, damages under title VII were limited to compensation for lost salary and benefits (*back pay*), injunctive relief such as reinstatement, and pay for a limited period of time in lieu of reinstatement (*front pay*). However, compensatory damages (e.g., for emotional distress or damage to reputation) or punitive damages were not available. The Civil Rights Act of 1991 expanded the remedies under title VII to include compensatory and punitive damages subject to caps based on the size of the employer. In addition to amounts for back pay and front pay (which are not capped), the Civil Rights Act of 1991 allows combined amounts of compensatory and punitive damages not to exceed $50,000 against employers with between 15 and 100 employees; not to exceed $100,000 against employers with between 101 and 200 employees; not to exceed $200,000 against employers with between 201 and 500 employees; and not to exceed $300,000 against employers with more than 500 employees.

Litigation under title VII has produced two distinct legal theories of discrimination: disparate treatment and disparate impact.

Disparate Treatment A plaintiff claiming *disparate treatment* must prove that the employer intentionally discriminated against him or her by denying employment or a benefit or privilege of employment because of his or her race, religion, sex, or national origin. The Supreme Court has established a three-step analysis of proof in such cases. First, the employee must make a prima facie case. This means that he or she must prove that (1) he or she is a member of a class of persons protected by title VII; and (2) he or she was denied a position or benefit he or she sought and was qualified for, and which was available. If the employee proves this prima facie case, the employer then must present evidence (but need not prove) that it had legitimate, nondiscriminatory grounds for its decision. If the employer meets this burden of producing evidence, the employee then must prove that there was discrimination and that the grounds offered by the employer were only a pretext for unlawful discrimination.

For example, an employee who is a member of a minority may claim that he was fired because of his race. He would show in the first instance that he is a member of a minority ethnic group, he was fired, and he possessed at least the minimum qualifications for the job. Some courts may require that he also show that his job was not eliminated but was filled by someone else after his termination. Once he proves this, his employer might present evidence that the employee was terminated for excessive absenteeism. The employer might produce the employee's attendance records and a supervisor's testimony that his attendance record was unacceptable. The employee may then attempt to prove pretext in a number of ways. He may show that his supervisor uttered racial slurs from time to time. He may show that his employer's attendance policy requires a written warning about poor attendance before the employee can be terminated on that ground, and that he received no such warning. He may show that nonminority employees with similar attendance records were not fired. The employee has the burden of proving that his employer fired him because of his race.

Disparate Impact   The *disparate impact* theory arose out of title VII class actions brought in the 1970s against large employers. These suits challenged testing and other selection procedures, claiming they systematically excluded women or particular ethnic groups from certain types of jobs. It is not necessary to prove intentional discrimination to prevail in a disparate-impact case. Discrimination can be established by proving that an employment practice, although neutral on its face, had a disparate impact on a protected group.

For example, suppose an employer has a policy that it will only hire persons for security guard positions who are 5 feet 8 inches or taller, weigh 150 pounds or more, and can pass certain agility tests. This policy would appear to be a neutral policy. It does not, for example, expressly exclude women or Asian males. However, if the number of women or Asian males who are refused employment is proportionately greater than the number of white males refused employment, then that policy has a disparate impact.

To prove disparate impact, the plaintiff must demonstrate that the specific employment practice, policy, or rule being challenged has, in a statistically significant way, disproportionately affected different groups. The employer then has the burden to produce evidence that the challenged practice is job related for the position in question and consistent with business necessity. Inconvenience, annoyance, or expense to the employer will not suffice. For example, a Latino applicant who is denied employment because he failed an English-language test may challenge the language requirement. If he has applied for a sales job, the employer may justify the requirement on the grounds that ability to communicate with customers is an indispensable qualification. On the other hand, if he has applied for a job on the production line, that justification may not suffice. As with disparate-treatment analysis, the ultimate burden of proof rests with the plaintiff.

Historically, disparate-impact analysis has been limited to objective selection criteria, such as tests and degree requirements. However, the Supreme Court has held that this analysis may also apply to subjective bases for decisions, such as interviews and supervisor evaluations. Thus, if, for example, an employer makes hiring decisions on the basis of interviews alone, and if the percentage of qualified women or African Americans hired differs significantly from the percentage of qualified women or African Americans in the relevant labor pool, then a claim may be made that this process is unlawful under title VII. The issue then will be whether the process is justified by business necessity.

Statutory Defenses Under Title VII   Title VII sets forth several statutory defenses to claims of discriminatory treatment. Statutory defenses absolve the employer even if the employee can prove that discrimination occurred. Of these defenses, the one most frequently cited is the defense of bona fide occupational qualification.

Bona Fide Occupational Qualification   Title VII provides that an employer may lawfully hire an individual on the basis of his or her religion, sex, or national origin if religion, sex, or national origin is a *bona fide occupational qualification (BFOQ)* reasonably necessary to the normal operation of that particular business. This is known as the *BFOQ defense*. The BFOQ defense is not available if discriminatory treatment is based on a person's race or color. Because BFOQ is an affirmative defense, the employer has the burden of showing a reasonable basis for believing that persons in a certain category (e.g., women) excluded from a particular job were unable to perform that job.

The BFOQ defense has been narrowly construed. For example, regulations promulgated by the Equal Employment Opportunity Commission (EEOC) provide that gender will not qualify as a BFOQ if a gender-based restriction is based on (1) assumptions of the comparative employment characteristics of women in general (such as the assumption that women have a higher turnover rate than men); (2) stereotyped characterizations of the sexes (e.g., that men are less capable of assembling intricate equipment than women); or (3) the preferences of co-workers, employers, or customers for one sex over the other. Gender will be considered a BFOQ, for example, if physical attributes are important for authenticity (as with actors) or if a gender-based restriction is necessary to protect the rights of others to privacy (as with rest room attendants).

Sexual discrimination suits can be brought by men as well as women. For example, an Atlanta-based restaurant chain, Hooters, was the target of a class action suit charging it with discrimination against men by hiring only female food servers, bartenders, and hosts. If the Hooters

---

FROM THE TRENCHES

Johnson Controls Inc., a battery manufacturer, adopted a policy barring all women from working in the manufacturing plant at jobs involving actual or potential lead exposure above a certain level. The policy was intended to protect fetuses from unsafe levels of lead exposure. The only exception to the policy was for women whose infertility was medically documented. A class action suit was filed on behalf of female employees affected by the policy. They claimed that the policy constituted sex discrimination in violation of title VII.

The Supreme Court held that the policy was illegal discrimination under title VII. First, the Court found that the policy was discriminatory against women on its face because it did not apply to men even though there was evidence that lead exposure was also harmful to the male reproductive system. Because the policy involved disparate treatment through explicit discrimination, the Court evaluated the policy under the bona fide occupational qualification (BFOQ) standard.

The Court rejected the BFOQ defense because the capacity of a woman to become pregnant does not affect her ability to perform on the job, and because fertile women can participate in the manufacture of batteries as efficiently as men. Finally, the Court said that the potential tort liability should not change the result because it doubted the company would be liable for harm to a woman or her fetus so long as it fully informed the women of the potential risk and did not act negligently.

Source: International Union v. Johnson Controls, Inc., 499 U.S. 187 (1991).

---

case were tried, the issue would be whether the essence of the restaurant chain's business is selling food or selling entertainment. The courts have held that gender, specifically female, is a BFOQ in some entertainment and fashion jobs. According to the EEOC, however, Hooters cannot claim that gender is a BFOQ because the main focus of the business is selling food, not atmosphere. Hooters counters that its business is the ambiance and entertainment created for men by the Hooters girls. The Hooters girls usually wear shorts and tank tops or crop top T-shirts with a large-eyed owl on the front. Some shirts read "more than a mouthful" on the back.

In the 1970s, Southwest Airlines lost a similar case when it hired only female flight attendants. The U.S. District Court for Northern Texas found that the airline could not make gender a BFOQ merely because it wished to exploit female sexuality as a marketing tool. Because the main business of the company was transportation, not entertainment, the court held that Southwest Airlines could not bar males from becoming flight attendants.

Seniority and Merit Systems Bona fide seniority and merit systems are not covered by title VII, as long as such systems do not result from intentional discrimination. This is considered an exemption rather than an affirmative defense. Consequently, the plaintiff has the burden of proving a discriminatory intent or illegal purpose. Moreover, although a disproportionate impact may indicate some evidence of a discriminatory intent, such an impact is not in itself sufficient to establish discriminatory intent.

Sexual Harassment Sexual harassment has emerged as one of the more complex and emotional issues in antidiscrimination law. Early on, the courts recognized that a specific, job-related adverse action (such as denial of promotion) in retaliation for a person's refusal to respond to a supervisor's sexual advances was a violation of title VII. Such retaliation is referred to as *quid pro quo harassment*. In 1986, the Supreme Court ruled that the creation of a hostile environment by sexual harassment (*hostile environment harassment*) is also a form of discrimination barred by title VII.[2]

Unwelcome sexual advances, requests for sexual favors, and other verbal or physical conduct of a sexual nature constitute sexual harassment when (1) submission to such conduct is made either explicitly or implicitly a term or condition of an individual's employment; (2) submission to or rejection of such conduct by an individual is used as the basis of employment decisions affecting such individual; or (3) such conduct has the purpose or effect of unreasonably interfering with the individual's work performance or creating an intimidating, hostile, or offensive working environment. An illegal hostile environment can exist even if the employee does not suffer psychological injury.

FROM THE TRENCHES

Teresa Harris, a manager, sued her former employer for sexual harassment under title VII, claiming that the conduct of the company's president, Charles Hardy, created an abusive work environment.

Hardy often insulted Harris because of her gender and subjected her to unwanted sexual innuendoes. At one point Hardy suggested that he and Harris "go to the Holiday Inn to negotiate [her] raise." Hardy also sometimes asked Harris and other female employees to take coins from his front pants pocket, and would throw objects on the ground in front of Harris and ask her to pick them up.

Eventually Harris complained to Hardy about his conduct. Hardy claimed he was only joking and apologized. A few weeks later, however, he resumed his insulting behavior. Shortly thereafter, Harris quit and sued the company.

A lower court dismissed the case because the conduct in question was not so egregious so as to cause Harris psychological damage. The Supreme Court reversed the decision, and held that although merely offensive behavior would not constitute an abusive work environment, conduct may be actionable under title VII even if it does not seriously affect the psychological well-being of, or cause injury to, the plaintiff. In the words of the Court, "Title VII comes into play before the harassing conduct leads to a nervous breakdown." Instead, the Court took a middle ground, ruling that so long as the environment would be reasonably perceived, and was perceived by the plaintiff, as hostile or abusive, the conduct violates title VII.

Source: Harris v. Forklift Systems, Inc., 510 U.S. 17 (1993).

Under certain circumstances, the employer may be liable for sexual harassment by a supervisor or coworker even if the employer was not aware of the conduct. An employer is absolutely liable for a supervisor's *quid pro quo* harassment. Similarly, the employer is liable for hostile environment harassment by a supervisor or coworker if it knew or should have known of the sexual harassment and failed to take reasonable steps to remedy it.

Age Discrimination in Employment Act (ADEA)

The Age Discrimination in Employment Act (ADEA) applies to all companies that affect interstate commerce and have at least twenty employees. (Some states have adopted comparable legislation that applies regardless of the number of employees employed by the business.) The ADEA prohibits employers, employment agencies, and labor unions from age-discrimination employment practices. The act covers workers age forty and older, and applies to applicants for employment as well as to current employees. Independent contractors are excluded from ADEA coverage.

If an employee age forty or older is fired, he or she can state a claim under the ADEA by showing that he or she was replaced by someone substantially younger. The burden then shifts to the employer to present evidence that it had legitimate, nondiscriminatory grounds for its decision. The burden then shifts back to the employee to prove that there was discrimination and that the grounds offered by the employer were only a pretext for unlawful discrimination.

One case involved a 56-year-old man who alleged that he had been terminated and replaced by a 40-year-old person on account of his age. The lower court ruled that because the replacement employee also was in the age-protected category, the 56-year-old plaintiff could not state a claim as a matter of law. The Supreme Court reversed and ruled unanimously that it was not necessary for a plaintiff to show that he or she had been replaced by someone under age forty to state a claim under the ADEA. Rather, a plaintiff need show only that he or she was replaced by someone substantially younger, whether or not the replacement was under age forty. Based on this reasoning, the Supreme Court reinstated the action of the 56-year-old employee for further proceedings. However, the Supreme Court suggested that the replacement of a 68-year-old employee by a 65-year-old person, for example, would not satisfy the ADEA because the 68-year-old was replaced by another worker who was not significantly younger.[3]

Americans with Disabilities Act (ADA)

The Americans with Disabilities Act (ADA) covers all employers that have fifteen or more employees who work at least twenty or more calendar weeks in a year. (Some states have adopted comparable legislation that applies regardless of the number of employees employed by the business.) The ADA prohibits discrimination against qualified individuals with disabilities in job application procedures, hiring, promotions, training, compensation, and discharge. A *disability* is defined as a mental or physical impairment that substantially limits one or more of a person's major life activities. The ADA requires the employer to provide reasonable accommodations so the disabled employee can perform his or her job, unless doing so would constitute an undue hardship for the employer. Independent contractors are excluded from ADA coverage. Available remedies for a violation of the ADA include back pay, reinstatement or hiring, and reimbursement of attorneys' fees and court costs.

Employers must exercise caution regarding any employee health issues that might be deemed to be disabilities because of the broad way in which the term "disabilities" is defined under the ADA. For example, a female employee who was missing work to undergo medical treatment for fertility problems was deemed to be a qualified individual with a disability. Although the employee had no physical or mental impairment preventing her from performing any of her job responsibilities, the federal district court reasoned that the fertility problems impaired her ability to be physically present in the workplace. The court further reasoned that childbearing qualified as a major life activity within the statutory definition of a disability. The lesson from this case is that the ADA definition of disability may be much broader than the more readily recognizable forms of disability. The employer in this case made the mistake of disciplining the absentee employee as if the situation were a routine absenteeism problem rather than a disability-related problem requiring reasonable accommodation under the ADA.

Reasonable Accommodation The ADA requires that employers make reasonable accommodations to an employee's disability, so long as doing so does not cause the employer undue hardship. Thus, even if a disability precludes an individual from performing the essential functions of the position, or presents a safety risk, the employer is required to assess whether there is a reasonable accommodation that will permit the individual to be employed despite the disability. The ADA includes a non-exhaustive list of what might constitute reasonable accommodation, including the following: (1) making work facilities accessible; (2) restructuring jobs or modifying work schedules; (3) acquiring or modifying equipment or devices; (4) modifying examinations, training materials, or policies; and (5) providing qualified readers or interpreters or other similar accommodations for individuals with disabilities.

Undue Hardship   Reasonable accommodation is not required if it would impose an undue hardship on the employer. The ADA defines undue hardship to mean an activity requiring significant difficulty or expense when considered in light of (1) the nature and cost of the accommodation needed; (2) the overall financial resources of the facility, the number of persons employed at the facility, the effect on expenses and resources, or any other impact of the accommodation on the facility; (3) the overall financial resources of the employer and the overall size of the business with respect to the number of employees and the type, number, and location of its facilities; and (4) the type of operation of the employer, including the composition, structure, and functions of the workforce, the geographic separateness, and the administrative or fiscal relationship of the facility in question to the employer.

Because strict compliance with the ADA can be costly, an employer may have an incentive to try to avoid falling under its purview by hiring independent contractors. However, any attempt to alter the characterization of existing employees solely to avoid compliance with the ADA will be viewed by the courts as a clear violation of the act. Thus, the use of any contractual arrangements to circumvent the act, if the effect is to screen out qualified individuals with a disability, will be considered an ADA violation. The choice to use independent contractor services must be made prior to the start of a working relationship. Additionally, such service providers must be economically independent businesses.

Establishing Nondiscriminatory Reason for Termination   An employee with a disability may still be terminated if the reason for the termination is unrelated to the individual's disability. For example, an assistant football coach at the University of Tennessee was terminated because of a well-publicized incident in which he was arrested for driving under the influence of alcohol. The coach was an alcoholic, a disability expressly protected under the ADA. However, the court found that the coach was not terminated because of his disability, but rather because of his criminal conduct and behavior, and the significant amount of bad publicity surrounding him and the school.[4]

Likewise, other courts have found that absenteeism unrelated to an individual's disability can provide the grounds for disciplinary action up to and including discharge. Similarly, the ADA will not protect individuals disabled due to drug addiction who sell illegal drugs on company property.

Family and Medical Leave Act

The Family and Medical Leave Act requires employers with fifty or more full-time employees to provide eligible employees up to twelve weeks of unpaid leave per year if such leave is requested in connection with (1) the birth of a child; (2) the placement of an adopted or foster child with the employee; (3) the care of a child, parent, or spouse; or (4) a serious health condition that renders the employee unable to do his or her job. To be eligible, an employee must have worked for the employer for at least twelve months and for at least 1,250 hours per year. The act requires the employer to restore the employee to the same position, or one with equivalent benefits, pay, and other terms and conditions of employment, following the expiration of the leave, unless the employee is a key employee (among the top 10% based on salary) and substantial and grievous injury will result from reinstatement. As soon as the employer determines that reinstatement would cause such injury, the employer must notify the employee that the company intends to deny job restoration and give the employee a reasonable time to return to work. Some states, such as California, require employers with fewer than fifty employees to grant family and medical leave.

An employee cannot contract out of his or her right to leave time under this act. However, the employer may require, or an employee may choose, to substitute any or all accrued paid leave for the leave time that is provided for under this act. The act should be considered a floor, not a ceiling, as to what employers can provide their employees in terms of a leave option.

Fair Labor Standards Act (FLSA)

The Fair Labor Standards Act (FLSA) covers all employers who participate in interstate commerce, regardless of the size of the business or the number of people employed. The FLSA was enacted in 1938 with the primary goal of regulating the minimum wage, overtime pay, and the use of child labor. Independent contractors are not covered by the statute, which requires that employees be paid for all hours worked. The employer must pay all nonexempt employees a minimum wage ($4.75 per hour as of October 1, 1996, with a scheduled increase to $5.15 after September 1, 1997).[5] The employer must pay for hours worked in excess of forty in a workweek at a rate equal to one and one-half times the regular rate of pay. Some types of employees, such as salespersons and executive, administrative, and professional employees, are exempt from the minimum-wage and overtime provisions of the FLSA. To be exempt, the employee must have job responsibilities that he or she fulfills without supervision.

In addition to the federal statute, most states have adopted their own provisions regulating wages and overtime pay. Generally, if there is a discrepancy between the federal and state statutes, the employer must abide by the law that is most favorable to the employee.

Workers' Compensation

Workers' compensation statutes provide for coverage of income and medical expenses for employees who suffer work-related accidents or illnesses. The statutes are based on the principle that the risks of injury in the workplace should be borne by industry. Coverage applies to accidents as well as to gradual onset conditions, such as carpal tunnel syndrome, and illnesses that are the gradual result of work conditions, such as heart disease or emotional illness. The system is no-fault, and an employee is entitled to benefits regardless of the level of safety in the work environment and the degree to which the employee's carelessness contributed to the incident. In exchange for the no-fault nature of the system, the monetary awards available to employees are generally lower than those that might be obtained in lawsuits for negligence and other torts. This arrangement is commonly referred to as the *workers' compensation bargain*. Independent contractors are generally excluded from workers' compensation coverage.

Workers' compensation can be provided in one of three ways. Some states allow an employer to self-insure by maintaining a substantial cash reserve for potential claims. This option is often an impossibility for small businesses. Some states require an employer to purchase insurance through a state fund. Other states give the employer the choice of going through a state fund or buying insurance from a private insurer. State funds and private insurance companies have attorneys who usually resolve legal questions of whether an employee is entitled to coverage.

A properly implemented workers' compensation insurance program for all employees provides employers with a basis for arguing that workers' compensation should be the exclusive remedy for workplace injuries and that it precludes liability for broader tort claims. Accordingly, it is very important for the employer to determine the status of all workers to ensure that all eligible employees are covered. If workers' compensation insurance is not properly obtained, an injured employee has a right to claim tort damages rather than the more limited payments available under workers' compensation. Some states may impose substantial fines on employers who fail to obtain workers' compensation insurance or even

---

FROM THE TRENCHES

A firefighter had worked his way through the ranks to become both a captain in the fire department and the union representative responsible for dealing with management on contract interpretation issues. He alleged in a lawsuit that management engaged in a campaign of harassment against him that caused him to suffer from high blood pressure, and ultimately to suffer a severe stroke, rendering him unable to move, care for himself, or communicate except by blinking. The alleged campaign of harassment included falsely accusing him of dishonesty, requiring him to attend a kangaroo court disciplinary hearing, publicly stripping him of his captain's badge, demoting him to an entry-level position, and filing an application to require him to involuntarily retire.

The California Supreme Court ruled that the firefighter's lawsuit for intentional infliction of emotional distress was completely barred by the exclusive remedy provided by the workers' compensation statutes. The employer was thereby spared a jury trial in which the firefighter might have obtained a large verdict on the basis of sympathy for his extreme physical condition.

In contrast, the Washington Supreme Court refused to ban a claim by employees who were injured by exposure to toxic chemicals in a fiberglass cloth used in constructing airplanes. The employer allegedly knew that the cloth would make them sick, yet refused to transfer employees with work-related medical symptoms, and cleaned and ventilated the workplace prior to government testing. Although an emotional-distress claim would ordinarily be barred by workers' compensation exclusivity, the court concluded that the alleged employer conduct amounted to a deliberate intent to injure, which was exempt from the exclusivity rule.

Sources: Cole v. Fair Oaks Fire Protection District, 729 P.2d 743 (Cal. 1987); Birklid v. Boeing Co., 904 P.2d 278 (Wash. 1995).

---

shut down the business until such insurance is obtained. Thus, not having workers' compensation insurance can be very costly for the employer.

Occupational Safety and Health Act (OSHA)

Businesses must comply with the federal Occupational Safety and Health Act (OSHA) as well as its state-law counterparts. OSHA requires employers to establish a safe and healthy working environment for their employees. However, OSHA does not apply to (1) self-employed persons who have no other employees; (2) farm businesses that employ only immediate family members; and (3) businesses in industries covered by other safety regulations and statutes, such as mining.

An employer governed by OSHA must provide a place of employment that is free from recognized hazards that are causing or are likely to cause death or serious physical harm to employees. What constitutes a recognized hazard is not entirely clear. However, its reach is broad and includes anything from sharp objects to radiation. Employers regulated by the act are also subject to the requirements of the Occupational Safety and Health Administration, also known as OSHA. This agency is authorized by Congress to govern additional workplace issues, including exposure to hazardous chemicals, first aid and medical treatment, noise levels, protective gear, fire protection, worker training, and workplace temperatures and ventilation.

Businesses regulated by OSHA are subject to many requirements. For example, businesses with ten or more employees are required to maintain an injury-and-illness log, medical records, and training records. The only types of businesses exempt from this requirement are certain retail trade and service businesses, and real estate, insurance, and financial businesses. The act also authorizes OSHA to conduct surprise inspections at work sites. If a violation is found, the employer must correct the problem immediately. OSHA may seek a court order to ensure compliance. OSHA can also impose fines for more egregious violations. Serious violations resulting in the death of an employee may lead to criminal prosecution of the company's management.

National Labor Relations Act (NLRA)

The National Labor Relations Act (NLRA) covers all enterprises that have a substantial effect on commerce. The NLRA requires employers to negotiate with labor unions representing the employees and makes it unlawful for an employer to discharge an employee solely for participating in union activities. The NLRA provides a remedy for an unlawfully discharged union employee by mandating his or her reinstatement and payment of back pay for the time off work. However, its protection extends only to employees, not to supervisors or independent contractors.

Entrepreneurs sometimes risk having their employees attempt to organize a labor union in response to the employer's failure to comply with basic employment regulations; such a failure often arises out of a desire to minimize expenses or streamline operations. Lack of compliance with employment regulations may cause employees to believe that banding together in a union is the only means to protect themselves. If an entrepreneur decides to oppose union organization efforts, doing so may require hiring labor consultants or attorneys; the process itself can be a major disruption to normal business operations. Thus, failure to address employee-relations issues may cause a long-term problem in the form of union organizing efforts.

EQUAL EMPLOYMENT OPPORTUNITY COMMISSION (EEOC)

The EEOC is the federal administrative agency created for the purpose of enforcing title VII and related federal antidiscrimination statutes. An individual with a grievance must first follow (*exhaust*) the administrative procedures of the EEOC before filing a lawsuit under title VII or related federal statutes. Because many employment disputes involve promotions, pay raises, and other issues regarded as less extreme than termination of employment, the theory is that the administrative process of the EEOC may help to resolve employment discrimination issues without the parties involved having to resort to time-consuming and expensive litigation.

Exhaustion of the EEOC process requires that an individual file a sworn document called a *charge of discrimination*, which lists the particulars of the alleged discrimination, harassment, or retaliation. The EEOC then investigates the charge, typically by sending to the employer a copy of the charge, a request for a written response to the charge, and any documentation regarding the allegations in the charge. The EEOC is authorized to make a finding that reasonable cause exists to believe that a violation has occurred, and if so, to attempt to resolve the charge by the informal process of conciliation and persuasion.

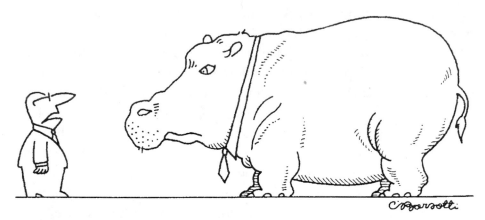

"The bunny did not get the job because the bunny is cute. The bunny got the job because the bunny knows WordPerfect."

Drawing by C. Barsotti, © 1994 The New Yorker Magazine, Inc.

The EEOC is permitted but not required to commence litigation on behalf of anyone who has filed a charge. Due to limited resources, such lawsuits brought by the EEOC are the exception rather than the rule. The EEOC may also find that no cause exists to believe that a violation occurred. If the EEOC fails to complete its investigation within certain time parameters, the individual involved is permitted to request a *right-to-sue* letter, which authorizes the commencement of a lawsuit within a ninety-day time period. Such right-to-sue letters are issued at the conclusion of the EEOC process as well. Exhaustion of the EEOC's process and obtaining a right-to-sue letter are necessary prerequisites to commencement of lawsuits under title VII or related federal statutes. Many states have analogous agencies that enforce parallel state antidiscrimination laws and specify similar exhaustion requirements before litigation may commence.

PREEMPLOYMENT PRACTICES

The laws described above affect not just employment practices but also certain preemployment practices.

Job Advertisements

Many employers begin the recruitment process by posting or publishing a "Help Wanted" notice. Title VII and the ADEA prohibit employers from publishing or printing job notices that express a preference or limitation based on race, color, religion, sex, national origin, or age, unless such specifications are based on good-faith occupational qualifications. For example, an advertisement for a "waitress" implies that the employer is seeking a woman for the job. If there is no bona fide reason why the job should be filled by a woman rather than a man, the advertisement might be considered discriminatory. Similarly, terms such as "young woman" or "girl" should never be used because they discourage job candidates from applying for positions because of their sex or age.

Many state laws also prohibit discriminatory advertisements. For example, Massachusetts and Ohio prohibit notices that express, directly or indirectly, any limitations or specifications concerning race, color, religion, national origin, sex, age, ancestry, or disability.

Word-of-mouth recruitment practices can also be discriminatory. Word-of-mouth recruiting normally takes the form of current employees informing their family and friends of job openings. When information is disseminated in this way, it may tend to reach a disproportionate number of persons of the same ethnicity as the employer's current employees. Thus, reliance on word-of-mouth recruiting practices may perpetuate past discrimination. If word-of-mouth recruiting is used, it should be supplemented with other recruiting activities that are designed to reach a broader spectrum of people.

Employers advertising for jobs should avoid placing advertisements in publications with sex-segregated help-wanted columns. They should indicate that the employer is an equal-opportunity employer, and should use media designed to reach people in both minority and nonminority communities.

Applications and Interviews

Employers use the application and interview process to gain information about an individual's personal, educational, and employment background. Unless there is a valid reason, an employer should avoid making inquiries on an application form, during a preemployment interview, or in some other manner that identify the protected characteristics of a job candidate. Although federal laws do not expressly prohibit preemployment inquiries concerning an applicant's race, color, national origin, sex, marital status, religion, physical traits, medical condition, or age, such inquiries are disfavored because they create an inference that these factors will be used as selection criteria. These inquiries may be expressly prohibited under state law.

Often the line between permissible and impermissible areas of inquiry is not clear. Because the actions of recruiters, interviewers, and supervisors can expose an employer to legal liability, it is crucial that they understand which questions should and should not be asked. As a general rule, recruitment personnel should ask themselves, "What information do I really need to decide whether an applicant is qualified to perform this job?"

Sex Any preemployment inquiry that explicitly or implicitly indicates a preference or limitation based on an applicant's sex is unlawful unless the inquiry is justified by a bona fide occupational qualification. In rare cases, a candidate's sex may be a valid criterion for a job, as in the case of actors, actresses, or fashion models. Normally, however, questions concerning an applicant's sex, marital status, or family should be avoided. For example, application forms and interviewers should not inquire:

- whether an applicant is male or female;
- the number or ages of an applicant's children;
- how an applicant will arrange for child care;
- an applicant's views on birth control;
- whether an applicant is pregnant or plans to become pregnant;
- whether a female applicant prefers to be addressed as Mrs., Miss, or Ms.; and
- the applicant's maiden name.

In addition, an interviewer should not direct a particular question, such as whether the applicant can type, to only the female or the male applicants.

Some of the above information eventually will be needed for benefits, tax, and EEOC profile purposes, but it can be collected after the applicant has been hired.

There are exceptions to this general rule. For example, state law may require employers to collect data regarding the race, sex, and national origin of each applicant, and the job for which he or she has applied. Certain government contractors are also obligated to collect applicant-flow data. Such data are collected for statistical and recordkeeping purposes only and cannot be considered by the employer in its hiring decision. In general, if an employer is required to collect such data, the employer should ask applicants to provide self-identification information on a form that is separate or detachable from the application form.

Age Application forms and interviewers should not try to identify applicants aged forty and older. Accordingly, job candidates generally should not be asked their age, their birth date, or the date that they completed elementary or secondary school. An employer can inquire about age only if (1) age is a bona fide job requirement, as for a child actor; or (2) the employer is trying to comply with special laws, such as those applying to the employment of minors. The fact that it may cost more to employ older workers as a group does not justify differentiation among applicants based on age.

Race Employers should not ask about an applicant's race. Questions concerning complexion, skin color, eye color, or hair color should be avoided, and applicants should not be asked to submit photographs.

National Origin An interviewer should not ask an applicant about nationality or ancestry because title VII prohibits discrimination on the basis of national origin. In addition, the Immigration Reform and Control Act of 1986 (IRCA) makes it unlawful for an employer with four or more employees to discriminate against applicants or employees on the basis of either their national origin or their citizenship status. (If the employer has fifteen or more employees and therefore is covered by title

VII, charges of national-origin discrimination must be filed under title VII, not the IRCA.)

The IRCA also makes it unlawful for an employer of any size to knowingly hire an individual not authorized to work in the United States. Violators can face civil and criminal penalties. However, employers cannot discriminate against persons solely because they have a foreign appearance or speak a foreign language. The act specifies the correct procedure for determining whether an applicant is authorized to work.

Under the act, any newly hired employee is required to complete form I-9 certifying that he or she is authorized to work in the United States and has presented documentation of work authorization and identification to the employer. After examining the documents presented, the employer must complete the remainder of the form, certifying that the documents appear genuine, relate to the employee, and establish work authorization. Form I-9 must be completed within a prescribed period of time.

Religion An employer generally should not ask questions regarding an applicant's religion. An employer can tell an applicant what the normal work schedule is but should not ask which religious holidays the applicant observes or whether the applicant's religion will interfere with his or her job performance. Title VII's ban on religious discrimination encompasses more than observance of the Sabbath. It applies to all conduct motivated by religion, such as dress or maintenance of a particular physical appearance. Title VII imposes a duty on employers to make reasonable accommodation to their employees' religious practices so long as such accommodation will not cause undue hardship to the employer's business.

An employer may ask about a candidate's religious beliefs if the beliefs are a bona fide occupational qualification. For example, a school that is owned, supported, or controlled by persons of a particular religion may require that its employees have a specific religious belief. In an extreme case, a federal district court ruled that a helicopter pilot could be required to convert to the Moslem religion in order to fly over certain areas of Saudi Arabia that are closed to non-Moslems. The court ruled that the requirement was a bona fide occupational qualification justified by safety considerations, because Saudi Arabian law prohibits non-Moslems from entry into Mecca, and non-Moslems who do so risk being beheaded if caught.[6]

Disability and Physical Traits The Americans with Disabilities Act prohibits all discrimination on the basis of disability and prohibits employers from questioning applicants about their general medical condition or any disabilities. After an employer has described a job's requirements, the employer may ask the applicant if he or she has any physical condition or disability that would limit his or her ability to perform the job. If the applicant answers yes, the employer should ask if there is any way to accommodate the applicant's limitation. An applicant also may be told that the offer is contingent on passing a job-related medical exam.

Applicants generally should not be asked questions regarding their height or weight. Height and weight requirements have been deemed unlawful where such standards disqualify physically disabled persons, women, and members of certain ethnic or national origin groups, and the employer could not establish that such requirements were directly related to job performance.

Conviction Record Although employers may ask applicants if they have ever been criminally convicted, this question should be followed by a statement that the existence of a criminal record will not automatically bar employment. Because in many geographical areas a disproportionate number of minorities are convicted of crimes, the use of conviction records as an automatic exclusion may have a disparate effect on minorities and therefore may be unlawful.

Consideration of a criminal record generally will be lawful only if the conviction relates to the requirements of the particular job. For example, an employer may be justified in rejecting an applicant convicted of theft for a hotel security position. Where a job applicant has been convicted of a crime involving physical violence, the employer may be faced with a delicate problem. Some courts have held the employer liable where an employee with a record of violent behavior later assaulted another employee or a third party. Liability is based on the theory that the employer was negligent in its duties to protect the health and safety of the injured person by hiring such an employee. If the employee is operating in a jurisdiction that recognizes this *negligent-hiring theory*, a policy against hiring any person with a criminal conviction for a violent act is justified.

Although employers should exercise caution in asking about criminal convictions, there may be compelling reasons to ask about them nonetheless. Asking about convictions may have the benefit of providing a basis for defending claims of wrongful termination of employment if an employee fails to disclose the conviction when asked during the hiring process.

Employers generally should not ask applicants if they have ever been arrested. Some states, such as Washington and Illinois, prohibit or restrict employers from asking applicants about arrests or detentions that did not result in conviction.

FROM THE TRENCHES

A husband and wife worked in support positions for a law firm that had asked them in the hiring process if they had been convicted of a felony. The husband and wife said they had not. The law firm did business with government agencies that required the firm to certify that it had no employees who had been convicted of felonies as a condition of contracting with the agency. The law firm so certified based on the false statements of the husband and wife. When their employment was terminated for performance reasons, the husband and wife sued for wrongful termination.

During the course of the litigation, the law firm discovered their felony convictions and their earlier false statements denying that they had been convicted. The court held that the husband's and wife's false statements denying that they had been convicted acted as a total bar to their claims, reasoning that their unclean hands prevented them from seeking relief in court regardless of whether their terminations were wrongful.

Source: Camp v. Jeffer, Mangels, Butler & Marmaro, 35 Cal. App. 4th 620, 41 Cal. Rptr. 2d 329 (1995).

Education and Employment Experience Employers may ask applicants questions regarding their education and work experience, but all requirements, such as possession of a high school diploma, must be job related. Inflated standards of academic achievement, language proficiency, or employment experience may be viewed as a pretext for unlawful discrimination.

Credit References Rejection of an applicant because of a poor credit rating may be unlawful unless the employer can show that the decision not to hire the applicant was due to business necessity. Because the percentage of minority-group members with poor credit ratings generally is higher than that of non-minority-group members, rejection of applicants on this basis can have a disparate impact on minority groups.

EMPLOYMENT AT-WILL AND WRONGFUL DISCHARGE

Employers are generally advised to hire employees on an at-will basis. *At-will* means that an employee is not guaranteed employment for a fixed period of time. Rather, both the employee and the employer remain free to terminate the employment relationship at any time for any reason, with or without cause or advance notice.

Wrongful Discharge

Significant inroads on the traditional doctrine of employment at-will have been made resulting from judicial decisions as well as legislation. Employers would be well advised to consider whether the reasons for any termination will pass muster as good cause.

The Public-Policy Exception Even an individual employed on an at-will basis cannot be discharged for a reason that violates public policy. For example, an employee cannot be lawfully discharged for (1) refusing to commit an unlawful act, such as perjury or price fixing, at the employer's request; (2) alleging that the company has violated a law; (3) taking time from work to serve on a jury or for military leave; (4) filing a workers' compensation claim; or (5) joining a union. An employee terminated in violation of public policy can recover both contract and tort damages, including damages for pain and suffering and, in egregious cases, punitive damages.

For example, in Michigan, the discharge of an employee for refusing to manipulate the sampling results for state pollution reports was held to give rise to a tort cause of action because it violated public policy.[7] However, the courts have shown restraint in defining what constitutes a public policy. The Colorado Court of Appeals found no cause of action for a nurse discharged for refusing to follow an order to reduce overtime in an intensive-care ward.[8] The nurse had relied on a licensing statute that required nurses to act in a manner consistent with public health and safety. The court found this statute was not sufficient to constitute a clear statement of public policy that would justify refusal to obey the order.

This judicially created cause of action exists alongside those specific statutory provisions that prohibit retaliatory discharge. For example, the Fair Labor Standards Act prohibits discharge for exercising rights guaranteed by the minimum-wage and overtime provisions of that act. The Occupational Safety and Health Act prohibits discharge of employees in retaliation for exercising rights under the act, such as complaining about work procedures or health and safety violations in the workplace. Many state acts contain similar provisions. A more recent development has been the adoption of whistle-blower statutes, which prohibit employers from discharging or retaliating against an employee who has exercised the right to complain to a government agency.

Implied Contracts The second judicial exception to the at-will rule arises from the willingness of courts to interpret the parties' conduct as implying a contract limiting the employer's right to discharge, even though no written contract exists. Such a contract is known as an *implied contract*. Some of the factors that can give rise to an implied obligation to discharge the employee only for good cause are that (1) he or she had been a long-term employee; (2) the employee had received raises, bonuses, and promotions throughout his or her career; (3) the employee was assured that employment would continue if he or she did a good job; (4) the employee had been assured before by the company's management that he or she was doing a good job; (5) the company had stated that it did not terminate employees at his or her level except for good cause; and (6) the employee had never been formally criticized or warned about his or her conduct. A personnel manual, together with oral assurances, can give rise to a reasonable expectation that an employee will not be terminated except for good cause.

Implied Covenant of Good Faith and Fair Dealing The third prong in the developing law of wrongful discharge is the recognition of an implied covenant of good faith and fair dealing in the employment relationship. In one case, the court found that termination of a twenty-five-year employee without good cause in order to deprive him of $46,000 in commissions was not in good faith and was a breach of contract.[9] A start-up that fired an employee on the eve of the date his stock was to vest might be found to have violated the implied covenant of good faith and fair dealing. This is one reason why many companies vest stock monthly after some initial period (usually six months to one year).

REDUCING LITIGATION RISK

An employer can minimize misunderstandings, decrease the likelihood of work-related disputes or union organizing efforts, and increase the chances of winning a wrongful discharge or discrimination lawsuit by taking certain simple steps. Such steps will also increase productivity and decrease turnover.

First, the employer should exercise care in the selection of employees. Companies in a growth mode may fall victim to the tendency to hire individuals quickly to satisfy a compelling need, rather than to hire individuals thoughtfully and deliberately regardless of how long the process may take. Many employment lawsuits stem from a lack of care in hiring. To

---

FROM THE TRENCHES

A consumer-products company terminated one of its executives in 1995. The company and the executive signed a letter of agreement that was intended to cover outstanding issues such as severance pay and vesting of stock options. Due to a number of technical glitches, however, the agreement had to be reworked several times. Meanwhile, as the former executive began to get wind of the company's plans to conduct an initial public offering (IPO), progress on ironing out the details of the settlement became slower and slower, and eventually stopped altogether. It became apparent to the company that the former executive had decided to stall the settlement in the hope that the company's reluctance to disclose the dispute in its prospectus would drive up the value of his claim. Litigation is pending.

Comment: This situation is, unfortunately, typical. Claims against companies often materialize "out of the woodwork" as the filing date for an IPO nears. Companies are well advised to recognize and resolve potential claims as early as possible to avoid the actual or perceived leverage that comes with an imminent public filing.

---

the extent possible, companies should know whom they are hiring, based on thorough screening, interviewing, and reference checks.

Second, once the employer decides whether a worker is an employee or independent contractor, the employer should formalize the working relationship in a written document signed by both the contractor/employee and the employer. The writing will delineate most, if not all, of the working conditions and benefits. For an employee, this includes job title, duties, and hours; term of employment or at-will language; compensation, benefits, and stock options; and the company's right to modify job duties and compensation. For an independent contractor, this includes the project description and milestones; fees; a recitation of the independent contractor relationship; assignment of inventions and protection of proprietary information; indemnification; and language regarding the contractor's right to control the manner and means of performing the work.

Employers should begin their legal compliance efforts at the interview and hiring stage and continue them throughout the employee's career. For example, the employer can target appropriate candidates by ensuring that all of its recruiting materials accurately describe job requirements and omit non-job-related criteria. The company must then hire or promote the candidate who best fits the criteria for the job, without respect to age, race, or any other protected classification. When evaluating an employee's performance, the supervisor must be timely, honest, and tactful. Evaluation criteria must be objective and job related. A copy of all performance appraisals should be signed by the employee and kept in his or her personnel file.

If the employee complains about a failure to promote, the employer should promptly and thoroughly investigate the circumstances surrounding the claim. The company should choose an appropriate investigator—one whom the employee believes and trusts. A supervisor should document the results of the investigation and report the results to the employee.

When a high-level employee such as an executive is terminated, it is often desirable to enter into a written settlement agreement. It is important to negotiate and finalize such an agreement promptly before the executive changes his or her mind.

THE EMPLOYMENT AGREEMENT

Employers should memorialize the terms of the employment relationship in a written document—either an offer letter or a formal employment agreement. (For ease of discussion, both the offer letter and

DILBERT reprinted by permission of United Feature Syndicate, Inc.

employment agreement will be referred to as the employment document.) The employment document will clarify the terms and conditions of the employment relationship, and will serve as an indispensable tool if a dispute later arises concerning the employment or its termination. Although there are numerous terms that an employer may wish to include, the following terms are essential.

Duties

The employment document should briefly describe the employee's duties. The description should be general enough so that the company retains the flexibility to expand the employee's duties and responsibilities, or to make modifications if necessary. If the employee works on an hourly basis (and is therefore governed by the wage and hour laws), the regular work schedule should be described.

Compensation and Benefits

The employee's base salary should be stated in the employment document. If the employee is eligible for a bonus, the employment document should clarify whether the granting of a bonus is at the employer's discretion or pegged to a specific formula or performance milestone. If possible, milestones should be described in objectively measurable terms to limit future misunderstandings or disputes.

The employment document should also briefly describe the benefits an employee may be entitled to receive, such as health, dental, and life insurance; retirement benefits; vacation; sick leave; stock options; and an automobile allowance. However, it need not provide too much detail as the terms and conditions of coverage should be delineated in separate, formal benefit plan documents. To avoid future confusion and litigation, the employment document should expressly state that the benefits are subject to the applicable plan documents, which are controlling.

The employment document should also state that the company reserves the right to modify compensation and benefits from time to time as it deems necessary or appropriate. This provision helps prevent the company from being locked into certain compensation and benefit levels as circumstances change.

Stock Options

One reason employees opt to join an entrepreneurial company is the opportunity to receive equity incentives such as stock options. It is important that the employment document specifically state that the terms of such stock option grants are subject to the company's incentive stock option plan and that the stock options are subject to a vesting schedule. This provision helps prevent litigation over the issue of whether an outright grant of stock was intended, as opposed to a stock option, which is subject to forfeiture if the employee leaves before the end of the vesting period. Companies should consider including clauses in their stock option documents stating that nothing in the stock option documents shall be construed to alter the terms of employment set forth in each employee's employment agreement, or in any employment handbook or personnel manual.

Termination of Employment

Guaranteeing employment for a specified period of time should be done only in extenuating circumstances and only after consultation with legal

---

FROM THE TRENCHES

An employee of a software company sued the company for more than $1 million upon termination of his employment. He alleged that the stock he had been granted was not subject to a vesting schedule but rather that the company had issued him an outright grant of stock. The company had neither an employment agreement nor an option agreement stating that the stock he was receiving was subject to a vesting schedule. The company could have avoided hundreds of thousands of dollars in both legal fees and settlement costs had it used a written employment agreement referring to the company stock option plan and grant.

counsel. Should an employer wish to obtain the services of an employee for a specified amount of time, the employer should still enter into an at-will employment relationship with the employee. The employer may, however, provide for severance in the event it elects to terminate the employment relationship prior to the end of the contemplated term of employment. An employer cannot force an employee to work (the Thirteenth Amendment abolished involuntary servitude), but the employer can prohibit an employee subject to a valid employment agreement from working for someone else before the term of the agreement expires.

Mandatory Arbitration

Increasingly, employers, especially in California, are requiring new employees to sign a document in which they agree not to sue the company but

---

FROM THE TRENCHES

Adrienne Magee, a cofounder of NewX, a consumer-products start-up, tried to convince her friend and former colleague, Bob Stein, to join NewX. At the local pub one Friday evening, Adrienne said to Bob, "Hey, you won't need to worry about a job because this company is going to take off." She added, "We'll bring you on as a marketing representative, but next year you'll become Vice President of Sales and Marketing." Bob was convinced of the wonderful opportunities awaiting him at NewX. The following Monday Bob resigned his employment at Happening Company. After all, Adrienne had just promised him employment for at least a couple of years. Six months after starting work at NewX, Adrienne decided that Bob really wasn't making the grade. Not only was Bob not going to be promoted to Vice President of Sales and Marketing, his employment was terminated. Bob sued NewX, alleging that he had been promised employment for at least two years, if not permanently, based on his conversation at the pub with Adrienne. In fact, Bob alleged that Adrienne promised him the Vice President of Sales and Marketing job.

NewX now faced expensive litigation, with uncertain results. All of this could have been avoided had NewX and Bob entered into a written employment agreement, memorializing all terms of employment, including the at-will nature of the employment relationship.

rather to submit all work-related disputes to binding arbitration or non-binding mediation. Such a provision protects the employer from the often unpredictable results of a jury trial, and provides a faster and less costly way to resolve disputes. However, it deprives employees of their day in court before a jury of their peers.

Employers should consider whether to require arbitrations to be conducted confidentially. Unless agreed to by the parties, there is no reason why an employee might not attempt to publicize the fact that an arbitration is pending, or the result of an arbitration.

Some employers do not believe that mandatory arbitration is the best approach to resolving work-related disputes. Intel Corp., the largest manufacturer of semiconductors in the world, has an open-door policy, whereby employees are encouraged to bring any problems to the attention of a manager. An internal investigator handles a wide range of work-related concerns and makes a recommendation in twenty-one business days.[10]

Entire Agreement

The employment document should contain an *integration clause* stating that the document constitutes the entire agreement with regard to the employment relationship and that the employee is not relying on any prior or contemporaneous oral or written promises that are not delineated in the document. This provision will help a company defeat a later claim that certain promises or commitments were made regarding terms and conditions of employment. Without such a provision, the employee may later claim that the company orally promised a promotion after six months or a guaranteed year-end bonus.

Immigration Status

As required by federal immigration laws, the employment document should require the employee to verify that he or she has the right to work in the United States by virtue of citizenship, permanent residency, or a work visa.

AGREEMENTS NOT TO COMPETE

Employers often desire to include noncompetition clauses in employment documents. These provisions prohibit an employee from competing with the company both during and after the termination of employment. As explained in chapter 2, although noncompetition covenants are enforceable during the term of employment, the enforceability of postemployment non-competition covenants varies state by state. For instance, although some states (e.g., Colorado, Massachusetts, Oregon, and Washington) will generally uphold reasonable restrictions on postemployment competitive activities, other states (such as California) will not, except in a few narrowly defined circumstances (e.g., when the noncompete clause is executed in connection with the sale of a business). It is advisable to consult legal counsel prior to attempting to preclude a prospective or current employee from engaging in post-employment competitive activities.

WORKS MADE FOR HIRE

The federal Copyright Act provides statutory protection for all of the writings of an author. In the case of works made for hire, the term

---

FROM THE TRENCHES

Upon commencement of employment, a major nationwide retailer requires all of its management-level employees to sign a noncompetition agreement. The agreement precludes the employee, during the term of his or her employment, and for one year thereafter, from working for the retailer's competitors. The retailer's Vice President of Sales and Marketing resigned his employment to join one of the retailer's major competitors. The retailer successfully prevented the vice president from joining its competitor by obtaining, from a state court, a permanent injunction that upheld the retailer's noncompetition agreement. Now, not only did the vice president not have the new position at a new company, he didn't even have his former position.

"author" is broadly interpreted to include an employer. Thus this definition means that in the absence of an agreement to the contrary, there is a presumption that the employer owns the copyright to any works created by employees. However, an employer is entitled to the copyright only when the work arose from an employer-employee relationship and when it was created by the employee within the scope of employment. Such a work is called a *work made for hire*.

The courts consider the following factors in determining whether an employee created the particular work within the scope of employment:

- right to control—whether the employer had the right to direct and to supervise the manner in which the work was being performed;
- who initiated the creation of the work;
- at whose expense the work was created;
- time spent on the project;
- who owned the facilities where the work was created; and
- the nature and amount of compensation received by the employee for the work.

If the court finds that no employment relationship existed and the creator of the work was an independent contractor, the creator (not the employer) would be granted the copyright ownership of the work. For example, a sculptor who used his own tools, worked in his own studio, had only one project that lasted a short period of time, and had total discretion in hiring and paying assistants was found by a court to own the copyright to the work rather than the organization that commissioned the sculpture.[11]

Copyright ownership disputes can often arise between the parties if the relationship is not clear. Such disputes can occur in relation to musical compositions, trade catalogs and pamphlets, pictorial illustrations, scientific and technical writings, photographs, works of art, and translations of foreign literary works. To avoid possible problems, the parties should enter into a written contract that specifies their intentions and relationship, and that assigns to the employer the right to the copyright ownership of the work to be created. (See, for example, section 4.6 of the Independent Contractor Services Agreement in "Getting It in Writing" at the end of this chapter.)

NONDISCLOSURE AND INVENTION ASSIGNMENT AGREEMENTS

All employees, at all levels with the company, should be required to sign detailed nondisclosure and invention assignment agreements, sometimes called proprietary information and inventions agreements. Such agreements provide broad protection for the company's proprietary information by prohibiting employees from the unauthorized use or disclosure of the company's proprietary information, and by requiring an assignment to the company of all rights and title that the employee may have to inventions created during the period of employment. The agreements should include the terms outlined below.

Nondisclosure and Nonuse of Proprietary Information

The nondisclosure agreement should obligate the employee to refrain from unauthorized *disclosure* of the company's proprietary information and from unauthorized *use* of proprietary information. The provision should also state that the obligation to refrain from unauthorized use or disclosure of the company's proprietary information continues indefinitely after the employee terminates his or her employment with the company.

Other Provisions

A company may also wish to include the following provisions in its nondisclosure agreement:

- a broad definition of proprietary information, which includes personnel information about employees;
- a commitment not to disclose or use third-party proprietary information, including information from joint venture partners or previous employers;
- an agreement that precludes the employee from participating in business activities other than those activities that the employee is performing for the company;
- a commitment to return all company materials upon termination of employment with the company, including any embodiment of

proprietary information such as notes or computer-recorded information;

- an acknowledgment that signing the nondisclosure agreement does not breach any other agreement that the employee may have with other entities;
- an acknowledgment that employment with the company is at-will; and
- an agreement not to solicit coworkers for a defined period after leaving the company.

Assignment of Inventions

The assignment of inventions agreement should require the employee to assign to the company all rights to any invention that results from work performed for the employer or work that relates to the employer's current business or demonstrably anticipated research or development. Any invention made on the employer's time, or using the employer's materials, equipment, or trade secrets, should also be assigned to the company. The assignment agreement should be as broad as the law allows. Some states, such as California and Washington, have statutes carving out an exception for inventions unrelated to the employer's business that the employee develops on his or her own time, and without use of the employer's material, equipment, or trade secrets.[12] Such carve-outs should be expressly referenced in the agreement.

It is important that the agreement include an actual assignment of inventions (e.g., "I hereby assign to the company . . .") rather than an agreement to assign (e.g., "I agree that I *will* assign to the company . . ."). Although this distinction may seem to be a mere technicality, an agreement to assign connotes that some further act is necessary to document the assignment; as a result, the employee can allege, at some point in the future, that the actual assignment never took place.

Disclosure of Preemployment and Postemployment Inventions

The assignment of inventions agreement should require the employee to identify preexisting inventions to which the employee claims ownership rights. This will help eliminate disputes regarding employee claims to ownership of an invention allegedly made prior to joining the company. To ensure that inventions belonging to the company do not sneak out the door, the agreement should also obligate the employee to disclose all of his or her inventions during employment, as well as those invented for a specified period of time after employment (e.g., six months or one year). This provides the company with an opportunity to determine whether a particular invention rightly qualifies as the company's property.

FOREIGN EMPLOYEES

Foreign Nationals and U.S. Citizens Working Abroad

Companies hiring foreign nationals or U.S. citizens to work in a foreign country should arrange for the employee to sign a detailed employment agreement. Employment laws in countries vary widely, and employment relationships are often heavily regulated by statute. Consequently, a

---

FROM THE TRENCHES

SoftPro employed a software engineer to develop source codes for various software products. In her free time and using her own equipment, the engineer developed a source code for a different, but related, software product that, unbeknownst to her, SoftPro had R&D plans to design. The engineer, believing she owned the new source code, resigned from SoftPro to start her own company, CopiPro. SoftPro initiated legal action against the engineer and CopiPro, claiming ownership rights to the new source code. SoftPro's invention assignment agreement, signed by the engineer, specifically stated that the engineer agreed to assign any invention developed while employed by SoftPro (excluding certain narrow exceptions). As a result of its strong position, SoftPro negotiated a very favorable resolution to the matter.

company cannot rely on a standard American employment document to provide sufficient protection or to ensure that it is in compliance with foreign law. It is advisable to engage foreign legal counsel prior to entering into relationships that involve employees residing in foreign countries.

Likewise, it is crucial to have the company's nondisclosure and invention assignment agreements reviewed by foreign counsel to ensure that the employee is both contractually and legally obligated to assign his or her rights to company inventions and to refrain from making unauthorized use or disclosure of the company's proprietary information.

Foreign Nationals Working in the United States

Employers wishing to hire foreign nationals to work in the United States must comply with U.S. immigration laws and procedures prior to hire. In most situations, the employer must file a visa petition with the Immigration and Naturalization Service (INS) and obtain approval on behalf of the foreign national desiring employment in the United States. These employment-based visas range from temporary nonimmigrant visas to immigrant visas. Immigration laws are very specific, and at times complex, and they require the expertise of an immigration specialist. Thus, employers are well advised to consult with an immigration attorney prior to promising employment to foreign nationals.

FROM THE TRENCHES

A Texas company was opening sales offices in several European and Asian countries, and planned to hire foreign nationals to help staff the offices. The company wanted to use its standard employment agreements. However, after quickly researching the employment law of these countries, the company learned that its standard employment agreements would violate the statutes of two of the countries as they related to the amount of notice to be given prior to terminating an employee's employment and the obligation to make severance payments. Had the company used its standard employment agreements, it would have been in violation of the statutes and may have been subject to government fines and penalties.

EMPLOYER LIABILITY FOR EMPLOYEES' ACTS

An employer is liable for his or her own negligence in supervising or hiring an employee. As explained in chapter 12, the employer may also be vicariously liable for the employee's wrongful acts, even if the employer had no knowledge of them and in no way directed them, if they were committed while the employee was acting within the course and scope of his or her employment. For example, an employer will be liable for an auto accident caused by an employee driving on a work-related errand.

An employer is bound by a contract entered into by an employee with authority to enter into it. Authority can be actual or apparent. An employee has *actual authority* when the employer expressly or implicitly authorizes the employee to enter into the agreement. Even if an employee does not have actual authority, he or she can still bind the employer if the employer engages in conduct (e.g., leaving the employee alone or giving the employee the title "manager" in a store) that would reasonably lead a third party to believe that the employer has authority. This is known as *apparent authority*. Thus, it is extremely important to delineate to employees and to third parties the acts that an employee or an independent contractor may undertake so that misunderstandings regarding the scope of a worker's authority are kept to a minimum.

EQUITY COMPENSATION

Compensating employees in a start-up company has special challenges and opportunities. Cash is a precious commodity in a start-up company and is typically best used in product research and development efforts. Therefore, base salaries are usually significantly lower than those talented individuals could earn doing comparable work for a mature business. Benefits, such as health insurance or a retirement package, are not used to attract and retain employees because, for the most part, the purchase of these benefits would require the company to use its cash.

To attract good employees, companies must use their own stock as compensation. There are a number of advantages to using company stock as an integral part of the business's total compensation strategy. First, using stock rather than cash helps conserve cash for research and development efforts. Second, compensation with stock aligns the interests of employees with those of investors in a collaborative effort to produce value for everyone's stock holdings. Third, use of stock compensation is a signaling device that helps attract individuals who are willing to make shorter-term financial sacrifices in exchange for the opportunity to succeed financially along with the business, the very type of individual a start-up business needs. As a result, the significant use of stock helps to reinforce the typical start-up company's strategic business objectives of rapid product development for commercial success.

Equity compensation can take a bewildering variety of forms, but, as explained in chapter 5, for most employees in entrepreneurial companies, the opportunity to acquire a stake in the business will usually come in the form of a stock option. The most important terms of an option are (1) the number of shares that may be purchased; (2) whether the option will be a tax-advantaged incentive stock option or not; (3) the exercise price; (4) the maximum duration of the option; (5) the permissible form or forms of payment; and (6) any contractual restrictions on the purchase or transfer of stock.

Number of Shares

Typically a start-up business will establish a collective pool of shares under a formal stock option plan that has been approved by the shareholders and out of which options to purchase the stock may be granted. For an individual award, the only formal limit is the number of uncommitted shares left in this pool. However, as a practical matter, a business will need to manage its share reserve pool carefully to ensure adequate grants for all employees and other personal service providers (such as nonemployee directors, consultants, and advisors). A reasonable rule of thumb is to earmark about 20% of the shares of a business for issuance to employees and other service providers. In making this calculation, the number of shares in the option pool is included in the total number of shares; any convertible securities (such as preferred stock that is convertible into common) are treated as if they had been converted; any other outstanding options or warrants are treated as if they had been exercised; and stock issued to the founders upon the formation of the business is generally excluded.

Types of Stock Options

Two types of options may be granted to eligible individuals: *incentive stock options* and *nonqualified stock options*. Although a stock option plan may be designed to grant one type of options, most will provide for the grant of both types of options. As explained in chapter 5, the difference between these two types of options relates to their income tax attributes.

Exercise Price

Most options in a start-up business are generally granted at an exercise price equal to 100% of the fair market value of the stock that may be acquired, valued as of the date of the option's grant. A plan may be designed to allow the grant of options with a lower exercise price (a so-called *discounted stock option*). However, the use of discounted stock options is limited to selective situations because of accounting charges and securities law restrictions.

Maximum Duration

Incentive stock options may not be granted with a term longer than ten years. A special rule applies to optionees owning more than 10% of the corporation, for whom the maximum term for incentive stock options is reduced to five years. Most plans provide for options with a maximum term of ten years. Many companies have found through bitter experience that five years can be too short a period of time if the business does not develop as rapidly as originally projected. Consequently, the company that wants to extend the term of an option due to expire may create accounting charges and cause the loss of incentive-stock option treatment for outstanding options.

A related issue is under what circumstances an option will terminate prior to the expiration of its term. Most plans provide for expiration of an option only upon the termination of an individual's service with the company. Typically, individuals have thirty to ninety days after termination of service within which to exercise their options. This period is typically extended to six to twelve months if the optionee's termination of service is attributable to disability, and to twelve to eighteen months if the optionee's termination of service is attributable to death.

Permissible Forms of Payment

There are four basic forms of payment that stock option plans use to allow optionees to purchase stock when exercising their options: (1) cash or cash equivalents, such as checks; (2) shares of the company's stock already owned by the optionee; (3) proceeds from the immediate sale of stock upon the exercise of an option (which, as a practical matter, is only available to companies with publicly traded stock); and (4) a promissory note. Most plans permit the use of all four forms of payment, or a combination of those forms, but the standard form of option agreement by which the option is actually granted will typically limit the permissible forms of payment to either cash and cash equivalents, or previously owned shares of the company's stock.

Contractual Restrictions on the Purchase or Transfer of Stock

Most option plans provide for a period of time during which an optionee must continuously perform services in order to acquire a contractually unrestricted right to purchase stock upon the exercise of an option. Shares that are not subject to contractual restrictions in favor of the company are called *vested shares*. Although the exact features of vesting schedules differ among plans, a typical vesting period is four years, with no vesting for the first twelve months (called *cliff vesting*) and vesting in equal monthly increments thereafter over the remainder of the vesting period.

Some companies tie vesting to the achievement of performance goals. The primary reason that this practice is not more widespread is the potential adverse financial accounting consequences associated with performance vesting for stock options. Under current accounting rules, if the vesting restrictions imposed on a stock option disappear with the passage of time and continued service, and if the option is granted with an exercise price of at least 100% of the fair market value of the company's stock on the date of grant, then accountants will routinely not calculate any charge to earnings for financial accounting purposes. However, if the vesting restrictions on an option are performance based, then the accountants will wait to calculate any possible charge to earnings for financial accounting purposes until the time that the performance objective has been satisfied, if at all. As a result, a company has a difficult time managing these charges to its earnings for financial accounting purposes because it cannot determine in advance the fair market value of the company's stock at the time that a performance objective is achieved.

A stock option plan may be designed to permit an individual to exercise an option immediately, even if the optionee would acquire only unvested shares. Alternatively, an option plan may be designed to permit optionees to acquire only vested shares. It is administratively simpler to restrict the exercise of options to vested shares, and most stock option plans sponsored by private companies do exactly that. However, for certain optionees, the ability to exercise options on unvested shares may produce some tax advantages. For example, the spread on exercise of an incentive stock option is included for purposes of calculating an individual's alternative minimum tax; an early exercise typically results in a smaller spread that is potentially subject to this tax. More significantly, optionees acquiring *qualified small business stock* within the meaning of section 1202 of the Internal Revenue Code can generally exclude 50% of any capital gains recognized upon sale if they have held the stock for at least five years. An option providing for early exercise permits the optionee to initiate that five-year holding period sooner. In addition, at the time that a company's stock is publicly traded, immediately exercisable options may provide officers and directors of the company, who are subject to various securities law restrictions, greater flexibility in acquiring and disposing of company stock.

A company designing a stock option plan needs to decide whether or not it will give itself the right to reacquire shares owned by an optionee that the optionee wishes to transfer at a time when the company's stock is not publicly traded. As discussed in chapter 5, most companies do provide for a right of first refusal in favor of the company. Often this right is extended to the other shareholders if the company does not exercise the right in full itself.

A company that wishes to maintain tight control over the ownership of its shares while the stock is not publicly traded may retain the right to reacquire even vested shares upon an individual's termination of service. Such a repurchase right enables a company to restrict ownership of shares acquired through its stock option plan to only current service providers. However, the price paid by the company on the repurchase of vested shares is generally the greater of the individual's purchase price or the stock's fair market value on the date of termination. Problems can arise because making a determination of the stock's fair market value in connection with such a repurchase may set a benchmark as to the stock's fair market value for other purposes (e.g., for awarding future stock options). In addition, a repurchase provision for vested shares produces an economic disincentive for the optionee.

OTHER EMPLOYEE BENEFITS

Although for most start-up businesses most of an employee's total compensation will be provided in the form of base salary and performance incentives (usually through stock options), broad-based employee benefits are a necessary part of a well-designed, competitive total compensation strategy.

Health Coverage

Adequate health insurance is the broad-based employee benefit on which employees place the most importance. Small businesses generally should not self-insure, so they will typically buy health coverage from an insurance company or health-maintenance organization through an insurance broker or consultant. The health-care services industry is going through some wrenching changes, so it is important that the business owner spend some time identifying a knowledgeable and responsive broker to help the company select appropriate health coverage. Tax law also creates an incentive for businesses to deliver health-care coverage to their employees because the receipt of these benefits does not create taxable income for the employees (except for partners in a partnership, members of a limited liability company, or 2% or greater shareholders in a subchapter S corporation) and is tax deductible as a business expense by the business.

Even with these tax advantages, given the stubborn persistence of health-care inflation in recent years, businesses are looking for methods to control their health-care costs. As a result, most businesses share the cost of health-care coverage with their employees, particularly the cost for covering an employee's family. A popular way of reducing the after-tax cost of the employee's share of the cost of health-care coverage is for the business to adopt a pre-tax premium plan. Such a plan allows employees to pay their share of health-care costs with before-tax rather than after-tax dollars. Having these costs paid through a pre-tax premium plan can produce income and employment tax savings of up to about 50% of the employee's before-tax cost. The business can reap tax savings as well, as these payments are generally not subject to payroll taxes such as Social Security taxes.

Retirement Benefits

How young businesses provide retirement benefits to their employees is perhaps the best illustration of the overall strategy that many businesses with limited cash employ in offering employee benefits in general. Start-ups cannot afford expensive employer-funded benefits, so instead they offer flexible tax-advantaged plans that permit employees to decide how to split their pay between taxable cash compensation and tax-deferred or tax-exempt employee benefits.

In the area of retirement benefits, the primary type of plan that offers this flexibility coupled with tax advantages is the *section 401(k) plan.*

Such a plan allows employees to authorize nontaxable contributions through payroll withholding into a special tax-exempt trust account. The contributions are invested in the trust account without tax liability to permit a more rapid accumulation of retirement assets. The employee may withdraw those accumulated assets at a later time (typically upon retirement) and will only incur a tax liability at the time of distribution. Meanwhile, the business is entitled to take a tax deduction immediately at the time that the employee authorizes contributions to the trust account. Although the tax treatment is basically the same as for other types of tax-qualified retirement plans, section 401(k) plans offer employees a high degree of flexibility in determining the level of their contributions subject to an annual maximum ($9,500 for calendar year 1996) and certain other legal limitations. (For companies with twenty-five or fewer employees, an even simpler and less expensive 401(k) plan look-alike, known as a *salary reduction SEP*, is available.)

In its simplest form, a business makes no contributions to the section 401(k) plan, so its only costs are the costs associated with establishing and administering the plan. Employees make all contributions through authorized payroll withholding. However, companies may find that plans funded solely through payroll withholding have more difficulty passing relevant nondiscrimination tests imposed by federal tax law. In particular, one test limits the permissible contributions for the benefit of highly compensated employees in relation to those made for the benefit of all other employees. The most popular response to safeguard the tax-qualified status of the plan in this situation is for a company to introduce a matching contribution. This contribution is designed to encourage enough lower-paid employees to authorize contributions through payroll withholding in sufficient amounts to pass the nondiscrimination test. Recent surveys indicate that a typical matching contribution design is $0.50 for each $1.00 contribution, up to a maximum matching contribution of 2% to 4% of a participant's base pay. The proper matching contribution formula for a particular company's section 401(k) plan is likely to differ from this typical formula, as the appropriate formula is affected by workforce demographics, actual contribution rates, and other variables.

At a later stage in development, some companies also consider making performance-oriented profit-sharing contributions to their tax-qualified retirement plans. Frequently, these contributions take the form of contributing a portion of the company's annual incentive bonus to the plan for the benefit of employees, rather than paying it to them directly in cash. The contribution may also be made in shares of company stock. Because tax law has requirements on important issues such as which employees must be eligible to share in these contributions and how the contributions must be allocated (requirements that cash bonuses paid directly to employees need not satisfy), whether or not a company diverts some of its bonus payout to the plan invariably depends on the degree of adjustments that must be made to satisfy the tax laws. Many companies with broad-based profit-sharing plans with contributions based on a formula find that they can make contributions to their retirement plan while preserving the basic integrity of the incentives built into their annual cash-incentive bonus plan. Furthermore, many employees, particularly more highly compensated employees concerned about generating an adequate retirement income, appreciate having a portion of this bonus contributed to the plan instead of being paid to them directly in cash. These company contributions may be conditioned on satisfying vesting requirements similar to those imposed on stock options to encourage employees to stay with the company.

Other Benefits

Even if a young company offers basic health and retirement benefits, it typically will refrain from introducing significant additional benefits in favor of using the cash for more important purposes. Of course, some vacation and holiday time off is usually provided from the outset, as well as some basic level of group-term life insurance (at least to take advantage of the tax law that allows businesses to provide their employees with up to $50,000 of life insurance coverage without creating any taxable income for the employees). The next benefit introduced that has a significant cost is disability insurance. Companies may either pay for this benefit themselves or arrange for employees to pay for some or all of the cost through a pre-tax premium plan, in which case any disability benefits are taxable income when received. Alternatively, if employees pay for these benefits with after-tax dollars, any disability benefits ultimately received are not taxed at all. The use of a pre-tax premium plan in this fashion gives employees a measure of flexibility in determining the tax treatment of their disability premiums and benefits, at least within the confines of some rather broad nondiscrimination tax requirements that govern these types of plans.

Putting It into Practice

When Alexandra hired workers to build the prototype, the first issue she had to decide was whether to hire such workers as independent contractors or employees. From an economic perspective, she preferred to engage contractors, rather than hire employees, because the contractor, not the employer, is liable for taxes. Classifying workers as independent contractors also would have allowed WebRunner to escape paying for unemployment insurance, workers' compensation insurance, and other employee-related expenditures. However, Alexandra knew that the government favors classifying workers as employees, not independent contractors, and that substantial fines and penalties might be assessed against WebRunner for misclassifying workers.

After reviewing the relevant criteria for classifying workers with Josh Austin, Alexandra decided to hire them as employees. Although several workers would be using their own computers and working at home, the programming was central to WebRunner's business and was subject to coordination and supervision by Alexandra and Paul. Also, the programmers would be working exclusively for WebRunner for a substantial period of time.

Alexandra worked with Josh to prepare a standard at-will employment agreement, which each of the workers signed. The agreement provided for a salary but no extra pay for overtime. Because she fully expected the programmers to work more than forty hours per week, Alexandra had checked with Josh to confirm that the programmers were exempt employees under the federal and California Fair Labor Standards Acts. They concluded that the programmers' status as well-paid professionals doing largely unsupervised tasks over which they had substantial decision making authority caused them to be exempt from the hourly-wage and overtime requirements applicable to nonexempt employees.

Shortly after the incident with James Ward, Alexandra was faced with two more problems. The first involved Guadalupe Garcia, a 41-year-old Hispanic employee who had been laid off due to her inability to write efficient code. Although Guadalupe's code worked, it required too much memory and ran too slowly because it was poorly written. Guadalupe had been warned of the need for improvement, but despite extensive tutoring by fellow employees, Guadalupe's code still was not acceptable. Finally, she was dismissed for poor job performance.

continued

continued

About three months later, Alexandra was served with papers from Guadalupe's lawyer alleging employment discrimination. The lawsuit claimed that Guadalupe was fired in violation of title VII because of her race, national origin, and gender, and in violation of the ADEA because of her age.

Alexandra immediately called Michael Woo, who initiated a conference call with Jill Calderon, a senior employment litigator. Jill explained that Guadalupe could establish a prima facie case by proving that she was a member of a protected group (by means of her race, national origin, gender, and age) and had been fired from a job for which she was arguably qualified. The burden would then shift to WebRunner to present evidence that it had legitimate, nondiscriminatory grounds for its decision.

Fortunately, Guadalupe's poor code writing was well documented. Alexandra had given her timely and honest feedback based on objective and job-related criteria. Copies of all performance appraisals were signed by Guadalupe and kept in her personnel file. However, Jill warned that there was a subjective element to the determination that Guadalupe failed to write elegant code. She might argue that this was a pretext for firing her and try to prove that the real reason she was fired was because she was a 41-year-old Hispanic woman. Because there was no evidence that Guadalupe had in fact been discriminated against (no one had complained of her Spanish accent, for example), Jill believed that WebRunner would ultimately prevail if the case went to trial. However, it would be expensive and time-consuming to litigate her claims. Jill explained that this was a typical strike suit and that it was likely that Guadalupe would settle for a small but significant amount of money. Alexandra and Jill agreed that Jill would contact Guadalupe's attorney to try to negotiate a settlement.

A week later Jill called Alexandra to report that Guadalupe's attorney had offered to settle all claims for $10,000. Jill recommended that Alexandra accept the offer because the legal fees to fight the suit would be at least twice that, and even more if the case went to trial. Although Alexandra hated to settle because she knew she was in the right, she could not afford the distraction it would cause and decided to simply chalk the settlement up to the cost of doing business.

The second problem was potential sexual harassment by a female supervisor named Brooke Barnes of an employee named Alan Raskovich.

continued

continued

Brooke, who had just moved from Atlanta, frequently called Alan "babe" and made comments about Alan's physique. One day Brooke grabbed Alan's arm, squeezed his biceps, and cooed, "I like my men with muscles." It was after this last incident that Alan had come to Alexandra to complain.

Alan said that Brooke's ongoing behavior embarrassed him and made him feel uncomfortable. He was afraid his coworkers might get the wrong idea. He was also concerned that Brooke was becoming more aggressive and felt that it was just a matter of time before she propositioned him. Alexandra asked Alan if he would like to have a different supervisor, and he said that he would.

Alexandra thanked Alan for coming to her and assured him that she would take care of the problem. Alexandra next spoke with several of Alan's coworkers, who confirmed the incident. Alexandra then called Brooke into her office, and told her that her behavior was inappropriate and that a reprimand letter would be placed in her personnel file. Brooke's face became flushed, and she said that she had not meant anything by her comments, noting that everyone in her former firm in Atlanta called each other "babe." Alexandra said that that was no excuse for behavior that in California, at least, created a hostile environment for an employee. Alexandra concluded by telling Brooke that Alan would no longer report to her as she was being shifted to a different programming group. Alexandra warned Brooke that she would be fired if she engaged in similar conduct with Alan or any other employee. Brooke apologized and assured Alexandra that it would never happen again.

After finishing her meeting with Brooke, Alexandra turned her attention to deciding what steps WebRunner should take to protect its intellectual property.

GETTING IT IN WRITING

SAMPLE INDEPENDENT CONTRACTOR SERVICES AGREEMENT

Contractor Name:
Effective Date:_____, 19__
("Effective Date")

INDEPENDENT CONTRACTOR SERVICES AGREEMENT

THIS AGREEMENT is between _____, a _____ [corporation] and its successors or assignors ("Client") and the undersigned (the "Contractor").

1. ENGAGEMENT OF SERVICES. Client may from time to time issue Project Assignment(s) in the form attached to this Agreement as Exhibit A. Subject to the terms of this Agreement, Contractor will, to the best of its ability, render the services set forth in Project Assignment(s) accepted by Contractor (the "Project(s)") by the completion dates set forth therein. The manner and means by which Contractor chooses to complete the Projects are in Contractor's sole discretion and control. Contractor agrees to exercise the highest degree of professionalism, and to utilize its expertise and creative talents in completing such Projects. In completing the Projects, Contractor agrees to provide its own equipment, tools, and other materials at its own expense. Client will make its facilities and equipment available to Contractor when necessary. Contractor shall perform the services necessary to complete the Projects in a timely and professional manner consistent with industry standards, and at a location, place, and time which the Contractor deems appropriate. Contractor may not subcontract or otherwise delegate its obligations under this Agreement without Client's prior written consent. **If Contractor is not a natural person, then before any Contractor employee or consultant performs services in connection with this Agreement, the employee or consultant and Contractor must have entered into a written agreement expressly for the benefit of Client and**

continued

continued

containing provisions substantially equivalent to this section and to Section 4 below.

2. COMPENSATION. Client will pay Contractor a fee for services rendered under this Agreement as set forth in the Project Assignment(s) undertaken by Contractor. [Contractor shall be responsible for all expenses incurred in performing services under this Agreement.] [Contractor will be reimbursed for any reasonable expenses incurred in connection with the performance of services under this Agreement provided Contractor submits verification of such expenses as Client may require.] Upon termination of this Agreement for any reason, Contractor will be paid fees and expenses on a proportional basis as stated in the Project Assignment(s) for work which is then in progress, up to and including the effective date of such termination. Unless other terms are set forth in the Project Assignment(s) for work which is in progress, Client will pay the Contractor for services and will reimburse the Contractor for previously approved expenses within thirty (30) days of the date of Contractor's invoice.

3. INDEPENDENT CONTRACTOR RELATIONSHIP. Contractor's relationship with Client will be that of an independent contractor and nothing in this Agreement should be construed to create a partnership, joint venture, or employer-employee relationship. Contractor is not the agent of Client and is not authorized to make any representation, contract, or commitment on behalf of Client. Contractor will not be entitled to any of the benefits which Client may make available to its employees, such as group insurance, profit sharing, or retirement benefits. Contractor will be solely responsible for all tax returns and payments required to be filed with or made to any federal, state, or local tax authority with respect to Contractor's performance of services and receipt of fees under this Agreement. Client will regularly report amounts paid to Contractor by filing Form 1099-MISC with the Internal Revenue Service as required by law. Because Contractor is an independent contractor, Client will not withhold or make payments for Social Security; make unemployment insurance or disability insurance contributions; or obtain workers' compensation insurance on Contractor's behalf. Contractor agrees to accept exclusive liability for complying with all applicable state and federal laws governing self-employed individuals, including obligations such as payment of taxes, Social Security, disability, and other contributions based on fees paid to Contractor, its agents,

continued

continued

or employees under this Agreement. Contractor hereby agrees to indemnify and defend Client against any and all such taxes or contributions, including penalties and interest.

4. Trade Secrets - Intellectual Property Rights.

4.1 Proprietary Information. Contractor agrees during the term of this Agreement and thereafter to take all steps reasonably necessary to hold Client's Proprietary Information in trust and confidence. By way of illustration but not limitation **"Proprietary Information"** includes (a) trade secrets, inventions, mask works, ideas, processes, formulas, source and object codes, data, programs, other works of authorship, know-how, improvements, discoveries, developments, designs, and techniques (hereinafter collectively referred to as **"Inventions"**); and (b) information regarding plans for research, development, new products, marketing and selling, business plans, budgets and unpublished financial statements, licenses, prices and costs, and suppliers and customers; and (c) information regarding the skills and compensation of other employees of the Client. Notwithstanding the other provisions of this Agreement, nothing received by Contractor will be considered to be Client Proprietary Infor-

mation if (1) it has been published or is otherwise readily available to the public other than by a breach of this Agreement; (2) it has been rightfully received by Contractor from a third party without confidential limitations; (3) it has been independently developed for Contractor by personnel or agents having no access to the Client Proprietary Information; or (4) it was known to Contractor prior to its first receipt from Client.

4.2 Third Party Information. Contractor understands that Client has received and will in the future receive from third parties confidential or proprietary information (**"Third Party Information"**) subject to a duty on Client's part to maintain the confidentiality of such information and to use it only for certain limited purposes. Contractor agrees to hold Third Party Information in confidence and not to disclose to anyone (other than Client personnel who need to know such information in connection with their work for Client) or to use, except in connection with Contractor's work for Client, Third Party Information unless expressly authorized in writing by an officer of Client.

4.3 No Conflict of Interest. Contractor agrees during the term of this Agreement not to accept work or enter into a contract or

continued

continued

accept an obligation inconsistent or incompatible with Contractor's obligations under this Agreement or the scope of services rendered for Client. Contractor warrants that to the best of its knowledge, there is no other existing contract or duty on Contractor's part inconsistent with this Agreement, unless a copy of such contract or a description of such duty is attached to this Agreement as Exhibit B. Contractor further agrees not to disclose to Client, or bring onto Client's premises, or induce Client to use, any confidential information that belongs to anyone other than Client or Contractor.

4.4 Disclosure of Work Product. As used in this Agreement, the term **"Work Product"** means any Invention, whether or not patentable, and all related know-how, designs, mask works, trademarks, formulae, processes, manufacturing techniques, trade secrets, ideas, artwork, software, or other copyrightable or patentable works. Contractor agrees to disclose promptly in writing to Client, or any person designated by Client, all Work Product which is solely or jointly conceived, made, reduced to practice, or learned by Contractor in the course of any work performed for Client (**"Client Work Product"**). Contractor represents that any Work Product relating to Client's

business or any Project which Contractor has made, conceived, or reduced to practice at the time of signing this Agreement (**"Prior Work Product"**) has been disclosed in writing to Client and attached to this Agreement as Exhibit C. If disclosure of any such Prior Work Product would cause Contractor to violate any prior confidentiality agreement, Contractor understands that it is not to list such Prior Work Product in Exhibit C but it will disclose a cursory name for each such invention, a listing of the party(ies) to whom it belongs, and the fact that full disclosure as to such Prior Work Product has not been made for that reason. A space is provided in Exhibit C for such purpose.

4.5 Ownership of Work Product. Contractor shall specifically describe and identify in Exhibit C all technology which (a) Contractor intends to use in performing under this Agreement, (b) is either owned solely by Contractor or licensed to Contractor with a right to sublicense, and (c) is in existence in the form of a writing or working prototype prior to the Effective Date (**"Background Technology"**). Contractor agrees that any and all Inventions conceived, written, created, or first reduced to practice in the performance of work under this Agreement shall be the sole and exclusive property of Client.

continued

continued

4.6 Assignment of Client Work Product. Except for Contractor's rights in the Background Technology, Contractor irrevocably assigns to Client all right, title, and interest worldwide in and to the Client Work Product and all applicable intellectual property rights related to the Client Work Product, including, without limitation, copyrights, trademarks, trade secrets, patents, moral rights, contract, and licensing rights (the **"Proprietary Rights"**). Except as set forth below, Contractor retains no rights to use the Client Work Product and agrees not to challenge the validity of Client's ownership in the Client Work Product. Contractor hereby grants to Client a non-exclusive, royalty-free, irrevocable, and world-wide right, with rights to sublicense through multiple tiers of sublicenses, to make, use, and sell Background Technology and any Prior Work Product incorporated or used in the Client Work Product for the purpose of developing and marketing Client products [**but not for the purpose of marketing Background Technology or Prior Work Products separate from Client products**].

4.7 Waiver of Assignment of Other Rights. If Contractor has any rights to the Client Work Product that cannot be assigned to Client, Contractor uncondi-

tionally and irrevocably waives the enforcement of such rights, and all claims and causes of action of any kind against Client with respect to such rights, and agrees, at Client's request and expense, to consent to and join in any action to enforce such rights. If Contractor has any right to the Client Work Product that cannot be assigned to Client or waived by Contractor, Contractor unconditionally and irrevocably grants to Client during the term of such rights an exclusive, irrevocable, perpetual, worldwide, fully paid, and royalty-free license, with rights to sublicense through multiple levels of sublicensees, to reproduce, create derivative works of, distribute, publicly perform, and publicly display by all means now known or later developed such rights.

4.8 Assistance. Contractor agrees to cooperate with Client or its designee(s), both during and after the term of this Agreement, in the procurement and maintenance of Client's rights in Client Work Product and to execute, when requested, any other documents deemed necessary by Client to carry out the purpose of this Agreement. Contractor agrees to execute upon Client's request a signed transfer of copyright to Client in the form attached to this Agreement as <u>Exhibit D</u> for all Client Work Product subject to

continued

continued

copyright protection, including, without limitation, computer programs, notes, sketches, drawings, and reports. In the event that Client is unable for any reason to secure Contractor's signature to any document required to apply for or execute any patent, copyright, or other applications with respect to any Client Work Product (including improvements, renewals, extensions, continuations, divisions, or continuations in part thereof), Contractor hereby irrevocably designates and appoints Client and its duly authorized officers and agents as its agents and attorneys in fact to act for and in its behalf and instead of Contractor to execute and file any such application and to do all other lawfully permitted acts to further the prosecution and issuance of patents, copyrights, mask works, or other rights thereon with the same legal force and effect as if executed by Contractor.

4.9 Enforcement of Proprietary Rights. Contractor will assist Client in every proper way to obtain, and from time to time enforce, United States and foreign Proprietary Rights relating to Client Work Product in any and all countries. To that end Contractor will execute, verify, and deliver such documents and perform such other acts (including appearances as a witness) as

Client may reasonably request for use in applying for, obtaining, perfecting, evidencing, sustaining, and enforcing such Proprietary Rights and the assignment thereof. In addition, Contractor will execute, verify, and deliver assignments of such Proprietary Rights to Client or its designee. Contractor's obligation to assist Client with respect to Proprietary Rights relating to such Client Work Product in any and all countries shall continue beyond the termination of this Agreement, but Client shall compensate Contractor at a reasonable rate after such termination for the time actually spent by Contractor at Client's request on such assistance.

In the event Client is unable for any reason, after reasonable effort, to secure Contractor's signature on any document needed in connection with the actions specified in the preceding paragraph, Contractor hereby irrevocably designates and appoints Client and its duly authorized officers and agents as its agent and attorney in fact, which appointment is coupled with an interest, to act for and on its behalf to execute, verify, and file any such documents and to do all other lawfully permitted acts to further the purposes of the preceding paragraph with the same legal force and effect as if executed by Contractor. Contractor

continued

continued

hereby waives and quitclaims to Client any and all claims, of any nature whatsoever, which Contractor now or may hereafter have for infringement of any Proprietary Rights assigned hereunder to Client.

5. CONTRACTOR REPRESENTATIONS AND WARRANTIES. Contractor hereby represents and warrants that (a) the Client Work Product will be an original work of Contractor and any third parties will have executed assignment of rights reasonably acceptable to Client; (b) neither the Client Work Product nor any element thereof will infringe the Intellectual Property Rights of any third party; (c) neither the Client Work Product nor any element thereof will be subject to any restrictions or to any mortgages, liens, pledges, security interests, encumbrances, or encroachments; (d) Contractor will not grant, directly or indirectly, any rights or interest to third parties whatsoever in the Client Work Product; (e) Contractor has full right and power to enter into and perform this Agreement without the consent of any third party; (f) Contractor will take all necessary precautions to prevent injury to any persons (including employees of Client) or damage to property (including Client's property) during the term of this Agreement; and (g) should Client permit Contractor to use

any of Client's equipment, tools, or facilities during the term of this Agreement, such permission shall be gratuitous and Contractor shall be responsible for any injury (including death) to any person or damage to property (including Client's property) arising out of use of such equipment, tools, or facilities, whether or not such claim is based upon its condition or on the alleged negligence of Client in permitting its use.

6. INDEMNIFICATION. Contractor will indemnify and hold harmless Client, its officers, directors, employees, sublicensees, customers, and agents from any and all claims, losses, liabilities, damages, expenses, and costs (including attorneys' fees and court costs) which result from a breach or alleged breach of any representation or warranty of Client (a "Claim") set forth in Section 5 of this Agreement, provided that Client gives Contractor written notice of any such Claim and Contractor has the right to participate in the defense of any such Claim at its expense. From the date of written notice from Client to Contractor of any such Claim, Client shall have the right to withhold from any payments due Contractor under this Agreement the amount of any defense costs, plus additional reasonable amounts as security for

continued

continued

Contractor's obligations under this Section 6.

Contractor, at its sole cost and expense, shall maintain appropriate insurance with Commercial General Liability Broad Form Coverage, including Contractual Liability, Contractor's Protective Liability and Personal Injury/Property Damage Coverage in a combined single limit of not less than $3,000,000. A Certificate of Insurance indicating such coverage shall be delivered to Client upon request. The Certificate shall indicate that the policy will not be changed or terminated without at least ten (10) days' prior notice to Client, shall name Client as an additional named insured, and shall also indicate that the insurer has waived its subrogation rights against Client.

7. TERMINATION.

7.1 Termination by Client. Client may terminate this Agreement at its convenience and without any breach by Contractor upon fifteen (15) days' prior written notice to Contractor. Client may also terminate this Agreement immediately in its sole discretion upon Contractor's material breach of Section 4 or Section 7.3.

7.2 Termination by Contractor. Contractor may terminate this Agreement at any time that there is no uncompleted Project Assignment in effect upon fifteen (15) days' prior written notice to Client.

7.3 Noninterference with Business. During and for a period of two (2) years immediately following termination of this Agreement by either party, Contractor agrees not to solicit or induce any employee or independent contractor to terminate or breach an employment, contractual, or other relationship with Client.

7.4 Return of Client Property. Upon termination of the Agreement or earlier as requested by Client, Contractor will deliver to Client any and all drawings, notes, memoranda, specifications, devices, formulas, and documents, together with all copies thereof, and any other material containing or disclosing any Client Work Product, Third Party Information, or Proprietary Information of the Client. Contractor further agrees that any property situated on Client's premises and owned by Client, including disks and other storage media, filing cabinets, or other work areas, is subject to inspection by Client personnel at any time with or without notice.

8. GOVERNMENT OR THIRD PARTY CONTRACTS.

8.1 Government Contracts. In the event that Contractor shall perform services under this Agreement in connection with

continued

continued

any Government contract in which Client may be the prime contractor or subcontractor, Contractor agrees to abide by all laws, rules, and regulations relating thereto. To the extent that any such law, rule, or regulation requires that a provision or clause be included in this Agreement, Contractor agrees that such provision or clause shall be added to this Agreement and the same shall then become a part of this Agreement.

8.2 Security. In the event the services of the Contractor should require Contractor to have access to Department of Defense classified material, or other classified material in the possession of Client's facility, such material shall not be removed from Client's facility. Contractor agrees that all work performed under this Agreement by Contractor which involves the use of classified material mentioned above shall be performed in a secure fashion (consistent with applicable law and regulations for the handling of classified material) and only at Client's facility.

8.3 Ownership. Contractor also agrees to assign all of its right, title, and interest in and to any Work Product to a Third Party, including without limitation the United States, as directed by Client.

9. GENERAL PROVISIONS.

9.1 Governing Law. This Agreement will be governed and construed in accordance with the laws of the State of California as applied to transactions taking place wholly within California between California residents. Contractor hereby expressly consents to the personal jurisdiction of the state and federal courts located in _____ County, California for any lawsuit filed there against Contractor by Client arising from or related to this Agreement.

9.2 Severability. In case any one or more of the provisions contained in this Agreement shall, for any reason, be held to be invalid, illegal, or unenforceable in any respect, such invalidity, illegality, or unenforceability shall not affect the other provisions of this Agreement, and this Agreement shall be construed as if such invalid, illegal, or unenforceable provision had never been contained herein. If, moreover, any one or more of the provisions contained in this Agreement shall for any reason be held to be excessively broad as to duration, geographical scope, activity or subject, it shall be construed by limiting and reducing it, so as to be enforceable to the extent compatible with the applicable law as it shall then appear.

continued

continued

9.3 No Assignment. This Agreement may not be assigned by Contractor without Client's consent, and any such attempted assignment shall be void and of no effect.

9.4 Notices. All notices, requests, and other communications under this Agreement must be in writing, and must be mailed by registered or certified mail, postage prepaid and return receipt requested, or delivered by hand to the party to whom such notice is required or permitted to be given. If mailed, any such notice will be considered to have been given five (5) business days after it was mailed, as evidenced by the postmark. If delivered by hand, any such notice will be considered to have been given when received by the party to whom notice is given, as evidenced by the written and dated receipt of the receiving party. The mailing address for notice to either party will be the address shown on the signature page of this Agreement. Either party may change its mailing address by notice as provided by this section.

9.5 Legal Fees. If any dispute arises between the parties with respect to the matters covered by this Agreement which leads to a proceeding to resolve such dispute, the prevailing party in such proceeding shall be entitled to receive its reasonable attorneys' fees, expert witness fees, and out-of-pocket costs incurred in connection with such proceeding, in addition to any other relief it may be awarded.

9.6 Injunctive Relief. A breach of any of the promises or agreements contained in this Agreement may result in irreparable and continuing damage to Client for which there may be no adequate remedy at law, and Client is therefore entitled to seek injunctive relief as well as such other and further relief as may be appropriate.

9.7 Survival. The following provisions shall survive termination of this Agreement: Section 4, Section 5, Section 6, and Section 7.3.

9.8 Export. Contractor agrees not to export, directly or indirectly, any U.S. source technical data acquired from Client or any products utilizing such data to countries outside the United States, which export may be in violation of the United States export laws or regulations.

9.9 Waiver. No waiver by Client of any breach of this Agreement shall be a waiver of any preceding or succeeding breach. No waiver by Client of any right under this Agreement shall be construed as a waiver of any other right. Client shall not be

continued

continued

required to give notice to enforce strict adherence to all terms of this Agreement.

9.10 Entire Agreement. This Agreement is the final, complete, and exclusive agreement of the parties with respect to the subject matter hereof and supersedes and merges all prior discussions between us. No modification of or amendment to this Agreement, nor any waiver of any rights under this Agreement, will be effective unless in writing and signed by the party to be charged. The terms of this Agreement will govern all Project Assignments and services undertaken by Contractor for Client.

IN WITNESS WHEREOF, the parties have caused this Independent Contractor Services Agreement to be executed by their duly authorized representative.

Client:

_____
(Printed Name)

By:
Title:
Address:

Contractor:

_____
(Printed Name)

By:
Title:
(if applicable)
Address:

For copyright registration purposes only, Contractor must provide the following information:

Date of Birth:
Nationality or Domicile:

continued

EXHIBIT A
PROJECT ASSIGNMENT

SERVICES   MILESTONES

Payment of Fees. Fee will be: (cross out inapplicable provisions)

a fixed price for completion of $ _____

based on a rate per hour of $ _____

other, as follows: _____

_____

       If this Project Assignment or the Independent Contractor Services
Agreement that governs it is terminated for any reason, fees will be paid
based on: (cross out inapplicable provisions)

contractor time spent

the proportion of the deliverables furnished Client, as determined by Client

other, as follows: _____

_____

Expenses. Client will reimburse Contractor for the following expenses:

_____

NOTE: This Project Assignment is governed by the terms of an Independent
Contractor Services Agreement in effect between Client and Contractor. Any
item in this Project Assignment that is inconsistent with that Agreement is
invalid.

Signed: _____   _____

              for Client   Contractor

Dated: _____

EXHIBIT B

CONFLICT OF INTEREST DISCLOSURE

EXHIBIT C

PRIOR WORK PRODUCTS DISCLOSURE

1. Except as listed in Section 2 below, the following is a complete list of all Prior Work Products that have been made or conceived or first reduced to practice by Contractor alone or jointly with others prior to my engagement by Client:

    ____ No inventions or improvements.

    ____ See below:

    ____ Additional sheets attached.

2. Due to a prior confidentiality agreement, Contractor cannot complete the disclosure under Section 1 above with respect to inventions or improvements generally listed below, the proprietary rights and duty of confidentiality with respect to which Contractor owes to the following party(ies):

Invention or Improvement	Party(ies)	Relationship
1. _____	_____	_____
2. _____	_____	_____
3. _____	_____	_____

____ Additional sheets attached.

BACKGROUND TECHNOLOGY DISCLOSURE

The following is a list of all Background Technology that Contractor intends to use in performing under this Agreement:

EXHIBIT D

ASSIGNMENT OF COPYRIGHT

For good and valuable consideration that has been received, the undersigned sells, assigns, and transfers to Client, a _____ [**corporation**], and its successors and assigns, the copyright in and to the following work, which was created by the following indicated author(s):

Title: _____

Author(s): _____

Copyright Office Identification No. (if any): _____

and all of the right, title, and interest of the undersigned, vested and contingent, therein and thereto.

Executed this _____ day of _____, 19___.

Signature: _____

Printed Name: _____

NOTES

1. *Vizcaino v. Microsoft Corp.*, 97 F. 3d 1187 (9th Cir. 1996). *See also* Charles McCoy, "Microsoft Temps Win Full-Time Benefits," *The Wall Street Journal*, Oct. 14, 1996, at B7.
2. *Meritor Savings Bank, FSB v. Vinson*, 477 U.S. 57 (1986).
3. *O'Connor v. Consolidated Coin Caterers Corp.*, 116 S.Ct. 1307 (1996).
4. *Maddox v. Univ. of Tenn.*, 62 F. 3d 843 (6th Cir. 1995).
5. Some states, such as Washington, have set the minimum wage at an hourly rate higher than the FLSA. Employers should check with their local state wage-and-hour office for differences between the FLSA and state wage-and-hour laws.
6. *Kern v. Dynalectron Corp.*, 577 F.Supp. 1196 (N.D. Tex. 1983), *aff'd*, 746 F.2d 810 (5th Cir. 1984).
7. *Trombetta v. Detroit, Toledo and Irontown Railroad Co.*, 265 N.W.2d 385 (Mich. 1978).
8. *Lampe v. Presbyterian Medical Center*, 590 P.2d 513 (Colo. 1978). *See also Foley v. Interactive Data Corporation*, 765 P.2d 373 (Cal. 1988) (an employee could be fired for reporting to his superiors that his incoming supervisor was under investigation by the FBI for embezzlement from a former employer because no fundamental public policy was involved).
9. *Fortune v. Nat'l Cash Register Co.*, 364 N.E.2d 1251 (Mass. 1977).
10. *See* Michelle Quinn, "Bosses' New Code: A No-Sue Policy," *San Jose Mercury News*, June 21, 1996, at C1.
11. *Community for Creative Non-Violence v. Reid*, 490 U.S. 730 (1989).
12. *See* Cal. Labor Code section 2870 and Wash. Rev. Code section 49.44.140.

Intellectual Property
14

Many entrepreneurs assume that intellectual property issues are important only to high-technology companies with large scientific staffs. In fact, virtually all businesses, even start-ups, have knowledge and information that are important to competitive success. Does the company have a name? A business plan? A logo? Advertising materials? Product literature? Customized software? A new invention? A training video? A new way of doing things? These may be among a company's most valuable assets. Intellectual property laws can help protect these assets. Likewise, all businesses should take precautions to avoid violating others' intellectual property rights. Even unintentional violations can result in time-consuming and costly litigation that can ruin a business.

The law of intellectual property is vast and complex. Obviously, no general businessperson can or should try to grasp all of its subtleties and nuances. Still, every entrepreneur needs to understand the basic rights that can be protected and the limitations on the protections available under the law. This basic understanding is critical to knowing when experienced help is needed.

Protecting intellectual property assets, and avoiding infringement of others' rights, requires the entrepreneur and his or her employees to act to prevent missteps. Experienced counsel can provide guidance, but the ultimate responsibility rests with the company itself. This chapter will give the entrepreneur an important leg up in meeting these challenges.

The authors gratefully acknowledge the contributions of Paul M. Work to this chapter. Mr. Work holds J.D. and M.B.A. degrees from Stanford University and is General Counsel and Product Marketing Manager for Digital Tools, Inc., a Silicon Valley software firm.

The chapter begins with a discussion of the important area of trade secrets. Trade secret law can help to protect confidential business information that is vital to competitive success. Trade secrets can protect broad classes of information, but concrete steps must be taken to preserve confidentiality.

Next, the chapter addresses copyrights. Copyrights have moved beyond their traditional role of protecting published literary works, musical compositions, and works of art into the realm of computer software and cyberspace, where challenging new issues are emerging. Discussion then moves to patents. A patent gives an inventor very powerful rights that last for twenty years from the date the patent application is filed. The chapter next outlines the basics of trademarks and service marks, which are important tools to protect logos, brand names, and other identifying slogans and trade dress.

The chapter then presents an overview of key business and legal issues for transactions involving intellectual property. This discussion includes both licenses and acquisitions of intellectual property rights in the course of larger transactions, such as in the sale of an entire business. Finally, the chapter provides an illustration of how many of these principles come into play by analyzing the evolving role of intellectual property laws in the software industry.

TRADE SECRET PROTECTION

Most businesses have important confidential information that helps them to compete in the marketplace. Such information may take the form of business and marketing plans, customer lists, financial statements, supplier terms, product formulas, custom software, and key contracts. Once competitors gain access to these company secrets, their value is often destroyed. Thus, the law of trade secrets can help to preserve a company's business secrets when patent and copyright protection cannot.

Trade secret disputes arise most often when an employee leaves a company to join a competitor and is accused of taking valuable competitive information with him or her. For example, a recent hire in a medical equipment firm brings to her new job a presentation she created for her former employer that outlines an as-yet-undisclosed marketing strategy for a new diagnostic medical instrument. Even if the new hire merely intends to show her new boss the presentation to demonstrate her skill in creating effective presentations, her actions would likely constitute misappropriation of her former employer's trade secrets. Violations of trade secret rights, both inadvertent and intentional, are common and are often costly.

Trade secret laws differ in other countries; the following discussion covers only U.S. trade secret law. If confidential business information is to be used or kept abroad, it is important to consider retaining foreign counsel. An experienced U.S. attorney can help to determine whether the often considerable expense of hiring a foreign attorney is justified and can often provide referrals.

What is a Trade Secret?

General Definition Although trade secret laws vary somewhat from state to state, the general principles are quite similar. A *trade secret* is (1) any information, including any formula, pattern, compilation, program, device, method, technique, or process, that (2) provides a business with a competitive advantage, (3) is not generally known by a company's current or potential competitors and cannot be readily discovered by them through legitimate means, and (4) is the subject of reasonable efforts to maintain its secrecy. A trade secret is protected for as long as each of these criteria is met.

Types of Information That Can Be Protected Virtually any type of information can be protected as a trade secret so long as the other requirements listed above are met. Sales and marketing plans, customer lists and data, software, computer files, manufacturing techniques, formulas, recipes, research and development results, survey information, sales data, secrets embodied in products, circuits on computer chips, and almost any other type of information can qualify, so long as the information provides the business with some competitive advantage. Thus, it is crucial to think in the broadest possible terms when assessing what information may qualify as a trade secret. The biggest risk is failing to take appropriate measures to protect less obvious forms of trade secrets and thereby losing trade secret protection.

Trade Secrets Must Not Be Generally Known or Discoverable
Information that is generally known or discoverable through proper means by competitors cannot constitute a trade secret. Thus, trade secret protection does not extend to information that is in the public domain or is otherwise generally available to customers or competitors. This includes information contained in a company's own product and promotional materials (even technical specifications) that are distributed freely to the public. It also includes information that is disclosed by mistake, such as when a document is left on top of a desk in plain view of a visitor to the company's offices, or when an employee in an elevator is overheard by a customer. In addition, trade secret protection is unavailable for information that competitors or others obtain through legitimate reverse engineering of a hardware product. (*Reverse engineering* is the process of breaking down a product and examining its inner workings.) Thus, once a product containing trade secrets is released for sale, trade secret protection is generally lost. However, if the trade secret cannot be ascertained from the product, as for example is the case with the formula for Coca Cola, then release of the product will not cause the loss of trade secret protection. In addition, prototypes and information destined for public release can still be protected as trade secrets before they are released.

Reasonable Efforts to Maintain Secrecy   Simply stated, a court will not protect trade secrets unless the owner does also. It is not necessary to take every conceivable precaution, but the owner must make reasonable efforts under the circumstances. In assessing reasonableness, courts examine the value of the information, the resources available to the company to protect its trade secrets, the difficulty and expense required for a competitor to develop the information on its own, and how broadly the information is known, both inside and outside the company. Elements of a sample trade secret protection program are discussed below.

Enforcing Trade Secret Rights

Legal remedies can protect the owner of a trade secret against improper disclosure and use by others. Improper means of acquiring trade secrets include theft, misrepresentation, bribery, breach of contract, and espionage. Perhaps more important, improper disclosures also include disclosures that violate a duty of confidentiality owed to the owner of the trade secret. This duty of confidentiality may arise because an employee, customer, consultant, independent contractor, banker, or other person has signed a *nondisclosure agreement* (also referred to as a *confidentiality agreement*) with the trade secret owner, in which the person to whom trade secrets are disclosed promises not to disclose them to others or to use them. A duty of confidentiality may also arise by operation of law, that is, merely because of a person's status as an officer, director, or employee of a company owning the trade secret.

When a person discloses or uses a trade secret in violation of a duty of confidentiality, the trade secret owner can use the courts to protect his or her trade secret rights. Just as important, if a company acquires a trade secret from someone such as an ex-employee of a competitor, and that company knew or had reason to know that the ex-employee violated a duty of confidentiality in disclosing the information, then the trade secret owner may have legal rights against the company. Note, however, that if no duty of confidentiality exists, then, absent improper means (such as theft), legal protections generally will not be available. This is why confidentiality agreements are so important.

Legal relief can include a court order preventing disclosure or use of the trade secret information, money damages, and, in some cases, punitive damages. The state may also bring criminal charges. Although the filing of criminal charges remains relatively rare in trade secret cases, increasing recognition that trade secrets are valuable company property (often far more valuable than physical property) may lead to greater use of criminal sanctions in trade secret theft cases. If trade secret rights may have been violated, it is prudent to contact an attorney immediately.

Even when trade secrets become public in violation of the owner's rights, once they are public, they cease to be trade secrets. This is true even though the owner is entirely innocent. Damages may be available, but winning them requires victory at trial, which is never a certainty. Even with a victory at trial, court-awarded damages may not provide full compensation for the harm to the business. If the wrongdoers are unable to pay the damages, there may be no effective remedy. Thus, an entrepreneur's best course is to take steps to prevent both improper and inadvertent trade secret disclosures. A trade secret protection program should form the centerpiece of this effort.

Establishing a Trade Secret Protection Program

Taking reasonable steps to protect trade secrets is legally necessary to secure the protection provided by the trade secret laws. Developing a program to protect company secrets usually makes good business sense as well. The company's trade secret policies should be in writing, be made available to all employees and contractors, and be discussed thoroughly with every employee and contractor who has access to trade secrets.

An experienced attorney should help develop the trade secret protection program, but ultimately the entrepreneur is responsible for seeing that the program is carried out by all employees and contractors. The plan should be comprehensive, but not so complex and burdensome that employees or contractors refuse or are unable to implement it. What constitutes a reasonable trade secret protection program that meets the legal standard necessary to enforce trade secret rights will vary from business to business. An entrepreneur in a start-up business need not take the same precautions as IBM. Again, an attorney can help craft a balanced, effective plan that meets the legal requirements for a particular business. Because many elements of a trade secret protection program are quite similar across businesses, such legal advice should not be too expensive.

Although every business's circumstances are different, most trade secret protection programs will contain most of the following elements.

Identifying Trade Secrets The program should include guidance as to what constitutes a trade secret. The head of a small business is likely to be aware of many, but not all, of his or her company's important trade secrets. Employees and contractors must also shoulder responsibility for helping to identify a company's trade secrets. The trade secret protection plan should spell out general categories of information that are likely to be particularly important to the business. This could be source code, sensitive computer files, and documentation for a software company, or customer data for a telemarketing company. In addition, the plan should include appropriate catchall categories, such as any information that is not known outside the company and that might have value to competitors.

The plan should require employees to mark all documents that contain trade secrets as "Confidential." However, it is important not to treat all company information as trade secrets. If every document is marked "confidential," a court is likely to conclude that the company is not taking seriously the notion of confidentiality and may refuse to grant any trade secret protection, even for those elements that truly are confidential.

Securing Employee Commitment Securing employee commitment to protecting trade secrets is essential. Employees are the biggest source of trade secret leaks, both accidental and otherwise. Steps to achieve employee commitment include the following.

Preemployment Clearance As noted above, trade secret disputes commonly arise when an employee leaves one company to work for a competitor, taking sensitive information with him or her. When hiring an employee away from a competitor, it is important to stress that no trade secrets from the former employer are to be used on the job or shared with others in the company. In sensitive cases, an applicant should be required to sign an agreement to that effect as part of the recruiting process. The new employer should make sure that the new employee has not brought documents, computer disks, or other papers containing trade secrets to the job. The new employer should include promises to this effect in the employee's employment or confidentiality agreement. It is also prudent to review any employment or confidentiality agreement that the new employee had with the former employer. Finally, conducting a broad search for a new hire to fill a vacant job, rather than merely offering the position to a competitor's employee, can help show that a new hire was not singled out with the specific intent to acquire trade secrets from his or her former employer.

Confidentiality Agreements Many authorities consider confidentiality agreements to be the single most important element in a company's trade secret protection program. In brief, the agreement contains a promise by the employee to avoid unauthorized use or disclosure of the company's trade secrets and to use care to prevent unauthorized use and disclosures from occurring. In addition to strengthening the employer's legal rights, the confidentiality agreement impresses upon the new employee the seriousness with which the company guards its trade secrets. The agreement may be part of a more comprehensive employment agreement or an invention assignment agreement, or it may be a stand-alone document. Middle- and upper-level management, as well as engineers, technical employees, secretaries, janitors, clerks, and all others with access to trade secrets, even as an incidental part of their jobs, should be required to sign a confidentiality agreement before beginning work. Experience suggests that most new employees will readily sign such an agreement. If the employer did not require an employee to sign a confidentiality agreement as part of the hiring process, the employer should offer some consideration other than just continued employment in exchange for the employee's agreeing to sign a confidentiality agreement later.

Noncompetition Agreements Some companies use noncompetition agreements (also called covenants not to compete) to prevent employees who leave the company from using trade secrets and other sensitive information on behalf of a competitor. The key advantage of a noncompetition agreement is that it avoids the often difficult task of proving that a former employee actually stole and used trade secrets to help a competitor. For example, a former employee might use general knowledge of a company's long-range strategic plans to design a strategy for his or her new company. In such a case, it might be virtually impossible to prove that the former employee actually divulged trade secrets in designing the new strategy. With a noncompetition agreement, the employee is simply prevented from working for the competitor at all. Typically, only senior managers and technical staff are asked to sign noncompetition agreements, which usually have a limited duration, often one to three years.

The chief difficulty with noncompetition agreements is that many states, including California, make such agreements generally unenforceable (except when executed in connection with the sale of a business, as discussed more fully in chapter 2). In states in which noncompetition agreements are generally enforceable, many employees refuse to sign them. However, if a noncompetition agreement is used, experienced counsel should draft the contract to maximize the likelihood that it will be held to be fully enforceable.

Employee Education All employees should be provided basic information about the company's trade secret protection program. Periodic reminders in newsletters and at companywide functions will help to keep employees aware of the need to protect trade secrets. For example, Synopsys, Inc., a Silicon Valley software firm, created a sinister-looking caricature of a spy and put it up on walls and in newsletters to provide a vivid reminder of the importance of trade secret protection. Company executives even performed a brief skit at a companywide meeting showing how easy it can be to accidentally divulge sensitive information. Educational efforts should also stress to employees the dangers of improperly using others' trade secrets. Companies should require employees to acknowledge on an annual basis all of the company's policies, including its trade secret program. Unintentional trade secret disclosures are common, and employee education is a key to safe-guarding confidential information.

Other Protective Measures Other recommended measures to protect trade secrets include the following:

- marking as "Confidential" documents that contain trade secrets;
- disclosing confidential information within the company on a need-to-know basis;
- keeping confidential information on-site whenever possible;
- using appropriate passwords and security codes to protect sensitive computer files;
- maintaining a clean-desk policy and locking offices and file cabinets;
- protecting prototypes and other physical products that contain trade secrets;
- avoiding the discussion of sensitive topics when visitors are present, over unsecured telephone lines (especially cellular phones), and in public, especially in airplanes, elevators, restaurants, and other places where competitors could possibly be present;
- advising employees to use extra caution at trade shows, scientific conferences, and professional gatherings, at which competitors are almost always present and where the temptation is great to boast about new but confidential developments at informal social gatherings (especially in bars);
- using a shredder or otherwise destroying discarded confidential information before putting it in the trash;
- prohibiting personal software and personal computer files at work;
- keeping records of what software was checked out to whom and when; and
- using appropriate precautions when working at home or away from the office.

Technically oriented companies should have a policy of reviewing engineers' and scientists' speeches and publications to prevent inadvertent disclosures of company trade secrets. This can be especially important because many scientists and engineers are justifiably proud of their new discoveries and are eager to share their findings with colleagues. Precautions such as these cost little and are good business practice, but too many companies fail to implement them, with often unpleasant consequences.

Exit Interview/Exit Agreement Exit interviews should be conducted to ensure that departing employees do not take any trade secrets from the company and recognize their duty to refrain from taking any materials containing trade secrets. Personal files, computer disks, and other items employees remove should first be inspected for company trade secrets, and the company should confirm with employees that all such materials have been deleted from hard drives in home or laptop computers. Companies should try to get all departing employees to acknowledge these matters in writing. If an employee never signed a confidentiality agreement, this becomes even more important. If an employee is leaving to work for a competitor, the company should consider having its lawyer send a letter to the new employer, informing it that the employee had access to valuable trade secrets and warning it against using any trade secrets that may be brought into its possession by the new employee.

Dealing with Outsiders A trade secret protection program should also include precautions for dealing with outsiders.

Confidentiality Agreements Employers should require consultants, independent contractors, potential investors, and other outsiders with access to trade secrets to sign a confidentiality agreement before disclosing confidential information to them. Without such an agreement, these persons may have no duty to refrain from disclosing or using a company's trade secrets.

Building Security Security measures may range from steps as simple as keeping unattended doors locked, maintaining a visitor sign-in log, and providing employee escorts, to steps as elaborate as providing fully guarded and electronically protected access. In addition, many of the suggested employee precautions noted above can also serve to help prevent inadvertent leaks to outside visitors.

Conclusion In sum, it is important to develop and follow carefully an appropriate trade secret protection program. An experienced attorney can help develop a reasonable program that balances the need for protection with the costs of the program. But it is the entrepreneur's responsibility to ensure that the employees actually live up to the program. In the end, knowledgeable and conscientious employees are the most important line of defense against trade secret disclosure.

COPYRIGHTS

Copyrights provide important protections for many businesses, and they are relatively cheap and easy to obtain. Copyrights are critical to companies operating in the software, publishing, journalism, movie, entertainment, music, and multimedia industries, among others. Copyrights are also important to artists, writers, musicians, photographers, and architects. However, virtually all businesses have some materials that can be protected through copyright law.

What Is a Copyright?

A *copyright* gives the owner of a work of authorship the legal right to determine how the work is used and to obtain the economic benefits from the work. For example, the owner of a copyright for a book or a piece of software has the exclusive rights to use, copy, distribute, and sell copies of the work, including later editions or versions of the work. If another person improperly uses material covered by a copyright, the copyright owner can obtain legal relief.

What Can Be Protected by a Copyright?

Copyrights protect a wide range of works. In addition to protecting books, works of art, musical recordings, magazines, plays, dramatic performances, and movies, copyrights can also protect software, advertisements, photographs, videos, games, instruction manuals, sales presentations and client proposals, original labels, diagrams, architectural drawings, financial tables, business plans, and many other forms of creative work.

Copyrights can also be used to protect derivative works and compilations. A *derivative work* is a work that is derived from another work.

Derivative works can include adaptations and modifications of previous works such as a later edition of a book or a translation of the original work into another language. A *compilation* is an original gathering and presentation of other works in which there is some creativity expressed in the arrangement itself. For example, a particular listing of high-quality auto repair shops could be copyrighted, although the names of the shops themselves are not copyrightable.

The copyright owner has exclusive rights to reproduce copies of the work; to develop derivative works; to distribute, sell, or license copies; and to perform or display the work in public. These exclusive rights can be used to prevent others from using, copying, distributing, performing, or displaying the copyrighted work or any derivative works.

Copyrights Do Not Protect Ideas

A crucial point to understand about copyrights is that they cannot be used to protect an idea or a certain way of performing some function; copyrights protect only the particular way the idea or function is expressed in a tangible medium (such as printed on paper, recorded on tape, or coded on a disk). For example, this book is protected by copyright, but the ideas contained in it are not. A business plan may be copyrighted, but that does not prevent another person from developing a business that uses the ideas contained in the plan. However, such ideas may be protectable as trade secrets.

If an idea and the way it is expressed are inseparably bound, the idea and the expression are said to merge, and no copyright protection is available. For example, the maker of a karate video game cannot obtain a copyright on the karate moves made by the action figures in the game because the expression of the karate moves in the video game is inseparable from the moves performed in actual karate. The "H" pattern for a manual transmission cannot be copyrighted because it is inseparable from the basic functioning of the gearshift pattern employed in most manual transmissions. As discussed below, distinguishing between an idea or functionality and its expression can sometimes be quite difficult, particularly in the software arena.

Requirements for Obtaining Copyright Protection

For a work of authorship to be eligible for copyright protection, it must meet three basic requirements. First, the work must be fixed in a tangible medium of expression (e.g., written down, saved on a computer disk, or recorded on tape). Almost any medium from which the idea can be retrieved will qualify. Second, the work must be original; that is, it must have been created by the author claiming the copyright. However, the work does not need to be unique, novel, or of high quality. Third, the work must contain some minimal level of creativity. The standard of creativity required is quite low—no particular merit is required. Thus, the white pages of the telephone directory would not qualify, but the "Yellow Pages" with ads and text displayed would. Directions for how to use a beauty product displayed on a product label would also qualify. Thus, almost any original work of authorship developed for a business can qualify for copyright protection.

No action is required to obtain copyright protection. It automatically arises when an original work of authorship is first fixed in a tangible medium of expression. However, steps can be taken to strengthen copyright protections. It is always advisable to display a copyright notice, even though it is not legally required. This puts others on notice that the work is copyrighted and can prevent a third party from asserting innocent infringement to avoid liability. This notice should be in the form of the word "Copyright" or a "c" enclosed in a circle (©), followed by the name of the author and year of publication and the phrase "All rights reserved." The notice should be displayed prominently.

To file an infringement suit in the United States, the owner of the copyright must register it with the Register of Copyrights in Washington, D.C. Although the right to sue can be secured by registration after an infringement occurs, statutory damages and attorneys' fees are only available if the registration is made within three months of the date that the work is first published. Statutory damages are remedies provided by the Copyright Act and currently are limited to $20,000 for each ordinary infringement and $100,000 for each willful infringement. Statutory damages are typically sought when the actual damages suffered are less than these amounts or are very difficult to prove in court. A plaintiff who made a timely copyright registration can seek actual damages or statutory damages, but not both. Actual damages awarded in copyright cases can be much greater than these statutory amounts.

Registration is a relatively simple and inexpensive procedure and should be considered for any significant works of authorship. Registration requires filing a copy of the work, which is available to the public, but special rules may be invoked to help protect valuable software code.

Protections Available Through Copyright

Copyright protects the particular expression of an idea, not the idea itself. Thus, the thoughts, systems, policies, procedures, know-how, formulas, and facts contained in a work protected only by copyright may be used freely by another person. In practice, it can be very difficult to separate an idea from its tangible expression, so the degree of protection afforded by a copyright is often hard to predict with precision. In general, the more different ways there are to express an idea, the more likely the work is to be copyrightable. For example, a court held that the use of the "+" sign to indicate addition in a computer spreadsheet program is not copyrightable because there really is no other logical and feasible way to express the notion of addition on a computer keyboard. On the other hand, a basic literary plot such as love triumphing over adversity is capable of so many unique expressions that many different stories expressing the same basic idea can be copyrighted.

If a person copies, word for word, the copyrighted work of another, there is a clear violation of the copyright. Thus, unauthorized duplication of a magazine article or a piece of software constitutes a copyright violation. Copyright violations can also occur if a later work is found to be "substantially similar" to the copyrighted work. Disputes often arise when the expression of an idea in one work is similar but not identical to the expression of an idea in a copyrighted work. For example, creating a movie that parallels closely the characters and plot of a copyrighted book can constitute infringement.

Proving Copyright Infringement

Direct proof that a work was copied is not required to prove copyright infringement. All that is needed is a showing that the alleged infringer had access to the copyrighted work and that his or her work is substantially similar to the copyrighted work. A technique that is frequently used to prove copying of software is the embedding of useless pieces of software code within a program; if another program contains the useless code, it is almost certain that the original code was copied. Determining whether copying of protected expression has occurred in cases other than literal copying can be highly fact specific and costly to litigate. A company should contact an experienced attorney immediately if infringement of an important copyright is suspected.

Fair Use

Even if material does qualify for copyright protection, the law permits others to make limited use of copyrighted materials, including making copies, under the doctrine of fair use. *Fair use* includes criticism, comment, research, teaching, and news reporting. Whether an unauthorized use of a copyrighted work constitutes protected fair use is fact specific. However, in very general terms, if the use is commercial and diminishes the value of the copyright to the owner, the use is less likely to qualify as a fair use.

Courts sometimes interpret the fair use exception quite broadly. For example, one court held that using another's drawings of film frames of the assassination of President Kennedy in a book qualified as fair use because the public interest was served by making available information about the assassination. The Supreme Court held that the use of the copyrighted song "Pretty Woman" in a parody by rap group 2 Live Crew was fair use so long as the parody used no more of the lyrics and music of the original work than was necessary to make it recognizable.[1]

For many commercial business uses of copyrighted information, however, fair use will not constitute a defense to infringement. For example, Kinko's Graphics Corporation violated the copyrights of Basic Books, Inc. and other publishers when it copied without permission and sold portions of copyrighted works selected by professors to be used in student course readers. The court rejected Kinko's fair use claim, noting that Kinko's involvement was for the purpose of obtaining profits, even if the copied materials were used for educational purposes. Kinko's was ordered to pay $510,000 in damages, attorneys' fees, and court costs.[2] Similarly, the copying of articles in scientific and technical journals by a scientist at Texaco Inc. for his own files was held not to be fair use.[3]

Duration of Copyrights

A key advantage of copyrights is that protection typically lasts far longer than is needed for most commercial uses. The copyright for an individual creator lasts for the life of the creator plus 50 years. For a work owned by a corporation, the duration is 75 years from the date of publication or 100 years from the date of creation, whichever occurs first.

Ownership of Copyrights

As a general rule, the author of a work owns the copyright. However, under the doctrine of *work made for hire*, the employer owns works created by its employees in the scope of their employment. As discussed in chapter 13, it is not always clear whether a worker is an employee or an independent contractor and whether an employee is acting within the scope of his or her employment. Thus, employees who create copyrighted

---

FROM THE TRENCHES

Even big companies can fall into the copyright ownership trap. *The Computer Lawyer* reported that a large bank had hired a software developer to create a computer program that the bank believed would provide a major competitive advantage. The agreement between the bank and the developer failed to specify who owned the copyright to the software. When the developer announced plans to license the product to other banks, the bank threatened suit. The bank probably would have lost. Absent a written assignment agreement, the program's author (the developer) owned the copyright.

works should be required to sign an agreement assigning any rights they may have in the works to the employer.

If the creator of the work is an independent contractor, then the company that pays for the work will own it and the copyright only if (1) there is a written agreement that states that the work is a work made for hire, and (2) the work falls into one of nine legal categories of specially commissioned works made for hire (none of which includes computer software). Because not all copyrighted works fit within the statutory categories of works made for hire, independent contractors are typically asked to sign agreements assigning to the company that hires them all of their rights to any works they produce during their service. Such an agreement is particularly crucial for works such as computer software that do not fall within one of the nine listed categories. Without such a written assignment, the independent contractor will own his or her works, and the party that paid for them may be entitled only to a single copy.

Copyright in Cyberspace

The ease with which copies can be made on the Internet and the World Wide Web has caused a rash of suits by copyright owners against computer bulletin board services (BBSs) and on-line service providers. For example, the publisher of *Playboy* magazine successfully sued a small BBS for copyright infringement when a BBS subscriber uploaded files containing digitized pictures copied from *Playboy*; the files could then be downloaded by other BBS subscribers.[4]

Similarly, the Church of Scientology sued Netcom On-Line Communication Services, Inc., an Internet-access provider, for infringing its copyrights to the works of Church of Scientology founder L. Ron Hubbard. A former minister of Scientology and now vocal critic of the church had posted portions of these works on a Usenet news group by uploading them to a BBS that had gained access to the Internet through the facilities of Netcom. The court concluded that Netcom could be liable for contributing to the subscriber's copyright infringement if it knew or should have known of the infringement, yet still did not remove the posting.[5]

Owners of copyrighted music, sound recordings, films, photographs, magazines, and books that are available on the Web are expected to act aggressively to protect their rights against persons making or facilitating the making of unauthorized copies. An entrepreneur who uses copyrighted art or music on his or her Web site without permission is violating the law and is subject to suit by the owners of the copyrighted works.

International Issues

Unlike most other forms of intellectual property protection, U.S. copyrights generally are valid overseas through a treaty (the Berne Convention) signed by most major countries. However, enforcing copyrights in other countries may be far more difficult and costly than enforcing them in the United States. In some countries, enforcement of copyrights may not be practical at all. However, recent U.S. government initiatives to promote protection for U.S. intellectual property overseas (including pressure on China to stop software copying) have led some experts to conclude that enforcing copyrights in many foreign nations will become easier in the future. For now, however, obstacles to enforcement remain in many countries. A company's only recourse may be to obtain U.S. government assistance in protecting its rights, which can be difficult to do.

PATENTS

Any entrepreneur whose business involves the creation of new products or manufacturing processes must understand the basics of patent law. Patents can provide powerful protections for new products, inventions, and processes. Patents can also give a young business a legal monopoly over a new technology, and with it enormous advantages over even the largest competitors. For example, in 1994 Stac Electronics won a $120 million jury verdict against Microsoft Corporation for infringement of Stac's data compression software patents. Although Stac later settled the case for $43 million cash and the purchase by Microsoft of $40 million of Stac nonvoting preferred stock, the award was a monumental victory for Stac. Patents can also give a new business instant prestige and quick revenues from licensing fees.

Another benefit of patents is their use defensively as bargaining chips in patent disputes. If a competitor claims that a company's product violates a patent, it is very helpful if the company can claim that the competitor is violating one of the company's patents. This often results in a cross-licensing agreement whereby each party is permitted to use the other's patented technology, often on a royalty-free basis.

The government, however, does not grant these exclusive rights readily. Obtaining a patent is often a complex and costly undertaking, and violating another's patent rights, even innocently, can result in crushing damage awards. Savvy competitors use patents in strategic ways, such as securing patents for improvements on another company's patents. Recent legal trends favor the enforcement of patents, and patent law is becoming more critical in many industries, including software, biotechnology, and medical devices.

One note of caution: Patent law is a subspecialty within the legal specialty of intellectual property. (Even within the subspecialty of patent

Drawing by Chas. Addams; ©1991, The New Yorker Magazine, Inc.

law, attorneys often focus on a single industry, such as biotechnology, software, or telecommunications.) Patent law is particularly complex and technical. If patent issues arise, a company should consult a patent attorney. The following discussion presents an overview that will help in assessing when to contact patent counsel.

What Is a Patent?

A *patent* is an exclusive right granted by the federal government that entitles the inventor to prevent anyone else from making, using, or selling the patented process or invention in the United States. There are two main types of patents: utility patents and design patents. (Patents for certain plants are a third type.) Rights to utility patents (the most important and most common type) last for twenty years from the date the patent application is filed. Rights to design patents last for fourteen years from the date the design patent is issued. Patents cannot be renewed once these periods elapse.

The patent application must contain a detailed description of the invention sufficient to allow someone else who is reasonably skilled in the field to reproduce it. Once the patent is issued, this information becomes public. Thus, after the patent protection period lapses, anyone can use the information in the patent application to reproduce the invention.

Utility patents can protect several kinds of inventions. Utility patents can cover a machine, such as a machine for making auto parts, or a process, such as the process for filling an aerosol can or fabricating a computer chip. Utility patents can also protect articles of manufacture, such as an intermittent windshield wiper or a plastic paper clip. Utility patents can also cover new compositions of matter, such as a new chemical compound or a formula for mouthwash. Improvements to any of these types of inventions can also be protected with a utility patent.

If an invention falls into one of these categories (i.e., machine, process, article of manufacture, or composition of matter), it qualifies as patentable subject matter. The requirements and procedures for obtaining a utility patent are discussed in greater detail on the following pages, but the range of inventions that can be patentable is broad. Examples of nonpatentable subject matter include methods of doing business, mathematical principles (such as pure algorithms), and laws of nature (e.g., $e = mc^2$).

A *design patent* can be used to protect ornamental (as opposed to useful) designs that are both novel and original. Design patents can protect the shape or appearance of items such as computer icons, furniture, or a pair of running shoes. Design patents have become more popular in recent years. For example, Reebok International, Ltd. sued L.A. Gear, Inc. for violation of a design patent on its running shoe design and won.

Requirements for Obtaining a Patent

Not all new inventions qualify for patent protection. First, as noted above, the invention must consist of patentable subject matter. Second, the invention must be useful. This is rarely a problem because most companies will not invest the time and expense of seeking a patent for a useless invention. Third, the invention must be novel. An invention is considered to be *novel* if (1) it is neither patented, or known, or used by others in the United States, and (2) it was not previously patented or described in a printed publication in another country. Fourth, even if the invention is novel, it cannot be merely an obvious extension of previously existing technology (whether or not that technology is actively used today or is patented).

The Statutory Bar

A patent will also be denied if the invention is disclosed to the public more than one year before the date that the patent application is filed. For this purpose, "disclosed" means that the invention has been publicly used or sold in the United States or was described in a written publication anywhere in the world. This limitation on an inventor's ability to file a patent application is known as the *statutory bar*. Scientists and engineers frequently are eager to publish their results and share their learning with others, but doing so before a patent is filed can render the invention unpatentable. Similarly, even beta testing (trial use by select customers to ascertain product performance) can undermine patentability unless adequate safeguards are taken, particularly if any money is to be paid by the beta tester for the use of the product.

Equally troubling, no other country (except the Philippines) has even a one-year grace period. Thus, in other countries, *any* publication of the invention before filing may result in a loss of patentability. For example, if a scientist presents a technical paper describing a patentable invention to a conference in Tokyo before the patent is filed in Japan, then the invention may no longer be patentable in Japan. A Japanese patent will not be issued if there has been disclosure in Japan or to a Japanese national outside of Japan prior to the filing of the patent application. Disclosing the invention anywhere in the world is enough to prevent the invention from being patentable in most European countries, unless a U.S. patent application was filed prior to disclosure and a European patent application is filed soon thereafter. Thus, to preserve both U.S. and foreign patentability, it is usually best to file a U.S. patent application before allowing any public disclosure or sale of the invention.

Overview of Procedures for Obtaining a Patent

The Application   The procedures for obtaining a patent are usually time-consuming and expensive. A complex application must be filed with the U.S. Patent and Trademark Office (PTO). The application must describe the invention in detail and include a diagram or illustration of it. Most inventions contain both patentable and unpatentable elements. For example, Polaroid Corporation obtained many patents for its instant cameras, but elements of these cameras, such as the lens and the shutter, were not themselves patentable. The application must set forth in detail the specific *claims* of the patent, that is, the precise elements of the invention for which patent protection is sought. These patent claims must be written in highly stylized language. Skill and experience are required to draft claims that are sufficiently broad to achieve meaningful protections yet narrow enough to withstand scrutiny from a patent examiner. Thus, an experienced patent attorney should prepare the patent claims. However, as the inventor usually understands the novel aspects of the invention better than anyone else, the inventor can often reduce legal costs by producing an initial draft of the patent claims.

Search for Prior Art In addition, before filing a patent application, it is advisable for the applicant to conduct a search for prior art. *Prior art* refers to earlier inventions that may undercut the applicant's claims that the invention is novel and nonobvious. Prior art includes both patented and nonpatented technology that is in the public domain, whether incorporated in existing products or described in written materials. Searching for prior art is essential to avoid wasting time and money trying to patent an invention that is not novel. It also helps the inventor anticipate the PTO's response. The patent attorney uses the search results to craft the patent claims to avoid the prior art, and the patent examiner at the PTO uses them to help determine whether a patent should be issued. The applicant is required to disclose in the patent application all prior art of which it is aware. Although on-line databases can be accessed by anyone, it is usually advisable to have a professional search firm conduct the search. Failing to uncover prior art leads to wasted time and expense if the examiner (or a person challenging the patent's validity) later discovers relevant prior art that was missed in the search.

The Patent Examination Once the application is submitted, a patent examiner will be assigned to determine whether the invention is patentable. The patent examiner will conduct his or her own search for prior art and frequently will seek to modify the claims of the patent. Very few applications are approved without modification. This back-and-forth process between the applicant and the examiner (called *prosecution*) usually takes at least a year and often more than two years. In many cases, an inventor will want to begin using or selling the invention before the patent application is approved. Although doing so may result in important time-to-market advantages, the patent attorney should be called on to help weigh these benefits against the possibility that the invention will ultimately be determined to infringe another patented invention.

Costs Patents usually represent a major expense for a small business. However, many patent attorneys will provide a free initial consultation to determine whether pursuing a patent claim makes sense. Although a definite answer to the question of patentability is unlikely to emerge from a single consultation (unless the answer is a clear "no"), the entrepreneur can usually get a better idea of whether it is practical to pursue the patent process further.

As of 1996, the filing fee for individuals and companies with fewer than 500 employees is $365, with an additional fee of $605 due if and when the patent is issued. Fees are greater for large companies. Additional fees are required over the life of the patent to keep it in force; total fees currently amount to $3,865, and these have been rising regularly as the PTO attempts to overcome staffing shortages. Attorney and search firm fees can bring the total cost to $10,000 or more, depending on the complexity of the application and the level of modifications sought by the patent examiner. In assessing whether a patent is worth the cost, it is important to consider also that having strong patent protections can make it easier to raise money from outside investors.

Competing Claims for a Patent

If two inventors independently develop essentially the same patentable invention, the U.S. patent system awards the patent to the first person to invent the invention, not necessarily the first person to file the patent application. Determining who was the first to invent can be difficult. For example, in 1989 Calgene, Inc. was granted a patent covering a genetic engineering process to improve the flavor and shelf life of tomatoes. In 1992, another company, Zeneca Group PLC, won an opportunity for review of the patent, arguing that it had invented the process first. Although the dispute was settled in 1994, Zeneca would not have had a winning argument in a first-to-file country, because it had filed its patent application two weeks after Calgene. All other countries in the world (except the Philippines) award the patent to the first person to file the application, and there are proposals in the United States to move to a first-to-file system.

If two or more inventors file for patent protection at about the same time, then the first-to-invent gets the rights to the patent, unless he or she was not diligent in reducing the invention to practice. *Reduction to practice* occurs when an inventor (1) produces a working prototype, or (2) files a patent application that includes the required description of the invention in sufficient detail for someone else to reproduce it.

Thus, documenting the dates of invention and reducing the invention to practice can be critical for securing patent rights. To document dates of invention and reduction to practice, scientists, engineers, and others working on the invention must keep detailed running records of their progress. Often this information is kept in lab books. These records must be signed and dated by both the inventor and another witness not involved in the development process. Inventors often resent the paperwork, but these records can be the difference between securing a valuable patent and losing it to a competitor. An attorney can provide more detailed advice on setting up an effective invention recordkeeping program. In addition, it is always wise to file the patent application promptly.

Important Patent Issues

There are several other important points to note about the patent process. First, although patent examiners usually have some relevant training, many patent applicants have been frustrated by the unfamiliarity of examiners with pertinent technology and the slowness of the proceedings. Applicants should be prepared for frustrations and delays.

Second, patents are frequently challenged and overturned. The mere fact that a patent has been granted is not always the end of the story. Patents can be reviewed and overturned by the PTO and the courts. This can happen when prior art is uncovered (often by a competitor seeking to undermine the patent) that was not revealed in the initial patent search. Perhaps the best known recent case of a patent being overturned involved Compton's NewMedia, Inc. Compton's was granted a patent that, if upheld, was widely seen as giving it a monopoly over much of the emerging multimedia field. Competitors challenged the patent, and it was subsequently thrown out on the basis that it lacked novelty and failed the nonobviousness test given existing prior art.

Third, it is important to obtain a written transfer of ownership rights in inventions from employees and independent contractors. Absent an agreement, employees will personally own the patentable inventions they create. It is therefore crucial to have any employee involved with inventions sign a written agreement transferring any rights in the inventions to the employer. The same holds true for independent contractors.

International Issues

U.S. patents do not protect inventions in foreign countries, although they will prevent a foreign company from exporting to the United States a product that includes features that violate the U.S. patent. An inventor should consider obtaining patents in each foreign country where the patent may yield meaningful benefits. Each country usually requires a separate patent filing, but a single filing in the European Patent Office can provide protection in the nations in the European Union. In addition, as noted earlier, many countries will not grant a patent if the invention is disclosed before the patent application is filed in that country. Costs to prepare and file a foreign patent currently average about $5,000 per country, assuming that a U.S. patent application has already been completed. Even if a patent is granted, foreign patents may be difficult or impossible to enforce in some jurisdictions.

A crucial point to consider in weighing the desirability of foreign patents is that most foreign countries publish patent applications eighteen months after the patent application is filed. Given the time required to process a patent, the information contained in the patent application usually becomes public before the patent is issued. Once such information is public, trade secret protection is lost. Under the current U.S. system, patent applications remain confidential until the patent is issued so that trade secret protection continues until patent protection begins. However, the General Agreement on Tariffs and Trade (GATT), ratified in 1994, requires the U.S. to adopt an 18-month publication rule, and passage of such legislation appears probable as of this writing.

The decision to obtain foreign patents is an important strategic issue that should be discussed with a patent attorney if the invention may be used abroad. Even if there are no plans for overseas use, it may still be worth the considerable expense to block foreign competitors from gaining access to the invention.

Patent Infringement

The unauthorized making, use, or sale of a patented item or process constitutes patent infringement. This is true whether or not the infringer was aware of the patent at the time of the infringement. Infringement can also occur if someone knowingly induces another to infringe a patent or knowingly contributes to another's infringement. The damages that can be awarded are often substantial, and may include paying over all profits earned with the infringing product. Courts can triple damage awards for intentional infringement and can also award attorneys' fees. In recent years, courts have been increasingly willing to find infringement and uphold substantial damage claims, some running into the hundreds of millions of dollars. For example, in 1990 Eastman Kodak was ordered to pay Polaroid $909 million in damages and interest for infringing Polaroid's patents on cameras, film units, and photographic processes.[6]

When Does It Make Sense to Pursue a Patent?

Because of the time and cost required to obtain a patent, the decision to file a patent application merits careful thought. Some experts suggest

---

FROM THE TRENCHES

Robert Kearns, the inventor of the intermittent windshield wiper, has spent the last eighteen years in an all-consuming battle to enforce his patents against automobile manufacturers. Kearns came up with the idea in 1962 and received several patents for his design in 1967.

He shopped the idea around to various automakers but never reached a licensing deal. In 1978, he sued Ford Motor Company for patent infringement and won a judgment that was later settled for $10.2 million in 1990. He subsequently won an $18.7 million judgment against Chrysler Corporation.

The victories, however, have not come without a cost. Kearns's wife left him, and his lawyers quit during the Chrysler case because of disputes over money and strategy. His lawsuits against General Motors Corporation and twenty-two foreign manufacturers were dismissed after Kearns, who had been representing himself, failed to meet court deadlines for preliminary filings.

that, before seeking a patent, the entrepreneur first evaluate the core technologies that are key to the business's success. Technologies outside this core area are probably not worth the expense of patenting for a small business (unless the patent is being obtained for strategic reasons, as discussed below). If the technology is such that better-established competitors could review the patent and design a different invention that would not infringe the patent but would still convey the same benefits, then a patent may be of little value.

Experts caution against overlooking improvements to existing inventions. If an improvement is nonobvious and otherwise meets the standards of patentability, the improvement itself can be patented. However, such a patent will not give the inventor rights to the entire invention; only the improvement will be covered.

In deciding whether to seek patent protection, the entrepreneur should also consider other, less costly forms of protection. For example, trade secret protection may be adequate for some inventions, particularly those that involve a process employed in making a product, rather than a product that is sold to the public. However, trade secrets, unlike patents, cannot protect against a competitor that independently develops similar technology, even through reverse engineering. Patentable software can also benefit from copyright protection. Consulting an experienced patent attorney, particularly one with knowledge of the field in which the patent is sought, is usually advisable to assess the best strategy in the face of these complicated trade-offs.

Strategic Aspects of Patents

Because the rights granted through patents are so powerful, it is not surprising that patents are often used strategically, particularly by larger businesses. These strategic uses often affect small businesses. For example, in one practice, known as *bracketing*, a company will systematically review patent issuances and seek to obtain patents on improvements to the issued patents. With its patent on the improvement, the company may seek either to exact license fees from the company that holds the initial patent or block use of the improvement altogether. In some instances, it may be worthwhile to pursue additional patents to block potential bracketers.

Competitors frequently review patents with an eye to designing around the patent, that is, coming up with a functionally similar invention that avoids the precise patent claims of the initial patent. (This is another reason why an experienced patent attorney is needed to precisely tailor the claims of the patent.) Large companies can often beat entrepreneurs by designing around the patent and then using superior sales and marketing resources to capture the market. But, as in the Stac Electronics—Microsoft case noted earlier, the big guy doesn't always win.

Companies with foreign operations also review U.S. patents. If the U.S. inventor does not promptly file in other countries, another company can use the details of the U.S. patent to seek a patent in foreign jurisdictions.

On the other hand, patents can provide added benefits to small companies. Patents often convey prestige and can be used to help promote the image of a technologically innovative company. The familiar phrase "Patent Pending" on some products is thought to convey an image of technical superiority that can be useful in marketing. A strong patent portfolio can also make it easier to raise money from venture capitalists and other outside investors who are looking for a proprietary technology that creates a barrier to others who might otherwise enter the market. As noted earlier, having a portfolio of patents that can be cross-licensed gives a company something to trade in a patent dispute.

Understanding Competitors' Patents

Gaining knowledge of others' patented inventions can yield substantial benefits. The search for prior art conducted in the course of preparing the patent application can reveal important competitive information. Some companies that do not plan to file for patent protection nonetheless undertake a patent search to uncover competing technology and to reduce the risk of inadvertent patent infringement. If the search uncovers a competitor's patent for a different invention that achieves superior results, pursing a patent may make little sense. However, if the patent for that superior technology is owned by a company that is not a direct competitor, then a licensing arrangement, whereby the entrepreneur gets the right to use the invention for a noncompeting product, can frequently be worked out. Competitors' patent filings can also provide clues about future product and development directions. Search results have even been known to spark creative ideas in the minds of inventors, helping them come up with new noninfringing inventions.

TRADEMARKS

All businesses strive to develop a positive image in the minds of their customers. Many companies spend lavishly to build reputations for quality, reliability, innovation, performance, and value. These reputations and positive images can be among a business's most valuable assets. Trademarks like Mercedes Benz, the Nike swoosh, Intel Inside, and McDonald's golden arches all carry with them images and associations that boost sales and contribute to the bottom line. If a low-quality automaker could freely use the name "Mercedes," or something confusingly similar such as "Mircedes," or the familiar circled three-point-star hood ornament, consumers could be fooled into thinking that they were buying a genuine Mercedes. Mercedes Benz AG's sales and reputation could deteriorate as consumers wrongly conclude that Mercedes Benz has let its quality and performance slip. Trademark law helps to protect both trademark owners and consumers from the confusion that can result

Reprinted with special permission of King Features Syndicate.

when different companies use the same or confusingly similar identifying marks, either intentionally or unintentionally.

Trademarks are not the exclusive province of large, established manufacturing companies. Local businesses also develop goodwill in their markets, which can be embodied in trademarks. Selecting good trademarks early in the life of a business can help to ensure that those marks will not need to be changed later on, perhaps at great expense. A service business can protect its good image through the closely related law of service marks. *Service marks* identify not a product but a service, such as American Express Travel Services. Because the principles and laws relating to service marks are virtually identical to those of trademarks, the remainder of this section should be read as applying to service marks as well.

Trademark disputes arise most frequently when the owner of one trademark alleges that another's trademark is confusingly similar to its mark. For example, a small barbecue sauce company was forced to change its product name from "Uncle Harry's" to "Show-Me" after the makers of "Harry and David" barbecue sauce alleged that the "Uncle Harry's" name was confusingly similar to "Harry and David." Whether or not the allegation was correct, the maker of "Uncle Harry's" concluded that it was cheaper to absorb the cost of creating new labels than to attempt to fight the larger company in court.

Trademarks should not be confused with trade names. A trade name is the formal, legal name of a business, which typically must be registered with either local or state authorities. A trade name (or a portion of a trade name) that meets the requirements for trademark protection can become a trademark. For example, Lotus 1-2-3 is a trademark of Lotus Development Corporation.

Definition of a Trademark

A *trademark* is any word (or phrase), name, symbol, sound, or device that identifies and distinguishes one company's products from those made or sold by others. The key requirement is that the mark must identify and distinguish the product from those of competitors. The word "Apple" to describe computers, the multicolored Apple Computer, Inc. logo of an apple with a bite taken out of it, and "Macintosh" are all trademarks of Apple Computer. "It's the real thing" is a trademark of the Coca-Cola Company, and the distinctive AT&T "bong" is a trademark of AT&T. The team logo for the Washington Redskins is also a trademark. "CitiPhone Banking" is a service mark relating to banking services offered by Citibank N.A. Trademarks can also protect *trade dress*, such as packaging, which is purely ornamental. For example, Coca-Cola has a trademark for its "old-fashioned" six-ounce bottle. Even a distinctive color can serve as a trademark. Harley-Davidson, Inc. is currently seeking to obtain trademark protection for the distinctive roar of its motorcycles. The U.S. Supreme Court recently held that the universe of things that can qualify as a trademark should be viewed "in the broadest possible terms."[7]

Establishing a Trademark

Consider the Image The first step in selecting a trademark is to consider marks that convey an appropriate image for the business and that are protectable under trademark law. Many businesspeople choose their own marks, but professional advice from advertising agencies or marketing firms may be worth the cost, particularly for consumer goods. The degree of protection available under trademark law is determined by how distinctive the trademark is: the more distinctive, the better. The basic idea is that the more distinctive the mark, the more it uniquely identifies the products as belonging to a single company. Generic terms such as "plane," "software," and "designer" are not protectable.

   Inherently distinctive marks are the strongest form of trademark. They need no proof of distinctiveness and are immediately protectable. These marks have no meaning within an industry before their adoption by a company in that industry. There are three main types of inherently distinctive marks. *Fanciful marks* include made-up words such as "Exxon" for gasoline or "Kodak" for cameras. *Arbitrary marks* are real words that have nothing to do with the product category, such as "Apple" for computers. Note, however, that Apple or Macintosh could not be used as trademarks by a company that sells apples. *Suggestive marks* suggest something about the product but do not describe it.

Examples include "Chicken of the Sea" for tuna or "WordPerfect" for a word processing program.

Descriptive marks are not considered to be inherently distinctive. A mark that indicates characteristics of the product it identifies is a descriptive mark. Examples include "Rapid Seal" for a paint sealant and "cc:Mail" for an electronic mail program. Laudatory terms such as "Gold Medal" are also considered descriptive. Marks that indicate the geographic origin of the product, such as "California Lumber" or "Albany Roofing," are considered descriptive. Marks derived from a proper name, such as "Hilton Hotels," are also considered descriptive.

Descriptive marks are not immediately protectable but may become fully protectable once they acquire secondary meaning in the marketplace. *Secondary meaning* is acquired when a significant number of people come to associate the mark with a particular company or product. For example, in 1995 Microsoft was successful in registering "Windows" as a trademark for its PC operating system in part because the word had acquired secondary meaning; consumers had come to associate Windows with Microsoft's operating system. If a dispute over the ownership of a descriptive trademark arises, it can be expensive to establish the factual existence of secondary meaning in court.

Perform a Trademark Search The second step in acquiring a trademark is to perform a trademark search. The purpose of the search is to ensure that someone else has not already established rights in the proposed mark or one confusingly similar to it. The search should include both federal searches and state searches in any states in which business will be conducted. Computerized databases exist to conduct both federal and state trademark searches. NEXIS can be used to search for unregistered trademarks that are still entitled to protection under the common law. If the trademark is to be used overseas, the search should also include foreign countries where the mark may be used.

Although it is not necessary to hire an attorney to conduct a trademark search, it is often a good idea. A legal assistant can usually perform a full search for well under $1,000 and can help to assess the risk that the proposed mark infringes confusingly similar marks. At the very least, the entrepreneur should review on-line trademark databases. In addition, salespeople, suppliers, and others in the industry should be questioned to determine whether they are aware of any similar marks in use. A careful search reduces the risk of infringing another's mark and can limit any infringement damages by helping to show that the infringing use was undertaken in good faith.

Create Rights in the Trademark The final step in establishing a trademark is to create rights in the trademark. Certain rights are obtained merely by using the trademark in business. Attaching the trademark to goods for sale and using the mark in advertising and promotional materials constitute use. The use must be in good faith, meaning that the user must be unaware of anyone else with prior rights to the mark or a confusingly similar mark. Note that every user is deemed by the law to be aware of every valid federal trademark registration, so failure to conduct a proper trademark search is not a defense.

In the United States, if the trademark is inherently distinctive, the first person to use the mark becomes the owner. If the mark is a descriptive mark, using the mark merely begins the process of developing the secondary meaning necessary to create full trademark rights. For both inherently distinctive

---

FROM THE TRENCHES

An emerging software company, Storm Technology, Inc. (STI), acquired the U.S. trademark rights to the name "Storm" for use with software. As the company expanded overseas, it discovered that "Storm" is a common surname in many European countries. This created problems in obtaining some European registrations. Furthermore, a German company claimed that STI was infringing its German trademark rights held in the Storm name. A settlement allowed STI to use "Storm" in its trade name (i.e., the company name) but prohibited STI from using "Storm" as a trademark to describe a product (e.g., "Storm Picture Press"). Later, a partner of STI shipped product literature into Germany for a product called "ThunderStorm." The German company claimed that STI had violated the settlement, despite the fact that ThunderStorm was not an STI product. Issues with overseas trademarks continue to occupy STI management time.

and merely descriptive marks, greater use generally leads to stronger rights as the mark becomes more closely identified with a single business.

In most foreign jurisdictions, however, the first person to register the mark owns the rights to the mark. For example, when Timberland Company decided to export its shoes to Brazil, it discovered that a Brazilian generic shoe manufacturer already owned the trademark to "Timberland." Timberland was able to secure rights to the trademark in Brazil, but only after suing on the basis that Timberland's copyright and trade name rights overcame the generic manufacturer's trademark rights.

Creating Additional Trademark Rights: Trademark Registration

Although mere use can establish rights to a trademark in the United States under common law, federal registration of the trademark on the Principal Register of the U.S. Patent and Trademark Office offers important benefits. First, registration is evidence of ownership that can be useful if the trademark is ever contested. Second, everyone is presumed by law to be aware of a registered trademark, so no infringing use can be in good faith. This makes it easier to stop trademark infringers and can also make it possible to collect damages. Third, after five years of continuous use, the trademark can be declared incontestable, making it far more difficult for anyone to challenge it. Fourth, registration enables the owner to prevent importation of articles bearing the trademark. In general, federal trademark registration is strongly recommended for all important trademarks.

If a person has a genuine intent to use a trademark in the future, he or she can file an intent-to-use application. Once the intent-to-use application

FROM THE TRENCHES

A small perfume company established trademark rights for the name of a new line of fragrances. Some time later, a multinational cosmetics company rolled out a major new fragrance using the small company's trademarked name. The small perfume company successfully settled its trademark infringement claim against the large cosmetics company by requiring it to pay $1 million for the right to use the trademarked name.

is filed, the owner obtains the benefits of registration, but these benefits can be lost if the owner does not subsequently use the mark in business. If the mark is approved, the owner has six months to begin using it; this period can be extended for good reason for up to two years.

Not all trademarks are eligible for federal registration on the Principal Register. In particular, descriptive marks are generally not eligible. This is yet another reason to avoid using them. However, separate filing procedures for descriptive marks do exist that can offer some protections. An attorney can provide additional advice about protecting descriptive marks.

The process of obtaining federal trademark registration can be complex, and it is usually advisable to consult with an experienced attorney before proceeding. After the application is filed, a trademark examiner at the U.S. Patent and Trademark Office will search for prior filings of confusingly similar marks and will decide whether the trademark is sufficiently distinctive to qualify for trademark protection. The process can be drawn out and involve multiple filings, sometimes taking as long as months after the initial filing for a federal registration to issue. In the interim, it may be advisable to file a state registration.

International Issues

Trademarks, like patents, must be registered in each country in which protection is sought. Although the U.S. gives priority to the first to *use* the trademark, all other countries give priority to the first to *file* an application to register the mark. Registration in foreign countries can be expensive.

Protecting Trademark Rights

Once a trademark has been obtained, the owner must take certain steps to ensure that the trademark rights are not lost. Failure to use a trademark for two years may create a presumption of abandonment. Also, federal trademark registration currently lasts for ten years but can be renewed indefinitely. If a trademark becomes generic, thereby losing its distinctiveness, trademark protection can also be lost. "Escalator," "yo-yo," "aspirin," and "cornflakes" were all once trademarks that lost their

EXHIBIT 14.1

Xerox Ad

"But Mr. Carruthers, you said you needed forty Xeroxes."

Mr. Carruthers used our name incorrectly. That's why he got 40 Xerox copiers, when what he really wanted was 40 copies made on his Xerox copier.

He didn't know that Xerox, as a trademark of Xerox Corporation, should be followed by the descriptive word for the particular product, such as "Xerox duplicator" or "Xerox copier."

And should only be used as a noun when referring to the corporation itself.

If Mr. Carruthers had asked for 40 copies or 40 photocopies made on his Xerox copier, he would have gotten exactly what he wanted.

And if you use Xerox properly, you'll get exactly what you want, too.

P.S. You're welcome to make 40 copies or 40 photocopies of this ad. Preferably on your Xerox Copier.

XEROX

Reprinted with permission of Worldwide Strategic Advertising.

FROM THE TRENCHES

A Chinese athletic footwear maker produced nearly 50,000 more pairs of shoes than its license from Champion Footwear permitted. The Chinese manufacturer then attempted to sell the additional shoes back to Champion, implying that if Champion refused to purchase them, they would be sold to black market "diverters." In March 1995, shortly after China had agreed with the United States to strengthen enforcement of intellectual property rights, Champion contacted the Chinese authorities. Government officials promptly seized the shoes and told the manufacturer that the shoes would be destroyed if a settlement were not reached. The Chinese authorities actively assisted in mediating a settlement favorable to Champion.

---

protected status because of their owners' failure to police the use of them. Xerox Corporation won't make that mistake; it runs ads to remind consumers that Xerox is a trademark (see Exhibit 14.1).

Trademark Infringement

To prove trademark infringement, the trademark owner must prove, among other things, a likelihood that the allegedly infringing mark could create confusion in the minds of potential customers. Such a showing is easy in the case of counterfeit goods displaying another's trademark. However, if the marks are not identical, determining whether another's mark is confusingly similar is a highly factual matter that can be expensive and time-consuming to prove in court. If infringement can be proved, remedies may include a court order barring the infringer from using the infringing mark and the assessment of damages. In addition, some foreign governments appear to be treating trademark infringement more seriously than in the past.

COMPARISON OF TYPES OF PROTECTION

As explained in this chapter, different types of intellectual property protection are available and appropriate in different settings. The advantages and disadvantages of the four basic types of protection are set forth in Exhibit 14.2.

EXHIBIT 14.2

Advantages and Disadvantages of Different Types of Intellectual Property Protection

	Trade Secret	**Copyright**	**Patent**	**Trademark**
Benefits	Very broad protection for sensitive, competitive information; very inexpensive	Prevents copying of a wide array of artistic and literary expressions, including software; very inexpensive	Very strong protection; provides exclusive right to make, use, and sell an invention; protects the idea itself	Protects marks that customers use to identify a business; prevents others from using confusingly similar identifying marks
Duration	So long as the information remains valuable and is kept confidential	Life of author plus 50 years; for corporations, 75 years from date of first publication or 100 years from date of creation, whichever is shorter	20 years from date of filing the patent application	So long as the mark is not abandoned and steps are taken to police its use
Weaknesses	No protection from accidental disclosure, independent creation by a competitor, or disclosure by someone without a duty to maintain confidentiality	Protects only particular way an idea is expressed, not the idea itself; apparent lessening of protection for software; hard to detect copying in digital age	High standards of patentability; often expensive and time-consuming to pursue (especially where overseas patents are needed); must disclose invention to public	Limited scope; protects corporate image and identity but little else; can be costly if multiple overseas registrations are needed

EXHIBIT 14.2 continued

Advantages and Disadvantages of Different Types of Intellectual Property Protection

	Trade Secret	Copyright	Patent	Trademark
Required Steps	Take reasonable steps to protect—generally a trade secret protection program	None required; however, notice and filing can strengthen rights	Detailed filing with U.S. Patent and Trademark Office that requires search for prior art and hefty fees	Only need to use mark in commerce; however, filing with U.S. Patent and Trademark Office is usually desirable to gain stronger protections
U.S. Rights Valid Internationally?	No. Trade secret laws vary significantly by country, and some countries have no trade secret laws	Generally, yes	No. Separate patent examinations and filings are required in each country; however, a single filing in the European Patent Office can cover a number of European countries	No. Separate filings are required in foreign jurisdictions, and a mark available in the U.S. may not be available overseas

UNFAIR COMPETITION

The law of unfair competition is designed to prevent false, deceptive, and unauthorized business practices, particularly in the areas of sales and advertising. Many of these practices will strike the average businessperson as simply unfair, but some of them are close calls.

Types of Unfair Competition

There are many types of unfair competition. Some of the most common are outlined below.

Passing off involves attempting to fool customers into believing that one's goods are actually those of a competitor. In one case, the publisher of *National Lampoon* successfully sued ABC when the network used the word "lampoon" in the title of a television series without permission, after having attempted to negotiate for use of the name. The court held that ABC was trying to use the reputation of *National Lampoon* for its own benefit. Passing off often involves improper use of another's trademark or trade name, or of a confusingly similar mark or name.

False advertising occurs when untrue, unsupported, or deceptive claims are made in advertising. For example, Campbell Soup Company engaged in false advertising when it used in its advertisements photographs of bowls of soup into which clear glass marbles had first been placed to make the solid ingredients rise to the surface, thereby making the soup appear more appetizing.[8] False advertising is discussed further in chapter 11.

Disparagement includes untrue claims about a competitor that would tend to damage his or her business. Disparagement arises frequently when disgruntled former employees make untrue but damaging statements about their former employer's business. *Bait and switch* tactics include advertising a product for an unrealistically low price to lure consumers into a store and then pushing them to purchase a different, more expensive product.

Dilution involves using another's trade name or trademark to promote non-competing goods if the consumer might be confused about the true origin of the goods. For example, a computer disk-drive company that called itself "Micronsoft" might be guilty of dilution because consumers could wrongly conclude that the computer disk drive is a product of Microsoft Corporation, even though Microsoft does not manufacture or sell computer disk drives.

Right of publicity is the exclusive right to exploit commercially one's name or likeness. Typically, these cases involve unauthorized attempts to use a sports or entertainment celebrity's name or likeness for commercial gain. For example, Bette Midler successfully sued an automobile manufacturer who used a sound-alike singer in television advertising.[9] Woody Allen was successful in his lawsuit against a video rental chain that had used a look-alike model in print advertising.[10]

Remedies

A victim of unfair competition may be entitled to a court order to stop the activity, as well as actual and punitive damages. Some types of unfair competition also carry criminal penalties.

LICENSING AGREEMENTS AND OTHER TRANSFERS OF INTELLECTUAL PROPERTY

As with most other forms of property, intellectual property rights can be bought, sold, and transferred. This is often done by granting a license. A *license* gives a person the right to do something he or she would not otherwise be permitted to do. For example, a movie theater ticket is a license giving the holder permission to enter the theater. Licensing agreements are often used to grant limited, specified rights to use intellectual property. For example, an inventor who owns a patent that has uses in several different industries might license the rights to use the patent in the medical field to one company, the rights to use it in the chemical industry to another company, and retain the rights to use the patent in all other fields. Because of their great flexibility, licenses are a popular way to transfer intellectual property rights. Some of the most important and heavily negotiated terms of a typical license agreement are discussed below.

Transfers of intellectual property also occur in less obvious situations. When one company acquires another, patents, trademarks, and copyrights

---

FROM THE TRENCHES

Johnny Carson, former host of the "Tonight Show," successfully sued the maker of "Here's Johnny Portable Toilets," who was using the famous introductory "Tonight Show" phrase, "Here's Johnny," to sell toilets. The court held that the company had unlawfully appropriated Carson's identity as a celebrity. Carson subsequently won a damage award of $31,000 against the company.

Source: Carson v. Here's Johnny Portable Toilets, Inc., 698 F. 2d 831 (6th Cir. 1983).

FROM THE TRENCHES

Seeking to cash in on the success of the Taco Cabana restaurant chain, another company established a competing restaurant chain called Two Pesos that copied the design, decor, and product offerings of Taco Cabana. Taco Cabana sued Two Pesos for infringement of trade dress. An expert witness testified that the restaurants were nearly identical. The jury found for Taco Cabana and awarded it $306,000 for lost profits and $628,000 for lost income. The district court found the infringement to be deliberate, doubled the damage award, and further awarded attorneys' fees of $937,550. To drive home the point, the judge also ordered Two Pesos to display for one year a prominent sign in front of each of its restaurants acknowledging that it had unfairly copied Taco Cabana's restaurant concept. The U.S. Supreme Court affirmed the decision.

Source: Two Pesos, Inc. v. Taco Cabana, Inc. 505 U.S. 763 (1992).

---

may be among the most valuable assets in the transaction. Many employment and consulting agreements require the worker to transfer intellectual property rights to the company funding the work. In all of these situations, the entrepreneur must understand exactly what rights are being conveyed.

Equally important, the entrepreneur must carefully evaluate the role played by the people—inventors, technicians, and others—who work with and understand the technology. Acquiring the rights to a patent without securing the services of the inventors may be next to worthless if the inventors' experience and expertise are necessary to exploit the technology.

Transferring Rights to Intellectual Property

Trademarks, copyrights, and patents can be transferred in several ways. An *assignment* is typically used to transfer all of one's interests in an item of intellectual property to a new owner. For example, an inventor wishing to sell a patent to a corporation would transfer all of his or her "right, title and interest" in the patent to the new corporation through an assignment document. After the assignment, the inventor would have no rights to the patent, and the corporation could sue the inventor for infringement if he or she were to use any elements of the patent. Employment and independent contractor agreements frequently contain assignments that convey to the company paying for the work to be done all intellectual property rights developed in conjunction with the work. Assignments are also used to transfer intellectual property when a company sells some or all of its assets to another company.

When an owner wishes to retain some rights to or control over its intellectual property, a license agreement is commonly used. For example, software developers will typically license, not sell, their software to the customer. The license agreement will often contain many restrictions on how and by whom the software may be used. These restrictions can become extremely detailed. McDonald's licenses rights to its many trademarks, such as the "Golden Arches" and "Big Mac," to its franchisees, but the licenses provide that McDonald's can take back the rights to use the trademarks if the franchisees use them improperly. Indeed, to protect the owner's rights to its trademarks, the owner must police their use by others who are licensed to use them. Imagine the damage to McDonald's reputation if a franchisee were to operate a dirty restaurant with McDonald's trademarks displayed prominently throughout.

Key Terms in Licensing Agreements

The potential variety and complexity of licensing agreements are limited only by the ingenuity and business needs of the parties. Agreements can range from a few pages to several hundred pages in length. Because license agreements are so flexible, the entrepreneur should take an active role in structuring the arrangements.

Patent, trademark, and copyright licenses all have differing provisions that are of particular importance to each type of intellectual property. What follows is a very brief overview of key considerations common to many intellectual property licenses. A more detailed application of these basic principles is presented in the final section of this chapter covering computer software. One bit of terminology: The *licensor* is the party granting the license; the *licensee* is the party receiving the license.

Specification of What Is to Be Licensed

The *specification* sets forth the precise description of what intellectual property is covered by the license. The licensee does not obtain rights to anything not set forth in the description of what is to be licensed. Developing the specification can be straightforward, but traps abound. The licensee must be sure that the license conveys all rights the licensee needs to meet its business objectives. For example, are all necessary trademarks conveyed? If a developer of multimedia products licenses the rights to use scenes in a movie, does the license include the right to use the accompanying music in the soundtrack? A major issue in many software license agreements is whether the license includes improvements or enhancements to the licensed technology made by the licensor after the license agreement is signed, and whether these will be provided free of charge or require an additional fee.

Scope of License   The *scope* of the license is the most important provision in many license agreements. The scope-of-license provision describes what the licensee may do with the licensed intellectual property and spells out any limitations on the rights granted in the licensed intellectual property. Matters to address include the following:

- Is the license exclusive or nonexclusive? If the license is nonexclusive, the licensor can grant the same rights to another licensee.
- Is the license limited to certain geographic regions? To particular markets or products?
- Does the license include the right to modify or improve the licensed technology? To sublicense it to others? To share the license with affiliated corporations?
- How long does the license last?
- Are there performance criteria such as minimum sales requirements that, if not met, result in a termination of the license?
- On what terms, if any, can the license be renewed?

These and many other limitations on the use of the licensed intellectual property are contained in the scope-of-license provision.

Licensors must be careful to restrict the licensing of valuable rights to only those rights that the licensee truly needs. Otherwise, revenue opportunities may be lost. For example, if a licensor grants to a distributor exclusive rights throughout the United States to sell a patented invention, but the distributor has no operations in the Southwest, then the licensor may lose revenues that could have come from granting a separate license to a Southwest distributor.

The licensee must also consider carefully what rights it needs to meet its objectives, both now and in the future. For example, geographic restrictions can impede future growth. If the license does not cover improvements to the licensed technology made by the licensor, the licensee could end up with an exclusive right to obsolete technology. Lawyers can craft careful language to implement a deal, but it is up to the businesspeople to consider carefully the scope of the license.

Payments   Payments are most often in the form of up-front lump sums, installment payments, royalties, or some combination of these. Sometimes a licensor will accept equity in the licensee in exchange for the license grant. Royalties can be based on many different measures, including unit sales, percentage of gross revenues, or percentage of profits. Careful consideration must be given to choosing how royalties are calculated because the method of calculation will affect licensee behavior. For example, a license based on the number of units sold will give the licensee an incentive to sell fewer units but at a higher price than would be the case under a percentage-of-gross-revenues calculation. Similarly, basing royalties on a percentage of profits may require specifying exactly how profits are to be calculated because financial accounting principles allow for some leeway, especially in such areas as allocation of overhead across products. Many agreements include minimum royalty payments and sliding-scale royalties, under which the per-unit royalties decrease as sales increase.

Representations, Warranties, and Indemnification   The licensee wants to be sure that the licensor actually possesses all of the rights that the agreement requires it to transfer to the licensee and that performing the agreement will not infringe the rights of any other person. The licensee also wants to ensure that the licensor is not bound by any restrictions that prevent it from carrying out its obligations under the license agreement. The representations and warranties set forth the licensor's statements on these

FROM THE TRENCHES

A producer of boxing videos signed license agreements with five top former heavyweight champions, including Muhammed Ali, to use film footage of the boxers in a video. Each license included in the boilerplate a so-called *most-favored-nations clause.* If the financial deal for any one of the boxers were improved, this clause required the producer to offer the same improved deal to each of the other boxers. Some time later, Ali's representatives negotiated a highly favorable deal for Ali, giving him 20% of the revenues from the video. When the other boxers learned of this deal, they each invoked the most-favored-nations clause, obligating the producer to pay over to each of the five boxers 20% of the revenues from the video, leaving the producer with none of the revenues.

(and many other) matters. If these statements turn out to be incorrect, the indemnification provisions give the licensee the right to recover from the licensor the losses that resulted from these inaccuracies. Often there are limits on the total amount that can be recovered under the indemnification provisions. The obligation to indemnify usually terminates after a stated period of time.

Similarly, the licensor will often demand representations, warranties, and indemnification from the licensee. For example, a licensor may demand assurances that the licensee is financially sound and is not under any contractual or other restrictions that could prevent it from performing its duties under the license agreement. These provisions are also highly negotiated.

Covenants   Covenants are promises by a party to the license agreement to do (or not do) certain things. For example, in a trademark license, the licensee must agree to use the trademarks in ways that maintain their value as symbols of goodwill for the business. In a patent license, one party will usually promise to make the additional filings and payments necessary to keep the patents in force for the term of the agreement. Violations of covenants are usually covered by the indemnification provisions of the license agreement so that if the promise is not kept, the other party can recover its losses.

Covenants sometimes require a party to use reasonable or best efforts to accomplish a task, rather than require the party to make an absolute promise to do something. Such covenants are frequently used when the party making the promise does not have complete control over the outcome. For example, a party may be required to use its best efforts to obtain patent protections in certain foreign jurisdictions. Because the party cannot force the patent examiners to issue the required patents, the party will not have breached this covenant if it did everything legally possible to obtain the patents.

The licensee should be aware, however, that many courts interpret "best efforts" literally and will require a party under a best-efforts obligation to use extraordinary and costly measures if necessary to achieve the promised result. A reasonable-efforts standard requires the party to operate with diligence but introduces an element of cost-benefit analysis into the determination of whether the party has lived up to its promise. Extreme care should be exercised in agreeing to any best-efforts obligation.

Importance of Due Diligence

Although a well-crafted license or technology-sale agreement can provide many protections, it is no substitute for thoroughly investigating the technology and the other party to the transaction—*due diligence* in legal jargon. The amount of due diligence necessary often varies, depending on the representations, warranties, and indemnities provided and the financial condition of the licensor. For example, if IBM gave full indemnification for any intellectual property problems, the licensee would have less need to conduct extensive due diligence.

A company acquiring technology must investigate whether the seller or licensor actually has all rights in the technology that the agreement requires it to transfer. Sometimes another party (such as an inventor or another licensee) may have rights to the technology that the seller or licensor has no right to transfer. The acquiring company should also analyze whether the patents, trademarks, and copyrights to be conveyed cover fully all technology that is truly important to the acquiror. Too often a buyer or licensee will assume that just because a company has some patents, all of its key technologies are fully owned and protected. Frequently, this is not the case. The financial condition and reputation of the seller or licensor should also be investigated. This is particularly important if the relationship is expected to last for a long period of time.

A licensor should also conduct a thorough investigation of the licensee. The licensor should analyze the licensee's financial strength, reputation, and future prospects. This is particularly important if the licensee is required to pay royalties based on the level of the licensee's sales, or if the payments are to be made over a number of years. It is also critical to understand the licensee's technological and marketing capabilities to develop and sell products using the technology, as well as the strength of the licensee's desire to exploit the technology. An ill-equipped or under-motivated licensee is unlikely to generate substantial royalty revenue.

Technology and Human Capital

People are often key to making an acquisition of technology competitively successful. Rapid technological change means that successful technology acquisition frequently requires gaining the services of technical experts who can help bring products to market quickly, and who can improve and enhance the acquired technology to meet new market pressures. Frequently, companies acquiring technology will also hire key personnel who were involved in its development. Often these key personnel are asked to sign employment agreements with the acquiring company to ensure that their know-how will be available for a period of time. Acquiring the rights to use or sell technology may be of little value if a company does not have the expertise to develop it fully.

SAFEGUARDING COMPUTER SOFTWARE

This section synthesizes many of the intellectual property principles introduced earlier and applies them in concrete factual situations. It also highlights the difficulties in applying copyright and patent protections in the digital age, in which copying information is simple and information travels globally. Because the law in the area of computer software is evolving rapidly, it is particularly important to consult counsel with expertise in applying intellectual property rules in the computer software field.

Copyright Protection

For most software developers and publishers, copyright provides the most important protection for software. However, copyright has important limitations, and increasingly courts are cutting back on the protections that copyright can provide.

Protecting Software with Copyright Computer code is clearly protected by copyright as a literary work. This protection extends to both *source code* (the computer code as written by programmers in a language such as Pascal, FORTRAN or C++) and *object code* (the binary or machine language, translated from the source code, that the computer hardware uses to execute the programmer's instructions). Thus, one who makes unauthorized copies of a copyrighted software program is guilty of copyright infringement. Similarly, using the same program on more than one computer at a time may constitute a copyright infringement (depending on what the license allows) because using a software program requires each computer to make a copy of the program in the computer's memory. Indeed, copyright is the principal legal weapon used to counter software pirates. Similarly, copying an entire program except for minor changes so that the copy is substantially similar to the original constitutes infringement. Translating exactly a program written in FORTRAN to one written in C++ infringes the copyright owner's rights to produce derivative works.

Copyright can also protect computer databases. Typically, the key issue in protecting databases with copyright is whether the selection and arrangement of the data display the required originality and creativity to qualify for copyright protection. Most customer, financial, personnel, product, and other important corporate information databases will meet these requirements.

More difficult copyright issues arise when only certain elements of a software program are duplicated or paraphrased without permission. The difficulties arise in separating the idea or function of a program, which cannot be protected through copyright, from the particular expression of the idea or function, which can be protected.

Challenges in Applying Copyright to Software In trying to distinguish between protectable expression and unprotectable ideas or functions, various courts have developed legal tests that are complex and not always consistent. Broadly speaking, however, courts have been reluctant to offer copyright protection to elements of a software program that (1) are required by efficiency considerations or are purely functional; (2) are necessary for compatibility with hardware, other software, or specific user needs; or (3) have become standard within the industry.

Efficiency Considerations and Functional Elements Copyright cannot protect the best way to implement a particular program. Thus, in a spreadsheet program, the use of letters to label columns and numbers to label rows is nonprotectable. Use of the "Enter" key to enter data is nonprotectable as the most efficient means of entering data, even though it would have been easy to program another key (such as "e") to perform the same function. Moreover, using the "Enter" key can be seen as merely a *method of operation*, which is a function not protectable by copyright. Similarly, a program that instructs a computer to retrieve data from mcmory in the most efficient way possible could not be protected by copyright. This is

Doonesbury   BY GARRY TRUDEAU

because granting protection to the expression would be equivalent to protecting the idea underlying the expression. (But patent protection might be available to protect the idea if all of the patent requirements are met.)

Compatibility For a software program such as a spreadsheet to run on a computer's operating system, certain software code must be included in the program. If this software code could be copyrighted, then the copyright holder could prevent any other programmer from developing a competing product for that operating system. Courts have refused to protect software code required for compatibility with operating systems, as well as code required by the mechanical specifications of a computer or by other software programs.

Industry Standards Some elements of computer programs have become so common that it would be difficult to develop a commercially viable program without them. For example, the use of pull-down menus, icons to represent functions, and multiple windows is so prevalent that many consumers would refuse to purchase products lacking them. Courts are increasingly reluctant to protect such commonplace features.

These three features—pull-down menus, icons, and multiple windows—came into play in a series of cases involving how much protection to give to the graphical user interface or *look and feel* of the program. Although the law is evolving rapidly, the current trend appears to be toward less copyright protection for these elements on the grounds that they are purely functional, are dictated by efficiency, or have become industry standards. For example, Apple Computer was unsuccessful in claiming that major portions of Microsoft's Windows operating system software infringed on Apple's copyrights for its Macintosh computer. The court found that many of the key features of the Apple Macintosh graphical user interface, such as overlapping windows, menus, icons, and the ways they are manipulated, were dictated by industry standards or were mere methods of operation or functions and thus were not protectable.[11]

In another important case, Lotus Development Corporation sued Borland International, which had copied the menu command hierarchy (the user commands and the ways they are arranged) from the popular Lotus 1-2-3 spreadsheet program. This was done to make it easier for former Lotus users to switch to Borland's Quattro Pro spreadsheet program. Borland did not copy Lotus's source code but, rather, wrote its own software code to re-create the Lotus menu command hierarchy. The trial court found in favor of Lotus, holding that the menu command hierarchy was protected expression. The appeals court reversed and held that the menu command hierarchy was a method of operation, like the buttons on a VCR, and therefore was not protectable by copyright. The U.S. Supreme Court upheld, on a 4-to-4 vote, the appeals court ruling in favor of Borland.[12]

The bottom line: Except for cases of literal copying, the scope of copyright protection remains unclear. Indeed, this ambiguity, coupled with the extreme ease of physically copying computer programs, has led many experts to call for entirely new ways to protect software and has caused increasing reliance on patent protection when it is available.

Another challenging issue is the degree to which reverse engineering can constitute fair use. In one important case, Accolade, Inc. reverse engineered the object code in SEGA Enterprises, Ltd.'s video game cartridge player in order to develop games that would play on the popular SEGA system. To perform the reverse engineering, Accolade copied SEGA's object code without permission. SEGA sued Accolade, charging copyright infringement. The court rejected SEGA's claim, holding that copying SEGA's code was the only way to gain an understanding of the unprotectable ideas and functional concepts embodied in the code.[13] The unauthorized copying thus constituted a fair use. In finding fair use, the court also emphasized that Accolade's copying would expand the market for SEGA video games by enhancing consumer choice for game cartridges that could play on the SEGA system. One can speculate that the court would not have found the reverse engineering to be a fair use if it had been undertaken to produce a competing game system. Indeed, in other circumstances, courts have held that copying undertaken to reverse engineer a product does constitute copyright infringement. For example, one court found infringement when an independent computer repair person turned on a computer and thereby loaded operating system software that he was not licensed to use into random access memory (RAM) for long enough to check an error log.[14] It is

---

FROM THE TRENCHES

Smallsoft Co. came across a competing product sold by Bigsoft Inc. that seemed remarkably similar to Smallsoft's product. Smallsoft reverse engineered Bigsoft's product and discovered that nearly 85% of the code in the two programs was identical, including the coded initials of a Smallsoft engineer. Smallsoft sent a cease-and-desist letter demanding that Bigsoft stop selling the infringing product and turn over all profits from the product. Unfortunately, Smallsoft had not filed a copyright registration prior to discovering the infringement (and more than three months had elapsed since the release of the software to the public). Thus, Smallsoft could not recover attorneys' fees or statutory damages, a fact that Bigsoft's attorneys undoubtedly discovered. Because Bigsoft's product had sold poorly, recoverable profits were small. In the end, Smallsoft decided against filing suit and recovered nothing from this clear-cut case of willful infringement.

---

prudent to consult an experienced attorney before undertaking any reverse engineering of copyrighted software or other copyrighted materials.

Strengthening Copyright Protections   Software companies should take steps to strengthen their copyright protections. First, to ensure that the company and not the individual programmer owns the copyright to software, all employees and independent contractors should assign any rights they have to the copyright to the company paying for the work. Second, to be able to enforce a copyright in court, the owner must register the copyright with the U.S. Copyright Office. Registration, however, requires depositing a copy of the source code, which then becomes a matter of public record. To prevent sensitive portions of the software code from becoming public, the Copyright Office has special rules that allow portions of the deposited code to be blacked out. (This procedure is also necessary to protect any trade secret rights in the software.) Third, a copyright notice should be displayed prominently in the program's graphical user interface so that no one can successfully claim a defense of innocent infringement.

Avoiding Infringement To avoid copyright infringement claims, software users should ensure that employees understand the consequences of making or using unauthorized copies of software. Management must also ensure that employees understand and adhere to all of the company's software license agreements. As discussed below, license terms can differ significantly. Software developers should always avoid literal copying of another's software code. Reverse engineering or copying the structure, sequence, or operation of another's program should never be undertaken without first consulting experienced counsel.

Patent Protection

Emerging Trends Favoring Software Patents Recent trends in the courts and the U.S. Patent and Trademark Office clearly indicate an increasing willingness to afford patent protection to software. In response to complaints that its patent examiners were ill equipped to process software patents, the PTO has expanded its staff of patent examiners with software and computer backgrounds. The number of software patents issued has increased dramatically in recent years, rising from 1,908 in 1988 to 6,142 in 1995. The number of applications is up as well: 3,829 applications were filed in 1988, but more than 8,000 were filed in 1994. Microsoft has announced a goal of obtaining 100 software patents per year. However, backlogs remain, and receiving a software patent still requires significant attention from key company personnel. Nonetheless, the strength afforded by patent protection and the PTO's increasing willingness to grant software patents have led many observers to conclude that patent protection for software will continue to increase in importance.

Free Advice As noted above, many patent attorneys will provide a free initial consultation to discuss patentability. If newly developed software represents such a departure from current practice that competitors would be eager to copy it, the entrepreneur should contact a software patent attorney to discuss patent protection.

If patent protection appears promising, then it is crucial to contact a software patent attorney early on. Recall that, under the statutory bar, a

U.S. patent will be denied if the software is disclosed to the public more than one year before the date that the patent application is filed and that many foreign jurisdictions deny patents if there has been any public disclosure before filing.

Patentable Subject Matter A key obstacle to patenting software is the exclusion from patentable subject matter of mathematical formulas and algorithms. Recall that laws of nature, scientific principles, and mathematical formulas cannot be patented. However, software patents have been granted when the software algorithm was used to control a machine or specific process. For example, a patent was granted for a software program that improved the process of curing rubber by controlling the heating process. Patents have also been granted for software that compresses data so that they can be stored in a computer using less memory. Another patent covered software that uses an algorithm to analyze electrocardiograms to help doctors treating heart patients. Unfortunately, it is often hard, even for experienced attorneys, to determine whether a given software program will be deemed unpatentable because it is a pure algorithm.

Prior Art Compounding this uncertainty is the difficulty in searching for prior art. Conducting a software patent search can be tricky because of the difficulties of classifying software patents and understanding the applicable categories. Because prior art also includes products sold or used within the United States, the existence of comparable software in the U.S. marketplace will undermine a patent application or provide grounds for invalidating a previously issued patent. However, discovering the prior art embedded in software code can be difficult, because source code is rarely distributed to the public and understanding a program's functionality usually requires more than a quick examination.

Trade Secrets and Trademarks

Trade Secrets Trade secret protection for software is typically most important in the development phase, before the software has been released to the market. So long as the developer takes appropriate measures to maintain confidentiality, the software program can be protected. Protectable trade secrets include design specifications and flowcharts, technical documentation, data structures, software development tools, and any other information that provides a competitive advantage, is not generally known, and is subject to reasonable efforts to maintain secrecy.

To protect trade secrets in the human-readable, source code version of their software, most developers distribute software only in machine-readable, object code form. Developers of high-end software, who typically require each purchaser to sign a license agreement, usually include in their license agreements provisions prohibiting reverse engineering to obtain access to trade secrets revealed by the source code. Prohibitions on reverse engineering are not enforceable in the European Union or Japan.

Purchasers of mass-market software typically do not sign license agreements. Although bans on reverse engineering are often included in the shrink-wrap licenses that accompany mass-market software, as discussed below, these shrink-wrap licenses may not be enforceable even in the United States.

Trademarks Like other companies, software developers and publishers can use trademarks to develop a distinctive and protectable identity in the marketplace. Examples include IBM's OS/2 Warp and Adobe Systems Incorporated's Acrobat. The most important trademark issues facing software companies are generally the same as those facing nonsoftware companies: choosing strong marks and taking measures to protect them.

Software Licensing

Except for custom-produced software, virtually all software is licensed, not sold outright. Licensing permits the program's owner to retain important controls over the software's use and transferability. Software vendors use license agreements to limit their warranties and liabilities.

Software license agreements come in many varieties: end-user, distribution, beta, development, VAR (value-added reseller), and others. Most consumer software is sold without a signed license agreement under what are known as *shrink-wrap licenses*. These licenses are included with the software along with a statement to the purchaser that by opening the software packaging (i.e., tearing off the shrink wrap), the purchaser agrees to be bound by the terms of the included shrink-wrap license agreement. A more sophisticated version—the *boot-screen license agreement*—requires the user to scroll through the license agreement on the screen and to indicate acceptance of its terms by typing "I accept" or words to that effect before being able to access the program. Although some authorities consider the terms of such license agreements to be unenforceable, the U.S. Court of Appeals for the Seventh Circuit recently upheld a shrink-wrap license prohibiting resale of a database contained on a CD-ROM disk.[15] Addition of a proposed new article to the Uniform Commercial Code (article 2B) would make most consumer mass-produced software shrink-wrap licenses enforceable.

A thorough discussion of software licenses is well beyond the scope of this book, but important provisions in most negotiated software license agreements will address the following issues.

Definition of the Software to Be Licensed Is all software needed to perform the required functions included? Does the license include the rights to maintenance, bug fixes, patches, upgrades, and enhancements? Does the license cover both object and source code? Without source code, it is usually impossible to customize the software. Even so, licensors will rarely give out the source code. What documentation is included in the license? What training materials are included?

License Grant Is the license exclusive or nonexclusive? How long does the license last? What rights does the licensee have to copy, sublicense, or transfer the software? Is the software restricted to use by particular individuals, machines, or geographic locations? Can a large number of users on a computer network share a specified number of copies? Does the license include rights to improvements made by the licensor? Does it include a grant-back whereby the licensor becomes the owner of all improvements made by the licensee? The license grant is particularly important because any rights to the software not granted in the license agreement remain the property of the licensor.

License Fees How are fees calculated? Are all payments made up front or are they paid out over the duration of the license? Are there separate charges for support, maintenance, and upgrades? Increasingly, some software vendors are using additional software to meter use by licensees and are assessing charges based on actual hours of use. If software is licensed for inclusion in another product or software package for resale to third parties, royalty payments may be appropriate.

Support and Maintenance What are the licensor's obligations for providing support? These can range from answering the telephone to flying engineers to the customer's site. What training classes are offered? What are the requirements for bug fixes and product upgrades?

Intellectual Property Indemnification The licensee wants to ensure that, in using the licensed software, it will not be liable for infringing the intellectual property rights of others. For example, if an ex-employee, not the company granting the license, turns out to own the software, the licensee could be guilty of infringement. Typically, the licensee will demand indemnification for any infringement claims against it. However, the amount of such claims is potentially huge and can depend in part on actions taken by the licensee. Intense negotiations frequently surround the scope and duration of this indemnification obligation and any limits on the amounts that can be recovered. Sometimes the indemnification obligations will differ, depending on whether the licensor knew it was licensing infringing software.

A crucial point to remember about higher-end software licenses and lower-end software licenses for large quantities (and other intellectual property licenses as well) is that they are contracts that can be negotiated and structured in numerous ways. Although many parts of software license agreements are quite standard, entrepreneurs who license or use software should take advantage of the flexibility offered by license agreements to structure creative arrangements that best meet their needs.

Putting It into Practice

CCS had previously assigned to WebRunner all of its rights to the Internet Rapid Retrieval System (IRRS) in exchange for equity pursuant to a written agreement Josh Austin had prepared under Michael Woo's supervision. WebRunner now had to act promptly to protect these intellectual property rights.

WebRunner set up a basic trade secret protection program. WebRunner's board of directors insisted that Alexandra and Paul and Sheryl Eagle sign nondisclosure agreements. In addition, potential investors and others with whom any key technologies were to be shared were asked to sign nondisclosure agreements. However, the venture capitalists had refused to sign them. Alexandra had decided to take a different tack. She had investigated the reputations of potential investors and refrained from describing any key facets of the technology until discussions reached a serious stage with Centaur Partners, at which point the technology experts who examined the IRRS on behalf of Centaur had been persuaded to sign. All WebRunner employees signed assignment of invention agreements.

CSS had already assigned to WebRunner the copyright to the IRRS software and documentation. WebRunner strengthened its copyright protection by filing a copyright registration for the IRRS software and the documentation. These two steps were inexpensive and provided important protections for IRRS. Trademark protection for the names "WebRunner" and "Internet Rapid Retrieval System" was investigated early on as well.

Alexandra consulted a patent attorney at Michael's firm to explore whether WebRunner could patent all or part of the IRRS source code. An initial consultation helped Alexandra determine whether the time and expense of pursuing a patent were worthwhile. Because IRRS solved the significant problem of moving large blocks of proprietary content rapidly across the Internet, and was critical to WebRunner's success, Alexandra did not hesitate to devote the resources necessary to hire a software patent expert to advise on patentability.

It was also critical that Alexandra and the other computer programmers had documented the timing of their progress in developing the IRRS, because the U.S. patent rights go to the first to invent, not necessarily the first to file the patent application. However, prompt filing was still advantageous, and as Alexandra had developed plans for a working prototype,

continued

continued

she began the lengthy patent application process. The IRRS had sales potential overseas, and Alexandra and WebRunner's patent attorney considered filing patent applications in key foreign countries. Alexandra decided to file applications in Japan and the European Union. In developing her funding requirements, Alexandra budgeted for the considerable expense of obtaining the U.S. and foreign patents. Having a patent pending would help in fund-raising efforts.

Alexandra reviewed the findings of the patent search for helpful ideas about possible enhancements. Even if she had not pursued a patent, the novelty of the invention suggested that WebRunner should undertake a patent search to ensure that the IRRS did not violate anyone else's patent rights.

Once the patent application was filed, WebRunner released the IRRS for public distribution. Sales were brisk. A patent for key elements of the IRRS was issued about eighteen months after the application was filed. With that in hand, Alexandra and the WebRunner board of directors turned to the matter of deciding whether to sell WebRunner to a larger company or to take it public in an initial public offering.

NOTES

1. *Campbell v. Acuff-Rose Music, Inc.*, 114 S.Ct. 1164 (1994).
2. *Basic Books, Inc. v. Kinko's Graphics Corp.*, 758 F.Supp. 1522 (S.D.N.Y. 1991). In a later case with similar facts, an appeals court in Michigan reached the opposite result. *See Princeton University Press v. Michigan Document Services*, 74 F.3d 1512 (6th Cir. 1996), *aff'd in part, vacated in part, remanded, en banc*, 99 F.3d 1381 (6th Cir. 1996), *petition for cert. filed* (1997).
3. *American Geophysical Union v. Texaco, Inc.*, 60 F.3d 913 (2d Cir. 1994).
4. *Playboy Enterprises, Inc. v. Frena*, 839 F.Supp. 1552 (M.D. Fla. 1993).
5. *Religious Technology Center v. Netcom On-Line Communication Services, Inc.*, 907 F.Supp. 1361 (N.D. Ca. 1995).
6. *Polaroid Corp. v. Eastman Kodak Co.*, 789 F.2d 1556 (Fed. Cir. 1986), *cert. denied*, 479 U.S. 850 (1986). *See* Lawrence Ingrassia and James S. Hirsch, "Polaroid's Patent-Case Award, Smaller than Anticipated, Is a Relief for Kodak," *The Wall Street Journal*, Oct. 15, 1990, at A3.
7. *Qualitex Co. v. Jacobson Products Co.*, 115 S. Ct. 1300 (1995).
8. *See* 77 F.T.C. 664 (1970).
9. *Midler v. Ford Motor Co.*, 849 F.2d 460 (9th Cir. 1988), *cert. denied*, 506 U.S. 1080 (1993).
10. *Allen v. National Video, Inc.*, 610 F.Supp. 612 (S.D.N.Y. 1985).
11. *Apple Computer, Inc. v. Microsoft Corp.*, 35 F.3d 1435 (9th Cir. 1994), *cert. denied*, 115 S.Ct. 1176 (1995).
12. *Lotus Development Corp. v. Borland International, Inc.*, 49 F.3d 807 (1st Cir. 1995), *aff'd*, 116 S.Ct. 804 (1996).
13. *Sega Enterprises, Ltd. v. Accolade, Inc.*, 977 F.2d 1510 (9th Cir. 1992).
14. *MAI Systems Corp. v. Peak Computer, Inc.*, 991 F.2d 511 (9th Cir. 1993).
15. *See ProCD, Inc. v. Zeidenberg*, 86 F.3d 1447 (7th Cir. 1996).

Going Public

15

For many entrepreneurs, the company's *initial public offering (IPO)* is the realization of a dream. This first offering of the company's securities to the public represents recognition of the entrepreneur's vision as well as access to the capital required for the company to achieve its potential. It also can create substantial wealth for the entrepreneur, at least on paper.

This chapter first explores the reasons to consider going public, identifies certain disadvantages of being a public company, discusses matters to consider in deciding whether to sell the company, and outlines several factors to consider in determining whether a company is a good candidate for an IPO. The chapter then presents an overview of the public offering process, summarizes the contents of the prospectus, and describes what is usually done to prepare for an IPO. It continues with a discussion of contractual and securities law restrictions on the sale of shares not being sold in the IPO. The chapter concludes with a brief summary of the ongoing responsibilities of a public company and its board of directors.

WHY GO PUBLIC?

Initially, an entrepreneur finances the company's operations through private financing transactions, often involving the sale of preferred stock to venture funds and sophisticated individual investors, or alliances with corporate partners. Although the timing varies by industry, most companies decide to go public when (1) the company has reached the point at which initial investors have invested the total amount of capital that they are willing to provide and are focused on *liquidity* (a return on their investment) and (2) the company has made sufficient progress to make a public offering viable. The company may need significant additional capital for research and development or product launches, or working capital to expand operations. However, as the company's value increases, the company may encounter difficulty in attracting new investors, who would rather target earlier-stage companies with a lower valuation.

A public offering of securities provides a company access to broader financial markets to fund capital requirements. Once the company goes public, it can use its stock instead of cash to acquire strategic pieces of technology or other businesses. The company will also have the benefit of public visibility, and, so long as the company is performing well and the market is receptive, the company can return to the public market to raise additional capital. Finally, the IPO will value the company's shares at many (if not hundreds of) times the price paid by the founders and will afford them access to the public market for sale of their shares.

However, there is also a significant number of disadvantages to going public. As explained in more detail below, a public company must meet a host of legal obligations that are inapplicable to private companies, including disclosure obligations and fiduciary duties owed to hundreds of shareholders whom the entrepreneur and the board have never, and will never, meet. The company will forever be in the fishbowl of public scrutiny. Disclosure requirements will apply not only to the company but also to officers and directors, who must inform the marketplace of the amount of the company's stock they and their family own and of any sales, gifts, purchases, or other changes in ownership of that stock, including stock option grants and exercises.

In addition, the going-public process is expensive, often costing more than $1,000,000 in SEC filing fees, state securities filing fees, stock exchange or over-the-counter registration fees, legal fees, accounting fees, printing costs, and increased premiums for director and officer liability insurance. Also, the process consumes an enormous amount of management time. Once public, the company will spend significantly more in legal, accounting, and printing fees than in the past.

In addition, an entrepreneur contemplating a public offering because of the desire for liquidity for his or her stock should be aware of the restrictions on the sale of that stock, even if it is fully vested. As discussed below, the first impediment to sale is that the investment banks that manage the public offering will require the entrepreneurs and all other significant shareholders to agree to not to sell their stock for at least six months after the offering. Second, after the lock-up period has expired, rules against insider trading will severely limit when the stock can be sold without risk. Third, because the entrepreneur likely is an *affiliate* (an officer, director, or owner of more than 5% to 10% of the outstanding shares), the amount of the stock that can be sold during any three-month period is limited by rule 144 under the federal securities laws to, in most circumstances, 1% of the company's outstanding stock.

IPO VERSUS SALE OF THE COMPANY

Because of the disadvantages of going public, an entrepreneur considering a public offering may wish to think about selling the company instead. Indeed, the sale alternative is a far more common path to liquidity for the entrepreneur, particularly one with a company experiencing slow but steady growth, or in an industry not currently favored by investment bankers. (Contracts for the sale of the enterprise are discussed briefly in chapter 10.)

FROM THE TRENCHES

A well-known maker of athletic equipment began the IPO process. The investment banks had advised the company that the public marketplace would value the outstanding shares at $125 million. Because of the disadvantages of being a public company, including the many restrictions on selling their own stock in the public marketplace after the offering, the founders seriously considered a third-party offer to buy the company for $95 million in cash, which was made after the offeror learned the public offering process had begun. The founders ultimately decided to go forward with the public offering, and after three years the public market valuation of the company was more than $800 million.

Often a larger corporation in the same general line of business will be interested in the purchase. For example, Boston Scientific, an integrated manufacturer of medical products, has purchased or offered to purchase several companies (including Cardiovascular Imaging Systems, EP Technologies, and Vesica) during the past few years, either as the companies were contemplating public offerings or soon after their IPOs. The purpose was to expand Boston Scientific's product line. A buyout by an acquisition firm such as McCown De Leeuw & Co. or Genstar Capital is often an option for companies with assets against which the purchaser can borrow. Finally, direct competitors of the company may have an interest.

Potential buyers often surface about the time a company is ready to go public because they are well aware that once a company is public, they will have to pay a 15% to 30% premium over the public market price to induce the target company's board to approve the sale. In any event, there are many professionals available to help the interested entrepreneur find an appropriate buyer, including business brokers and corporate finance personnel at investment banks.

The sale of the company can offer several advantages compared to a public offering. In a cash sale, the shareholders of the target corporation can lock in their gains and have immediate liquidity, although they will have to pay taxes on their gain. The target shareholders will not be subject to the risk that stock market conditions will change and the IPO will be called off, or to market risk on their shares if the IPO does proceed.

If the sale is to be for stock of the acquiring company, the sellers will face certain restrictions on disposition of the stock, particularly if the transaction is to be tax free. A significant amount of the stock received must continue to be held by the target's shareholders to satisfy the tax-free reorganization requirements (the so-called *continuity of interest rule*). If the shares issued to shareholders of the target are registered, rule 145 (the analog to rule 144 [discussed below] for stock acquired in a merger or acquisition transaction) will prohibit affiliates of the target from selling in any three-month period more than the greater of 1% of the acquirer's outstanding shares and its average weekly trading volume in the past four weeks. If the shares are not registered, then all shareholders of the target must hold the shares for at least one year. If the acquisition is structured as a *pooling of interests* under financial accounting rules, additional limitations on disposition of the acquired stock may apply.

Although market risk remains in a stock-for-stock deal because the entrepreneur now holds stock of a public company, the market price of a more established company is usually less volatile than that of a newly public company whose price can be depressed for years if early quarterly earnings do not meet the expectations of the market. In addition, the entrepreneur acquiring stock in a merger or acquisition can engage in certain hedging activities against market risk that would be precluded by a lockup agreement with investment banks. But perhaps most important, the sale of the business enables the entrepreneur to avoid having to deal with the myriad pressures of being a public company, including meeting or exceeding revenue and earnings estimates quarter after quarter, dealing with stock analysts who are constantly seeking information and assurances, and communicating with and owing duties to shareholders the entrepreneur has never met.

Arguing against the sale of the business is the limitation on return. First, the price paid per share by a buyer will usually be less than the company could obtain in a public offering. Second, the entrepreneur's *upside* (potential profit) is capped at the purchase price if the consideration is cash, or is determined by the stock market performance of the acquiring company if the consideration is stock. Many entrepreneurs do not want to let control of their upside slip from their own hands.

Is the Company an IPO Candidate?

The entrepreneur and the board must determine whether the company should pursue an immediate IPO or an alternative strategy, such as waiting until the company has made additional progress so that it can command a higher valuation in an IPO or pursuing a merger with a private or public company. Factors to consider include the nature of the company's existing products and product pipeline; the strength and depth of the company's research, development, and management teams; the competitive landscape; and the company's anticipated capital requirements.

The timing of an IPO is often dependent on conditions outside of the company's control, such as general market receptivity to IPOs at the time; whether the relevant industry is "hot"; whether major institutional investors have exceeded the proportion of their portfolios reserved for investment in the relevant industry; and whether there has been an announcement of disappointing financial or regulatory results by a competitor in the industry that causes the market to be wary of the industry as a whole. When faced with less than ideal conditions, some companies elect to seek bridge financing from existing investors or mezzanine (later stage) financing from new investors to raise enough capital to permit the company to wait until market conditions improve or product milestones are achieved. If bridge financing is not available on acceptable terms and the IPO window closes, making it very difficult to get deals done (as happened in July and August 1996 after a very active IPO market in 1995 and the first six months of 1996), the company may want to reevaluate its decision to go public and instead try to find a buyer for the company.

THE IPO PROCESS

Overview

The first four weeks of the IPO process are typically spent in a series of intensive drafting sessions to prepare the registration statement for filing with the Securities and Exchange Commission (SEC). The registration statement includes a detailed selling document called a *prospectus*, which describes the company and its business and management. *Due diligence*, which is a review of the company's business and legal affairs that is done to ensure the accuracy of the prospectus, is also conducted during this period. After the registration statement is filed, 20,000 or more copies of the *preliminary prospectus* are printed, then distributed by members of the underwriting syndicate to potential buyers. The preliminary prospectus, which is preliminary because the SEC's comments have not yet been incorporated, is also known as the *red herring* because it contains a red legend mandated by the SEC on its front cover, warning of its preliminary nature.

Once the registration statement has been filed, the company will work with the underwriters to prepare a presentation about the company for the road show. The *road show* is arranged by the underwriters and consists of a series of meetings, large and small, with potential investors in a number of major cities during a two- to three-week period. Approximately thirty days after the registration statement has been filed, the SEC staff will send a letter with its comments on the registration statement to the company. Meanwhile, the road show will have commenced. The goal of this part of the process is to complete the road show at about the same time as the company's and underwriters' counsel have satisfied the SEC by filing a series of *pre-effective amendments* to the registration statement. These amendments are pre-effective because the registration statement has not yet been *declared effective* by the SEC, which is the point at which the SEC gives permission for trading in the company's stock to commence. These pre-effective amendments typically revise the registration statement and the prospectus contained therein.

Once the SEC has declared the registration statement effective, the underwriters and the company, having completed the road show, agree on a final price and the final number of shares for the offering. Trading in the stock generally commences the next day.

The closing of the purchase and sale of the shares occurs three business days after trading commences. Following effectiveness, between 10,000 and 12,000 copies of the *final prospectus* will be printed and, as required by law, distributed to purchasers of the stock in the offering. The final prospectus includes the final price and number of shares offered and reflects changes to the preliminary prospectus suggested by the SEC or necessitated by events occurring subsequent to the date of the preliminary prospectus.

Selecting the Managing Underwriters

If the company is a suitable public offering candidate and the market is generally receptive, the first step is to establish a relationship with a financial institution that will assist the company with the offering. Virtually all public offerings are managed by investment banks that arrange for the purchase of the company's stock by institutions and individual investors in exchange for a commission. (In contrast, commercial or merchant banks lend their capital in exchange for interest.) A relationship with an investment bank also provides analysts to publish ongoing research reports on the company's progress, which can foster investor interest after the offering.

Typically, the company will select two or even three investment banks to act as managing underwriters. One bank is usually designated the *lead underwriter*. If there are to be other managing underwriters, they are known as *co-managers*. The company should seek underwriters that are willing to underwrite the offering on a firm commitment (as opposed to a best-efforts) basis. In a *firm commitment offering*, the underwriters actually purchase the shares from the company for resale to investors, thereby assuming some (albeit minimal) market risk in the transaction. In contrast, investment banks conducting a *best-efforts offering* are required only to use their best efforts to sell the securities.

The role of the managing underwriters is to position the company in the public market and to form a *syndicate* (a group of investment banks) to participate in the offering. The primary purposes for syndication of an offering are risk sharing and marketing. The syndicate will be composed of multiple underwriters that share liability under the securities laws and share in the underwriting component of the gross spread. In an IPO, the underwriters buy stock from the company at a discount (usually 6% to 7% of the public offering price), then sell it to the public at the full price. The *gross spread* is an amount equal to the difference between the offering price to the public and the proceeds to the company. The syndicate may also include selling group members or dealers who do not share liability with the underwriters. Selling group members or dealers agree only to purchase a specific number of shares at the public offering price less a selling commission (typically 55% to 60% of the gross spread). Unless otherwise indicated, references in this chapter to underwriters mean the managing underwriters.

To be effective, a managing underwriter must be familiar with the company's industry and be able to differentiate the company and its products or services from others in its industry. The company should consider the reputation and experience of the underwriter in the relevant industry, its level of commitment to the deal, its ability to staff the offering appropriately with experienced and knowledgeable personnel, its marketing strength, and the quality of postpublic offering support (e.g., research analysts, market-making capabilities, and experience in mergers and acquisitions). The managing underwriters should have complementary strengths. For example, one might be stronger in making sales to institutional buyers and another might have stronger retail distribution or a better-known analyst.

A company will often hold what has come to be called a *beauty contest* or *bake-off* among four or five investment banks before selecting the managing underwriters. In this process, each investment bank brings a team of three to five people to make a presentation to the board of directors. The investment bankers prepare and distribute elaborate bound materials (referred to as *books*). The books detail the strengths of the investment banking firm, its recent relevant IPOs, the post-IPO price performance of the companies it has taken public, and, perhaps most importantly, its preliminary views on how the market will value the company. These valuations are typically based on past and projected future earnings (initially supplied by the company but massaged by the bankers before the presentation), the *price/earnings ratio* (market price per share divided by earnings per share) of comparable public companies, and the strengths and weaknesses of the company compared with its competitors. Despite the similarity of approach, the valuations among investment banks can vary tremendously. Following the presentations, the company will select the lead underwriter and one or more co-managers.

Timing

IPOs typically take ten to fourteen weeks from start to finish, although it is sometimes possible to accelerate the schedule. The underwriters typically prepare a time and responsibilities schedule setting out who does what and when those tasks must be completed. This schedule will be handed out at the first *all-hands* or *organizational meeting*, which is attended by all of the key participants. Companies well prepared to move quickly will be in the best position to control the IPO timing and minimize market risk. For example, well-organized company counsel frequently will

---

FROM THE TRENCHES

A Silicon Valley company invited six prestigious investment banks to engage in a beauty contest for the IPO. Although all the firms made impressive presentations, the company was attracted to the winner for two principal reasons. First, the bank had the industry's best analyst, which the company felt was important both for completing the IPO successfully and for providing ongoing research writing about the company. Second, the bank had completed many deals as a co-manager but only recently had begun to be selected as a lead underwriter in the particular industry. The company felt that the bank, intent on building its reputation, would give them excellent service during the offering and make certain their deal attracted significant attention in an overcrowded market. The offering was wildly successful as the preliminary orders exceeded the shares available in the offering by ten times.

---

distribute a first draft of the registration statement before the organizational meeting. Exhibit 15.1 sets forth a sample timetable. Exhibit 15.2 is a sample agenda for the organizational meeting.

Registration Statement

The rules and regulations of the SEC require that an offering of securities to the public be made pursuant to a form of registration statement filed with and reviewed by the SEC. In the case of an initial public offering by the company of its stock, the prescribed form will be form S-1, which is filed with the SEC in Washington, D.C. Smaller companies may qualify for filing on form SB-2, which requires somewhat less disclosure. The SEC staff reviews the registration statement for compliance with SEC rules, and reviews the substance of the disclosure in the prospectus, which is the part of the registration statement that will be printed and distributed to the public.

Participants in the IPO Process

The management of the company plays a central role in the offering, guided by the underwriters, counsel, and the auditors. As discussed above, the major task of this *working group* is the preparation of the prospectus.

EXHIBIT 15.1

Sample Timetable

SAMPLE INITIAL PUBLIC OFFERING TIMETABLE

April							May							June							July						
S	M	T	W	T	F	S	S	M	T	W	T	F	S	S	M	T	W	T	F	S	S	M	T	W	T	F	S
	1	2	3	4	5	6				1	2	3	4							1		1	2	3	4	5	6
7	8	9	10	11	12	13	5	6	7	8	9	10	11	2	3	4	5	6	7	8	7	8	9	10	11	12	13
14	15	16	17	18	19	20	12	13	14	15	16	17	18	9	10	11	12	13	14	15	14	15	16	17	18	19	20
21	22	23	24	25	26	27	19	20	21	22	23	24	25	16	17	18	19	20	21	22	21	22	23	24	25	26	27
28	29	30					26	27	28	29	30	31		23	24	25	26	27	28	29	28	29	30	31			
														30													

WebRunner, Inc. . . . . Company
Representatives of the Underwriters . . . . UW
Company Counsel CC
Underwriter's Counsel . . . . UC
Auditors . . . . AU

SUMMARY

April 18 and 19	Organizational meeting and due diligence sessions
April 26	First draft of Registration Statement distributed
April 29	All hands drafting sessions at CC at 8:00 a.m.
May 2 and 3	All hands drafting sessions at CC at 8:00 a.m.
May 6 and 7	All hands drafting sessions at CC at 8:00 a.m.
Week of May 13	All hands drafting sessions at the printer
May 16	File Registration Statement with SEC
Week of May 27	Preparation of road show
Week of June 3	Road show presentation finalized
Weeks of June 10 and 17	Domestic and international road shows
June 20	Registration Statement effective; pricing
June 21	Commence trading
June 26	Closing

EXHIBIT 15.2

Sample Agenda

SAMPLE AGENDA FOR ORGANIZATIONAL MEETING

I. Review and Complete Working Group List
II. Review Time Schedule
    A. SEC review period
    B. Drafting sessions and due diligence
    C. Shareholder communications
        1. Piggyback rights
        2. Proposed lockup
    D. Board of Directors meetings
    E. Filing/offering timing
    F. Road show
    G. Other lead-time items
III. Discuss Proposed Offering
    A. Size of offering
    B. Primary and secondary components
    C. General discussion of use of proceeds
    D. Green Shoe option
    E. Review existing shareholder list
        1. Registration rights
        2. Rule 144 stock
    F. Number of shares authorized
    G. Lockup agreement with principal shareholders
    H. Distribution objectives
    I. Directed shares
    J. Possibility of confidential treatment being requested
IV. Review Legal Issues
    A. Outstanding claims
    B. Loan agreement restrictions or other consents needed to offer the shares
    C. Blue Sky issues
        1. Shareholder notes
        2. Cheap stock
        3. Stock options
        4. Employment agreements
    D. Board Meetings
        1. Preparation of resolutions and appropriate board authorizations
        2. Filing registration statement
        3. Officers' and directors' questionnaires
        4. Pricing committee
    E. Disclosure of confidential agreements
    F. Related party and certain transactions disclosures
    G. Required shareholder approvals
    H. Expert opinions

Exhibit 15.2 continued

Sample Agenda

   V.   Discuss Financial and Accounting Matters
       A. Audited financials
       B. Availability of quarterly financials
       C. Comfort letter
       D. Management letters
       E. Any special accounting issues
  VI. Discuss Publicity Policy
       A. Pre-filing, post-filing/pre-effective, post-offering periods
       B. Pending newspaper/magazine articles to be published
       C. Other corporate announcements
       D. Filing press release(s)
 VII. Discuss Printing of Documents
       A. Selection of printer and bank note company
       B. Use of color, pictures
       C. Volume requirements
VIII. Due Diligence Review
       A. Management interviews
       B. References for customer/supplier due diligence
       C. Detailed competitive analysis
       D. Projected financials (revenues, earnings, backlog)
       E. Methodology and models for financial planning
       F. Product brochures, trade press, other public relations materials
  IX. Discuss Form and Contents of Registration Statement
   X. Discuss Road Show Presentation
  XI. Legal Due Diligence/Review of Corporate Records

The managing underwriters actively participate in the drafting of the prospectus and are responsible for the selling effort. They put together the syndicate of investment banks that will participate in the offering, organize the road show and marketing meetings, and coordinate other matters relating to the marketing and sale of the securities.

Company counsel, in addition to advising the company on compliance issues, coordinates the drafting of the registration statement and shepherds it through the SEC review process. He or she also helps the company select and coordinate with other participants in the process, such as stock exchange representatives, the printer, the transfer agent, and the bank note company. Company counsel participates in the negotiation of the *underwriting agreement* between the company and the managing underwriters, which covers all aspects of the offering, including the amount of the gross spread. Typically, company counsel will review the company's charter documents and legal records to determine what actions the company should take prior to becoming a public company. Company counsel also conducts a detailed review of the business, addressing any legal problems that may emerge and identifying items that require disclosure in the prospectus. If the company has separate patent counsel or regulatory counsel, such counsel may be asked to participate in discussions with the working group and to review, and, in many cases, render an opinion to the underwriters regarding, sections of the prospectus in their area of legal expertise.

Underwriters' counsel participates on behalf of the underwriters in the drafting process and the due diligence effort, advises the underwriters on legal issues that arise, and prepares the underwriting agreement. Underwriters' counsel also coordinates the review of the underwriting arrangements by the National Association of Securities Dealers (NASD) and the review of the offering by state securities authorities.

The company's auditors provide accounting advice in connection with the offering and work closely with the company's chief financial officer in the preparation of the prospectus as it relates to accounting issues and financial disclosure. The auditors also address SEC comments related to accounting issues and prepare comfort letters. A *comfort letter* summarizes the procedures the auditors used to verify certain financial information in the prospectus and describes the scope of their review of the prospectus. It is delivered to the underwriters when the offering becomes effective and again at the closing.

Generally, the prospectuses are printed by a financial printer. The printer must be experienced; able to produce a high-quality, timely, and accurate product; and cost-effective in responding to revisions prepared by the working group. A company should expect to spend more than $100,000 to print approximately 20,000 preliminary prospectuses and 10,000 final prospectuses, and should obtain quotes from two or three reputable financial printers with extensive IPO experience.

In addition, the company will need a transfer agent, which is typically a specialized stock transfer company or a commercial bank, to issue and effect transfers of the company's shares and to coordinate mailings to shareholders. The company will also need to select a bank note company to help design and then print the new stock certificates that will be issued to the shareholders after the public offering.

Due Diligence

The company, the underwriters, and their respective counsel assemble and review the information about the company in the registration statement, thereby conducting a legal audit of the company and its business. This time-consuming process, along with the data and backup materials used by the company, its underwriters, and their counsel to verify the accuracy of this information, is called *due diligence*. Due diligence is also used to determine what additional information should be disclosed and to uncover any problems or risks that need to be addressed or disclosed in connection with the public offering. The company must make sure that all participants are aware of the importance of complete candor in the due diligence process to ensure that the information in the prospectus is complete and accurate.

The underwriters, their counsel, and company counsel ask numerous questions of the company's officers and key employees in order to understand thoroughly the company's business, its products and markets or potential markets, and their inherent risks. The due diligence review often includes discussions with key customers and suppliers; a review of environmental issues; analysis of projections, business plans, and product strategy; a review of industry publications; and consultations with patent counsel, technology advisors, and regulatory counsel. It also includes a legal audit of company records, including minutes of board and shareholder meetings, charter documents, qualifications to do business, and all material contracts.

The company must be prepared to back up the claims it makes in the prospectus. Even if stated as opinion, such as its belief that it is becoming the industry leader, the company must be able to demonstrate the

---

FROM THE TRENCHES

Due diligence in a recent offering revealed a situation that the investment bankers concluded had to be changed before they were willing to proceed. It turned out that the two founders had transferred patents to the company in exchange for future royalties. If the company met its sales projections, the royalties would amount to several million dollars a year, commencing in three years. These royalties would have significantly reduced the company's earnings per share. The underwriters refused to try to market the company unless these royalties were eliminated. The company reached a settlement with the founders, and the offering proceeded.

---

reasonableness of this belief. Industry publications and market surveys are common forms of support for statements regarding market size and the company's position in the market. The information collected in the due diligence process is useful in responding to the SEC if it asks for support for the company's assertions, which is common.

A company should expect the unexpected during the due diligence process. Matters of personal and professional character can become significant issues. The entrepreneur should discuss with counsel any and all issues, both real or perceived, that could affect the offering.

Determination of Stock Price and Offering Size

Although underwriters generally like the company's offering price to be more than $10 and less than $20 per share, the offering price and the size of the offering will be determined by negotiations between the company and its underwriters. The company often will need to effect a stock split of the outstanding stock prior to the offering to bring the expected price per share into this range.

The valuation of the company takes into account market conditions, comparable companies in the industry, past and projected financial performance, product and technology position, the management team, the potential for growth, and new products in development. As noted above, the valuation of the company will have been preliminarily proposed by

FROM THE TRENCHES

For one company's officers, the prospect of personal liability for misstatements prompted the disclosure of unorthodox accounting practices by the chief financial officer and patterns of sexual harassment on the part of the chief executive officer. The revelations slowed the offering process and proved highly embarrassing when they were disclosed. The issues should have been discussed with company counsel before the offering process commenced so that counsel could have framed them for the bankers at the outset of the IPO process.

the managing underwriter at the outset of the IPO process. Additional due diligence by the underwriters' financial analysts and revisions to the company's financial models will take place before the registration statement is filed. This may result in a valuation in the red herring different from that initially proposed. This valuation is still preliminary, and is reflected in a *price range* set forth on the cover of the red herring, such as $14–$16 per share.

The final offering price is usually set after the SEC review process is completed and just before the commencement of the offering. The determination of the final price is based on the market and the reaction of potential purchasers to the offering, which is reflected in nonbinding indications to the underwriters of potential investors' intent to purchase shares (commonly referred to as the *underwriters' book*). Typically, underwriters would like a book equal to at least seven times the offering size. The underwriters generally will try to price the shares slightly below the price at which the underwriters predict the stock will trade in secondary trading after the initial sale by the underwriters (the *target price*) to give the stock room to move up in the aftermarket. This *IPO discount* is typically 15% of the target price.

The size of the offering is based on the company's capital needs, dilution to existing shareholders, the level of *public float* (shares held by investors other than officers, directors, and 10% shareholders) desirable to achieve an active trading market and to provide liquidity for existing shareholders, market receptivity, and the proposed price per share. The underwriters are typically granted an overallotment option, called the

---

FROM THE TRENCHES

The relationship between the IPO price and subsequent trading prices is anything but predictable. Amgen, perhaps the most successful biotechnology company in history, remained at (and even below) its IPO price for several years, before going on to give investors extraordinary returns. By contrast, Netscape Communications, originally priced at $13 per share, was raised to $28 on the eve of the IPO as demand continued to grow. On the first day of trading, the stock soared to $75 before coming to rest at $52 a few days later.

---

green shoe, to purchase additional shares at the IPO price. The option typically gives the underwriters the right to purchase an amount of additional shares equal to 15% of the amount originally offered, within a set period after the offering commences, usually thirty days. The option may be exercised only to cover overallotments, that is, to cover the underwriters' short positions when the offering has been oversold.

If the underwriters want to sell more shares than the company is willing to sell, the underwriters may invite certain shareholders to offer shares they own for resale as part of the initial offering. Moreover, some shareholders may have registration rights entitling them to sell shares in the offering pursuant to agreements entered into with the company at the time of their initial investment. These registration rights can usually be limited if the underwriters do not want to include selling shareholders because they believe that an offering limited to company shares is optimal or that management or significant investors may be perceived as bailing out if they make substantial sales. (Registration rights are discussed in more detail in chapter 8.)

Confidential Treatment of Material Agreements

Generally, all of the company's material contracts must be filed as exhibits to the registration statement. These filings are public documents, and copies can be obtained by anyone. However, when documents contain information that could harm the company's legitimate business interests if disclosed, the company can seek to protect such information from public disclosure. In response to a narrowly framed request, the SEC may grant confidential treatment, for a limited number of years, of select portions of the agreements, such as royalty rates, payment amounts, volume discount rates, proprietary technical data or chemical compounds, and fields of research. A copy of the exhibit with the confidential portions carefully excised will then be available to the public. Requests for confidential treatment must be cleared with the SEC prior to effectiveness of the IPO. Prolonged negotiation with the SEC, or a third party who might be affected by such disclosure, may delay this clearance and thus delay the offering.

Exchanges, Nasdaq, and Blue Sky Laws

Each exchange has its own listing requirements, which must be satisfied for a company, upon application, to be listed on that exchange. Underwriters will typically recommend that companies list their shares for trading on the Nasdaq Stock Market National Market System (*Nasdaq/NMS*) concurrently with the public offering. When stock is traded on the Nasdaq/NMS, brokers and traders are able to obtain real-time trading information. Listing on the Nasdaq/NMS is generally viewed as preferable to the Nasdaq Small Cap Market because of the greater information available for Nasdaq/NMS companies, the larger following by analysts and shareholders, and the availability of broad state securities law exemptions and corporate governance benefits.

To list its stock on the Nasdaq/NMS, the company must file an application and satisfy specified criteria. It is important to begin the application process as early as possible in the offering. The requirements for being listed on the Nasdaq/NMS are generally more stringent than those for the Nasdaq Small Cap Market, and include financial as well as corporate governance requirements. As part of its Nasdaq/NMS listing application, the company must select a unique four-letter trading symbol.

Alternatively, if the company satisfies the more stringent listing requirements of the New York Stock Exchange or the different requirements of the American Stock Exchange, the company may file a listing application and become approved for listing.

Early-stage companies may have difficulty meeting the Nasdaq/NMS listing requirements. A special appeal process is available to permit the company to present additional facts to support its application. For example, one company, unable to satisfy the three-year operating history requirement, was able to demonstrate that the period of preincorporation research and development conducted by the company's founder should be taken into account.

Trading on the Nasdaq/NMS or an exchange requires the company to register under the Securities Exchange Act of 1934 (the *1934 Act*), which subjects the company and its officers and directors to certain additional securities law requirements. Company counsel usually files to register the company under the 1934 Act at the time of the initial filing of the IPO registration statement with the SEC. Registration under the 1934 Act takes effect simultaneously with the commencement of trading on the Nasdaq/NMS or an exchange. Such registration would typically not otherwise be required for a number of months after a company's IPO.

The company must also comply with the securities or Blue Sky laws of each state in which shares are offered or sold except to the extent that such state laws are preempted by federal law. Underwriters typically ask a company to qualify in each state in which the underwriters may offer the shares, as well as in Guam and Puerto Rico. Blue Sky qualification is usually handled by underwriters' counsel. The fees and expenses incurred in this process are typically paid by the company, subject to a cap on attorneys' fees. However, designation for trading on the Nasdaq/NMS or certain exchanges allows the company to avoid time-consuming merit review by state regulators (whereby regulators evaluate the fairness of the terms of the offering) and eliminates the need for any pre-offering state filings.

The Road Show

After the registration statement is filed, the underwriters organize a series of informational meetings at which company management makes presentations to institutional investors and other prospective investors about the company, its business, and its strategy. This is called the *road show*. The underwriters typically time the road show to take place in the last weeks of the SEC review period. The meetings are set up for large audiences at select cities throughout the United States and sometimes

Europe and Asia, and are often followed up by one-on-one meetings with certain potential investors. The road show can take two or three weeks and generally ends just prior to the expected effective date of the offering. The material presented in the road show must be consistent with, and cannot go beyond, the information contained in the prospectus, and no written materials other than the preliminary prospectus should be distributed to the potential investors.

SEC Comments

The SEC's internal policies provide that comments to the prospectus be delivered within thirty days after filing; however, during extremely busy periods, the comments may be delayed. The company responds to the SEC's staff comments by filing a pre-effective amendment to the registration statement, usually within a week after receiving the comments. The amendment is typically reviewed by the SEC examiner within a few days after receipt. If there are no additional comments, the examiner will indicate that an acceleration request to declare the registration statement immediately effective will be accepted from the company and the managing underwriters. It is not unusual to file more than one pre-effective amendment, particularly if the initial comments are numerous or broad in nature. As the company is filing its amendments, the underwriters are finishing the road show and finalizing their book of nonbinding commitments.

Pricing and Commencement of Trading

After the SEC review process is completed, the company and its underwriters each request that the SEC declare the registration statement effective by submitting a request for acceleration. The underwriters and a subcommittee appointed by the board of directors to act as a pricing committee negotiate the final price, usually after the stock market has closed on the day before the offering is to commence. This actual price is usually, but not necessarily, within the price range set out on the cover page of the preliminary prospectus. The company may reject the price proposed by the underwriters and elect not to proceed with the offering, although this rarely happens. Once the registration statement has been declared effective, the deal priced, and the underwriting agreement between the company and the underwriters signed, trading in the stock will commence, usually on the Nasdaq/NMS or an exchange, depending on where the stock is listed. Trading typically commences the morning after the pricing.

The Closing

The offering is not *closed* (consummated) until the stock certificates are delivered and the funds are received. The closing usually takes place on the third business day after trading has commenced.

RESTRICTIONS ON SALES OF SHARES

Lockup Agreements

The possibility of having additional shares of the company's stock come onto the market creates a very significant risk for the underwriters, the

---

---

company, and the investors. Referred to as the *overhang*, an excess supply of shares in the marketplace can substantially depress stock prices. As a condition to the offering, underwriters typically require most shareholders, including all employees of the company, to sign *lockup agreements*, restricting their ability to sell any shares for a specified period of time, generally 180 days from the effective date of the IPO. As explained in chapter 8, in many cases investors agree in advance to such a lockup at the time of their initial investment.

Most underwriters believe that unless the company secures lockups for at least 90% of the shares, an IPO could be jeopardized. Because of the risk, the underwriters may be reluctant to file the registration statement until sufficient lockup agreements have been obtained.

Trading of Stock Not Issued in Offering and the Impact of Rule 144

In addition to the lockup agreement provisions, trading of company stock acquired prior to the IPO is restricted under the federal securities laws. Consequently, common stock issued to employees and common stock issued when preferred stock is converted may not be sold in the open market unless certain conditions are satisfied. Employee shares issued prior to the IPO under written compensatory plans may be sold, pursuant to rule 701 of the 1933 Act, ninety days after the IPO by employees who are not affiliates of the company and are not otherwise locked up. Employee shares held by affiliates, such as directors, executive officers, and significant shareholders of the company, may also be sold ninety days after the IPO pursuant to rule 701, subject to the volume limitations described below. After the IPO, stock issued pursuant to employee plans is often registered with the SEC on form S-8.

Restricted stock (i.e., stock not sold in a public offering) that was not issued under employee plans or for compensatory purposes must generally be resold in compliance with rule 144 under the 1933 Act. Rule 144 generally requires that the securities be held for at least one year after purchase and be sold in limited quantities (*dribbled out*) through brokers or market makers. Rule 144 limits the amount that may be sold in a three-month period to the greater of 1% of the outstanding shares and the average weekly trading volume in the preceding four weeks. A form 144 notice must be filed with the SEC when the order to sell is placed. However, non-affiliates who have held their restricted stock for more than two years may sell their shares pursuant to rule 144(k) without complying with any of these requirements.

Sales by affiliates must generally be made pursuant to rule 144 even if they are selling stock acquired on the open market that was previously registered. However, sales by affiliates of stock acquired pursuant to employee plans under an S-8 registration statement or pursuant to rule 701 are not subject to the one-year holding period requirement of rule 144.

CONTENTS OF THE PROSPECTUS

The prospectus begins with a one-page summary of the offering, referred to as the *Box Summary*, which summarizes the key elements of the company's business and financial statements. Following the Box Summary is an extremely important section entitled *Risk Factors*, which alerts investors to the key risks and challenges faced by the company. It is important that risks specific to the company be identified. Additionally, some of the risks that are universally addressed in an IPO prospectus include the absence of an extended operating history or profitable operations; the fact that the nature of the business is inherently risky; the dependence on a sole supplier or particular customers; the uncertainties regarding technology or regulatory

---

FROM THE TRENCHES

The underwriter and its counsel often must exert great effort to convince the company's chief executive officer to make the risk factors in a prospectus as strong as possible. The CEO may believe that strong risk factors will have a negative effect on the offering; the CEO also may disagree with what he or she perceives as trashing the company's business in a public document. The underwriter, of course, wants to make certain that all possible risks are disclosed. In a recent offering, the CEO initially refused to permit certain risk factors to be included. It was only after the managing underwriter offered to write him a letter to the effect that the inclusion of the factors would not have a negative impact on the IPO that the CEO relented.

---

approvals; the uncertainty of proprietary rights; intense competition from more mature companies; and the lack of manufacturing or marketing experience, all of which make the stock particularly speculative. The Risk Factors section is not intended to produce a balanced view of the company; rather, it highlights potential risks and serves as important protection in the event of shareholder litigation.

The *Use of Proceeds* section describes how the company intends to use the proceeds of the offering in its business. The company should be able to support, by projections or otherwise, the proposed uses. The SEC staff has recently been insisting on fairly detailed discussions of the proposed uses of the funds, despite resistance by companies that want to avoid specific commitments to the extent possible or that might not have specific uses planned.

The *Management's Discussion and Analysis of Financial Condition and Results of Operations (MD&A)* section contains an analysis of the financial statements for at least the three most recent fiscal years and any applicable interim periods (unless the company has been in business for a shorter period of time). The analysis provides a year-to-year and period-to-period comparison, focusing on material changes and the reasons for those changes, as well as unusual or nonrecurring events that could cause the historical results to be a misleading indicator of future performance. This section has been the subject of heightened SEC scrutiny. Although projections per se are not required, the MD&A section does require a forward-looking analysis of the effect of known trends, events, or uncertainties, including information that may not be evident on the face of financial statements. As part of the MD&A, the company's historical and projected sources of funds for the business must be discussed.

The *Business* section provides a narrative description of the company, its strategies and goals, products or products in development, technology, manufacturing, and marketing. Within certain limits, this section can be customized both in terms of presentation and substance. Potential risks, such as technological uncertainties, shortages of raw materials, timing of new product introductions, or reliance on sole suppliers, are highlighted throughout. This section will reflect the tension between the need to provide complete risk disclosure of the investment and the desire to describe the company in a manner that is attractive to investors and does not reveal sensitive or competitive information.

The *Management* section provides biographical information about officers, directors, and key employees, and describes executive compensation,

"Would everyone check to see they have an attorney? I seem to have ended up with two."

Drawing by Maslin; ©1989 the New Yorker Magazine, Inc.

FROM THE TRENCHES

One way to persuade the SEC that a cheap stock charge is inappropriate (or to reduce the amount of such a charge) is to obtain a valuation report from an independent expert concluding that the stock was issued at fair market value. In a recent deal, several hundred thousand shares of stock were issued seven months before the IPO at a price of $1 per share. The proposed public offering price was $15 per share. Knowing that the SEC might argue that the company should recognize $11 per share of compensation expense (based on 80% of $15), amounting to several million dollars of charges over time, the company hired a valuation expert after the IPO process commenced to value the company's stock as of the issuance seven months before. The expert concluded, based on the company's precarious financial condition at that time, that a value of $3 per share was appropriate. The company took a charge based on this amount and filed the report with the SEC. No additional earning charges were required.

---

employee benefit plans, and insider transactions. Disclosure of executive compensation is quite comprehensive and must follow certain prescribed tabular formats designed to facilitate comparisons among companies.

Audited Financial Statements are also required, including balance sheets as of the end of the last two fiscal years and income statements for the three most recent fiscal years. Unaudited interim financial statements are required for offerings that become effective 135 or more days after the end of the most recent fiscal year. All financial statements must conform to generally accepted accounting principles (GAAP) and to SEC accounting requirements.

If the company has recently (i.e., within twelve months prior to effectiveness) granted stock options or otherwise issued stock at a price significantly below the IPO price, a charge to earnings to reflect the issuance of this so-called *cheap stock* may be required. The theory is that cheap stock is actually additional compensation to the employee and should be accounted for as such. Cheap stock is often the subject of SEC comment on the prospectus, and, if the proposed charge is significant, can jeopardize the offering. It is important to discuss this issue with the company's auditors prior to the organizational meeting.

The company need not but often does include photographs, illustrations, and graphs in the prospectus. Although color photographs or illustrations add to the cost of printing and require additional lead time, many companies and underwriters believe that they assist readers who lack a technical background to understand the company's business and products. The SEC staff has commented negatively on the use of professional models rather than employees in product photographs. Photos of prototype products, fully disclosed as such, may be used in the prospectus.

Liability for Misstatements in the Prospectus

Securities laws regulating IPOs and other registered public offerings of securities are geared, in large part, toward ensuring that sufficient disclosure of relevant facts is made to permit potential investors to make informed investment decisions. To further this goal, section 11 of the 1933 Act makes certain persons associated with a registered offering of securities (including the company, its officers who sign the registration statement, the directors, the named nominees for director, and the underwriters) civilly liable to the purchasers of the shares for any untrue statement of a material fact contained in a registration statement and for any failure to state a material fact necessary to make the other statements not misleading. The auditors are liable for any material misrepresentation or omission in the financial statements.

The company is absolutely liable for any material misrepresentation or omission, regardless of the degree of care that was used in preparing the prospectus. A director or an underwriter may avoid liability by establishing that he, she, or it exercised due diligence; that is, that, after undertaking a reasonable investigation, such person reasonably believed the statement at issue to be accurate. This *due diligence defense* is technically available to officers as well, but it is much more difficult for officers to demonstrate that they would not have been aware of the inaccuracy or omission if they had exercised due diligence. Underwriters, directors, and officers are often named as defendants in section 11 lawsuits, and even a successful defense is expensive, time-consuming, and unpleasant.

Preparing for an IPO

Prefiling Publicity

Any publication of information or publicity effort made in advance of a proposed public offering that has the effect of conditioning the public mind or arousing public interest in the issuer or its securities may constitute an impermissible offer to sell securities under federal securities laws. This type of impermissible activity during the *prefiling period* (the period before the registration statement is filed) is referred to as *gun jumping*. Disclosures that may run afoul of the securities laws include marketing letters, press releases, speeches, presentations at seminars or conferences, articles in the financial press, and other forms of advertising. Gun-jumping violations, in addition to embarrassing the issuer and its underwriters, may delay the marketing of the securities, because the SEC may refuse to declare a public offering registration statement effective until the effect of the violations has dissipated. Such violations may also result in criminal and civil actions against the issuer and underwriters.

Companies in the registration process must be careful to avoid inappropriate publicity. During the prefiling period, it is illegal for the company to offer to sell any securities pending registration. Therefore, during this period, the company's communications are most significantly restricted. For example, the company may not issue forecasts, projections, or predictions about its expected future performance. The only

---

FROM THE TRENCHES

After years of unsuccessful attempts to attract press coverage, Amgen and its founder and then CEO, George Rathman, were unexpectedly featured in a prominent article published by *Business Week*. The article appeared on the day that the SEC received the company's registration statement. Counsel for the company spent a long weekend drafting a letter of explanation to the SEC, emphasizing that the interview was granted well before the offering process began, explaining that the company had no notice of publication, and requesting that the offering not be delayed. Fortunately, the request was granted.

communication about the offering permitted during this period is a notice of proposed offering, the contents of which are narrowly prescribed by regulation. These notices are rarely used in connection with IPOs.

However, the company need not completely discontinue its normal public relations activities. It is permitted to continue advertising that is consistent with past practices, to send out its customary reports to shareholders, and to make routine press announcements with regard to factual business developments, so long as such activities can be conducted without having an impact on the offering. The company should remember that newspaper and magazine articles often have a long lead time. Thus, an article currently being researched and written may not be published until many months later, when the public offering process is in full swing.

The company should consider setting up an internal control procedure to ensure that all public disclosures are properly reviewed and coordinated in advance. Counsel for the company and the underwriters should review all press releases and publicity, including product announcements, to be released for publication, broadcast, or distribution during the registration period. In addition, the company should establish a policy prohibiting employees, officers, and directors from recommending the company's securities, offering their opinions or forecasts regarding the company or, without the advice of counsel, providing any information regarding the IPO.

Postfiling Publicity

After the registration statement is filed but before it is declared effective by the SEC, the company is in the period called the *registration period* or *waiting period*, during which the company can offer its securities for sale but cannot actually sell them. The offer of securities must be made by means of the preliminary prospectus or through oral communications. During this time, the company and the underwriters will conduct the road show. Antifraud provisions of the securities laws still apply, and selective disclosure of material not included in the prospectus is problematic. Members of the press are typically excluded from the meetings with potential investors during the road show.

Industry conferences are extremely important opportunities for the company to meet the investment community. These conferences are planned long in advance, and invitations to present at them are intensely sought after. After discussion with counsel and the underwriters, a company may go forward with previously arranged conference presentations provided that the red-herring prospectus is available at the conference (and no other written materials are given out because they would be considered offering materials not included in the prospectus). The presentation should be the same as the road show presentation; the company will typically not participate in one-on-one or breakout sessions.

Posteffective Quiet Period

The 25-day period after effectiveness of the registration statement and commencement of the IPO is called the *quiet period*. During this period, sales of the securities can begin and the final prospectus is delivered. Distribution of other written literature is permitted, provided that it is accompanied or preceded by a prospectus. It is also traditional for the underwriters to issue a tombstone advertisement in the financial press to announce the commencement of the sale of the securities. This tombstone advertisement is governed by both regulation and custom.

Even though the offering may be complete from the company's perspective once the closing has occurred, publicizing the offering may be considered by the SEC as an inappropriate attempt by the company to

---

FROM THE TRENCHES

In a recent proposed IPO involving a Salt Lake City company, a significant shareholder (who owned 25% of the stock) had the contractual right to elect a majority of the company's board of directors. The shareholder wanted to maintain this right even after the IPO to protect its investment. The underwriters felt that board control by a single investor would adversely affect the marketability of the IPO. After extensive discussions, the investor agreed that it would retain only the right to elect one-third of the board. The offering proceeded.

encourage the public to purchase shares from dealers who are still required to deliver a prospectus during this quiet period. As a result, issuers are generally careful to remain quiet, releasing information only as necessary in bare factual form. If, during this period, material developments do occur, it may be necessary to supplement, or sticker, the prospectus to reflect the new developments or, in some cases, to file a posteffective amendment with the SEC.

Board Composition

The company should review the composition of its board of directors prior to the offering. Public investors occasionally will have a concern if there are not enough *outside* or *independent directors* on the board, that is, persons who are not officers or employees of the company or its subsidiaries or who do not otherwise have a relationship to the company that would interfere with the exercise of independent judgment in carrying out the director's responsibilities. To be listed on the Nasdaq/NMS, a company must have at least two independent directors. (Independent directors and board composition are discussed in chapter 9.)

Board committees, such as audit and compensation committees, become much more important once a company goes public. A company listed on the Nasdaq/NMS or the New York Stock Exchange must have an audit committee composed solely of independent directors. The audit committee, which reviews the company's independent auditors and evaluates the company's accounting system and internal controls, is perceived as having a critical oversight role in preventing and detecting fraudulent financial reporting. The SEC's proxy rules require a report from the compensation committee (or the full board if there is no such committee) on how the compensation of the company's executive officers was set. Additionally, a committee composed of at least two non-employee directors generally must administer most of the company's employee stock plans if the company intends to take advantage of the favorable treatment afforded those plans by certain exemptions from liability under section 16 of the 1934 Act, discussed later in this chapter.

Reincorporation in Delaware

As explained in chapter 5, there are a number of reasons companies choose to incorporate in Delaware. Delaware law generally provides broader powers and flexibility to companies to indemnify their directors, officers, employees, and agents, and there is more extensive case law in Delaware regarding the interpretation of indemnification provisions than in other states. For example, Delaware permits companies to eliminate monetary liability even for gross negligence, while California law requires directors to remain liable under certain circumstances for acts or omissions that constitute an unexcused pattern of inattention or reckless disregard of their duties. In addition, Delaware law is often viewed as more receptive to shareholder protection measures designed to reduce a corporation's vulnerability to hostile takeover attempts than other states, which either do not permit such measures or restrict their use.

Accordingly, companies not already incorporated in Delaware frequently reincorporate there as part of the IPO process. Shareholder protection measures available in Delaware are often adopted at the same time.

RESPONSIBILITIES OF A PUBLIC COMPANY AND ITS BOARD OF DIRECTORS

The realities of being a public company include heightened public scrutiny and disclosure obligations which a private company does not face. Once public, a company must file a number of periodic reports and other documents with the SEC disclosing information about its business, management, and financial results and condition. The company's officers, directors, and principal shareholders must file documents with the SEC that disclose their ownership of and transactions in the company's securities. The company, as well as its directors and officers, also face increased potential liability as a result of their fiduciary responsibilities to public shareholders and their disclosure obligations.

The periodic reporting requirements, together with the practice of issuing press releases and managing the expectations of securities analysts and public shareholders, add significant pressure to achieve short-term results at the expense of long-term goals, and may limit the flexibility of management and the board of directors in making strategic corporate decisions. Finally, the periodic reporting requirements bring additional costs to a public company in the way of increased legal, accounting, and printing expenses. The company may also need to hire additional management personnel to handle its expanded reporting and other obligations.

Periodic Reports

Public company status increases a company's responsibilities to its shareholders and to the trading market. In addition to describing in the prospectus how the company plans to use the net proceeds from the offering, the company must file with the SEC an initial report on form SR within ten days after the end of the first three-month period following the effective date of the offering. Form SR must specify how the proceeds have been used and explain any material deviations from the plan of use described in the prospectus. Subsequent periodic reports on form SR must be filed until all of the offering proceeds have been fully applied, with the final report on form SR filed within ten days after all of the offering proceeds have been used.

The company will also be required to file certain periodic reports with the SEC (e.g., annual reports on form 10-K, quarterly reports on form 10-Q, current reports on form 8-K, and reports by Nasdaq/NMS issuers on form 10-C). In addition, companies that trade on the Nasdaq/NMS must file with Nasdaq copies of documents filed with the SEC, and companies that trade on the New York and American Stock Exchanges must file copies with the applicable exchange. Additionally, public companies must comply with the SEC's proxy regulations when soliciting a vote or consent of shareholders.

Form 10-K The report on form 10-K is an annual report filed with the SEC that provides a continuing update of information about the company and its management substantially similar to that contained in the company's prospectus. It will include a description of the company's business for the preceding fiscal year, audited financial statements, and an MD&A section relating to the periods covered by those financial statements.

Form 10-Q The report on form 10-Q is a quarterly report filed with the SEC and includes summary unaudited quarterly financial statements, an MD&A section covering those results, and certain other specified disclosures, such as information concerning new developments in legal proceedings or shareholders' actions taken within the quarter.

Form 8-K A report on form 8-K is intended to supplement the normal recurring filing requirements (e.g., form 10-K and form 10-Q) when material events occur that should be brought to the prompt attention of the investing public, such as a merger, change in control, sale of significant assets, bankruptcy, or a change in accountants.

Form 10-C If the company's shares will be quoted on the Nasdaq/NMS, the company must file form 10-C with the SEC within ten days after (1) an aggregate increase or decrease of 5% or greater in the amount of its outstanding shares as last reported, or (2) a change of corporate name.

Effect of Proxy Rules

A company registered under the 1934 Act must comply with the SEC proxy rules when soliciting a shareholder vote or consent. Generally, these rules require that a proxy statement be mailed to each shareholder of record in advance of every shareholders' meeting. The proxy statement must set forth detailed information regarding the company's management and the matters to be voted on. For example, a proxy statement relating to the election of directors must include a report of the compensation committee (or the full board, if there is no such committee) explaining how executive compensation was determined and the relationship between pay and performance; it also must include a graph comparing performance of the company's stock against a broad-based index and an industry-group index. In some cases, such as a shareholder vote on a merger, the proxy statement and form of proxy must first be submitted to the SEC for review and comment. Because of the filing and other procedural requirements applicable to proxy solicitations, the company should plan all meetings of shareholders well in advance.

Insider Trading

Definition Insider trading liability may arise as a result of trading by someone who has material nonpublic information about a company and owes a duty to that company, its shareholders, or others, either by reason of employment by the company or some other fiduciary relationship. Directors, officers, employees, accountants, attorneys, and consultants are considered insiders with a fiduciary duty to the company. An insider in possession of material nonpublic information must either disclose it before trading in the company's securities (which is often impossible for a variety of reasons) or refrain from trading. Failure to observe these restrictions may subject the individual (and perhaps the company) to both civil and criminal liability, including treble damages, fines of up to $1 million, and prison sentences. In past court cases involving insider trading, what the insider thought or knew, or later claimed he or she thought or knew, has not necessarily provided a successful defense if, in hindsight, the insider's personal securities transaction created the impression that the insider was in fact taking advantage of undisclosed information about the issuer. Thus, it is important that insiders avoid even the appearance of impropriety.

Insiders are also prohibited from disclosing material inside information to others who might use the information to their advantage in trading in the company's securities. Both the person who discloses the information (the *tipper*) and the person who receives it (the *tippee*) may be liable under the insider trading laws. Assume, for instance, that a director is also a partner in a venture capital partnership and knows of a significant unannounced contract the company has won. Although the director-partner has not communicated this information to anyone, one of his or her partners, based entirely on public information, purchases securities of that company. Shortly thereafter, the company's securities increase substantially in value. Because it would be possible for an objective fact finder to find, based on appearances, that the director-partner had tipped the nondirector-partner, the partners and the fund could have significant exposure to litigation and potential liability, despite not having actually violated the law. Accordingly, persons with special relationships with insiders of a company are well advised to check with the insider before trading in the company's stock to make certain the insider is not in possession of material nonpublic information about the company.

Company Liability   Legislation adopted in 1988 extends potential liability for insider trading violations to employers under certain circumstances. The Insider Trading and Securities Fraud Enforcement Act of 1988 (ITSFEA) provides that any controlling person who knew or recklessly disregarded the fact that a controlled person was likely to engage in acts constituting an insider trading violation and failed to take appropriate steps to prevent such acts before they occurred may independently be liable for a civil penalty of up to the greater of $1 million or treble the profits resulting from the violation. This penalty provision theoretically would permit a court to assess a company a penalty of $1 million even if the insider trading by the employee involved only a few thousand dollars.

FROM THE TRENCHES

In a recent SEC insider trading investigation, the son of the president of MCA Corporation overheard his father discussing the pending sale of MCA to Matsushita. The son heeded his father's warning not to trade on the information, but passed on the information to his ex-wife and her boyfriend. They traded for their own account and passed the information on to others who also traded. Following public announcement of the sale, MCA's stock rose sharply, and the SEC launched an investigation. Those who traded as a result of the son's tip settled with the SEC by disgorging their profits, plus penalties; the son settled by paying the SEC $418,000 in penalties, even though he hadn't traded and had not made a dime on the information he passed on.

Adopting a written policy prohibiting insider trading can reduce the company's exposure for controlling-person liability. A well-drafted policy educates employees on the law of insider trading and establishes internal procedures to safeguard against both intentional and unintentional illegal trading. In the event that an employee does violate the law, the policy and related procedures reduce the risk that the company itself will be liable under the ITSFEA.

Some companies go beyond a simple insider trading policy applicable to all employees and adopt an additional policy limiting the times when directors, officers, and principal shareholders can sell or purchase stock. These so-called *window period policies* typically prohibit the person from trading in the company's stock during a period commencing four weeks before the end of a quarter and extending through a point seventy-two hours after the company has released its earnings report for that quarter (typically three weeks after the quarter has ended). The company usually retains the right to close the trading window early or not open it at all if there exists undisclosed information that would make trades by insiders inappropriate. The theory of these policies is that the company does not want to be sued because an officer or director traded stock at a time when the insider might have known how the quarter was going to turn out and the market did not. It takes management time and company resources to defend such lawsuits, and they can bring ill repute to the company. A window period policy lessens the possibility of such a lawsuit.

Liability for Short-Swing Profits   Section 16 of the 1934 Act provides for the automatic recovery by the company of any profits made by executive officers, directors, and greater-than-10% shareholders on securities purchased and sold, or sold and purchased, within a six-month period (i.e., on *short-swing trading*). Section 16(b) is mechanically applied and liability is imposed regardless of the trader's intent to use, or actual use of, inside information. Furthermore, the reports filed by executive officers, directors, and greater-than-10% shareholders pursuant to section 16(a) are monitored by professional plaintiffs' attorneys for indications of short-swing trading violations. Thus, even if a company might choose to ignore the short-swing trading of its insiders, insiders who have violated the strictures of section 16(b) will still be pursued by plaintiffs' attorneys in shareholder derivative suits. Complex rules exist for the attribution to insiders of purchases and sales by persons and entities related to insiders for the purposes of section 16(b).

Insider Reports Executive officers and directors of public companies are subject to a number of reporting requirements designed, among other things, to provide to the investing public information regarding their holdings and trading activity in the securities of the companies by which they are employed or on whose boards they serve. Section 16(a), for instance, requires that each executive officer and director of a company involved in an IPO file a form 3 detailing his or her beneficial ownership of the securities of that company. The form 3 is typically filed at the same time as the public offering becomes effective. (A public company must also file a form within ten days of the election of any new director or officer of the company.) A form 4 must be filed within ten days after the end of any month in which a change in beneficial ownership occurs, including gifts and transfers to trusts. Finally, a form 5 must be filed annually to report certain transactions that were not otherwise reportable or reported. It should be noted that, for purposes of these reporting requirements, complex rules exist regarding what constitutes beneficial ownership of securities.

The SEC has the power to seek monetary fines from individuals for violation of the securities laws up to the following limits: (1) up to $5,000 ($50,000 for entities) per violation for plain vanilla violations, such as a late filing or a nonfiling of a required form under section 16; (2) up to $50,000 ($250,000 for entities) per violation for violations involving fraud, deceit, manipulation, or deliberate or reckless disregard of the law; and (3) up to $100,000 ($500,000 for entities) per violation for violations that not only involve fraud or reckless disregard of the law, but also result in, or create a substantial risk of, substantial losses to others or a substantial gain to the individual involved. According to the SEC, a new violation may occur for each day a filing is made late or not corrected. The SEC recently announced that it is increasing its scrutiny for late filing or nonfiling of section 16 forms.

Post-IPO Disclosure and Communications with Analysts

A public company should establish and follow the practice of prompt and complete disclosure through the press of all material developments, both favorable and unfavorable, that, if known, might reasonably be expected to influence the market price of the company's shares. However, disclosure may sometimes be delayed for valid business reasons or if it is otherwise premature.

Disclosure Obligation   The duty to disclose material information imposed by securities laws will arise as a result of a number of events or circumstances. Some examples are (1) when necessary to satisfy a company's SEC reporting requirements or obligations under listing agreements with Nasdaq or an exchange; (2) when the company or its insiders are trading in the company's own securities; (3) when necessary to correct a prior statement that the company learns was materially untrue or misleading at the time it was made; (4) when a company is otherwise making public disclosure and the omission of material information could be misleading; or (5) when necessary to correct rumors in the marketplace that are attributable to the company. A company may incur liability under the antifraud rules adopted by the SEC pursuant to the 1934 act to any person who purchases or sells the company's securities in the market after issuance of a misleading proxy statement, report, press release, or other communication.

Information is considered *material* if its dissemination would be likely to affect the market price of that company's stock or would likely be considered important by a reasonable investor who is considering trading in the company's securities. In the event of nondisclosure for any reason, officers, directors, and other insiders should be advised against trading in the company's securities until the information has been adequately disseminated. Otherwise, a plaintiff's attorney will use the fact that insiders were trading as evidence of intent to deceive the market. For example, if a company expects its earnings to be less than the analysts have projected and insiders are selling, then when the earnings are announced and the market price drops, it may appear that insiders misled the market so they could sell their stock at an artificially high price.

Communications with Analysts Discussions with market analysts, who write reports following the progress of the company and generally keep the public informed of business developments, are inherently risky.[1] No information given to an analyst is ever off the record. Casual or ill-considered disclosure to an analyst of material inside information can lead to shareholder lawsuits and SEC investigations for securities fraud and insider trading. Although it is important to maintain good relations with the press and analysts, it is also critical to avoid selective disclosure of material information. *Selective disclosure* is simply the release of material information on an individual basis without its simultaneous release to the public generally.

In most cases, however, it is permissible in dealing with analysts and the press to provide general background information or to fill in incremental details regarding a matter that has been disclosed in all material respects. In an attempt to avoid selective or premature disclosure problems, many companies observe a consistent no-comment policy with respect to certain material undisclosed corporate developments, such as acquisitions. The company should always consult with counsel to determine whether a press release is appropriate when material developments occur that may require disclosure through formal mechanisms or when the company becomes aware of rumors circulating in the marketplace.

Caution also should be taken in informal meetings with members of the business community not to make inadvertent disclosure of nonpublic information that might be considered material. The SEC has stated that the antifraud provisions of the federal securities laws apply to all company statements that can be expected to reach investors and trading markets, not just to SEC filings or press releases.

Liability for an Analyst's Report If an analyst provides an inaccurate projection regarding the company, it is generally considered to be the analyst's assessment and not the company's unless the company confirms the information or otherwise becomes entangled in the analyst's report. Companies should always consult carefully with counsel whenever they are tempted to comment on an analyst's report. Disclaimers, warnings, and generalities can reduce risk if a decision is made to comment.

However, any spokesperson talking to analysts must understand that, if he or she comments on projections and forecasts, the company may be held liable if the projections prove incorrect or if the analyst uses the information to engage in trading before the information is released to the public. Generally, the safest course is for the company not to comment.

Safe Harbor for Forward-Looking Statements Federal legislation adopted in December 1995 increased the opportunity for companies to protect themselves from litigation concerning certain disclosures made after an IPO. In passing the legislation, Congress established a safe harbor for certain oral and written forward-looking statements, such as projections, forecasts, and other statements about future operations, plans, or possible results. For a company to be protected, a statement must disclose that it is forward-looking and that the company's actual results may differ materially. In addition, the company must, in the case of a written statement, provide a detailed discussion of the factors that could result in a discrepancy and, in the case of an oral statement, refer the audience to a readily available written statement that contains such a discussion. The scope of the safe harbor's protection has yet to be tested in the courts. Disclosure issues continue to be sensitive and should be discussed thoroughly with counsel.

Directors' Responsibilities in a Public Company

Because directors have a fiduciary relationship to both the company and its shareholders, they are bound by the duties of loyalty and care imposed by the law of the state where the company is incorporated. These duties are applicable to directors of all companies, whether public or private, and are discussed in chapter 9.

Director Liability for Securities Claims Companies and their officers and directors are subject to damage claims for securities fraud under the antifraud rules if their regular quarterly and annual disclosures to the SEC and the public are inaccurate in any material way. Similarly, the securities laws make it unlawful for any person to solicit proxies in contravention of the rules and regulations of the SEC. In this context, directors may be held liable if they knew, or in the exercise of due diligence should have known, that a proxy solicitation issued on their behalf contained material false or misleading statements or omissions. Beyond required disclosures, it is possible to incur liability for securities fraud in connection with the issuance of misleading press releases, reports to shareholders, or other communications that could be expected to reach investors and trading markets.

Indemnification and Liability Insurance for Directors   Under the law of most states, companies are given broad and flexible powers to indemnify directors who are made parties to proceedings and incur liability by reason of their status as directors. A sample indemnity agreement is provided in "Getting It in Writing" at the end of chapter 9. In addition, companies can acquire directors' and officers' (D&O) liability insurance. Most companies secure D&O liability insurance prior to completion of an IPO or consider increasing the company's current coverage while still a private company.

FROM THE TRENCHES

Not long ago, a company facing a disappointing earnings announcement decided that it might be able to soften the impact on the market by disclosing the news to two analysts who followed the company several days before the issuance of a press release. One of the analysts decided to tell his firm's favored clients the news, and the company's stock began to fall rapidly. Not only did the company have to issue a press release quickly to respond to calls from panicky investors, it also had to defend itself in an SEC insider trading investigation.

NOTES

1.   For a general discussion of legal issues associated with dealing with analysts, *see* Dale E. Barnes, Jr. and Constance E. Bagley, "Great Expectations: Risk Management Through Risk Disclosure," 1 *Stanford Journal of Law, Business & Finance* 155 (1994). *See also* Dale E. Barnes, Jr. and Karen L. Kennard, "Greater Expectations: Risk Disclosure Under the Private Securities Litigation Reform Act of 1995—An Update," 2 *Stanford Journal of Law, Business & Finance* 331 (1996).

Putting It into Practice

Soon after the successful product launch of IRRS, Alexandra met with the other WebRunner directors to decide whether to proceed with an initial public offering or to sell the company. They knew that additional funds were needed for WebRunner to accelerate its growth and continue to leapfrog over its competitors. Alexandra and her board felt it would be relatively easy to find a buyer for the company, given the enormous interest in the Internet area. In fact, two customers had already made unofficial overtures. But the directors also felt that WebRunner had a huge potential for growth that would not be reflected even in the IPO price, much less the price they would be able to command as a prepublic company. In the end, they were unwilling to cap this upside by selling for cash or by taking stock in a larger company whose stock price would be determined in large part by the performances of businesses other than WebRunner. They also were excited by the challenge of taking WebRunner to the next level of growth as an independent company. They decided to proceed with an IPO.

Once Alexandra and her board reached this decision, Alexandra assembled a team of investment bankers, lawyers, and accountants. The first step in picking an investment banking firm was to update and assemble a corporate profile to present to potential underwriters. This consisted of a business plan, marketing literature, and audited yearly and unaudited quarterly financial statements for the three years WebRunner had been in existence. Next, Alexandra compiled a list of suitable and likely candidates for underwriters. She wanted to consider firms with expertise in and commitment to companies involved in the Internet, firms that employed respected analysts who were likely to support the company by providing research reports to the investment community in the future, and firms that would not have any conflicts of interest. The list of potential underwriters included firms that had expressed interest in the company in the past and others that were likely to be receptive to the company. Michael Woo and other experienced securities counsel at his firm were helpful in providing leads and introductions.

Prior to the first organizational meeting, Alexandra met with Michael and the company's auditors to determine whether there were any corporate or financial cleanup items that could affect the timing or success of the offering. At the organizational meeting, attended by Alexandra, Paul,

continued

continued

and Sheryl on behalf of WebRunner, Michael as company counsel, the underwriters, underwriters' counsel, and the auditors, all such issues were fully aired and thoroughly discussed. By discussing these issues up front, the group was able to develop a realistic time line.

In addition to disclosure and timing issues, the WebRunner working group also discussed a number of other important issues at the organizational meeting, including the size of the offering, the price range, a required stock split, the length of lockup agreements and who would be required to execute them, reincorporation in Delaware, and other corporate matters. Finally, the various executive officers and key employees of WebRunner introduced themselves and each gave a short (thirty-minute) presentation on his or her respective area of responsibility. Alexandra had reviewed the content of the presentations with the officers in advance. At a minimum, she wanted them to include an overview of the business, a review of the intellectual property portfolio, a description of significant corporate partners and strategic relationships, and a review of the company's current financial condition and projections.

After the organizational meeting, company counsel produced the first draft of the registration statement with significant input from Alexandra and her partners. Alexandra had prepared the first draft of the Business section. Because all prospectuses have a particular tone and set of language conventions with which Alexandra and her partners were unfamiliar, Michael substantially revised the Business section to reflect standard prospectus language. Once the first draft was completed and distributed, the working group met for a series of all-hands meetings. The dates for these meetings had been confirmed at the organizational meeting and took place at the offices of Michael's firm.

Once the draft had progressed sufficiently, a smaller group met at the financial printer to finalize the document and file it with the SEC. Alexandra chose a printer early in the process based on competitive bids and recommendations of the underwriters and counsel. Given the SEC requirement that all documents be transmitted to the SEC electronically (through a system referred to as EDGAR), it was important that Alexandra retain an experienced financial printer that could meet the company's proposed schedule.

After the registration statement was filed with the SEC, Alexandra and her partners turned their attention to corporate matters that required

continued

continued

completion prior to the closing of the offering. For example, the company needed to undertake a shareholder mailing to obtain written shareholder consents to amend charter documents, reincorporate in Delaware, and effect a stock split. In addition, the underwriters worked with Alexandra and her partners to develop the road show presentation and also recommended a consultant to assist in that process. The road show was timed so that the first set of SEC staff comments would be received approximately halfway through the road show. If all went well, this would put the parties in a position to complete the road show and price the offering very soon thereafter. Alexandra planned to spend at least two or three weeks on the road show, making her presentation twenty to thirty times in as many as fifteen different U.S. cities. (The road show would have been even longer if Europe had been included.)

After approximately thirty days, the SEC staff provided comments on the registration statement. At this point, the working group reassembled at the printer to prepare the first amendment to the registration statement to respond to the comments. The group believed that certain of the SEC's comments were not clear or reflected a misunderstanding on the part of the SEC staff. In those cases, the company explained supplementally in a letter to the SEC why the company believed that the registration statement should not be revised in response to those comments. In addition, the SEC requested certain supplemental information to determine whether other comments were appropriate. A number of the comments related to accounting matters. Alexandra obtained from the auditors a realistic estimate of the time they needed to revise any numbers, draft additional disclosures, and prepare any required supplemental response.

After filing the amended registration statement, Alexandra expected one or more additional sets of oral or written comments from the SEC, each of which generally would require another amendment to the registration statement. These comments were delivered within a few days after the filing. Each amendment was signed on behalf of the company and included an executed consent of the auditors. Once the SEC had no further comment, the company requested that the SEC declare the registration statement effective. This was done by means of a letter filed electronically with the SEC. The underwriters joined in the request with their own letter.

continued

continued

The underwriters set up a telephonic conference call on the day the offering was declared effective, after the close of the market. The underwriters first congratulated Alexandra on a successful road show, and then proposed the final size of the offering, the offering price, and the underwriters' gross spread (commission). Alexandra wanted to try to negotiate with the underwriters about the gross spread and the price, so she came to the meeting armed with the latest information about WebRunner's competitors, particularly recent trends in their stock prices and price/earnings ratios. Because WebRunner was considered "hot," she was able to negotiate a slightly higher price, although the underwriters would not budge from a 7% gross spread. Once the deal was struck, the underwriting agreement was executed that same day. Trading commenced the following morning. The final prospectus was then prepared based on the final price information, and the offering closed three business days following the commencement of trading.

After the offering closed, Alexandra invited Michael to visit the company to meet with her and the other executive officers to set up procedures to implement the company's insider trading and window period policies, the SEC and Nasdaq/NMS compliance procedures, and the investor relations strategy. Michael then spoke to the employees about the implications for them of owning stock in a public company and applicable restrictions on trading.

After Michael finished, Alexandra addressed the employees. She thanked them for their long nights and weekends of toil to get the IRRS ready for the product launch. She also reminded the longtimers of the dark days before venture financing, when WebRunner's creditors were hounding the company and it almost failed. Finally, she spoke of the future. WebRunner had made remarkable progress from the time when it was merely a dream of Alexandra, Paul, and Sheryl, but it was now time for the next stage. The challenges of entrepreneurship had been met, and now the challenges of becoming a successful public company lay ahead. "But first," she declared, "break out the champagne—it's time to party!"

Index

A

Advertising, 332–335
Age Discrimination in
    Employment Act (ADEA),
    373
Americans with Disabilities
    Act (ADA), 374–376
Angel investors, 102
Antideficiency laws, 146
Antidilution provisions,
    119–120, 212–218
    and pay-to-play provi-
        sions, 120, 218
    and preemptive rights
        (right of first refusal),
        212–213
    and price protection, 213–
        218
    ratchet method, 120,
        214–216
    structural antidilution
        provisions, 119, 212
    weighted average method,
        120, 216–218
Antipiracy clause, 14
Applications and interviews,
    383–389
Article 9, 148
Articles of organization, 60
Assumption of risk,
    330–331
Attorneys,
    and client privilege, 44–45
    billing costs, 36–39
    billing process, 42–44

B

Bankruptcy, 164–167
    and creditors committee,
        174
    and effect on contracts,
        295–296
    and effect on director liti-
        gation and indemnifica-
        tion, 176–177
    and loss of control,
        185–186

and preference claims,
    172–173
and running a business in,
    174–175
business combination
    through chapter 11,
    184–185
creditor claims, 168–171
involuntary, 166–167
prenegotiated, 183
prepackaged, 182–183
pros and cons, 186–187
Blank check preferred stock,
    75
Blue Sky laws, 124,
    129–130, 512–513
    and merit review, 130
Board of directors,
    business judgment rule,
        246–247
    independent, 238–239
    information needed, 249–
        252
    responsibilities, of, 243–
        246
    size of, 240
    type of representation,
        241–243
Business
    choosing and protecting a
        name for, 65–66
    conducting in other states,
        64–65
    forms of, 50–51
    insurance
    local licenses, 64–65
Business plan, 110–111
    avoidance of unsupported
        statements, 114
    backup (due diligence)
        files, 114
    further requirements,
        114–115
    identification of risks,
        113–114
    requirements of, 112–115
Buy-sell agreements, 93–94
Bylaws of incorporation,
    77–79

C

Cash (stock) holdback, 314
Certificate of formation, 60
Certification of incorpora-
    tion (articles of incorpora-
    tion), 75–76
    blank check preferred
        stock, 75
    indemnification, 76
    preemptive rights, 76
    supermajority voting
        requirements, 76
    the incorporator, 76
Chapter 7 reorganization
    (straight bankruptcy), 165
Chapter 11 bankruptcy, 165,
    167–174, 177–182
    absolute priority rule,
        180–181
    and cramdown issues,
        180–181
    and loss of control, 185–
        186
    business combination
        through, 184
    creditors committee, 174
    debtor-in-possession, 167
    executory contracts and
        leases, 171–172
    fraudulent transfer claims,
        173
    impaired and unimpaired
        claims, 178
    new value exception, 181
    plan voting requirements,
        179
    preference claims, 172
Charter amendment,
    120–121
Cheap (founders) stock, 87,
    520
Cliff vesting, 90
Closing date, 121
Collateral, 146, 149–150
Common law 17, 268
    and advertising, 332
Common stock, 116
Comparative risk, 330

Compensation and bene-
fits, 394–395
Compensatory (actual)
damages, 355
Computer software,
safeguarding, 481–491
copyright protection,
482–487
patent protection, 487–
488
trade secrets and trade-
marks, 488–489
software licensing,
489–491
Consideration, 272–273
Consideration for stock,
85–86
Contract law, 268–275
Contracts,
implied, 268, 390–391
effects of bankruptcy
on, 295–296
illusory promise, 274
output contract, 274
promissory estoppel,
301–302
quantum meruit, 303
remedies for breach of,
296–301
requirements contract,
274
sales of goods, 315
special, 303–315
unilateral, 274–275
written, 279–292
Contribution and indem-
nification, 357
Conversion, 348
Conversion price, 120,
210–211
Conversion rights, 119,
210–211
Copyrights, 443–450
duration of, 448
fair use, 447–448
in cyberspace, 449–450
international issues,
450
ownership of, 448–449
protections available
through, 446
proving infringement,
447
requirements for
obtaining, 445–446

works protected by,
443–444
Corporations, 51–55
C Corporations, 51
S Corporations, 53–55
Covenant not to compete
(see also non-compete
covenant), 8
and legitimate interests,
15
exceptions to legisla-
tion, 17
limitations, 15
post employment
restrictions, 14–18,
398
public interests, 17
state legislation, 17
Covenants, 122
affirmative covenant,
122
negative covenant, 122
Creditors, types of and
rights, 155–158
Cumulative voting, 74
Cumulative dividend,
205–206

D
Debtor, 148
obligations, 151
Defamation, 345
Defective product,
326–328
Dilution, 116, 473
Directors, board of,
238–239
responsibilities in a
public company,
535–536
Disclosure of preemploy-
ment and postemploy-
ment inventions,
401–402
Dividend preference, 118
Dragnet clause (cross col-
lateralization), 151
debtor-in-possession,
167
Due diligence, 196, 311,
499, 508
defense, 521

E
Employee benefits,
409–413
Employee compensation
plans, 117–118
Employees versus inde-
pendent contractors,
362–365
Employer liability for
employees acts, 404
Employment
agreements, 95–96
393–397
at-will, 13, 96, 389
Employment legislation,
major 366–381
Age Discrimination in
Employment Act
(ADEA), 373
Americans with
Disabilities Act
(ADA), 374–376
Family and Medical
Leave Act, 376–377
Immigration Reform
and Control Act of
1986 (IRCA), 385
National Labor
Relations Act
(NLRA), 380–381
Occupational Safety
and Health Act, 379–
380
Title VII of the Civil
Rights Act of 1964,
366–372
workers' compensa-
tion, 378–379
Equal Employment
Opportunity
Commission (EEOC),
381–382
Equity compensation,
404–409
Equity, issuing, 83–85
Exchanges, Nasdaq, and
Blue Sky laws,
512–513
Nasdaq/NMS, 512
Executory contracts, 162
Exemplary (punitive)
damages, 355
Express warranty, 321

F

Fair Labor Standards Act (FLSA), 377
Fair use, 447–448
False advertising, 473
Family and Medical Leave Act, 376–377
Federal securities registration requirements and exemptions, 123–129
    Blue Sky laws, 124
    Regulation A, 128
    Regulation D: Safe-Harbor Exemptions, 125–127
    Rule 701, 128
    Securities Act of 1933, 123–124
Financial crisis, responses for, 158–164
    general considerations, 159–160
    out-of-court reorganization, 160–162
    out-of-court liquidation, 162–164
    secured creditors and foreclosure, 164
Floating lien, 151
Foreclosure, 146, 151
Foreign employees, 402–403
Forgotten founder, 72
Form 10-C, 528
Form 10-K, 527–528
Form 10-Q, 528
Form 8-K, 528
Forward triangular merger (D reorganization), 310
Founders (cheap) stock, 87
Fraudulent misrepresentation, 349
Full warranty, 325
Funding,
    and the business plan, 110–111
    and the private placement memorandum, 111,112
    private (angel) investors, 102–104
    self-financing and credit, 105–108

    sources of, 101–110
    strategic alliances and joint ventures, 108–110
    venture-capital financing, 104–105

G

General creditors, 146
General partnership, 55
Green shoe option, 511

I

Implied warranty of fitness, 324
Implied warranty of merchantability, 321–323
Incentive stock options (ISOs), 88, 226
Incorporation, 72–80
    action by incorporator, 79
    action by unanimous written consent, 80
    bylaws, 77–79
    certificate of incorporation, 75–76
    charter documents, 73
    division of equity, 80–83
Indemnification and liability insurance for directors, 536
Independent contractors, versus employees, 362–365
Initial public offering (IPO), 494
    closing, 515
    confidential treatment of material agreements, 511–512
    due diligence, 508–509
    determination of stock price and offering size, 509–511
    exchanges, Nasdaq, and blue sky laws, 512–513
    IPO process, 499–515
    pricing and commencement of trading, 514–515

    registration statement, 503
    road show, 513–514
    SEC comments, 514
    selecting the underwriters, 500–502
    timing, 502–503
    versus sale of the company, 496–498
Insider trading, 529–532
    company liability, 530–531
    insider reports, 532
    Insider Trading and Securities Fraud Enforcement Act of 1988 (ITSFEA), 530
    liability for short-swing profits, 531–532
Insider Trading and Securities Fraud Enforcement Act of 1988 (ITSFEA), 530
Integration (merger) clause, 277, 397
Intellectual property, 432–433
    transferring rights to, 475–476
Intentional torts, 343–351
Invention Assignment Agreement, 22–24
Investment securities, 115–123
Investors' rights, 122–123
Involuntary redemption rights, 119
Involuntary bankruptcy, 166–167
Intellectual property, 432–433

L

Liability defenses, 330–331
Liability, employer for employees' acts, 404
    actual authority, 404
    apparent authority, 404
Liability for defective products, 325–331

Liability for misstatements in prospectus, 521
due diligence defense, 521
Liability of multiple defendants, 356–357
contribution and indemnification, 357
joint and several liability, 356–357
Licensing agreements, 474–481
Lien creditor, 153
Limited partnership, 55–56
Limited liability companies, 59–61
articles of organization, 60
certificate of formation 60
choice of, 61–64
operating agreement, 60
Limiting liability, 324–325
Liquidation preference 84, 118, 204–208
Litigation, reducing risk of, 391–393
Loan agreements, 147
Loans, types of, 145–146
secured loans, 146
term loans, 145

M
Magnuson-Moss warranty act, 325
Mandatory arbitration, 396–397
Milestones, 221

N
Nasdaq Stock Market National Market System (Nasdaq/NMS), 512–513
National Labor Relations Act (NLRA), 380–381
Negligence, 339
defenses to, 341–343
No-moonlighting clause, 8

Non-compete covenant (see also covenant not to compete), 10, 96
Nondisclosure agreement (NDA), 20, 400–402, 436
and invention assignment agreements, 400–402
and nonuse of proprietary information, 400
assignment of inventions, 401
disclosure of preemployment and postemployment inventions, 401–402
Nonstatutory (nonqualified) stock options (NSOs), 88
Nuisance, 347–348

O
Occupational Safety and Health Act (OSHA), 379–380
Operating agreement, 60
Option contract, 270
Options, stock, 226–227, 406
Out-of-court liquidation, 162–164
executory contracts, 162
Out-of-court reorganization, 160
Ownership of copyrights, 448–449

P
Partnerships, 55–59
choice of, 61–64
general partnership, 55
limited partnership, 55–56
Patents, 450–462
competing claims for, 456–457
design patents, 453
important issues, 457–458
infringement, 459

international issues, 458
procedures for obtaining, 454–456
requirements for obtaining, 453
statutory bar, 453–454
strategic aspects of, 460–461
understanding competitors, 461–462
utility patents, 452–453
Perfecting a security agreement, 152–154
Personal guaranties, 158
Placement agent, 102
Post employment restrictions, 14–18
Postpetition (debtor-in-possession) financing, 175
Preemployment practices, 382–389
Preemptive rights, 76
Preferred stock, 116
rights of, 118–121, 202–225
series, 204
Preparing for an IPO, 522–526
board composition, 525
posteffective quiet period, 524–525
postfiling publicity, 523–524
prefiling publicity, 522–523
reincorporation in Delaware, 526
Price antidilution provisions, 120
Price/earnings ratio, 502
Prior art, search for, 455
Private investors, 102–104
Private offerings (placements), 124–125
Private placement memorandum, 111–112
Promissory estoppel, 301–302
Property, contributions of, 85–86

Proprietary rights agreement, 95–96
Prospectus, 499–500, 517–521
Proxy rules, 528
Public company, responsibilities of, 526–536
Public float, 511
Punitive (exemplary) damages, 355–356
Purchase-money security interest, 153

R

Reasonable accommodation, 374–375
Redemption rights, 118–119, 208–210
Red herring, 499
Reducing tort risks, 357–358
Reduction to practice, 456
Registration rights, 123, 222–223
and demand rights, 222
Registration statement, 503
Regulation D: Safe-Harbor Exemptions, 125–127
and accredited investors, 124
Regulation A, 128
Regulatory law and advertising, 333–335
Replacement lien in bankruptcy, 175
Representations and warranties, 121
Restrictions on sales of shares, 515–517
impact of Rule 144, 516
lockup agreements, 515–516
trading of stock not issued in offering, 516–517
Retirement benefits, 410–412
Reverse triangular merger (E reorganization), 310

Revolving loan (revolving line of credit), 145
Right of first refusal, 92–93
Road show, 222, 500, 513–514
Rule 144, 517
Rule 504: Offerings up to $1 Million in a Twelve-Month Period, 126
Rule 505: Offerings up to $5 Million in a Twelve-Month Period, 126–127
Rule 506: Limited Number of Investors who Understand Risks, 127
Rule 701: Offerings to Employees, 128–129

S

Schedule of exceptions, 313
Secured creditors, 156
and foreclosure, 164
Section 83(b) election, 226
Secured party, 148
Secured transactions under the UCC, 147–148
Securities Act of 1933, 123–124
Securities Exchange Act of 1934, 124
Security agreements, 148–152
Self-financing and credit, 105–108
Seniority and merit systems, 371
Sexual harassment, 371–372
hostile environment harassment, 371
quid pro quo harassment, 371
Shares, transfer of, 92–94
Short-swing trading, 531
Software licensing, 489–491

boot-screen license agreement, 490
intellectual property indemnification, 491
license fees, 491
license grant, 490
shrink-wrap licenses, 489–490
support and maintenance, 491
Sole proprietorship, 50
Special contracts, 303–315
Standard form contracts, 280–281
Statute of frauds, 275–277
Statutory bar, 453–454
Statutory law and advertising, 332–333
Stock (cash) holdback, 314
Stock options, 395, 406
Stock price and offering size, determining, 509–511
green shoe option, 511
IPO discount, 510
price range, 510
public float, 510
target price, 510
underwriters' book, 510
Stock purchase agreement, 121–123
conditions to closing, 121–122
covenants, 122
description of security, 121
investors' representations, 123
investors' rights, 122–123
representations and warranties, 121
Stock,
types of, 84–85
and substantial risk of forfeiture, 90–91
cheap (founders), 87
classes of, 116–117
common, 116
consideration for, 85–86

contributions of property, 85–86
convertible preferred, 117
liquidation preference, 84
preferred 116
qualified small business, 87–88
versus stock options, 86–89
Strategic alliances and joint ventures, 108–110
Strict liability, 352
ultrahazardous activities, 352
Successor liability, 330
Supermajority voting requirements, 76

T

Tax-free reorganization, 309–311
Term loans, 145
Title VII of the Civil Rights Act of 1964, 366–372
disparate impact, 367–369
disparate treatment, 366–367
statutory defenses under, 369–371
sexual harassment, 371–372
Torts
defenses to negligence, 341–343
duty, 340
elements of negligence, 339–341
intentional, 343–351
liability of multiple defendants, 356–357
reducing tort risks, 357–358

remedies, 354–356
standard of conduct, 341
toxic, 352–353
Trade secrets, 19–22, 434–435, 488–489
and reverse engineering, 435
enforcing rights, 436–437
establishing a protection program, 437–443
protection, 433–443
Trademarks, 462–470, 489
establishing, 464–465
infringement of, 470
international issues, 468
protecting rights of, 468–470
trademark registration, 467–468
Transfer of shares, 92–94
Trespass, 345–348

U

Underwriters, 500–502
Unfair competition, 350–351, 472–474
Uniform Trade Secrets Act (UTSA), 22
Unilateral contract, 274–275

V

Valuation, determining, 197–202
Venture capital financing, 104–105
deciding to seek, 190–191
finding, 191–193
stages of development 193

Venture capitalist,
and due diligence, 196
selecting, 194–197
Vested shares, 407
Vesting, 89–92, 225–226
and section 83(b) election, 91–92
cliff vesting, 90, 407
Voluntary bankruptcy, 164–165
Voluntary redemption rights, 118–119
Voting agreements, 95
Voting rights, 120, 218–220

W

Warranties, 320–325
express, 321
implied warranty of fitness, 324
implied warranty of merchantability, 321–323
limiting liability, 324
Magnuson-Moss Warranty Act, 325
Warrants, 115, 117
Window period policies, 531
Workers' compensation, 378–379
Works made for hire, 398–399, 448–449
Written contracts, 279–292
effects of bankruptcy on, 295–296
form, 280–282
remedies for breach of, 296–301
terms to consider, 282–292
Wrongful discharge, 389–391